Challenges to Democracy in the 21st Century

Series Editor
Hanspeter Kriesi
Department of Political and Social Science
European University Institute
San Domenico Di Fiesole, Firenze, Italy

Democracy faces substantial challenges as we move into the 21st Century. The West faces malaise; multi-level governance structures pose democratic challenges; and the path of democratization rarely runs smoothly. This series examines democracy across the full range of these contemporary conditions. It publishes innovative research on established democracies, democratizing polities and democracy in multi-level governance structures. The series seeks to break down artificial divisions between different disciplines, by simultaneously drawing on political communication, comparative politics, international relations, political theory, and political economy.

More information about this series at
http://www.palgrave.com/gp/series/14889

Giacomo Delledonne • Giuseppe Martinico
Matteo Monti • Fabio Pacini
Editors

Italian Populism and Constitutional Law

Strategies, Conflicts and Dilemmas

palgrave
macmillan

Editors
Giacomo Delledonne
Scuola Sant'Anna
Pisa, Italy

Giuseppe Martinico
Scuola Sant'Anna
Pisa, Italy

Matteo Monti
Scuola Sant'Anna
Pisa, Italy

Fabio Pacini
Scuola Sant'Anna
Pisa, Italy

Challenges to Democracy in the 21st Century
ISBN 978-3-030-37400-6 ISBN 978-3-030-37401-3 (eBook)
https://doi.org/10.1007/978-3-030-37401-3

Cover illustration: Photo 12 / Alamy Stock Photo

This Palgrave Macmillan imprint is published by the registered company Springer Nature Switzerland AG.
The registered company address is: Gewerbestrasse 11, 6330 Cham, Switzerland

Acknowledgement

Funded by the
European Union

This volume is part of the Jean Monnet Module—European Public Law-IUS (EUR.PUBL.IUS) coordinated by Prof. Giuseppe Martinico and held at the Scuola Sant'Anna, Pisa, Italy.

Contents

1 **Introduction: A Constitutional Viewpoint on Italian Populism** 1
Giacomo Delledonne, Giuseppe Martinico, Matteo Monti, and Fabio Pacini

2 **Populism and Constitutional Reform. The Case of Italy** 11
Paul Blokker

Part I 39

3 **Is There a Populist Turn in the Italian Parliament? Continuity and Discontinuity in the Non-legislative Procedures** 41
Cristina Fasone

4 **Populism and Referendum: The Italian Debate from a Comparative Perspective** 75
Giuseppe Martinico

5 **Populism and Constitutional Amendment** 97
Pietro Faraguna

6 **Populism and Law-Making Process** 119
Fabio Pacini

7 **Populism and Government: Continuity and Paradoxes in the Yellow-Green Experiment** 135
Giacomo Delledonne

8 **"Kicking the Can Down the Road" Deferring Fiscal Adjustment as a Premise for Italian Budgetary Populism** 153
Giovanni Boggero

Part II 175

9 **Italian Populism and Fake News on the Internet: A New Political Weapon in the Public Discourse** 177
Matteo Monti

10 **Rise of Populism and the Five Star Movement Model: An Italian Case Study** 199
Marco Bassini

11 **Populism, Science and the Italian Democracy** 223
Marta Tomasi

12 **"Le cose sono un po' più complesse": Constitutional Law and Religion in Italy and the Populist Challenge** 241
Pasquale Annicchino

13 **The Italian Way to Migration: Was It 'True' Populism? Populist Policies as Constitutional Antigens** 255
Simone Penasa

14 **Does a Sub-State Dimension of Populism Exist?** 277
Alessandro Sterpa

15 Populism and Criminal Justice in Italy 291
Nicola Selvaggi

Index 311

Notes on Contributors

Pasquale Annicchino is an Associate Researcher at the FBK Centre for Religious Studies. He has also affiliations with the Robert Schuman Centre for Advanced Studies at the European University Institute (EUI) and the Cambridge Institute on Religion & International Studies, Cambridge University.

Marco Bassini is a postdoctoral researcher in Constitutional Law at Bocconi University, Milan.

Paul Blokker is Associate Professor of Sociology in the Department of Sociology and Business Law, University of Bologna.

Giovanni Boggero is Assistant Professor in Constitutional Law, Università degli Studi di Torino.

Giacomo Delledonne is a postdoctoral researcher in Comparative Public Law at the Scuola Sant'Anna, Pisa.

Pietro Faraguna is Assistant Professor in Constitutional Law, University of Trieste.

Cristina Fasone is Assistant Professor of Comparative Public Law in the Department of Political Science at Libera Università Internazionale degli Studi Sociali (LUISS) Guido Carli in Rome and a visiting professor at the Nicolaus Copernicus University of Toruń.

Giuseppe Martinico is Associate Professor of Comparative Public Law at the Scuola Sant'Anna, Pisa.

Matteo Monti is a researcher in the Faculty of Law at the Scuola Sant'Anna, Pisa.

Fabio Pacini is a postdoctoral researcher in Constitutional Law at the Scuola Sant'Anna, Pisa.

Simone Penasa is Assistant Professor of Comparative Public Law, University of Trento.

Nicola Selvaggi is Associate Professor of Criminal Law and Director of the Research Center on Preventive measures and organized crime (CeRPEC) in the Department of Law and Economics at the "Mediterranea" University of Reggio Calabria.

Alessandro Sterpa is Associate Professor of Public Law at Tuscia University, Viterbo.

Marta Tomasi is a postdoctoral researcher at the Free University of Bozen-Bolzano.

CHAPTER 1

Introduction: A Constitutional Viewpoint on Italian Populism

Giacomo Delledonne, Giuseppe Martinico, Matteo Monti, and Fabio Pacini

Concept Behind the Book

The aim of this edited volume is to explore the relationship between constitutionalism and populism in the Italian context. The Italian experience with populism is interesting both to domestic and comparative lawyers for many reasons. First, the country has a long-lasting tradition of anti-parliamentarism over the course of its history as a unitary state. In the post-war constitutional setting, dissatisfaction with political parties and their perceived self-serving attitudes (*partitocrazia*, in Italian) was widespread among scholars and in specific circles. After the end of the Cold War, populism has characterised many of the new parties and movements that have come to the forefront in Italian politics (Tarchi 2015, 2018; Bressanelli and Natali 2019). After the 2018 general election, Italy turned into the first European country in which two self-styled populist parties with very different agendas and voting constituencies formed a coalition

G. Delledonne (✉) • G. Martinico • M. Monti • F. Pacini
Scuola Sant'Anna, Pisa, Italy
e-mail: giacomo.delledonne@santannapisa.it; giuseppe.martinico@santannapisa.it; matteo.monti@sssup.it; fabio.pacini@sssup.it

G. Delledonne et al. (eds.), *Italian Populism and Constitutional Law*, Challenges to Democracy in the 21st Century,
https://doi.org/10.1007/978-3-030-37401-3_1

government. In this respect, Italy has not only been marked by populist politics for many decades: by that time, it became an experiment of a self-styled populist coalition government. The first Conte government, formed after the 2018 election, resigned in August 2019: however, many issues that it raised are still there.

Second, the Italian case is of the greatest interest because the country is a founding member of the European Communities (now European Union). Therefore, the constitutional implications of populist politics have to be considered not only within the national framework but also in the wider context.

In this book it will be argued that the relationship between populism and constitutionalism should not be seen in terms of mutual exclusion and perfect opposition (Müller 2016). Indeed, it is possible to say that populism frequently relies on concepts and categories belonging to the language of constitutionalism (majority, democracy, people), trying to reshape them and offering a sort of constitutional counter-narrative (Corrias 2016). This kind of approach can be described in the light of two concepts: mimesis and parasitism. Meanwhile, populists do not normally acknowledge the distinction between constitutional and non-constitutional politics, since they do not conceive the constitution as neutral. This reveals a sort of legal scepticism that can be traced back to what Blokker (2019: 548–51) calls "legal resentment". This element is connected to what Arato (2013: 148) would call the "regeneration of the people" and to the tendency of populism "to occupy the space of the constituent power" (Arato 2017: 5). This also explains why populists tend to perceive limits and procedures as obstacles in the path of establishing the democratic principle. Moreover, populists depict courts and independent agencies as biased and non-neutral since "independent judges and courts are understood as an illegitimate constraint on majority rule, and hence legal means are to be employed to counter this situation" (Blokker 2019: 547). These considerations clarify why populists seem to be on a permanent political campaign. Against this background, present-day populisms do not emerge completely out of the blue, since they are the consequences of long-standing issues that have characterised the political contexts in which they operate.

Building on these ideas, some scholars have drawn a parallel between political constitutionalism and populism, as they both question the political engagement of unaccountable constitutional courts and the status of judicial review (Blokker 2019). Nevertheless, important differences exist between political constitutionalism and populism, as the latter is deeply rooted in a kind of pre-political understanding of the "people", seen as the direct and automatic source of political truth, and this inevitably results in questioning representative institutions as well. This is an element that does not necessarily characterise political constitutionalism as such.

Structure of the Volume

Bearing in mind this framework, the edited volume develops a comprehensive analysis of constitutional issues related to the rise of Italian populism. In order to do so, we have structured the book in two parts. In the first part, the impact of populist claims on Italian institutions is addressed. The second part, in turn, focuses on the constitutional implications of the populist approach to the elaboration of policies. All chapters consider both recent developments and their long-term antecedents.

The two parts are preceded by an opening essay, in which *Paul Blokker* considers the weight of populist arguments in the season of constitutional reform in Italy since the early 1990s. His understanding of populism is based on a dualistic perspective, in which democracies are subject to a fundamental tension between constitutionalism and populism. Blokker considers two failed reform projects—respectively undertaken by the Berlusconi government in 2004–6 and the Renzi government in 2014–16—in the light of three typical aspects of the interplay of populism and public law: majoritarianism, instrumentalism, and legal resentment. Those attempts at constitutional reform were unsuccessful; however, a populist attitude seems to have become the prevalent flavour in Italian constitutional politics debates.

The first part includes contributions by Cristina Fasone, Giuseppe Martinico, Pietro Faraguna, Fabio Pacini, Giacomo Delledonne, and Giovanni Boggero.

Cristina Fasone addresses the impact of the populist turn in Italian politics on the non-legislative functions of the Parliament. In her view, the latest wave of populism has contributed to further marginalising the national legislature. However, a number of relevant elements point at continuity with the past: in this respect, some trends that were already in place have escalated. Aside from this, at least three significant shifts are directly related to the spectacular rise of populist parties in the last two legislative terms. First, the contestation of the alleged "privileges" of the members of Parliament may lead to a radical devaluation of the status of MPs. Second, the claim to provide total transparency, coupled with a massive resort to the new media, is intimately at odds with certain distinctive traits of the traditional mission of the Parliament. Third, the spectacularisation of politics, which is an integral part of the populist strategy, has led to an overexploitation of some traditional instruments of parliamentary oversight, like investigating committees and parliamentary questions.

Giuseppe Martinico considers the current Italian debate about direct democracy, in which populist claims play a crucial role. In his chapter, the starting point is a draft constitutional bill introduced by the first Conte government and aiming to enhance direct democracy and to enhance a type of legislative referendum. In the populist discourse, emphasis on direct democracy and referendums generally goes hand in hand with questioning representative democracy and its instruments. In the light of the possible anti-parliamentarian inspiration of referendums, a comparative analysis suggests that constitutional law tends to limit the political risks that are connected to them. In the Italian constitutional order, where referendums have long played an important role, the rationalising function of the case law of the Italian Constitutional Court deserves close attention and provides guidelines for "taming" some of the most controversial aspects of the recent constitutional amendment proposals.

The chapter by *Pietro Faraguna* explores the relations between populism and constitutional amendment. By analysing the use, misuse, and abuse of constitutional amendment by populists, the chapter argues that populists tend to reject any distinction between "constitutional" and "day-to-day" politics. Therefore, if the notion of constitutional amendment is correctly understood, populists in power usually stay at large from constitutional amendments in a strict sense: they rather prefer constitutional replacement or constitutional sabotage. Subsequently, the chapter explores possible constitutional remedies against the populist use and abuse of constitutional change. Finally, the designed conceptual map is tested on constitutional developments in the never-ending debate on constitutional change in Italy. Apparently, there are some similarities between the populist approach to constitutional change and the Italian debate on constitutional reforms. Nevertheless, the amendment procedure provided for by the Italian Constitution successfully tamed most of the populist impulses.

Fabio Pacini looks into another natural target of populism: law-making processes. Due to its complex structure, the legislature procedure is accused of complicating the decision-making process unduly. However, it is necessary to distinguish between two scenarios, and Italy has given interesting examples of both, depending on whether populist movements are in the opposition or in the majority. In the first case, the opposition (populist) movement tends to exacerbate the use of obstructionism and generally transforms the moment of decision into that of a performance, as the Five Star Movement, the Northern League and the Radical Party did at different stages. However, developments since 2018 have been even more interesting from an Italian perspective in order to study the behaviour of populist movements when they are in the government. In fact, emphasis on performance remains, thus leading to an extreme spectacularisation of the legislative activity, systematically sacrificing its good functioning.

Giacomo Delledonne considers whether and how the Italian executive has been affected by the rise of populist parties and movements or, more broadly, by populist arguments and discourse. The chapter points at an inherent paradox. On the one hand, a strengthened constitutional role of the executive lies at the heart of the populist constitutional project or, less ambitiously, constitutional discourse. On the other hand, the first Conte government, labelled as the first purely populist experiment in Western Europe, was based on an unusual understanding of government activity. Government formation was preceded by the elaboration of a "contract" between the leaders of the Five Star Movement and the League, with a very marginal role for the person who would be picked to serve as Prime Minister. Meanwhile, executive leadership was split into two, with no serious attempt to reconcile the opposing claims of the two parties in the majority.

Giovanni Boggero shows that in Italy a populist approach seems to prevail in budgetary matters. Indeed, budget constraints have long been considered as an obstacle to the legitimate implementation of fiscal and social policies by leaders who claimed to truly act in the name of a unified will of the people. This attitude harks back to how questions of public finance have been dealt with by both right- and left-wing cabinets over the last 40 years. An attempt to reverse the weakening of the financial constitutional framework caused by a bipartisan populist course of action has been made with a number of reforms passed between 2009 and 2012, which aimed to strengthen the entrenchment of the Italian normative framework into the European one. However, this attempt backfired, as it appears that the parliamentary budgetary process still lacks faithful abidance by constitutional and EU legal prescriptions. Therefore, the Constitutional Court has been most recently unleashed to act as the "last bastion" against the typical populist strategies.

In the second part, the focus of the analysis shifts from institutions to policies. This part of the book includes chapters by Matteo Monti, Marco Bassini, Marta Tomasi, Pasquale Annicchino, Simone Penasa, Alessandro Sterpa, and Nicola Selvaggi.

Matteo Monti explores the instruments and possible solutions available in Italian constitutional law to confront the populist use of fake news. As a preliminary, Monti frames the fake news problem and its use by populist movements. The current spread of fake news seems to be connected with two correlated phenomena: the rise of "mediated populism" and the novel role of Internet platforms in the news ecosystem. Populist fake news is an actual challenge for constitutionalism and is having an impact on the freedom of information, one of the most important components of democratic theory. Against this background, it seems necessary to prepare new legal tools for Internet platforms and to (co)regulate them in accordance with the well-established paradigm of the freedom of information as enshrined in the Constitution, although it should not be taken for granted that this will work.

Marco Bassini studies a very peculiar case of political participation through the use of the Internet. From the very beginning, the Five Star Movement has seen the Internet as a means to reshape the essence of political representation in that of delegation and to allow direct democracy to flourish. Unlike other populist movements in Italian history, the Five Star Movement has brought about an unprecedented constitutional challenge affecting political representation. After analysing the status of political parties in the Italian constitutional system, including anti-party and anti-establishment parties, Bassini looks into which measures may be taken to respond to the populist surge and to revitalise representative democracy. His conclusion is that given the tolerant attitude of the Italian Constitution vis-à-vis anti-system parties, this phenomenon can be marginalised but is unlikely to be defeated.

Marta Tomasi addresses the highly problematic impact of anti-elitist ideologies and populism with regard to scientific and health-related issues, where scepticism and suspicion risk compromising the relationship between political institutions and the scientific community, and may actually threaten fundamental rights. Her chapter presents some paradigmatic examples of how, when expert and popular knowledge come into conflict, the political discourse is often contaminated, creating impasses and making good policy outcomes significantly less likely. The decade-long Italian debate around compulsory vaccinations and the contentious "Stamina" case (which involved a non-validated therapy) exemplify the challenges posed by populist trends to the effective informing of government policy by objective scientific expertise and advice, and the consequences of this dynamic for a democratic society.

In order to analyse the role of populism in the Italian constitutional context, *Pasquale Annicchino* makes specific reference to the relationship between religions and the state. Populist parties seem to adopt an anti-pluralist stance that contradicts the basic principle of the Italian constitutional order, among them the "supreme principle" of *laicità* as defined by the Constitutional Court since the 1980s. The Italian model of secularism that has emerged in the last few decades is quite respectful of religious pluralism and it has been able to adjust and evolve. So far, the populist challenge has not affected it strongly. Under the first Conte government, relationships between religions and the state have not been a priority action, but rather, a narrative used to frame political positioning. In this narrative, Catholicism is sometimes transformed into a quasi-ideology and used to create a shared political identity.

Simone Penasa assesses the "constitutional sustainability" of populist policies implemented in the context of migration within the Italian constitutional order. The starting point is that migration as a global, European, and national phenomenon undoubtedly represents a privileged context where populism may find expression. The management of migration flows involves legal concepts that are traditionally related to populist trends: national security, border defence, and national identity. Against this background, the populist season experienced in Italy can be seen as an antigen rather than a parasite within the constitutional system, as it has been able to activate antibodies that are traditionally linked to the core of constitutionalism: the central role of counter-majoritarian bodies, separation of powers, the limitation of popular sovereignty, and a truly pluralistic social and cultural debate.

In the chapter by *Alessandro Sterpa*, the focus of the analysis moves from the national layer to the subnational one. Populism being based on the presumed superiority on the contingent will of the people independently of any legal restrictions, the popular will of one regional community can also formalise political choices at odds with the Constitution. The chapter addresses the following research questions: Is national unity a value and a constitutional obligation qualifying a certain political choice that undermines it as populist? Or rather, is it something that is not a value to be considered like others, but that simply represents a mere material presupposition (as opposed to an axiological principle) of the national state? In this respect, populism and souverainism are symptoms of the crisis of the nation-state to the extent that they would recover the previously existing conditions of state authority.

The chapter by *Nicola Selvaggi* shows how the interplay between populism and criminal justice may bring the risk of a real retrograde step and fuel a kind of "penal extremism". The starting point of Selvaggi's analysis is that in relation to social problems of varying degrees of gravity, criminal justice is constantly being called for in order to deal, in the most politically advantageous way, with the problems posed by security and the need for collective reassurance. And while the primacy of criminal justice unleashes a dangerous chase after ever harsher punishments and ever stricter treatment of offenders, the associated penal legislation tends to divert from classical and liberal principles. In the wake of the Tangentopoli scandals, the criminal justice system has become a major actor in the legal and political system, and mass popular expectations have been placed on it. In recent years, the moralising attitudes of populisms have fuelled a kind of "penal extremism".

We would like to thank wholeheartedly all the authors who have enthusiastically joined this project and contributed to making this book possible. In their diversity, the chapters of this book map the relationship between populism and the Italian constitutional order in all its complexity. Furthermore, they show that the Italian case is particularly relevant in a comparative perspective too. In prospective terms, we hope that this book will enrich the discussion about how to deal with the populist challenge in contemporary constitutional democracies.

References

Arato, A. (2013). Political Theology and Populism. *Social Research, 80*(1), 143–172.

Arato, A. (2017). *How We Got Here? Transition Failures, Their Causes, and the Populist Interest in the Constitution*. Available at https://papers.ssrn.com/sol3/papers.cfm?abstract_id=3116219

Blokker, P. (2019). Populism as a Constitutional Project. *International Journal of Constitutional Law, 17*(2), 535–553.

Bressanelli, E., & Natali, D. (2019). Special Issue: Politics in Italy. *Contemporary Italian Politics, 11*(3), 206–354.

Corrias, L. (2016). Populism in a Constitutional Key: Constituent Power, Popular Sovereignty and Constitutional Identity. *European Constitutional Law Review, 12*(1), 6–26.

Müller, J.-W. (2016). *What Is Populism?* Philadelphia: University of Pennsylvania Press.

Tarchi, M. (2015). Italy: The Promised Land of Populism? *Contemporary Italian Politics, 7*(3), 273–285.

Tarchi, M. (2018). *Italia populista. Dal qualunquismo a Beppe Grillo*. Bologna: Il Mulino.

CHAPTER 2

Populism and Constitutional Reform. The Case of Italy

Paul Blokker

Introduction

As Yves Mény and Yves Surel observed almost 20 years ago, all democracies are subject to a fundamental tension between their two main components: constitutionalism, on the one hand, and populism, on the other (Mény and Surel 2001: 42). In a similar manner, Shmuel Eisenstadt spoke of the constitutional and participatory conceptions of democracy (Eisenstadt 1998: 218). On this view, democracy is in many ways a balancing act between the 'order' and the 'popular' dimensions. In contemporary debates on populism, however, the relation is frequently portrayed in a different manner. Constitutionalism is predominantly presented as the only real form or basis of democracy, whereas populism is understood as essentially a threat to democracy.

The argument in this chapter returns to Mény and Surel as well as to Eisenstadt's insights, in that it departs from a dualistic understanding of democracy as grounded in both constitutionalism and popular

P. Blokker (✉)
Department of Sociology and Business Law, University of Bologna, Bologna, Italy
e-mail: paulus.blokker@unibo.it

G. Delledonne et al. (eds.), *Italian Populism and Constitutional Law*, Challenges to Democracy in the 21st Century,
https://doi.org/10.1007/978-3-030-37401-3_2

participation, in order to grasp the 'season of constitutional reform' in the context of Italy since the early 1990s. The presuppositions are that populism plays an important role in the so-called Second Republic, and equally so in the spirit and orientation of constitutional reforms that have become frequent since 1990. Understood from this dualistic perspective, the main question becomes: How are populist movements in general, and populists-in-government in particular, relating to constitutions? Is the populist approach to constitutions reducible to a destruction of constitutional institutions while attempting to entrench populist power? Is hence the constitutionalism-populism relation a zero-sum game? Or can we understand the populist approach to constitutions equally as attempts to rebalance the aforementioned dual dimensions of democracy in the context of hampering and delegitimated democratic institutions?

The general—political-scientific—approach towards populism argues that populism is about (1) a friend-enemy logic in its political mobilization of ordinary citizens, (2) the construction of a unified people, and (3) a critique of the liberal-democratic status quo in the people's name (cf. Möller 2018; Urbinati 2014). Liberal democracy, according to populists, is inadequate in promoting popular sovereignty. This general set of observations is accurate, I believe, but it leaves out one highly significant aspect, that is, the crucial role of *constituent power* in populist projects. As recently stressed by Kolja Möller, studies on populism tend to overlook that the 'invocation of "the people" is not only a matter of bolstering mere political discourse, but of constitutional politics addressing the higher-ranking dimension of the legal and political community, the distribution of powers, and the overall design of rule-making and application' (Möller 2018). As Möller rightly claims, '[p]opulism does not only refer to certain policy issues, but invokes "the people" as constituent power on which the political community relies' (Möller 2018; Corrias 2016). Different populisms draw on the 'multi-faceted character of foundational peoplehood', and in this, 'populists do not rely on a societal foundational force which checks and authorizes public institutions, but in fact can also turn the constitutional structure or the state against the "elites", supranational agreements, or economic powers' (Möller 2018: 17–18). The Italian case becomes highly relevant from this perspective. The frequent recourse to the instrument of constitutional reform since the early 1990s indicates a widespread conviction that the institutions of the First Republic were not functioning properly (were 'out of balance'). The delegitimated state of Italian democracy hence provides the background for attempts to change the fundamentals of Italian democracy in the name of the people. A key issue then becomes: Can we identify a distinctive orientation in Italian constitutional reform projects that indicates a different conception of the balance between order and participation? Are the constitutional reforms of the post-1990 period reducible to attacks on the 1948 Constitution or can we identify a distinctive project of a different, 'populist' democratic order?

It is in particular populism-in-power which shows an important relation to existing constitutions and constitutional reform. This relation—between populism and constitutionalism—is currently a central subject of debate (Halmai 2017; Mudde 2013; Müller 2016, 2017; Scheppele 2018; Landau 2018). The debate stresses the abusive and autocratic tendencies in populist dealings with constitutions, with an emphasis on the undoing of constitutional institutions by populists. This argument is equally taken up in this chapter, but it is also stressed that a populist approach to the constitution engages in the construction of an alternative constitutional order. It is hence important to identify the contours of such an alternative order, its understandings of the law, and to assess what the implications for constitutional democracy are.

The chapter will first discuss three important dimensions to populism and public law: majoritarianism, instrumentalism, and legal resentment. In the second part, it will discuss the Italian 'season of constitutional reform' (from 1990 onwards), focusing on two significant reform projects and exploring the relevance of the three populist dimensions mentioned in these projects. In conclusion, it will be argued that both the centre-left and centre-right forces in Italy have been engaging in populist constitutional reform, without, however, succeeding in bringing about a different, more stable *balance* to Italian constitutional democracy.

Populism and Constitutionalism

The suggestion in this chapter is that constitutionalism needs to be understood as one fundamental dimension of modern democracy, while popular participation constitutes an equally fundamental one. With regard to contemporary manifestations of populism, Luigi Corrias (2016) has argued that the relation between populism and constitutionalism can best be understood as a radicalization of the second fundamental dimension, that is, the idea of popular sovereignty. This makes populism part of a revolutionary tradition within democratic thought and practice.

The argument is that the populist approach to constitutions ought to be analysed as an integral part of populist projects. What is more, with relevance also for the Italian case, a distinctive populist legal mindset can be discerned, which equally affects political forces which are not nominally populist but pursue reforms which reflect populist concerns of the popular will, majoritarianism, and decisionism. Populist approaches to constitutionalism are then frequently reactions to what is portrayed as an unbalanced reality of constitutional democracy, in which judicial institutions and a legal understanding of constitutionalism have become excessive.

The populist approach to the law can be understood from the context of a wider set of critiques on liberalism (on both the left and right) regarding constitutionalism and the rule of law. Populists criticize liberalism's tendency to depoliticization and claim that the liberal model of constitutional democracy leads to an increased distance and potentially alienation of citizens from the institutions. Populist constitutionalism endorses, instead, a programme that promises to reduce the distance between ordinary citizens and the institutions. Populists hence want to directly link the people to the institutions, and to re-enchant democracy, to make it meaningful to its citizens.

An important thrust in populist constitutionalism is the claim to directly represent the people and to overcome the significant *constraints* to popular rule that they observe in liberal or legal constitutionalism. These constraints are inter alia related to the entrenchment of norms, judicial independence and activism, and the closed nature of the legal system. Here, I will briefly engage with three critical components of the populist constitutional approach.[1] These components can be understood as distinctive parts of the populist critique on liberal or legal constitutionalism. First, the populist project is based on an extreme form of *majoritarianism*, which is the way in which populists imagine their project politically (cf. Urbinati 2017). Second, the populists' practical approach to the law is based on *instrumentalism*, which mobilizes the law in the name of a collectivist project. Third, the populist attitude towards the law, or its main prescriptive and evaluative judgments of the law, consists of a critical, emotional stance, or what I call '*legal resentment*'.

[1] I have more extensively elaborated these dimensions—with an additional dimension of justification in the form of popular sovereignty—in Blokker (2019a).

Majoritarianism

Populists imagine political power as the expression of the will of a cohesive, unitary majority that coincides with the popular will. Political government hence means to govern in the name of the majority. Populism in power takes the form of a political project that wants to radically change the rules of the game, so as to correct alleged past wrongdoings to the people and to realize a more intimate relation between political institutions and larger society. Populists approach the majority as a durable and pre-political entity, and equate it with a material, social unity. In right-wing, conservative populism, this tends to take the form of an authentic people or the nation (Blokker 2005). This is in sharp contrast to the liberal understanding of the majority in procedural terms. In liberalism, the majority is a constructed and always again reconstructed set of political forces, which represents social interests. Populists deny conflict within society or they understand conflict as an inherently problematic phenomenon, rather than as a legitimate expression of different viewpoints and interests.

Instrumentalism

The practical approach of populists to the law is an instrumental one,[2] which mobilizes the law in the name of a collectivist project. There is a tendency in populist constitutionalism to collapse the distinction between ordinary and constitutional politics. In Ackermanian terms, this means that there is a permanent mobilization of constitutional norms and constitutional issues in daily politics. Frequently, this mobilization is not driven by popular mobilization from below, but rather by populist elite entrepreneurship from above. The populist constitutional attitude can be understood as the result of populism's overall negative evaluation of liberal

[2] The term 'instrumentalism' is used here in a (pejorative) sense akin to the one expressed by the Venice Commission, in its opinion on the fourth amendment of the Hungarian Fundamental Law, see Opinion on the Fourth Amendment to the Fundamental Law of Hungary, CDLAD(2013)012, Strasbourg, Council of Europe, 17 June 2013, www.venice.coe.int/webforms/documents/?pdf=CDL-AD%282013%29012-e. The Commission argued that '[f]requent constitutional amendments are a worrying sign of an instrumental attitude towards the constitution as is the resort to the exceptional two-thirds majority in constitution-making without a genuine effort to form a wide political consensus and without proper public debates' (2013: 30). The Commission decries the frequent and in-transparent nature of reforms and the abuse of the majority position of the government.

constitutionalism, and it manifests itself in the downplaying of the constitution's status as a rigid, higher law (a cornerstone of liberal or legal constitutionalism). An important dimension of the populists' instrumentalist approach is the *frequency* of constitutional interventions. Populists tend to engage on a frequent basis with constitutional revision, not least because they understand the existing order as tainted with legacies from the past (e.g. as facilitating 'partitocracy') and as an order which can be at best considered a 'façade democracy' which protects elite interests rather than the interests of the people.

Legal Resentment

The populist attitude towards the law is a critical attitude that could be labelled legal scepticism or 'legal resentment', a critical, emotional stance towards liberal and legal constitutionalism, and the latter's alleged juridification, depoliticization, and rationalization of society (Blokker 2013). Legal resentment is a crucial dimension of populist constitutional programmes and comes forth out of a distinctive populist reading of liberal constitutionalism. The populist approach regards liberal constitutionalism as both a mindset and a practice. The latter could be aptly described as the post–Second World War 'default design choice for political systems across Europe and North America', in the form of a constitutionalism that 'typically hinges on a written constitution that includes an enumeration of individual rights, the existence of rights-based judicial review, a heightened threshold for constitutional amendment, a commitment to periodic democratic elections, and a commitment to the rule of law' (Ginsburg et al. 2018).

The populists' critical attitude towards the liberal understanding of the law includes a critical evaluation of the idea of the law as *non-political and neutral.* Populists criticize what is perceived as a strong separation between law, on the one hand, and politics and morality on the other, in liberal constitutionalism. The populist understanding of the law denies its closed, self-sufficient, and self-referential nature, and emphasizes the ultimately always already political nature of the law. Hence, the law in the populist view becomes inseparable from extra-legal sources, such as political power and the societal community, and is in this repoliticized. As such, for populists the law always needs to be the expression of the 'national interest'. In addition, the liberal emphasis on individualism promotes a view of the demos as the basis of the democratic polity, which is rejected by populists, in order to be replaced by a collectivist view which emphasizes the belonging of the individual to a larger community, the ethnos. The function of the law changes in this perspective from one emphasizing constraints and rights (and the protection of vulnerable minorities) to one underlining duties and a distinctive cultural and sometimes religious ethos.

In the rest of the chapter, I will consider the populist mindset towards the law as it has emerged—and continues to—manifest itself in post-1990 Italy, by focusing on two of the most significant constitutional reform projects in the post-1990 period. Below, I will attempt to show that a distinctive populist-constitutional mindset has become intrinsic to Italian politics, and continues to push for reforms that propose to rebalance the democratic system towards a majoritarian system, which prioritizes the popular will and strong leadership, away from system centred on legal and constitutional guarantees.

Projects of Constitutional Reform in Italy

Italy is frequently portrayed as a laboratory of populism (Blokker and Anselmi 2019; Verbeek and Zaslove 2016; Revelli 2015; Tarchi 2015). It is no coincidence that the emergence of populism in the 1990s was accompanied by a heightened attention for, and actual engagement with, constitutional reform. The Italian case appears hence as a crucial one in the contemporary debate on populism and constitutionalism, but has not been often discussed in such terms (for an exception, see Prospero 2007).

Below, I will discuss the Italian 'season of constitutional reform' from the perspective of populism. While the argument is surely not that *any* reform proposal or attempt in the post-1990 period is populist, the general constitutional spirit of the era is a distinctive one, in which the focus in the understanding of Italian constitutional democracy shifts from one that prioritizes Parliament, parties, and the post-war 'guarantist compromise', in which none of the political forces is able to dominate, to one that prioritizes a close and direct relationship between the government and the people, the leader, and the singular party that holds a majority, to the detriment of Parliament (Urbinati and Ragazzoni 2016: 123, 180).

The post-1990 period also stands out in that the Italian Constitution of 1948 had not been object of any comprehensive attempt at reform before. Even if in the mid-1970s, extensive debate on constitutional reform emerged, this was largely of a scholarly nature (Ragazzoni and Urbinati 2016). Only in the 1990s, a range of actual political projects of constitutional revision were undertaken (Groppi 2013: 213–214). The various reform projects have their roots in a deep crisis of the democratic system, that particularly came to culmination with the major political rupture of the early 1990s, widely referred to as *Tangentopoli* ('bribe city'). The subsequently unfolding 'season of constitutional reform' consisted of more or less permanent political attention to the theme of constitutional reform, and the regular set-up of political reform projects: two bicameral commissions in 1993 and 1997, respectively, comprehensive reforms followed by constitutional referenda in 2001, 2006, and 2016 (with different outcomes).

The discussion will in particular focus on two reform projects that stand out in their populist approach to the reform process as well as the substance of the reforms (see more below), and differ from the other attempts in the same period in that they are government-driven rather than Parliament-driven (Urbinati and Ragazzoni 2016: 120–121). The two reform projects are the ones undertaken by the Berlusconi government in 2004–06 and the Renzi government in 2014–16, respectively. The two projects display a form of continuity in their attitude towards the Constitution, even if they were initiated by parties on opposite sides of the political spectrum. The discussion will highlight an extreme majoritarian logic to both projects, which sheds light on important dimensions in the relation between populist understandings of public law and constitutional reform. In the constitutional narrative in both reform projects, a number of key populist elements are evident (cf. Prospero 2007: 84–85). As argued by the Italian scholar Michele Prospero (here referring in particular to the centre-right reform of 2004–06),

> [a]n inclination to emphasize the image of a leader as supreme embodiment of an uncontrolled power has diffused in the Italy of the 1990s, in the aftermath of traumatic events which have undermined the historical subjects of mediation (parties and the parliament). The last fifteen years of the Italian republic are in reality to a large extent years of triumphing populism and of the erosion of spaces of representation. (Prospero 2007: 13)

The argument below is hence that the 'years of triumphing populism' have continued until the present (year 2019), attesting to a certain 'settling' or institutionalization of a populist mindset with regard to constitutional reform. Already from the 1970s onwards, the Italian Constitution has become increasingly object of a 'culture of revisionism', in which the

Constitution is portrayed as inadequate in a variety of ways. Valerio Onida has remarked:

> In the last decade of the past century, a wind of 'constitutional newism' was blowing, which ranged from proposals that intended to ameliorate the functioning of the system to a comprehensive criticism, if not a real and full-blown denigration, of the Republican Constitution – seen as a product from another 'era' and party system (the antifascist parties that had supported Italy from 1944 onwards) that were supposed to be overcome – and therefore as an 'old' and inadequate instrument for new times and new necessities. (Onida 2007: 125)

Onida distinguishes at least four main forms of critique that have become prominent since the 1970s, and in particular so since the 1990s. A first form of critique on the 1948 Constitution is that of 'governability' or '*governabilità*'. Here, the claim is that the form of government the 1948 Constitution institutionalizes is highly problematic and has led to great political instability, weakness of the government, and excessive powers of political parties ('partitocrazia') (Onida 2007: 124). One related discourse is the one invoking 'presidentialism' as a way out of instable governance. A second form of critique is that regarding a supposedly flawed and weak arrangement of regionalism in the 1948 document, a critique stemming not least from political forces from Northern Italy, most evidently the Lega Nord. A third form of critique, stemming from the centre-right, is focused on the theme of 'giustizia' and in particular on the status of judges, and the relation between politics and the judiciary, within the constitutional system. The main thrust here is a call for a weakening of the status and autonomy of the judiciary (Onida 2007: 125). A fourth form of critique is that related to the 'economic constitution', focusing on the rights and duties in the first part of the Constitution. Onida identifies here a critique of a neo-liberal kind that identifies a form of statism in the existing Constitution.

As mentioned, in Italy, a significant and evident change in political and social attitude towards the 1948 Constitution in the post-1990 period (and in many ways already since the 1970s) regards a move away from a form of *constitutional veneration* (cf. Levinson 2012), that is, generally, a relatively uncritical attitude towards as well as worship of the original document and its crafting (as expressed in notions of 'la più bella costituzione del mondo' and worship of the Founding Fathers of the *assemblea costituente*) towards a form of *constitutional engineering* or *instrumentalism*. The latter generally entails a critical and even negative view of the 1948 Constitution, as sketched above, and the perception that the Constitution keeps in place a form of government ('forma di governo') that inhibits efficient and modern governance (condemning the existing constitutional order as inter alia indicated by the pejorative notion of 'partitocrazia'; cf. Pizzorusso 1996: 24, fn47). The phenomenon of constitutional engineering is not unrelated to 'populist constitutionalism', which in the Italian case implies to a critical attitude towards extensive checks and balances, extensive parliamentary debate of legislation, and a desire to create a direct relationship with the people.

The trend towards constitutional engineering and instrumentalism, in which there is a heightened proclivity to use constitutional means for governance purposes, is not unrelated to the emergence of a distinctive, novel set of ideas on democracy (which had, in reality, always already been there as part of a peripheral, but potent and consistent critique of the 1948 Constitution) (Wolff 2012). The latter has close affinity to a populist view, which in some cases translates into the populist constitutional idea that the relation between political governance/the political leader and the people ought to be a direct one, unhindered by extensive constitutional constraints. In populism, important dimensions are anti-elitism and a promise of bringing politics closer to the people (cf. Mudde 2013). Populism 'opposes any institutions or procedures that impede the direct and full expression of the people's voice' (Mudde 2013: 3). Indeed, '[p]opulism deems that nothing supersedes the general will of the people, and consequently, no one should interfere with it'. 'For populism everything is political', '[t]he idea that certain things are non-political, in the sense that they are outside of the scope of majority rule, is alien to populism' (Mudde 2013: 4). The specific view of constitutional democracy is one in which the modern, mediated view of politics—of popular sovereignty through representation, political pluralism, and the insulation of political and legal power from wider society—is replaced by one in which popular sovereignty is expressed through a leader who directly reflects the People-As-One and in which political and legal power are at the 'service' of the people. This also means that the leader is absorbing constitution-making or constituent power (cf. Arato 2013). In the Italian context, the populist view has often been linked to a plebiscitarian idea of democracy, while the critique of the tendency to institutionalize a plebiscitarian model is indicated by the notion of a '*deriva autoritaria*' or authoritarian turn.

Below, I will use the three dimensions of populist constitutionalism introduced at the start of the chapter—extreme majoritarianism, instrumentalism, and legal resentment—as a lens through which to explore the two government-driven constitutional projects of Berlusconi and Renzi respectively. As extensively explored by Mauro Volpi, the two reform projects are different, but also show important similarities which exactly demonstrate my thesis, that is, a populist approach to the constitution[3] has become significantly entrenched in the Italian political system. As Volpi argues, there are a number of similarities in these two reforms, both of which included comprehensive reforms that finalized the 'iter' of the formal constitutional reform process but were subsequently rejected in a national referendum. In the case of the Berlusconi reform, it was originally elaborated by four politicians of the government parties in 2003, who met in a mountain cabin in Lorenzago. The Renzi reform originated from an extra-parliamentary deal between Berlusconi and Renzi in the so-called *patto del Nazareno* (Volpi 2016: 120). Both reforms were considered integral parts of the governments' political programme. This, according to Volpi, can be understood as having inflationary effects on the Constitution in that the constitutional law becomes part of a wider package of ordinary legislation, which 'any future government may decide to change as it wishes' (Volpi 2016: 120). Both texts were comprehensively addressing the second part of the Italian Constitution. Both reform processes lasted for roughly two years, while, however, in both cases, hardly taking into account propositions of the opposition (Volpi 2016: 121). Both reforms were backed by a fragile majority, in itself 'amplified' by electoral laws with majority premiums. And finally, as will also become clear from the account below,[4] both reform projects invoked an 'epochal change' and the significant strengthening of Italian 'governabilità', which would lead to highly significant change of Italian institutions, not least by creating a direct link between government/Prime Minister and the people, and finally (ostensibly) complete Italy's modernization process (Volpi 2016: 123).

[3] That this approach is not merely evident with regard to constitutional reform, but is equally visible in ordinary legislation is convincingly argued by Nicola Lupo (2019). In Lupo's discussion, a populist approach is identified as one in which the law becomes 'too close to the popular will', while the 'law of the state' and 'constitutional rights' tend to be marginalized (Lupo 2019: 253).

[4] The analysis of the two reforms can be found in an earlier version in Blokker (2019b).

Majoritarianism

The 1990s have frequently been described as years of a majoritarian turn. Indeed, Lupo speaks of a period of 'majoritarian legislatures' between 1994 and 2013 (Lupo 2019: 252). The attention for majoritarianism is equally visible in the various constitutional reform projects of the post-1990 period. Centre-right parties, in particular Forza Italia, the Lega Nord, and Alleanza Nazionale—consisting largely of new (and transformed) political formations emerging in the aftermath of *Tangentopoli*, the large corruption scandal in the early 1990s—were an intrinsic part of various constitutional reform attempts. The latter took the form of bicameral parliamentary commissions in the 1990s, unfailingly endorsing a 'majoritarianization' of the Italian political system. After a failed attempt of such a bicameral commission in the late 1990s, and the unilateral imposition of constitutional reform by the centre-left, the centre-right moved towards an independent, partisan constitutional agenda, which culminated in the constitutional reform of 2006 of the Berlusconi government. The centre-right criticized the centre-left for having used a partisan approach to constitutional reform and, what is more, claimed that it had used an 'illegitimate majority to change the Constitution' (Schifani, Senato della Repubblica, 16-11-2005, 39). From then on, the partisan approach to the Italian Constitution became a clear characteristic of both sides of the political spectrum. The partisan approach informed the two most significant reform projects— those of Berlusconi and Renzi—a tendency towards what Nadia Urbinati has called 'extreme majoritarianism', that is, the promotion of not merely the 'electoral majority' but a 'further, more intense majority'. This implies the attempt of 'freezing' a majority 'into a permanent one', in stark contrast to the temporary and changeable majority that is the outcome of elections (Urbinati 2017).

A majoritarian and antagonizing logic was clearly visible in the Berlusconi project. It is in fact undeniable that, more in general, the post-1990 'season of constitutional reform' was increasingly characterized by a *partisan* approach, in which different political parties competed for the claim to authentically represent the Italian people. From the failure of the 1997 Bicamerale onwards, the consensualist basis of the constitutional compromise of 1948 (which sought to widely include different parts of society) was left behind (cf. Prospero 2007: 127), in favour of a partisan approach that anyhow claimed to represent the Italian people *tout court*. Constitution-making was now understood as the prerogative of the incumbent government and majority, without a need to involve the opposition. The majority of the Berlusconi government clearly identified with the Italian people as such, and *against* the institutions. As minister for reform Calderoli, one of the authors of the constitutional reform, argued in the Senate: 'It may or may not please, but the principal aspect of this reform is that the people are counting more [now], even if the [institutions] do not like it' (Calderoli, n. 899, Senato, 16/11/2005). Calderoli further stated: 'The current majority… is [in contrast to that of the majority of the centre-left in the 2001 constitutional reform] a *real* majority that concludes a constituent pact with the people' (Calderoli, n. 899, Senato, 16/11/2005; emphasis added). The government hence turned into a 'constituent government' or the 'depository of the power of constitutional revision' (Prospero 2007: 127; cf. Prospero 2015: 6839). Constituent power, rather than being the power of the multitude (Loughlin 2004: ch. 6), becomes the power of the majority. In the case of the Berlusconi reform in 2003–06, it is hence fair to speak of an executive-driven project promoted by the governmental majority, pursuing its partisan interests while claiming the popular will.

The Berlusconi reform project reflected in particular the objectives of Forza Italia and the Lega Nord (even if many reform themes—bicameralism, regionalism—had been widely debated also in the 1990s; see Fusaro 2015). What is conspicuous in the reform of the Berlusconi government is the sheer number of articles of the constitution the reform touched upon (57 out of 139; see Prospero 2007: 128). An additional source of tensions was whether such a comprehensive revision is legitimate, that is, whether it can be promoted in purely partisan manner, without involving opposition. A large-scale revision entails the 're-awakening' of constituent power, and without the direct involvement of the opposition in the actual writing of the reform, the project needed other ways of enhancing a more generalized legitimacy (and hence the great importance put on a confirmatory referendum which would bestow popular legitimacy on the project).

A majoritarian thrust could equally be detected in the novel usage of the amendment rule of the Italian Constitution (Art. 138), used by the centre-right, but in a way preceded by the centre-left in 2001.[5] The rule stipulates, in case of the lack of a two-thirds majority in both parliamentary houses after a dual reading, that a popular referendum may be called for.

[5] In 2001, two groups of senators requested the referendum, from the centre-right, but also those belonging to the government majority, from the centre-left.

The latter was originally meant to provide an instrument for the opposition to oppose constitutional reform in case of a lack of consensus (as indicated by a lack of supermajority in favour of the reforms). The first constitutional referendum, held in 2001, was activated by both the opposition and government forces, in that both requests were accepted by the Central Office for the Referendum. The Berlusconi government, but in a way equally its predecessor,[6] turned the logic of the amendment rule upside down, by calling for a referendum in the guise of government majority.[7] In this manner (as was equally to occur with the constitutional referendum in 2016), the popular referendum obtained a plebiscitarian nature, searching for a popular confirmation of the will of the majority (Prospero 2007).

But it is not only in the process of constitutional reform, and the forces involved, that we can detect a majoritarian thrust in the Berlusconi reform. It was equally present in the substance of the reforms. A key dimension was the proposed strengthening of the role of the Prime Minister (some speak of 'absolute premiership'; cf. Fusaro 2015: 4949), at the expense of both the President of the Republic and the President of Parliament. The proposal was to 'designate the prime minister from the part of the electorate', in the form of a kind of 'immediate democracy' (Urbinati and Ragazzoni 2016: 159–160). In this view, the Prime Minister was to be directly indicated by the people, and is strictly linked to, or embodies, the political majority. The proposition reflected both a form of personalization of political power and a populist, direct form of leadership. The distinctive view of democracy emphasized the need for a powerful leader, in political terms understood as a Prime Minister who was to be directly chosen by the citizens and who was to have key decision-making prerogatives.

Let us now turn to the majoritarian dimensions in the Renzi project. In March 2014, Matteo Renzi and the new minister for constitutional reform, Maria Elena Boschi, presented a new constitutional reform proposal. The

[6] Admittedly, I wrongly attributed this governmental usage of the article 138 procedure merely to the Berlusconi government in an earlier discussion (Blokker 2019b).

[7] Four other requests had been presented by oppositional forces. Calderoli claimed in the Senate that this logic had already been used by the centre-left in 2001: 'We have been criticized for having used article 138 in an anomalous way, one does not understand, however, why that article may be valid for your reforms and cannot be valid for the changes that we want to bring about nor does the breadth of the reform count, because it is not true that an instrument is valid if I use it for a pound… but not [when I use it for a kilo]: an instrument is valid or not' (Calderoli, Senato, n. 899, 16/11/2005).

constitutional reform project was also in this case a governmental initiative, and took the form of a governmental 'disegno di legge' (the *Ddl Boschi*). Renzi's reform was embedded in the aforementioned 'patto del Nazareno', stipulated between Renzi and Berlusconi on a number of reforms in early 2014, including electoral and constitutional reform. The pact did not involve any of the opposition parties nor those of the governing coalition. Formally, however, the constitutional reform project was endorsed by a political majority of the Partito Democratico (PD), the centre-right party Nuovo Centro Destra, and some smaller parties, but without support of the largest opposition parties, in particular the Movimento Cinque Stelle (M5S) and later also Forza Italia, which broke with the 'patto del Nazareno' in early 2015.

In general, the involvement of the opposition in the process of constitutional reform was minimal (Volpi 2016: 121), while the logic of reform pursued by the government was a clearly bipolar one, dividing the political and social landscape between 'good Italians' (in favour of reform) and 'bad Italians' (the 'criticasters', 'conservatives'). As argued by Ida Dominijanni, there was a strong redemptive and Manichean claim in the constitutional reform project, that is, the reformers were going to 'save' Italy and the Italians,[8] while the forces who opposed the reform supposedly attempted to push Italy into crisis and disaster (Dominijanni 2016: 8). The reform saw a continuous polemic between Prime Minister Renzi and Reform Minister Boschi, on the one hand, and part of the scholarly, constitutional expert community, on the other (pejoratively referred to as 'professoroni') (Plutino 2015: 149–150). One of the constitutionalists, Gaetano Azzariti, spoke in an interview of a 'strategy of delegitimisation of all critical reflection' (cf. Plutino 2015: 150). Equally, from the side of trade unions (e.g. the main trade union, the Confederazione Generale Italiana del Lavoro (CGIL)), critical comments regarding the reforms

[8] Despite its claim to represent the 'ordinary people', the position of the political majority, and its search for popular legitimacy, was compromised by the fact, as frequently argued by the parliamentary and societal opposition, that the majority behind the reform could be understood as an 'illegitimate' one. This was due to the fact that the electoral law in vigour (the so-called Porcellum) created an artificial majority by means of an electoral premium (identified as unconstitutional by the Constitutional Court in January 2014). What is clear is that the majority behind the reform was relatively small and fragile (Volpi 2016: 121). As Ferrajoli argues, the majority of the government consisted in 25% of the votes, which corresponds to 15% of the electorate, which was however transformed in an absolute majority by means of the electoral law and its majority premium (Ferrajoli 2016: 18).

were raised as well as concern related to a lack of societal participation in the reforms.

The Renzi reform tended to be characterized by a top-down logic, and a general absence of public debate and insensibility to dissenting, critical views. This is not only clear in the way in which opposing views were rebutted (as forms of sabotage), but equally in the manner in which internal critique, within the centre-left itself, was being stifled and a strict party discipline imposed (Prospero 2016: 151). In the process of constitutional reform, the popular referendum became once again a vehicle for the government to identify its popular legitimacy in the form of a plebiscite, while bypassing any parliamentary and societal dissent. The reform process could hence be qualified as a reform by 'colpi di maggioranza' ('blows by the majority'), as further confirmed in the popular referendum organized at the end of the reform trajectory. The popular referendum, held on 4 December 2016, was initiated by the government itself, *qua* majority, in accordance with a by-now-consolidated majoritarian tradition in Italian politics.

In terms of substance of the reform, the *Ddl Boschi* focused in particular on the reform of the bicameral system (most importantly the Senate); a reduction of the number of parliamentarians, and a revision of Title V regarding relations between the state and the regions. The overhaul of the Senate, the most contentious part of the reform, involved its radical transformation, from an 'identical twin' of the Chamber of Deputies into a semi-federal, regional chamber (Ragazzoni and Urbinati, 2016: 172–173). The new Senate was to lose many of its prerogatives, including the power to unseat governments through the vote of no confidence, while retaining a voice in constitutional matters.[9] De facto, the proposition to radically change the nature of the Senate points to a democratic design in which counterbalances, the separation of powers, and popular sovereignty diminish, while the powers of the executive increase.[10] The original bicameral set-up was inspired by a 'guarantist' logic, in which the two chambers,

[9] A further, highly significant part of the reforms, even if formally not part of the Constitution, was electoral reform. In 2014, the Constitutional Court had struck down two parts of the (then) existing electoral law (referred to as the Porcellum): closed-list voting and the majority premium. The new law adopted in May 2015—the Italicum—did not, however, fully eliminate doubts concerning constitutionality, as raised by the Court.

[10] The reform was significantly criticized, also by opponents within the Democratic Party (PD), inter alia for compromising the democratic and representative quality of the Italian Parliament by eliminating the direct election of senators. For extensive discussions of the

supported by a proportional system, functioned as an instrument of control and 'cooling off' of the political process (Prospero 2016: 154). In the Renzi reform, the bicameral set-up was displayed in a very different, potentially populist manner, that is, the cumbersome procedures of bicameralism were identified as an obstacle to the lean type of efficient governance needed in modern, globalized societies.

The objective of the Renzi reform was in this not dissimilar to that of the Berlusconi reform of 2005 (cf. Volpi 2016). The emphasis was on lean institutions and a strong leader and government, this time combined with a centralizing move. One of the implications of the reform of the Senate, in the name of governability, was the weakening of the Parliament in relation to the government. In the reform, the latter was particularly strengthened by way of the position of its leader, that is, Renzi's reform (even if in a less explicit manner than was the case in the Berlusconi reform) formed an attempt to strengthen the relation between the leader and the people, by means of a directly elected 'prime minister', enhancing the latter's 'popular legitimacy' (Volpi 2016: 124). The Prime Minister became the key political institution in Renzi's reform, in a system with only one real parliamentary chamber, an electoral law (Italicum) that allowed for a direct relation between the Prime Minister/the government and the electorate, while the President of the Republic's role in government formation was reduced to a formality (Volpi 2016: 136). As argued by Volpi, the Prime Minister would become the 'Sindaco d'Italia' (the 'mayor of Italy'), 'directly elected by the people and in practice unreplaceable' (Volpi 2016: 137).

Instrumentalism[11]

In general, the season of constitutional reform that started in the early 1990s is characterized by a weakening of the distinction between

substance of the reform, see, for example, Ceccanti (2016), Fusaro (2015, 2016), Pasquino (2015), and Ragazzoni and Urbinati (2016).

[11] The term 'instrumentalism' is used here in a (pejorative) sense akin to the one expressed by the Venice Commission, in a recent opinion; see Opinion on the Fourth Amendment to the Fundamental Law of Hungary, CDLAD(2013)012, Strasbourg, Council of Europe, 17 June 2013, www.venice.coe.int/webforms/documents/?pdf=CDL-AD%282013%29012-e. The Commission argued that '[f]requent constitutional amendments are a worrying sign of an instrumental attitude towards the constitution as is the resort to the exceptional two-thirds majority in constitution-making without a genuine effort to form a wide political con-

constitutional politics and normal politics.[12] In particular the centre-right political formations that came to dominate politics in the 25 years after *Tangentopoli* are characterized by an absence of relation with the 1948 constitutional compromise. Whereas that compromise was still somehow carried forward by the centre-left coalitions, the centre-right had no relations to it, either because of its Fascist legacy (Alleanza Nazionale) or because of the only recent formation of the parties (Forza Italia and Lega Nord). This implied that these parties were rather indifferent to the 1948 Constitution, and were ready to change parts of the constitution which did not correspond to their political objectives (Pinelli 2006: 336). In itself, the 'constitutional acceleration', or the frequent attempts to change the constitution that emerged in the 1990s, indicates the emergence of a more instrumental view across the political spectrum. In Berlusconi's 2006 reform, this instrumental, 'ordinary politics dimension' is perhaps best indicated by the large amount of norms (57 of 139) the reform proposed to change, as well as in the clear partisan nature of the key dimensions of the reform ('devolution' and a strong premiership). The idea of the constitution as a widely endorsed higher framework for Italian politics was yielding to a partisan approach which sees the constitution as an instrument to be manipulated for party purposes[13] (Prospero 2007).

The centre-right discourse articulated a comprehensive critique of the 1948 Constitution and the 'First Republic' as being responsible for the *ingovernabilità* that allegedly defined the post-1948 period. The 1948 Constitution was in this criticized for its institutionalization of a party-based, pluralistic, and representative system. A key justification for the comprehensive reforms of the Second Part of the Italian Constitution provided by the centre-right was the designation of the 1948 Constitution as obsolete and in dire need of modernization. In the initial phase of the reform project in 2004, Minister for Reform Calderoli (Senato della Repubblica, 540a seduta, 3-8-2004, 66) argued:

sensus and without proper public debates' (at page 30). The Commission decried the frequent and non-transparent nature of reforms and the abuse of the majority position of the government.

[12] See for this distinction, Ackerman (1991).

[13] This was exactly the critique of the centre-left opposition: 'Simply for electoral convenience and for reasons of survival of the majority, you are changing the constitutional Charter in a partisan Constitution, the result not of a noble aspiration or a noble compromise, as was that of 1948, but of a confused, watered-down deal between yourselves' (Senator Paolo Giaretta, n. 899, Senato, 16/11/2005).

> The season of institutional reform has known a series of failures, if not centralizing counterreforms. With the modification of Title V of the Constitution – this merit has to be recognized – the system has really started to move. Today, we are surely in front of a further step towards the adaptation of the organization and functioning of our institutions to the exigencies of a modern democracy, which is able to represent the requests from society and to transform these in responsible and rapid deliberations.

In the concluding parliamentary debate in November 2005, when the extensive reform package of the centre-right was adopted, Senator Salvatore Lauro of *Forza Italia* stated that the reform was to 'contribute to the modification of the Constitution in order to bring it into alignment with the necessities and culture of our times' (Senato della Repubblica, 900a seduta, 16-11-2005, 5). In a debate on the same day, a senator from Forza Italia, Andrea Pastore (Senato della Repubblica, 899a seduta, 16-11-2005, xv), claimed:

> It is undeniable that the '48 Constitution has sustained a long phase of democratic development for the country, but it is necessary to look at the future with confidence, without regrets towards a season which has demonstrated serious institutional shortages and which has shown a strong instability as well as bitter social conflictuality.

Similar arguments and attitudes could be found in the Renzi reform project, in particular with regard to the need to update an obsolete constitutional document and the willingness to engage in comprehensive (rather than modest) reform. The Renzi reform corresponded to popular (and populist) calls for political change and the reduction in the costs of politics (the radical reform of the Senate, the abolition of the provinces) and the supposed increase in efficiency of governance. The objective of reform was neither the mere maintenance of the constitution, correcting malfunctioning norms, nor that of founding a polity anew, in a revolutionary sense. Rather, constitutional reform was approached in a partisan manner, and borrowed to the revolutionary grammar of 'epochal change' in a reform that allegedly had been awaited 'for 70 years', while in reality the reform pursued much more modest and partisan objectives. The affirmation by minister Boschi of a reform that the Italians 'had been awaiting for 70 years' perhaps best conveys the instrumentalist approach to the Italian Constitution (cf. Volpi 2016). When Boschi pronounced these words, technically, 70 years would have indicated a period that started 3 years before the actual adoption of the Italian Constitution in 1948. But what is more important is that the observation indicates a rather deep disqualification or delegitimation of the 1948 Constitution as such, which was apparently already obsolete at the moment of adoption, indicating an 'original defect' (Dominijanni 2016: 7–8).

From this instrumental perspective, there is hence no need to regard to the 1948 Constitution as a foundational document which reflects a robust societal consensus and inhabits a spirit of guarantee of the institutions and of (minority) inclusion. Instead, there is no particular normativity attributed to the Constitution, which becomes an object of competition in the game of Italian politics (Prospero 2016: 159). As argued by Prime Minister Renzi during the presentation of the reform project in the Senate in April 2014 (Senato della Repubblica, DDL 1429, 8-4-2014; emphasis added):

> After a debate of by now more than thirty years and after numerous failed or only partially successful reform attempts, but with results that almost everyone judges as controversial, the revision of the second part of the Constitution *cannot wait anymore*. In recent years, the institutional system has had to cope with powerful and sudden transformations... without, however, the adoption of direct interventions in an organic manner within a renewed constitutional framework to confront such transformations.

In its drive to pursue *governabilità*, also the centre-left perceives the Constitution as a set of obstructions for governments to produce the 'outcome' that citizens expect and request. This image of democratic politics grounded in output-oriented legitimacy understands the essence of politics to be one based on the 'delivery of the goods', not one of channelling conflict and ensuring the inclusion of a plurality of different viewpoints. As the representative of the centre-left in the Commission for Constitutional Affairs in 2014, Emanuele Fiano, argued in the Italian Parliament, '[Democracy's] values are still the right ones, but in a world that is changing at a speed that is so much faster than that of politics and to which our societies need to adapt continuously in order to keep up, democracy seems slow, bureaucratic, and weak'. He continued, 'it is time to ameliorate [the Constitution], to render it faster and stronger. It is time for reforms' (Camera, 16-12-2014, 74–76).

Legal Resentment

A final, significant dimension of constitutional reform on both left and right is that of a sceptical and even resentful approach towards legal procedures and constraints, an (excessive) division of powers, and a general juridification of politics. This becomes evident in the centre-right's constitutional reform project and in Berlusconi's attitude towards judicial institutions in particular (see Dallara 2015). Regarding the latter, Berlusconi displayed an 'orientation which could be defined as postmodern because of its decisive aversion vis-à-vis the intrinsic systemic rationality of "legal modernism"' (Taruffo 1998: 902). In Berlusconi's view of the law, 'Legal norms do not derive their existence and validity from the fact that they have been approved with the necessary procedures by the institutions of legislative power'. Rather, for Berlusconi, the idea of the separation of powers seems to be 'tainted by a positivistic formalism which is obsolete by now and is not anymore acceptable' (Taruffo 1998: 902). Berlusconi's theory of the law regards those norms that his electorate desires (Taruffo 1998: 902). Luigi Ferrajoli makes similar observations with regard to Berlusconi's perception of the law:

> But the Berlusconian ideology is not limited to an affirmation of the primacy of economics over politics, reduced to a serving role with respect to the private interests of the leader. Its inevitable corollary is the intolerance of juridical limits and constraints and forms of judicial control, identified as undue obstacles to private autonomy and to political sovereignty. Therefore, the central question in Italian politics has been for more than a decade the relation between politics and law, even more so than that between politics and the economy: whether the political powers of the new governors would need to be subjected to the law – to the constitution and even more to penal law – or whether the "democratic" legitimation which the governors enjoy renders them beyond the law. (Ferrajoli 2003: 26)

Ferrajoli touches here upon the essence of the notion of 'legal resentment', that is, a view in which the liberal understanding of the rule of law and constitutionalism are presented as deeply problematic. Ferrajoli goes on:

> The conflict between politics and law which has been at the core of the institutional question for years is essentially about these two theses: between the principles of the *Rechtsstaat*, according to which the incumbent rulers have to be subjects to the law, and the pretence of their impunity, or, in

other words, the claim of a neo-absolutism of the majority as much as that of the market. The electoral success of Berlusconi signals clearly that the first of these two theses, the one which defines the "*Rechtsstaat*", has been surpassed, in the common sense produced and interpreted by Berlusconi, by the second. (Ferrajoli 2003: 26)

The core of the centre-right approach to the law was hence based on a distinctive idea of democracy, and the relation between the principle of popular legitimation and the principle of legality, that is, the 'conviction that political power, which results from elections, is immune to control by jurisdiction; the one who wins the elections can do whatever he/she wants, even if it is on an illegal basis' (Zanchetta 2003: 1065).

This view of the law was prominent in the centre-right's constitutional reform project. A major objective of the reforms was to reduce constraints on the exercise of executive leadership, which should not be obstructed by institutional processes that 'slow down' the decision-making process (cf. Prospero 2007: 133). The core dimension of 'garantismo' of the 1948 Italian Constitution is replaced by a concentration of political power, in the government and in particular in the new figure of Prime Minister. As Calderoli sustained (Senato della Repubblica, 540a seduta, 3-8-2004, 68):

The institutional weakness of the government and of the prime minister have characterized Italian political life since 1948; this has indeed meant that the history of the Republic was subject to continuous governmental crises, related to fluctuations of parliamentary majorities and to party orientations, indifferent towards indications of the electorate.

In the words of Senator Francesco D'Onofrio, part of a centrist party which sustained the centre-right reform project, the constitutional reform was to lead to a direct relation between citizens and the government, and its Prime Minister, in this strengthening democracy and popular sovereignty (Senato della Repubblica, 900a seduta, 16-11-2005, 19):

Until now, Italians could not vote for a parliamentary majority and a prime minister. They vote for parliamentarians, who, after the elections, may decide what to do. From this constitutional reform onwards, this will not be possible anymore. The popular vote, for the first time with this constitutional reform, will allow the Italians to vote for the parliamentarians, for the head of government, and for the political programme.

While the criticism that post-1948 Italian politics has been rife with instability and lack of citizen participation is reasonable, the proposal in the centre-right reform to strengthen the head of government through direct election indicates a potentially problematic plebiscitarian dimension. The reform did not propose to strengthen the political system by expanding various participatory rights of citizens which would allow them to actively participate in politics, but rather reduces constraints on governmental prerogatives, to be legitimized by a one-off, direct indication of the majority and its leader through elections. As Elisabetta Wolff notes, '[c]onstitutional scholars noted that the reform would have made way for a sort of "absolute premiership" or "Prime Ministerial dictatorship" as opposed to the system of "checks and balances" (bilancia di poteri)' (Wolff 2012: 4).

The attitude towards the law that emerges from the Renzi reform is equally one that displays forms of legal scepticism or resentment to those present in Berlusconi's reform. The Renzi reform challenged the legal or normative constitutionalism ('costituzionalismo garantista') of the Italian post-1948 order (Prospero 2016: 154), as the argument was that the existing rules and checks and balances were too rigid in times of rapid societal change. The post-1990 constitutional revisionism identifies in the 1948 Constitution the responsibility for the malfunctioning of democracy and government (Ferrajoli 2016: 15). The main purpose of the constitutional reforms is hence to clear the way of governmental decision-making, putting at the heart of the democratic regime the necessity of rapid decision-making of the executive, rather than the necessity of inclusionary and pluralistic deliberation (cf. Urbinati and Ragazzoni 2016). In the words of senator Russo:

> Let us say that the great value of the 1948 Constitution today can be found, in my view, in particular in the first part, that of the principles. Because I count myself amongst those that, even if having a great respect for the Constitution, find that the second part today shows the signs of time. And even already at the time [of adoption], if one reads the papers of the constituents, it emphasizes that the Constitution was a child of a distinctive historical context and hence contained in itself already a number of problems, as in the organization of a perfect bicameralism and a certain weakness of the executive. (Russo 12-2-2014, Italian Senate)

The perception that the Constitution forms an obstacle to effective government is even more pronounced in Renzi's introductory speech to the reform, in the Senate on 8 April 2014:

> The *chronic weakness* of the executives in the implementation of the governmental programme, the *slowness and the complex nature of legislative processes*, the excessive usage – in quantity and heterogeneity of the substance – of decrees of urgency and the emergence of the usage of the vote of confidence for maxi-amendments, the change in sources of law and the growing normative entropy, the *difficulty in implementation of a smooth legislative process* and the too frequently instable and confused, heightened conflictuality between different levels of government: these are only some of the symptoms of the pathology that affects the Italian institutional system for years now and the removal of which need profound interventions of reform. (Senato della Repubblica, DDL 1429, 8-4-2014; emphasis added)

Concluding Remarks

If we return to the dualistic perspective mentioned in the introduction, and the question of whether we can understand the populist approach to constitutions as an attempt to rebalance the aforementioned dual dimensions of democracy in the context of hampering and deeply delegitimated democratic institutions, it appears that in the Italian case of the last 25 years, an already unbalanced system (party-centred politics with little citizen participation, embedded in the 1948 Constitution) increasingly moved towards a different, but equally unbalanced system (majoritarian politics with a more direct, but controlled participation of citizens, with an instrumental relation to the 1948 Constitution). Even if neither the centre-right nor the centre-left constitutional reform project was successful, in that both were rejected in popular referenda, a decisive change in (constitutional) politics has become visible. The relatively similar approach taken in the constitutional reform projects—with a strong emphasis on majoritarianism, executivism, and a strong leadership figure, an instrumental approach to the constitution, and forms of resentment towards liberal understanding of the rule of law—is by now shared across the political spectrum. This diffused populist attitude appears ill-equipped in its capacity to rebalance Italian constitutional democracy, not least with regard to a more meaningful inclusionary approach to citizens, in particular from a comparative perspective (Blokker 2017). The populist approach has rather provoked further instability and imbalance. If the First Republic was suffering from a lack of 'governability' but also from a lack of (possibilities for) bottom-up, civic engagement, and 'counter-democracy' (Rosanvallon 2008), the populist 'Second Republic' does not provide a conclusive answer but has rather activated a continuous, and potentially centrifugal, conflict between partisan interests.

The failure of significant reform also means that calls for constitutional reform have continued, for instance in the 2018–19 'green-yellow' government coalition, and equally in the current 'red-yellow' one.[14] In other words, the quest for a rebalancing of the Italian system, away from a legalistic-guarantist approach towards a majoritarian, popular sovereignty approach, remains prominent. In this respect, the various constitutional reform attempts since the early 1990s have had important consequences for the Italian democratic system, in particular for the Italian political and legal culture (cf. Pasquino 2018). One clear result of the entire 'season of constitutional reform' is the idea that it is the 1948 Constitution as such that prevents Italian democracy from operating properly. In this, the Italian reform process constitutes a kind of prelude to what by now is a wider contemporary trend. In various European countries, in particular in East-Central Europe, partisan politics have been dramatically reshaping constitutional orders in recent years. We may be witnessing in this a shift in constitutional imaginary, away from the legalist, anti-totalitarian hegemony of the post–Second World War period, towards a majoritarian, decisionist, and instrumental understanding of constitutions. Whether this shift is able to rebalance constitutional democracy in a more virtuous direction remains very much to be seen.

References

Ackerman, B. (1991). *We The People. Volume I: Foundations.* Cambridge, MA: Harvard University Press.

Arato, A. (2013). Political Theology and Populism. *Social Research: An International Quarterly, 80*(1), 143–172.

Blokker, P. (2005). Populist Nationalism, Anti-Europeanism, Postnationalism, and the East-West Distinction. *German Law Journal, 6*(2), 371–390.

[14]The main reform proposals relate to the reduction of the 'costs of politics' (reducing the number of parliamentarians) and instruments of direct democracy.

Blokker, P. (2013). *New Democracies in Crisis? A Comparative Constitutional Study of the Czech Republic, Hungary, Poland, Romania and Slovakia*. London: Routledge.

Blokker, P. (2017). The Grande Riforma of the Italian Constitution: Majoritarian Versus Participatory Democracy? *Contemporary Italian Politics, 9*(2), 124–141.

Blokker, P. (2019a). The Populist Assault on the Constitution. In P. Blokker & M. Anselmi (Eds.), *Multiple Populisms: Italy as Democracy's Mirror* (pp. 196–215). London: Routledge.

Blokker, P. (2019b). Populism as a Constitutional Project. *International Journal of Constitutional Law, 17*(2), 536–553.

Blokker, P., & Anselmi, M. (Eds.). (2019). *Multiple Populisms: Italy as Democracy's Mirror*. London: Routledge.

Ceccanti, S. (2016). *La transizione è (quasi) finita: Come risolvere nel 2016 i problemi aperti 70 anni prima. Verso il referendum costituzionale*. Torino: Giappichelli.

Corrias, L. (2016). Populism in a Constitutional Key: Constituent Power, Popular Sovereignty and Constitutional Identity. *European Constitutional Law Review, 12*(1), 6–26.

Dallara, C. (2015). Powerful Resistance Against a Long-Running Personal Crusade: The Impact of Silvio Berlusconi on the Italian Judicial System. *Modern Italy, 20*(1), 59–76.

Dominijanni, I. (2016). La deriva della politica costituzionale. *Democrazia e diritto, 2*, 7–13.

Eisenstadt, S. N. (1998). The Paradox of Democratic Regimes: Fragility and Transformability. *Sociological Theory, 16*(3), 211–238.

Ferrajoli, L. (2003). Il berlusconismo e l'appropriazione della sfera pubblica. Un nuovo caso italiano. *Democrazia e diritto, 1*, 21–35.

Ferrajoli, L. (2016). Dal bicameralismo perfetto al monocameralismo imperfetto. *Democrazia e diritto, 14*(2), 15–24.

Fusaro, C. (2015). Per una storia delle riforme istituzionali (1948–2015). *Rivista Trimestrale di diritto pubblico, 64*(2), 431–555.

Fusaro, C. (2016). La ragioni della riforma costituzionale. Una guida. Available at http://www.carlofusaro.it/materiali/Guida%20ragionata%2015052016.pdf

Ginsburg, T., Huq, A. Z., & Versteeg, M. (2018). The Coming Demise of Liberal Constitutionalism. *University of Chicago Law Review, 85*(2), 239–255.

Groppi, T. (2013). Constitutional Revision in Italy: A Marginal Instrument for Constitutional Change. In X. Contiades (Ed.), *Engineering Constitutional Change. A Comparative Perspective on Europe, Canada, and the USA* (pp. 203–228). London: Routledge.

Halmai, G. (2017). Is There Such Thing as 'Populist Constitutionalism'? The Case of Hungary. *Fudan Journal of the Humanities and Social Sciences, 11*(3), 1–17.

Landau, D. (2018). Populist Constitutions. *University of Chicago Law Review, 85*(2), 521–543.
Levinson, S. (2012). *Framed: America's 51 Constitutions and the Crisis of Governance*. Oxford University Press.
Loughlin, M. (2004). *The Idea of Public Law*. Oxford: Oxford University Press.
Lupo, N. (2019). Populismo legislativo?: continuità e discontinuità nelle tendenze della legislazione italiana. *Ragion pratica, 16*(1), 251–272.
Mény, Y., & Surel, Y. (2001). *Populismo e democrazia*. Bologna: il Mulino.
Möller, K. (2018). Popular Sovereignty, Populism and Deliberative Democracy. *Philosophical Inquiry, 42*, 14–36.
Mudde, C. (2013). Are Populists Friends or Foes of Constitutionalism? *The Foundation for Law, Justice and Society Policy Brief*. Available at https://pdfs.semanticscholar.org/a5b9/c00983c780d4e4f780f77cc32f9afa6c2651.pdf
Müller, J.-W. (2016). *What Is Populism?* Philadelphia: University of Pennsylvania Press.
Müller, J.-W. (2017). Populism and Constitutionalism. In C. R. Kaltwasser, P. Taggart, P. O. Espejo, & P. Ostiguy (Eds.), *The Oxford Handbook of Populism*. Oxford: Oxford University Press.
Onida, V. (2007). *La Costituzione. La legge fondamentale della Repubblica*. Bologna: il Mulino.
Pasquino, G. (2015). *Cittadini senza scettro: le riforme sbagliate*. Milano: EGEA.
Pasquino, G. (2018). The Disappearance of Political Cultures in Italy. *South European Society and Politics, 23*(1), 133–146.
Pinelli, C. (2006). The 1948 Italian Constitution and the 2006 Referendum: Food for Thought. *European Constitutional Law Review, 2*(3), 329–340.
Pizzorusso, A. (1996). *La Costituzione. I valori da conservare, le regole da cambiare*. Milano: Einaudi.
Plutino, M. (2015). Equilibri e squilibri costituzionale tra la tentata revisione costituzionale del 2005 e il d.d.l. costituzionale "Boschi". In V. Baldini (Ed.), *La Costituzione e la sua revisione* (pp. 117–172). Pisa: Pisa University Press.
Prospero, M. (2007). *La Costituzione tra populismo e leaderismo*. Milano: Franco Angeli.
Prospero, M. (2015). *Il nuovismo realizzato. L'antipolitica dalla Bolognina alla Leopolda*. Roma: Bordeaux.
Prospero, M. (2016). Una democrazia minore. *Democrazia e diritto, 2*, 148–164.
Ragazzoni, D., & Urbinati, N. (2016). *La vera Seconda Repubblica. L'ideologia e la macchina*. Milano: Raffaello Cortina Editore.
Revelli, M. (2015). *Dentro e contro: quando il populismo è di governo*. Roma/Bari: Laterza.
Rosanvallon, P. (2008). *Counter-Democracy: Politics in an Age of Distrust*. Cambridge: Cambridge University Press.
Russo, F. (2014, February 12). *Senato della Repubblica* (Interview).

Scheppele, K. L. (2018). Autocratic Legalism. *University of Chicago Law Review, 85*(2), 545–583.
Tarchi, M. (2015). *Italia populista: dal qualunquismo a Beppe Grillo*. Bologna: Il Mulino.
Taruffo, M. (1998). Berlusconi teorico del diritto, della giustizia, e d'altro. *Il Mulino, 5*, 901–912.
Urbinati, N. (2014). *Democracy Disfigured*. Cambridge, MA: Harvard University Press.
Urbinati, N. (2017). Populism and the Principle of Majority. In C. R. Kaltwasser, P. Taggart, P. O. Espejo, & P. Ostiguy (Eds.), *The Oxford Handbook of Populism*. Oxford: Oxford University Press.
Urbinati, N., & Ragazzoni, D. (2016). La vera Seconda Repubblica. L'ideologia e la macchina. Raffaello Cortina Editore.
Verbeek, B., & Zaslove, A. (2016). Italy: A case of Mutating Populism? *Democratization, 23*(2), 304–323.
Volpi, M. (2016). Riforma Renzi e Riforma Berlusconi: così lontane... così vicine. *Democrazia e diritto, 14*(2), 119–138.
Wolff, E. (2012). *Berlusconi's Attempt to Reform the Italian Constitution. Rehearsal of New (Post-modern) Authoritarian Politics or Same Old Habit?* Paper Presented in the Paper Prepared for the Conference 'Silvio Berlusconi and Post-modern Politics', University of Birmingham, December 14.
Zanchetta, P. L. (2003). Il governo Berlusconi, il sistema costituzionale, la giustizia (Lo studio del fenomeno in quattro raccolte di saggi). *Questione giustizia, 23*(5), 1053–1067.

PART I

CHAPTER 3

Is There a Populist Turn in the Italian Parliament? Continuity and Discontinuity in the Non-legislative Procedures

Cristina Fasone

The Italian Parliament: A Story of Gradual (Self-)Disempowerment

While for almost 40 years since the enactment of the new democratic Constitution, the Italian Parliament has generally been regarded as one of the most powerful Parliaments worldwide, especially as a legislature (Polsby 1975; Di Palma 1976), its decline started as early as the 1990s at least. Such a disempowerment is also part of a trend that has affected several Parliaments in the twentieth and twenty-first centuries, including those in liberal democracies, as an effect of processes of globalization and of supranational integration, of the crisis of the "political" (Orsina 2017) and the setting up of independent technocratic institutions, of executive dominance and, lately, of the rise and strengthening of populist forces that tend to see Parliaments as unresponsive to the voters and as big machineries slowing down the

C. Fasone (✉)
Department of Political Science, LUISS Guido Carli in Rome, Rome, Italy

Faculty of Law, University of Toruń, Toruń, Poland
e-mail: cfasone@luiss.it

G. Delledonne et al. (eds.), *Italian Populism and Constitutional Law*, Challenges to Democracy in the 21st Century,
https://doi.org/10.1007/978-3-030-37401-3_3

decision-making process (Taggart 2002; Issacharoff 2018). The story of the Italian Parliament, however, is somewhat peculiar in that for some decades, due to particular social and political conditions, it contributed to the myth of the 'parliamentary centrality' before turning to decline.

Indeed, the "success" of the Italian Parliament had clear political roots, beyond what the plain words of the Constitution, designing a system of symmetric bicameralism and of parliamentarism with a low level of rationalization, may have entailed (Manzella 2003: 69–76; Chessa 2019). The Christian democrats, the party gaining the relative majority of seats in Parliament, in alliance with some small centre-right and centre-left parties, ruled the country for almost 40 years, with the socialists until the 1960s and the communists until the 1990s excluded from the government (*conventio ad excludendum*)[1] because of their pro-USSR stance in the framework of an internationally divided scenario and the Italian alliance with Western partners. The arrangement could work and be accepted by all parties because there was the tacit agreement, always respected, that any reform or bills touching upon the constitutional compromise would have never been passed without the political consent of the three major political parties. Such an arrangement gave particular strength to the Parliament as locus of deliberation and place where the compromise amongst the three main political actors—two of which were excluded from the government for some time—could be reached. In contrast with the Executive, the Parliament really embedded the pluralism present in the Italian society.

It was only at the beginning of the 1990s, with the collapse of the political system (Bull and Rhodes 1997),[2] that the Italian Parliament entered its descendent phase, while a populist rhetoric, touching upon anti-elitist and anti-pluralist sentiments (e.g. see Pinelli 2011; Müller 2016), strongly entered the political scene and pervaded representative institutions. Due to the extensive corruption net between the élites of the major political parties (in particular Christian democrats and Socialists), the public administration and business corporations, the judiciary basically dismantled through criminal proceedings and convictions—and it could hardly be otherwise—an entire political class (Della Porta and Vannucci 2007). Public prosecutors and judges led a sort of political catharsis of the then élites in the name of the principle of legality (Guarnieri 1997). In the

[1] An effective formula coined by Elia (1970).

[2] Although the Constitution was not changed, many started to (improperly) talk about the consolidation of a "Second Republic", after the first established in 1948: see Sartori (1992).

coming years, this triggered a sort of backlash against both the judiciary and the Parliament in the public discourse, though for different reasons: on the one hand, there was the idea of a too activist judicial branch and, on the other, the view of a corrupted legislature.

In addition to this, also due to the end of the Cold War, new political actors emerged, amongst whom stood the former entrepreneur Silvio Berlusconi, who, thanks to the majority gained in Parliament, controversially managed at the same time to rule the country and to hold a large share of national media (Hibberd 2007). The domination of the media further fostered an anti-pluralist—populistic—rhetoric against his political opponents and minorities, in particular Muslim minorities and immigrants.[3] The allegation of a politicized judiciary and of a *fumus persecutionis* against him—convicted for several criminal offences—and against politicians in general became obsessive and further echoed by the media. Laws were passed aiming to extend, without clear limitations, the immunity from criminal proceedings for the highest public offices—laws that were subsequently declared invalid by the Constitutional Court.[4]

It is in this context that the marginalization of the Parliament in the system of government has gradually occurred. Every government, though with a different intensity, more or less oriented towards populism, has abused decree-laws, has shortened parliamentary debates and has made use of "maxi-amendments", composed of one article and a thousand commas and replacing the entire text of a bill, coupled with a confidence vote.[5] These tools have become a routine in Parliament. To some extent, the populist tone of the political struggle has never disappeared since the 1990s. While, luckily, not every government in office has promoted anti-élites and anti-pluralist discourses, elements like the personalization of politics and the engagement in a permanent electoral campaign have never abandoned the Italian political landscape, for example, also during Renzi's government (2014–2016), as the possible reasons behind the defeat of 'his' constitutional reform at the referendum held on 4 December 2016 show.

[3] For example, the criminalization of illegal migration was introduced during one of Berlusconi's governments, in 2009, and has remained in force since then. See Legislative decree no. 94 of 2009.

[4] See Law no. 140 of 2003 declared unconstitutional by the Constitutional Court in judgment no. 24 of 2004 and Law no. 124 of 2008 declared unconstitutional in judgment no. 262 of 2009.

[5] See F. Pacini's chapter in this volume.

Overall, the quality of the deliberative process in Parliament has been undermined, with very negative consequences in terms of representative capacity of the institution, in particular for what concerns the minorities. The Parliament has not been able to recover its position by strengthening its scrutiny and oversight powers. The increased transparency of parliamentary procedures, thanks to the Internet, has not been used to 'reconnect' with the citizens and orient the public debate, but rather act as 'shop windows' to feed the voters with empty promises ahead of the next elections. The two Chambers have not reacted to this path of disempowerment either. Indeed, both the Constitution and the rules of procedure could provide a bulwark against the misuse and the abuse of parliamentary procedures, but the Parliament has been passive towards abusive parliamentary practice. The Speakers of the Houses, in theory the guardians of their good functioning, have remained lenient to such a parliamentary decay if not prone to endorse a transformative and abusive reading of parliamentary rules of procedures (Torre 2001; Gianfrancesco 2007: 21–39; Ibrido 2015; 180–193).[6]

This chapter provides a critical analysis of if and how the populist turn of the Italian politics and government has affected the performance of the non-legislative functions of the Parliament.[7] In particular, after a brief review of how populist forces can influence the status of members of Parliament (MPs), the contribution deals with the expressive-informing functions of the Parliament,[8] linked to the transparency and publicity of its activity and to the ability to act as a representative institution. It then explores the impact of populist forces on the parliamentary function of scrutiny and oversight, in particular on whether this has been exercised in continuity with the past, of a Parliament not very keen to fully exploit its tools and of governments inclined to escape parliamentary control.

As for the time frame, the investigation covers the 17th (2013–2018) and the 18th (2018–2019) parliamentary terms until the collapse of the coalition government between the Five Star Movement (hereinafter 5SM)

[6] Despite the fact that from time to time Speakers have emphasized the centrality of the Parliament: see, for example, the opening speech of Robert Fico as President of the Italian Chamber of Deputies on 24 June 2018.

[7] Even though all parliamentary functions are intimately related one to another as the idea of "poli-functional" parliamentary procedures highlights (Manzella 2003: 409–410). On the legislative function of the Italian Parliament and populism, see F. Pacini's chapter in this volume.

[8] For this categorization, see Bagehot ([1867] 2001: 125 and ff).

and Lega in August 2019. Although, as anticipated, the marginalization of the Italian Parliament and the affirmation of a populist rhetoric is anything but new in the national context, the selected timespan can be explained by the fact that these two parliamentary terms have witnessed the alternation of political forces that have publicly described themselves as populist—the 5SM, Lega and Fratelli d'Italia—at the opposition and in government.[9] Therefore, this can assure proper coverage in the study of the parliamentary practice of populist groups, acting in different capacities, depending on how they have placed themselves vis-à-vis the executive.

Moreover, the year 2013 can be considered as a sort of watershed. The political elections and the new Parliament summoned featured for the first time the entry of the 5SM (and of Fratelli d'Italia, founded in December 2012) into the Parliament, saw the alternation of three centre-left governments in five years[10] and followed the most acute phase of the Eurozone crisis in Italy, with the experience of a full-fledged technical government led by Mario Monti that promoted crucial, yet controversial, austerity reforms. The reaction to the financial crisis has probably triggered a new 'populist wave' in the Italian constitutional system (Boggero in this volume) that seems worth exploring in its evolution from 'populist opposition' to 'populist government'.

Brief Reflections on How Italian Populist Forces Aim to Influence the Status of MPs

The view of an unresponsive political élite towards the citizens, keen to pursue its own self-interest rather than the "public good" and isolated in the "ivory towers" of Montecitorio and Palazzo Madama has fed the idea, promoted by the 5SM in particular, to revise the status and "privileges" of MPs. From this, it followed the idea of the 5SM to let its MPs renounce part of their allowance (*indennità*, Art. 69 Const.) or to declare themselves

[9] This, of course, does not apply to the parliamentary group Fratelli d'Italia that has never held governmental positions in the period considered.

[10] Thus showing a high degree of political instability even inside the ruling party. The government led by Enrico Letta remained in office from 28 April 2013 to 22 February 2014; the government led by Matteo Renzi, from 22 February 2014 to 12 December 2016; finally, the government led by Paolo Gentiloni, from 12 December 2016 till 1 June 2018. Although some prominent technical figures were appointed as ministers in these governments, by no means these governmental experiences can be considered as 'technical governments'. See Verzichelli and Cotta 2018.

strongly against the inviolability (Art. 68, sections 2 and 3, Const.),[11] disregarding the fact that those are not individual "privileges" but functional immunities, instrumental in assuring the good functioning—against corruptive practices—and the stable composition of the institution. The same goes for some attempts to overcome or revise the prohibition of a binding mandate for MPs.[12]

While with the rise of mass political parties and with contemporary Parliaments anchored to party group's discipline the free mandate risks becoming a sort of *fictio*, this principle is considered part of the *ius constitutionale commune* (Ciaurro 2006: 1289) and fulfils a fundamental function: namely, to balance the principle of popular sovereignty in that, by allowing MPs to deviate from the will of their constituents and from the position of their party, the free mandate tames the most extreme manifestations of the democratic principle (Zanon 1991; Pinelli 2011).[13]

Even though party domination of MPs' conduct represents a challenge to the free mandate, party discipline is nevertheless essential to let accountability mechanisms on the elected representatives properly work (e.g. Curreri 2004: 7 and ff.; Morelli 2018: 52–56). Moreover, party control on MPs is also crucial to reach the political compromise in parliamentary institutions that appear more and more fragmented and internally divided (Ridola 1994; Manin 1996).

A certain degree of constraint on the representative mandate is indeed instrumental to the operation of Parliaments. It is not by chance that, beyond the populistic discourse on the need to restore a binding mandate for MPs in front of the voters, for the sake of abiding to their preferences,[14] the debate on the limitation of the free mandate typically arises in constitutional systems, like Italy since the mid-1990s, featured by high level of

[11] Article 68 Const. had been already at the centre of the political debate at the time of the corruption scandals in the 1990s, leading to its reform and to abandon the tool of the prior parliamentary authorization to start judicial proceedings against MPs: see Constitutional Law no. 3/1993, Gazzetta Ufficiale no. 256 of 30 October 1993. It should be borne in mind, however, that even in its current formulation, being the inviolability a functional immunity, not an individual right, cannot be waived by individual MPs and it is the Chamber of which the MP is part that decides over its use.

[12] On which see also the Introduction in this volume by Delledonne, Martinico, Monti and Pacini.

[13] See also Art. 1 of the Italian Constitution, which clearly highlights such an inherent tension between popular sovereignty and democratic representation, the latter being one of the tools through which people's sovereignty is channelled: cf. Morelli (2018: 82–86).

[14] It goes also beyond this, for example, in countries where elected representatives can be subject to recall, under specific conditions.

parliamentary 'transfugism' (*transfughismo parlamentare*), that is the likelihood and the inclination of MPs to change political group or party once or several times since the electoral moment.

In general, the limitation of the free mandate is tolerated, though with a number of guarantees, to protect competing constitutional values that deserve protection in the legal system, like ensuring governmental stability and the well-ordered functioning of parliamentary procedures. Those limitations can take the form of constitutional clauses, for example, Art. 160 of the Portuguese Constitution (Scarciglia 2005; Orrù 2015), of provisions in the parliamentary rules of procedure, for example, Arts. 23.2 and 27 of the rules of Spanish Congress (Caretti et al. 2019: 1–70), or the balance between free mandate and other constitutional principles can be struck by case law, depending on where in the Parliament the limitation has occurred. For example, in the *Wüppesahl* case decided by the German Constitutional Tribunal in 1989, the court held that the norm of the rule of procedures foreseeing the automatic loss of the seat in a parliamentary committee for MPs who had exited their group, becoming non-attached members, was unconstitutional as it violated the principle of free mandate.[15]

In Italy parliamentary 'transfugism' is a serious issue, whose solution is not eased by the instability of the electoral legislation (Tarli Barbieri 2018). It suffices to say that during the 17th parliamentary term (2013–2018) more than 185 deputies (out of 630) and almost half senators (out of 315) have changed their group affiliation since the beginning of the term (Lupo 2018: 1). The situation has improved during the 18th parliamentary term (2018–)[16] perhaps as a consequence of the new electoral legislation (Law no. 165 of 2017) and, at the Senate, of the new Art. 14 of the rules of procedure. Indeed, this article, reformed in 2017 and implemented from the new term, allows the formation of a group only if it represents a political party or movement—also resulting from the aggregation of several parties and movements—that competed with their own candidates under the same symbol for seats in the Senate obtaining that at least some of them were elected. Despite the emphasis of the new provision on the relationship between the electoral moment and the creation of political groups, to avoid frequent changes in the groups' composition and creation, its implementation, as problematically interpreted by the President of the Senate, has recently bypassed the objective to counter

[15] BVerfGE 80, 188.
[16] Until October 2019 (Curreri 2019).

parliamentary ‘transfugism’. A new political group, *Italia Viva*, whose members previously formed part of a different group and party—the Democratic Party—competing at the 2018 elections, was considered as validly formed in September 2019 despite the absence of an electoral linkage.[17]

The problem of ‘transfugism’, coupled with the crisis of mass political parties, affecting the Italian political system, likewise most European countries, and generating a profound sense of disenchantment and of estrangement in the relationship between voters and elected representatives (Ignazi 2009; Mair 2013), have paved the way to several attempts to reform the constitutional clause where the principle of the free mandate is enshrined. Article 67 of the Italian Constitution, stating that “Each Member of Parliament represents the Nation and carries out his duties without a binding mandate”, is indeed placed amongst the constitutional provisions protecting the freedom and the autonomy of MPs (Zanon 1991).

In a clear attempt to counter governmental instability, a number of proposals to amend Art. 67 have been put forward over the last two decades, in particular since the 13th parliamentary term (1996–2001), when the problem of parliamentary ‘transfugism’ became particularly serious.[18] Although the idea to reform Art. 67 of the Constitution is anything but new, under the current populist twist of the Italian political system it has been subject to a more extreme interpretation. For example, during the 17th parliamentary term (2013–2018), possibly the most radical attempt of revision has been advanced with a view to introduce, as the constitutional amendment bill puts it, a “popular binding mandate” for MPs (De Fiores 2017: 19–41).[19]

[17] In fact, lacking such a requirement at the Chamber of Deputies, the new group was easily constituted at the lower chamber. The circumvention of Art. 14 of the Senate’s rules was, instead, possible thanks to one senator elected by the socialist party who, without any clear political affinity, accepted to join the force with the “expats” from the Democratic Party in exchange for the possibility to form a political group (Maestri 2019).

[18] See, for example, Chamber of Deputies, A.C. 5923, 6663 e 6718, 13th parliamentary term, jointly discussed by the Constitutional Affairs’ Committee on 8 March, 5 April, 10 May, 4 and 20 July and 7 December 2000 and on 18 January 2001.

[19] Cfr. Senate of the Italian Republic, 17th parliamentary term, A.S. 2759, “Modifica dell’articolo 67 della Costituzione, concernente il vincolo di mandato dei parlamentari”, presented on 23 March 2017, not approved. On the ongoing attempt to change Art. 71 of the Constitution as a form of limitation of the representative mandate’s exercise, when it contrasts with the “people’s will”, see Delledonne, Martinico, Monti and Pacini, in the Introduction to this volume.

Tabled by senators of the 5SM, according to the promoters, the presentation of the bill followed a proposal channelled by a private citizen through the 5SM platform 'Rousseau'. It aimed to keep the first part of Art. 67 Const., on the representation of the Nation, while it created a bond between the affiliation to a party group and the electoral candidacy, similarly to the revised Art. 14 of the Senate's rules. However, the constitutional amendment bill goes much further: it foresees the loss of the seat and the preclusion to run as candidate in the elections for MPs changing party group's affiliation during the term, compared to the party and group on whose lists she had been elected. Therefore, under the conditions set, the sanction for the MP who leaves the group is particularly far-reaching. Not only does she lose the representative mandate while the term is ongoing, like under Art. 160 of the Portuguese Constitution, but she is also excluded from future electoral contests (Morelli 2018: 101 ss.).

The very strict approach of the 5SM on party discipline and sanctions for 'disobedient' MPs is further confirmed by another controversial measure put forward, this time at the level of the Statute of the 5SM group in the Chamber of Deputies (with comparable provisions that had already appeared before at local and regional level: see Ceccanti and Curreri 2015; Caterina 2016; Grasso 2017).[20] Starting from the beginning of the 18th parliamentary term, in 2018, Art. 21.5 of the 5SM group's Statute imposes a penalty of 100,000 euro to deputies that are expelled from the group (due to deviations from the party's directives), who leave the group joining another one or resign in dissent with the group. Moreover, such a clause, which has to be signed by deputies elected within the 5SM's lists—hence, it can be considered as a 'contract'—confers to the group the power to define the procedure to impose the penalty. While the penalty is usually automatic—for instance, when the deputy is willing to join a different group—'in exceptional circumstances', upon indication by the 5SM political leader, the expulsion of the dissident deputy and therefore the imposition of the penalty can be decided through an online majority vote on the Rousseau platform by the registered users (Art. 21.4 of the Statute). This procedure clearly endorses the idea of a binding mandate conferred upon the elected representatives by the 'voters-Internet users', which can sanction the detour from such a mandate (Gianfrancesco 2018: 486).

[20] This circumstance highlights the underlying tension here between the principle of free mandate (Art. 67 Const.) and the requirement for an internal democratic structure of political party (Art. 49 Const.), which has never been fully implemented and followed.

This interpretation is in sharp contrast with the case law of the Italian Constitutional Court clarifying that MPs are free to vote according to the political directions of their party, but are also free to deviate from them: "No norm could legitimately impose any effect or sanction on an MP as a consequence of her voting against the party's directives".[21] Along this path, based on Art. 67 Const., scholars have excluded any legal effects for agreements and contracts signed by MPs that mandate them to follow specific instructions and that foresee sanctions in case of a lack of compliance (Caterina 2016; Carducci 2018; Conti 2018). Clauses, like Art. 21.5 of the 5SM Statute, that bind the mandate of MPs and make them subject to sanctions to this end, are null and void being in contrast with imperative norms, amongst which Art. 67 Const. can certainly be placed (*ex* Art. 1418 of the Civil Code) or are, at least, voidable (Ciaurro 2006: 1292). Indeed, it being patently in violation of Art. 67 Const. the relevant clause can be annulled by the Constitutional Court, most likely by means of a conflict of attribution (on this hypothesis, see Gianfrancesco 2018: 485).

While this measure is objectively problematic from a constitutional standpoint and the constitutional amendment bill on the popular binding mandate of MPs presented in 2017 provides a distorted interpretation of what an accountable and responsive MP is expected to fulfil, limitations of the reach and the scope of the representative mandate may not appear as necessarily driven by the last populist wave. Indeed, further proposals strongly supported by the 5SM like the limit of two parliamentary mandates or the reduction of the number of seats in both Houses, eventually approved by the Parliament,[22] though for different reasons and arguments, had been discussed for decades. While the limit to representative mandates has eventually materialized at local level, for example, for consecutive mandates of mayors, the lowering of the number of the seats in Parliament had been on the agenda since the 1990s,[23] though being often linked to

[21] See Italian Constitutional Court, judgment no. 14/1964, Considerato in diritto, § 2 (own translation from Italian).

[22] See Camera dei deputati, A.C. 1585-B, 18th parliamentary term, finally approved on 8 October 2019 and that may be subject to constitutional referendum pursuant Art. 138 Const. The constitutional revision, should it enter into force, will reduce the number of seats, in the Chamber of deputies, from 630 to 400 and in the Senate, from 315 to 200 (plus the life senators; those appointed cannot go beyond 5). On populism and constitutional revisions, see in detail, the chapter by P. Faraguna in this volume.

[23] See Camera dei deputati and Senato della Repubblica, Commissione parlamentare per le riforme istituzionali, A.C. 3597 and A.S. 1789, 11th parliamentary term, Progetto di legge

the reform of the bicameral system. Those measures, able to affect directly or indirectly the status of MPs, likewise previous attempts to reform Art. 67 Const., are not populistic in themselves and they can have a rationale to counter dysfunctions of the present political system, from out-of-control 'transfugism' to the never-reformed symmetric bicameralism. However, what are populistic are the arguments put forward to support these measures, the *finalité* proclaimed, the over-simplification of the debate (or lack thereof) on the effects of the reforms in the current scenario.[24]

Indeed, any measure affecting the status of MPs should be well thought through and thoroughly considered as it could potentially impair the autonomy of the Parliament in exercising its functions. The limitation of parliamentary representation is constitutionally problematic in itself. Moreover, in a comparative perspective, such limitation is usually put in place and justified mainly when there is a different type of representation between the two Houses of a bicameral Parliament; for instance, a non-elected Chamber, in a federal form of state, is expected to ensure the representation of Member States as for the *Länder* in the German *Bundesrat* or, depending on system of government, the representation of social formations is guaranteed in the upper house, as in the Irish and the Slovenian Senates.[25]

costituzionale. Revisione della Parte Seconda della Costituzione, Final Report of the Chairwoman, Nilde Iotti, 11 January 1994, p. 5.

[24] N. Lupo, La riduzione del numero dei parlamentari. Una riforma giusta con la motivazione sbagliata e F. Palermo, La riduzione del numero dei parlamentari. Riformare, ma con giudizio, bothpublished in la rivista Il Mulino online, 14 October 2019. A populist aurea has also featured the decisions to lower the pensions of former MPs, the so-called *rideterminazione dei vitalizi* adopted by the Bureau of the two Houses in 2018: see the deliberation of the Chamber of Deputies' Ufficio di Presidenza no 14 of 12 July 2018 and the deliberation of the Senate's Consiglio di Presidenza no 6 of 16 October 2018.

[25] Precisely because of their non-elected nature, the Irish and the Slovenian Senate in particular and, to some extent, also the German *Bundesrat* after 2006 have seen their powers reduced and reduced by law or by practice over the years compared to the Lower House.

The 'Populist Design' of Parliamentary Procedures: Transparency at Any Cost

The fulfilment of a free mandate by MPs can be put in relation to the publicity and transparency of parliamentary procedures. Article 64, second section Const. sets the general rule according to which parliamentary meetings are held in public, unless each House or the Parliament in joint sitting decide to meet in camera. Moreover, Art. 72, first section, Const., defers to the rules of procedure the choice regarding the transparency regime for committees during the legislative process, which ranges from full transparency when the committees pass legislation on behalf of the plenary to meetings recorded and diffused with closed-circuit television cameras. Beyond legislative procedures, usually, committee meetings offer reduced level of publicity of their work, if compared to the House. They meet in camera, especially the committee's bureau, and when informal hearings are organized. No one can enter the committee rooms except the committee members, the parliamentary officials working for that particular committee and potential guests invited for a hearing, just for the duration of the hearing. This places the Italian Parliament, in a comparative perspective, definitely not amongst the most transparent parliamentary institutions (Caretti and Morisi 2014; Fasone and Lupo 2015).

Transparency and secrecy of parliamentary activities are directly linked to the very sensitive balance to be struck between the autonomy of MPs from external and from party influence and democratic accountability to the voters (Gianniti and Lupo 2018: 331–341). Such a balance has become even more problematic since the Internet has provided access to parliamentary procedures through the institutional channels of the Houses and, furthermore, through the individual use of social media by MPs. Although the Internet is a neutral instrument in theory (Frosini 2019), it is easily misused for political purposes. Populist forces, and especially the 5SM in Italy, have strongly supported the idea of 'total transparency' of parliamentary procedures and this might become problematic for the correct functioning of the Parliament.

Indeed, on the one hand, there is a close relationship in place between the principle of transparency of parliamentary activities, the representative mandate and democratic accountability (see, though from different standpoints, Kelsen [1924] 1982: 195; Bobbio 1984). On the other hand, however, the Internet lends itself to extreme manifestations of such a relationship, in particular when it is instrumentally used by populist forces, adopting an anti-élitist and anti-pluralist discourse (Müller 2016: 7–74; Blokker and Anselmi 2019: 1–14). The idea of 'transparency at any cost' (Lessig 2009; Erkkilä 2012), which would allow to bring together again the political *casta* with the citizens, as promoted through the arguments put forward and the practice of the 5SM, takes advantage of digital tools to build up a dangerous narrative: by accessing all parliamentary procedures on the Internet, regardless of the decision to be taken and of the specific function fulfilled, the Parliament would be able to face the challenge of the disintermediation derived from the crisis of mass political parties as to reconcile representatives and those represented. However, the situation is slightly more complex than depicted by populists. Not every parliamentary procedure, or—better—not every stage of a parliamentary procedure, deserves the same level of transparency. Negotiating and forging the political compromise in committees typically requires a certain degree of secrecy to work properly, unlike scrutiny and oversight activities on the executive that probably deserve the highest level of transparency possible, particularly in the plenary, as to let the citizenry control the government via the Parliament.

The use of the Internet by the Parliament and by MPs individually in this context appears to create new challenges to the traditional configuration of the representative mandate. In the digital era, the level of transparency of parliamentary procedures does not rely exclusively—and, perhaps, not predominantly—on the Parliament as an institution and on the rules of procedure. As a consequence of social media, principally Facebook and Twitter, the institutional representation of the Parliament—expected to channel outside a coherent and unitary vision of its activities, despite the fragmentation of bodies and meetings along which its work is articulated—risks becoming inconsistent with the representation of the Parliament provided by deputies and senators, on an individual basis, through their own social media accounts (Judge and Leston-Bandeira 2018). Therefore, the Parliament loses, to a certain extent, the monopoly of the information over its activities and is bound to compete with a series of sources of information, potentially every single MP, that escape its institutional control. Indeed, once information on parliamentary procedures and activities are released on the Internet, then they reach millions of users. Individual MPs, in turn, can circulate 'their own' information on those procedures with a timing—often while the parliamentary meeting is taking place—and a way that is outside the control of the institution, claiming that such a conduct is consistent with their accountability duties towards the voters. This is patent, for example, when looking at the implementation of the rules on the secret vote in Parliament, a tool normally foreseen in deliberations dealing with elections by the Parliament of people to certain offices inside or outside the institution or with issues affecting fundamental rights and highly sensitive matters.[26] Through the secret vote the freedom of conscience of every MP is protected and MPs can easily vote against the official position of her party. However, as has been clearly reported (Biondi Dal Monte 2017: 16 and ff.), in a few cases MPs have used their social media accounts to make improper voting declarations and unveil how they voted.[27]

In the name of 'transparency at any cost', populist forces and their MPs tend to use the Internet and social media to break parliamentary rules. With this regard, in violation of the rules of procedure that makes summary reports the ordinary device to ensure the visibility of committee meetings in both Houses, from time to time MPs of the 5SM have provided streaming via Facebook or other social media of the committee meetings they are participating in. The streaming of committee meetings, however, may pose a series of problems to the good functioning of parliamentary procedures. Indeed, it can impair the quality of the preliminary analysis (*istruttoria*) and the negotiation preceding the decision. The closed venue of a parliamentary committee is expected to favour the in-depth and specialized examination of the issue at stake without the interference of the public, with a view to enhance the authenticity of the discussion and the achievement of a political compromise. The high degree of informality, which features the work of Italian parliamentary committees and that follows from the fact that usually they do not meet in public, is beneficial for the committees' deliberative process. By contrast, the attempt to instil a regime of forced transparency through the Internet can

[26] It should be borne in mind that at the Italian Chamber of Deputies the secret vote has remained the rule for the final deliberation on bills until 1989 (Manzella 2003: 41). A roll-call vote, instead, is prescribed by the Constitution (Art. 94 Const.) for deliberation engaging the confidence relationship with the executive.

[27] The author reports that this practice has manifested itself, for example, at the time of the approval of the bill on civil unions (Biondi Dal Monte 2017: 19) and improper voting declarations through social media have not featured only or mainly MPs from populist parties. Moreover, the opportunity for MPs to express their orientation in presence of a secret vote is generally admitted (see, also, Italian Constitutional Court's judgment no. 14 of 1964), even though it can prove to be politically problematic.

jeopardize the ability of these committees to provide an appropriate setting for political negotiations.

The same holds true for other collegial bodies of the Parliament, with even lower levels of transparency than committees. For example, the bureau of the House and of the parliamentary committees, in the framework of which informal hearings take place, as well as the Conference of Group Chairmen are marked by the secrecy of their deliberations. Indeed, not even a summary report of their meetings is provided by the Parliament with only the date and the time of the meeting known (Fasone and Lupo 2015). Perhaps, it is precisely because of the level of secrecy surrounding their activities that these bodies have become so powerful in the parliamentary procedures, where the real political bargaining in Parliament takes place. This notwithstanding, during the 17th (2013–2018) and the 18th (2018–) parliamentary terms, MPs of the 5SM have tried to offer the streaming of committees' and plenary's Bureau meetings as well as of meetings of the Conferences of Group Chairmen by using their own mobile phones. The aim pursued, also in this case, is always the same: to (improperly) use parliamentary transparency as a tool of political propaganda.

Do Populist Forces Trump or Contribute to Enhance Parliamentary Oversight?

Such a discourse regarding the instrumental use of parliamentary transparency by populist forces, in particular by the 5SM, can trigger some reflections on how this impacts the parliamentary oversight function on the government where the openness of parliamentary procedures is usually seen as particularly desirable (McCubbins and Schwartz 1984; Pelizzo et al. 2006).[28] Indeed, the use of parliamentary oversight powers by populists has been subject to little investigation so far, not just in Italy, while on the side of the legislative function there are already studies pointing to the strengthening by populist parties of previous trends already in place

[28] According to these authors, scrutiny is generally referred to parliamentary control exerted before the government takes a decision, as to shape the political directions ('fire alarm' function), while oversight is typically exercised *ex post* ('police patrol' function). In this section, the attention will be mainly devoted to traditional tools of oversight: parliamentary questions and committees of enquiry.

thereby favouring the marginalization of the Parliament as a legislature.[29] Could the populist turn have led to a sort of redemption of the parliamentary oversight? And, are there specific differences depending on whether populists are in opposition or in government?

Two typical tools of parliamentary oversight deserve specific analysis here, committees of enquiry and parliamentary questions, in particular the question time, as new trends can be detected at first sight, both going in the direction of an increasing use of the relevant procedures, following the rise of populist forces.

Committees of Enquiry

In the Italian constitutional system, committees of enquiry can be established by each House or by the two Houses jointly, "to conduct enquiries on matters of public interest" and are exclusively formed by MPs proportionally to the composition of political groups (Art. 82 Const.). They can proceed to "investigations and examination with the same powers as the judiciary". Thus, these committees are particularly powerful, able to fulfil a quasi-judicial function, but through political bodies, and they have been used extensively by the Parliament, thereby generating a series of disputes with the judiciary (Pace 1973, 2011; Piccione 2011). The Constitutional Court, called to solve those conflicts, has increasingly supported the "sincere cooperation" between committees of enquiry and judges when exercising their powers[30] and has clearly reminded that the autonomy of the former is structurally limited by their nature of parliamentary bodies.[31]

Committees of enquiry can be unicameral and, as such, established by means of a resolution, or bicameral, in which case they are set up following the approval of legislation. Unlike other constitutional systems, for example Germany, they are not created upon the (exclusive) initiative of a minority. Rather they need the endorsement of the majority to be established, either supporting the vote of the unicameral resolution or passing legislation.[32] However, empirical analyses show that, although a minority

[29] See, for example, F. Pacini's chapter in this volume and Lupo (2019).

[30] Compare judgment no. 26 of 2008 of the Italian Constitutional Court with one of the first constitutional judgments on committees of enquiry, no. 231 of 1975.

[31] See the Italian Constitutional Court's judgment no. 241 of 2007.

[32] The government can express its opinion on the setting up of a committee of enquiry, but cannot veto or obstacle its creation, for example, putting to a vote a question of confidence on it.

is not sufficient for their creation, unicameral committees of enquiry are typically set up with the support of minorities or of large coalitions, which also include minorities, and bicameral committees of enquiry have often been promoted by the majority and the minorities together (Malvicini and Lauri 2016: 12–15). Indeed, through the committees of enquiry minorities aspire to obtain privileged information to hold the government accountable and to challenge the majority (Celentano 2016: 5).

However, once established these committees usually do not implement a scheme that favours the minorities. The chairmanship of these unicameral or bicameral committees has been either assigned by the President of the House and by the two Presidents by common accord—a solution that appears to better protect the interest of minorities as it sees the Presidents as guarantors of the good functioning of parliamentary procedures—or among its members through an election taking place inside the committee. The practice has developed in favour of a majority chairmanship, which has been a constant in the bicameral committees of enquiry, while in unicameral committees the minority has been given the chairmanship on a few occasions, a bit more frequently in the Senate than in the Chamber (Malvicini and Lauri 2016: 14). These circumstances led to the conclusion that overall committees of enquiry in the Italian experience have traditionally not acted as bulwark to protect minorities, but rather to promote majority interests, with some exceptions.[33] Such a conclusion is quite remarkable if one takes into consideration the far-reaching investigative powers these parliamentary bodies have, their potential impact on constitutional rights and the risk of a purely political or propagandistic use of their role against individuals and groups.

The panorama of the 17th and the 18th parliamentary terms offer interesting insights into the role of enquiry committees during the last populist turn experienced by the Italian constitutional system. First, during the 17th parliamentary term, when the Lega and the 5SM were in opposition, the highest ever number of enquiry committees established in the Italian Parliament has been recorded. There were four bicameral enquiry committees, six enquiry committees at the Chamber and five at the Senate. Perhaps even more remarkable has been the number of

[33] The bicameral committee of enquiry against mafia and other criminal associations, established since the 1962 (Law no. 1720) and re-established at every term (see, lately, Law no. 99 of 7 August 2018), has been somewhat institutionalized, has become almost 'permanent' and is regarded as independent and highly authoritative (see Lupo and Gianniti 2018: 218).

proposals to establish enquiry committees presented, most of which did not get the support of the majority. More than 40 proposals were tabled unsuccessfully to set up unicameral enquiry committees at the Chamber and more than 20 at the Senate, while the (unsuccessful) proposals of bicameral enquiry committees went beyond 130 (Lauri 2018: 5–7). Such figures highlight a significant level of activism by MPs to promote enquiry procedures in the Parliament. Most attempts were put forward by minority groups, including the 5SM and the Lega, but did not get through and some of them have been proposed again during the 18th term. Interestingly, in the Senate the 5SM managed to let the plenary approve the creation of an enquiry committee on the reconstruction of the city of L'Aquila following the earthquake of 6 April 2009,[34] but this committee has never started to work due to the delay of some groups in appointing their members.

In the committees of enquiry established the chairmen were elected from within the committees and all of them, with the exception of the chairman of the Chamber's enquiry committee on the security of the cities, their decay and the safety of the suburbs, of Forza Italia, came from the majority, preferably from the Democratic Party and in a few cases from minor groups supporting the governmental coalition.

Given the criterion of proportional representation for the composition of enquiry committees and due to the size of political groups, neither the 5SM or the Lega have been particularly vocal in these committees' activities, even though the 5SM has probably been under-represented compared to the other groups. This low profile of MPs of the 5SM and Lega has also been confirmed with regard to enquiry committees that, in light of their portfolios, in theory, would have intersected the priorities of these parties, for instance for what concerns the committee on the reception, identification and expulsion of migrants and the use of public resources to this end. Therefore, except for the bicameral enquiry committee on the banking and the financial system—which has also undergone important developments during the 18th term—the activity of the enquiry committees in operation was not subject to adversarial politics and was not affected by the minority-opposition status of the 5SM and the Lega.[35] The enquiry

[34] See Delibera of the Senate of 10 November 2016, published in G.U. n. 268, 16/11/2016, errata-corrige published in G.U. n. 55 of 7th March 2017.

[35] It is worth clarifying here that, unlike other constitutional systems, in Italy no formal status is granted to the most significant minority force in Parliament as the 'Opposition'.

committee on the banking and the financial system,[36] chaired by Pier Ferdinando Casini, has been featured by heated debates since it was established. Its mandate was subject to high politicization not only because of the then recent crises of some Italian banks,[37] with significant implications for the protection of the right to savings (Art. 47 Const.), but also because of the alleged implications of relatives of members of the Government in these scandals. The rate of internal conflict inside the committee is indeed also confirmed by the report(s) it approved on 30 January 2018. Next to the report of the majority, three other minority reports were presented: by deputies and senators of Forza Italia-Popolo della Libertà, Fratelli d'Italia-Alleanza Nazionale and Lega Nord, the right-wing groups (Doc. XXIII, n. 37-bis); by deputies and senators of the 5SM (Doc. XXIII, n. 37-ter); and by the deputies and one senator of the left-wing group Liberi e uguali (Doc. XXIII, n. 37-quarter).

Beyond the activity of the enquiry committee on the banking and the financial system the presence of populist forces like the 5SM and the Lega has been irrelevant in terms of influence on the enquiry powers of the Parliament. On the contrary, one could have expected a much more active stance of these groups, then in a minority position, to use parliamentary enquiries 'against' the majority.[38]

Compared to the 17th parliamentary term, which lasted five years, in a year-and-a-half since 23 March 2018, when the new term started, there has been a higher number of proposals to establish enquiry committees: 94 bills have been presented to create bicameral enquiry committees, 22 proposals for unicameral enquiry committees have been tabled at the Senate, and 37 of those in the Chamber. The rate of success of these proposals and bills, however, seems to be lower than in the previous term and, in most cases, the issues covered by those proposals show a high degree of continuity with the 17th term (i.e. most proposals had already been tabled back then, or referred to committees of enquiry established in the past term at the same House or in the other Chamber). To date there is just one enquiry committee in operation at the Senate, against feminicide and gender violence—already in place in the previous term—and created with

[36] Established by Law no. 107 of 2017 as a bicameral committee.

[37] See, for example, the cases of the Banca Popolare di Vicenza and of Banca Etruria.

[38] Indeed, no significant changes could be observed in the 17th parliamentary term with regard to the procedures and activities of the bicameral enquiry committees that had been already in operation in other parliamentary terms, in particular those against mafia and on illegal activities linked to the waste cycle and to environmental crimes.

a bipartisan support, as the proposal for its creation came both from a majority party, the 5SM, and from minority groups, Forza Italia and Fratelli d'Italia. The same applies for the only committee set up in the Chamber of Deputies, to investigate the death of Giulio Regeni in Egypt, which resulted from a bipartisan attempt of the MPs from the 5SM, on the one hand, and of MPs from the Democratic Party and from Liberi and uguali (LEU), not yet part of the coalition government at that time,[39] on the other, to create such a committee, which however has not yet held its constitutive meeting.

A first element to be detected is the very low level of initiatives of the Lega regarding enquiry committees. In relation to this, the change of the party group position, in the majority from June 2018 to August 2019, has not transformed the attitude of the group vis-à-vis this tool (thereby confirming the low profile followed during the 17th term).[40] This is a sign that for the group parliamentary enquiries are not considered instrumental for building the populist discourse. By contrast, overall, MPs from 5SM have increased their rate of engagement with committees of enquiry, at least in terms of proposals. Although deputies and senators from Forza Italia have also been quite active to date, by far the most active group when it comes to proposals to establish committees of enquiry is Fratelli d'Italia, a small minority group with a strong populistic and sovereigntist rhetoric. By looking at the variety of issues MPs from this group would like to be covered by a parliamentary enquiry—from the national health care system and its financing, to provincial administration, banking crises, reception of migrants, child abuse, feminicide to single killings—it appears that Fratelli d'Italia is willing to use such enquiries as an ordinary tool to pursue its populist strategy.

As for bicameral enquiry committees, beyond the two committees systematically re-established at every term, the one against the mafia and the one on the waste cycle and environmental crimes,[41] both chaired by MPs from the 5SM, the creation of two new committees—on the banking and the financial system and to investigate the events that have occurred in the

[39] See Italian Chamber of Deputies, 18th parliamentary term, Doc. XXII, nos. 17 and 36.

[40] Just one proposal to create a committee of enquiry promoted by MPs from the Lega can be detected in this term, at the Chamber of Deputies, on the diffusion of counterfeit goods, illegal trade and digital piracy, Doc. XXII, no. 26.

[41] The relevant bills were presented by MPs of the Democratic Party and of the 5SM, respectively.

social community of Forteto—has been much more politically controversial.

The creation of the bicameral enquiry committee dealing with the community of Forteto relates to a sad story of abuse perpetrated against minors, and also the disabled, under the custody of the administrators of such a community and for which Italy was condemned by the European Court of Human Rights in 2000 for violation of Art. 8 ECHR.[42] Following several vain attempts to establish a committee of enquiry, always opposed by the Democratic Party, a bill was eventually passed in 2019 upon the joint initiative of the 5SM, Forza Italia and Fratelli d'Italia.[43] The operation of such a committee that has not yet held its first meeting at the time of writing, however, is still blocked by the Democratic Party since September 2019 in a coalition government with the 5SM, as it objects to populistic misuse of what has been already settled by means of judicial proceedings.

Even more disputed has been the setting up of the enquiry committee on the banking and the financial system, renewed in its composition on 1 August 2019, following the adoption of a new—contested—law establishing its mandate and remit[44] and that diverges quite significantly from those provided for the committee sharing the same denomination during the 17th term. The creation of this committee in the new term has been strongly advocated by the 5SM, but is in fact the result of a joint effort of the MPs from this party with those of Forza Italia and of Fratelli d'Italia.[45]

In contrast to a practice that had become the rule since the 1990s—that is, the election of the enquiry committee chairman from amongst its members—Law no. 28 of 2019 provides for the appointment of the chairman by common accord between the Presidents of the two Houses (Art. 2), who also ensure that every group present in at least one of the Houses of Parliament gets one seat in this committee, when appointing deputies and senators in proportion to political groups. This article, therefore, is meant

[42] See European Court of Human Rights, Grand Chamber, judgment of 13 July 2000, applications nos. 39221/98 and 41963/98, *Scozzari and Giunta v. Italy*.

[43] See Law no. 21 of 8 March 2019, which is the result of a bill originally proposed by MPs of the 5SM, then combined with bills proposed by MPs from Forza Italia and from Fratelli d'Italia.

[44] See Law no. 28 of 26 March 2019.

[45] Also in this case, one of the bills put forward by MPs from the 5SM has absorbed the bills tabled by MPs of Forza Italia and of Fratelli d'Italia.

to protect the impartiality of the committee's activities also ensuring that the minorities can play a role.

However, the mandate that through the Law the Parliament has accorded to this committee, in principle, could be subject to a populist twist, given its (too) broad scope of action that risks clashing with the Constitution. These concerns are clearly outlined in the letter that the President of the Republic Sergio Mattarella sent to the Presidents of the Chamber and of the Senate when the law was promulgated.[46]

First, the head of state highlights that, unlike the committee in operation during the 17th parliamentary term which looked after the banking crises, the new one is supposed to monitor the banking and the financial system in their entirety, including every bank and, thus, even those that do not face a crisis and that regularly deploy their tasks. Second, the law allows the enquiry committee to "analyse the management of credit and investment institutions" (own translation). The President of the Republic warns against the possibility that this committee could control banking operations and investment activities, in breach of Art. 41 Const., on the freedom of enterprise. To allow that political subjects, like the enquiry committee's members, could condition banks in the fulfilment of their functions would mean to overstretch the weight of politics in the private economic domain, a potentially dangerous populist twist.

Third, Art. 3 of the law, which appears to hint at a sort of supervisory authority of the enquiry committee on banks, should not lead to the idea that such a committee would interfere with the supervisory activity of national agencies and institutions set up (also) for this purpose, for example, the Bank of Italy and Consob, or of EU institutions and agencies like the European Central Bank or European Securities and Markets Authority, in violation of EU law.

Fourth, Art. 6 of the Law, regarding the circulation of information obtained by banking supervisory authorities, which remains rather vague on the point, should be read as to protect the right to saving (Art. 47 Const.). Leaking such sensitive information through the enquiry commit-

[46]The President could have chosen to send the bill back to the Parliament, under Art. 74 Const., for further considerations, should he have detected manifest violations of the Constitution, which was not the case. Yet he expressed a series of problems that might arise in the implementation of the law and he asked the two Presidents of the Chamber and of the Senate to carefully monitor the activities of the enquiry committee. The text of the letter, in Italia, is available here: https://www.quirinale.it/elementi/26206

tee activity could impair the functioning of financial markets and the interests of bank account holders.

Fifth, in the name of the principle of loyal cooperation, the political role of the committee cannot lead to ascertain the responsibility of the judiciary when investigating or adjudicating on the banking crisis and bankruptcy, following a certain bias that populists have concerning the relationships between politics and the judicial function, whereby the latter is subordinated to the former. Perhaps, also due to these controversial aspects and to the new governmental equilibria, the committee is not in operation yet, since its constitutive meeting, originally scheduled on 4 September, did not take place.[47]

To sum up, the 18th parliamentary term so far has witnessed an increasing attempt by populist forces—though not all of them, for example, the Lega has not contributed to this trend—to exploit parliamentary enquiries, with some degree of success, to pursue their own strategy. This has happened in the case of both a populist party shaping the governmental majority, like the 5SM, and a populist opposition party, like Fratelli d'Italia. However, as the experience with the committee on the banking and the financial system shows, enquiry committees should be handled with care. Indeed, if the powers of those committees are not clearly delimited, they might improperly interfere with other constitutional powers, starting from the judiciary, or institutions, ranging from independent authorities to the market, to undermine individual rights and liberties in an attempt to dominate the public debate and make it more extreme to maximize electoral support. At the same time, however, the change of the government, with the collapse of a first coalition and the creation of a new one, seems to have delayed or slowed down the activity of some enquiry committees.

Question Time

Parliamentary questions are amongst the traditional tools of parliamentary inspection, though not being in the Italian experience the most visible from outside of Parliament. Under the rules of procedure of the Chamber and of the Senate (Art. 128 r. C. and Art. 145 r. S.), a parliamentary question is a request put forward by an MP to the government on a specific

[47] Indeed, likewise the bicameral committee of enquiry on Forteto, the constitutive meeting was scheduled on the day before the new coalition government took office, on 5 September 2019.

occurrence, asking for precise information, details and documents or to express her own position on the facts (see Gianniti and Lupo 2018: 224). These questions can take the oral or the written form and can be presented both in the plenary and in committee. More than creating an effective exchange of views between an MP and the government (most likely, a Minister or an undersecretary) and to seek a clear answer, parliamentary questions are meant to draw the attention of the executive and to shed light on a specific problem.[48] That's why it is not considered as a serious problem that most questions, especially oral questions, never get an answer (Filippetta 1991; on the UK, see Saafeld 2011).

With a view to "revitalize" parliamentary questions as oversight instruments, following the "majoritarian (incomplete) turn" of the system of government in the 1990s (see, amongst many, Lippolis and Pitruzzella 2007), a particular form of questions for oral and immediate answer, within the so-called question time, where 'imported' from the UK Parliament with a series of adjustments. The question time has been regulated, at the Chamber of Deputies, both in the plenary and in committee since 1997 and, at the Senate, since 1999 in the plenary and, since the 2017 revision of the Senate's rules of procedures, also in committee.[49] The question time has a specific space reserved on the parliamentary agenda and, in theory, it should feature in alternation the participation of the President of the Council of Ministers (or the Vice President)—the Premier question time—and of the competent Minister, always informed about the questions to be asked beforehand.

In fact, question time has not served the purpose for which it was introduced, that is, to strengthen the accountability of the government through an active role played by MPs challenging the Premier or the competent Minister, especially—though not exclusively—from minority groups, in a vibrant exchange of questions and answers. The systematic lack of participation of the President of the Council of Minister in the relevant sessions, the presence of undersecretaries or of the Minister for the relationship with the Parliament rather than the competent Minister on the subject matter and the low engagement of MPs, (most of them are absent during question time), has led scholars to consider the question time and, even

[48] Indeed, the MPs asking an oral question can just declare herself satisfied with the answer provided by the government, without engaging in an articulated reply. Moreover, in the case of a written question, there is no chance for the MP to 'reply' in writing.

[49] At the Chamber of Deputies, see Arts. 135 bis and 135 ter r.C.; at the Senate, see Art. 151 bis.

more so, the Premier question time as a missed opportunity and a failed experience (Lippolis 2008; Rivosecchi 2008).[50]

If and how has the situation changed as an effect of the last populist wave?

First, it should be highlighted that there has been a general increase in the use of parliamentary questions since the 17th parliamentary term, which also affects the question time.[51] The increase has been uneven though, more prominent in the Chamber of Deputies than in the Senate, where during the 18th term so far about half of the question time sessions and questions are held in comparison to the Chamber.

Second, the situation has not been modified in relation to the Premier question time that still rarely happens. In contrast to the expectations created by the codification of the Premier question time in the Senate's rules of procedure in 2017 (Art. 151 bis, section 1 bis r. S.) and by the programmatic declarations of President Conte at the beginning of the 18th term,[52] no substantive change has been detected. Indeed, as Giuseppe Conte stated, "aiming to honour the centrality of the Parliament, I hereby anticipate that I am committed to give application to the question time, according to the rules of procedure of the Chamber and of the Senate".[53] In fact, to date during this term the Premier question time took place only twice at the Chamber of Deputies and once at the Senate.[54]

The question time in general, instead, has been somewhat 'revitalized' in the plenary. In committees it is regularly practised at the Chamber of

[50] Just during the 13th parliamentary term (1996–2001), the President of the Council of Ministers engaged with the Premier question time 21 times. In the following terms, the rate of appearance of the President before the Parliament for the question time has been from one to four times per term.

[51] Source: Databases of the Italian Chamber of Deputies and the Senate, in particular the Banche dati del sindacato ispettivo, showing a trend towards a gradual and steady increase since the 14th parliamentary term (2001–2006), thus starting from the second and the third Berlusconi governments.

[52] Similar expectations had been raised by the former Premier Letta, who remained in office from 28 April 2013 to 22 February 2014, almost at the start of the 17th parliamentary term, when he announced his firm intention to use the Premier question time to keep a proper and effective relationship between the Parliament and the government. See Italian Chamber of Deputies, 17th term, verbatim report of the plenary, session of 10 July 2013.

[53] Own translation. Senate of the Italian Republic, 18th term, verbatim report of the plenary, 9th session, of 5 June 2018.

[54] At the Chamber of Deputies, during the sessions held on 7 November 2018 and on 24 July 2019; at the Senate, on 21 February 2019.

Deputies, but not at the Senate, where it has never been applied, despite having been regulated in the rules of procedure since 2017. This is consistent with the trend towards the politicization and the 'spectacularization' of the question time, which sees in the plenary its natural place and on the Internet and social media two clear allies.

Perhaps to such a trend a further rationalization of the drafting style of parliamentary questions has contributed. In line with the letter of the President of the Chamber of 21 February 1996 on the matter (when question time was not yet in place though), on 3 August 2016 the Committee on rules of procedure of the Chamber of Deputies issued a new opinion that foresaw as one of the conditions for the admissibility of questions raised during the question time the maximum length of 400 words aiming to make those questions "brief, concise and direct" (Bargiacchi 2017: 1), and more effective and easier for the public to understand, in contrast to lengthy statements.

While the replacement of the competent Minister by the Minister for the relationship with the Parliament or by undersecretaries still remains quite widespread and is perceived as a problem by MPs,[55] during the first part of the 18th parliamentary term the main targets of the question time, though not through the Premier question time,[56] have been the two Vice Presidents of the Council of Ministers, Luigi Di Maio and Matteo Salvini, at the same time the Minister for Economic Development and Labour and the Minister of Interior, respectively. Indeed, the role of political chiefs of the respective party, the 5SM and the Lega, that of Vice Presidents and that of ministers, have been confused during the question time. Moreover, the question time sessions that have directly concerned them have been featured by particularly heated debates and an unusually high amount of conflict between the majority and the opposition on the use of the instrument which has required the two Presidents of the House to intervene, threatening the suspension of the televised broadcast of the session.[57] Such

[55] From the opposition, in particular. See, for example, Senate of the Italian Republic, 18th term, verbatim report of the plenary, 21st session, of 12 July 2018.

[56] In theory usable in this framework, as the Premier question time can be referred to both the President and the Vice President(s) of the Council of Ministers. See Art. 8, Law no. 400 of 1988.

[57] See, for example, at the Senate of the Italian Republic, 18th term, verbatim report, session no. 27 of 26 July 2018, when the President of the House—on that occasion the Vice President of the House Paola Taverna (M5S) replaced the President—described the question time session as a sort of "ring" and invited the Minister of Interior, who was taking pictures

a politicization of the question time with regard to the two Vice Presidents is in sharp contrast with the practice of the question time in relation to two other strategic ministries during the same term, namely the Minister of Economics and Finance and the Minister of Foreign affairs, who have been traditionally subject to a significant volume of parliamentary questions. Indeed, during the first year-and-a-half of the 18th term, the Minister of Economics and Finance has only been ranked sixth in terms of number of questions received in the framework of the question time, whereas the Minister of Foreign Affairs has been ranked last in this "competition".[58] Most likely, the technocratic figures appointed to these ministries back then (Verzichelli and Cotta 2018; Lupo 2019),[59] in contrast to the populistic approach to politics of the two vice Presidents, have played a role in explaining the relatively low number of questions the former have been asked.

Intra-majority dynamics between the two coalition partners of the first government led by Giuseppe Conte also show interesting developments. Especially in the presence of an extremely heterogeneous coalition between two populist parties, like the one in place from June 2018 to August 2019 between the 5SM and the Lega, parliamentary questions can be used by the majority forces to mutually control each other (Höhmann and Sieberer 2019). Even though during the question time most of the questions coming from either populist party from within the coalition were meant to highlight the merits and the achievement of their own party's minister rather than to oversee the minister's and the government's action, there are significant examples of MPs' intra-coalition control through the question time: for instance, representatives of the Lega asked critical questions to the 5SM Minister of Justice Bonafede with regard to the reform of the judiciary and to the Minister for Economic Development di Maio about the leeways to revising the basic income (*reddito di cittadinanza*) introduced.[60] By the same token, 5SM's MPs sought clarifications from the

of the House, in particular of the opposition benches, protesting against him, to end his provocation and not to use the self-phone to record the session.

[58] Source: databases of the Italian Chamber of Deputies and the Senate, in particular the Banche dati del sindacato ispettivo.

[59] In particular, Giovanni Tria as Minister of Economics and Finance and Enzo Moavero Milanesi, as Minister of Foreign Affairs, both academics, with previous institutional roles, but never elected as MPs or representatives nor affiliated to a party.

[60] See Italian Chamber of Deputies, 18th term, verbatim report, 75th session of the 31 October 2018 and Senate of the Italian Republic, 18th term, verbatim report, 107th session of 4 April 2019.

Minister of Economics and Finance Tria about banking accounting and put forward questions to the Minister of Interior Salvini—that sound like critical remarks—on his immigration policy.[61]

Maybe the most remarkable innovation in the use of the question time by populist forces has been the strategic management of its transparency regime, as the relevant sessions are broadcast on TV and available through streaming, combined with the use of social media, which has allowed the question time to gain a visibility it had never experienced before. The awareness about the presence of television cameras and of the fact that questions and answers are taking place with live broadcasting is evident also by the language used by ministers and MPs who have frequently referred in their interventions to the TV viewers watching the question time at home.[62] As highlighted above, the full disclosure of these procedures has also let the tone of the debate become more confrontational and, to some extent, more entertaining. At the same time, this distracts the question time from its original nature of being an oversight tool. Indeed, questions and answers have tended to become more and more vague and turned into instruments of political propaganda, praising or disapproving the government, the minister or a party.[63]

In relation to this, the use of the question time that a minority populist force, Fratelli d'Italia, has made during the past and the present terms is particularly telling, because it also includes social media in the propaganda strategy. Not only taking advantage of the TV cameras during question time sessions, MPs from this group from time to time have shown signs—a conduct that is forbidden by the rules of procedure—on related claims while one of their colleagues was formulating a parliamentary question aiming to raise the attention of it to the audience.[64] They have systematically reproduced on their own Facebook page, typically that of the leader

[61] For example, see Italian Chamber of Deputies, 18th term, verbatim report, 75th session, cit.

[62] See, respectively, Italian Chamber of Deputies, 18th term, verbatim report, 55th session of 3 October 2018 and Senate of the Italian Republic, 18th term, verbatim report, 101st session, of 21 March 2019.

[63] See, for example, during the plenary session held at the Italian Chamber of Deputies on 13 March 2019, the question asked by the MP Stefani (Lega) to the Minister of Interior of the same party, Salvini, which was only meant to provide the minister with an opportunity to promote the achievements of Decree Law no. 113 of 2018.

[64] See, for example, Chamber of Deputies, 18th term, verbatim report, 160th session of 10 April 2019.

Giorgia Meloni, and on the account of the party, the video of question time sessions where one of the group's members had intervened or, better, the relevant part of the session is made available live via Facebook on these accounts.[65] The aim is to increase the number of visualizations as much as possible and, to this end, the same video is also reposted subsequently. On Facebook, the question time has been treated by MPs from Fratelli d'Italia as a 'shop window' to seize the attention of the public.

Such 'spectacularization' of the question time, a path that starts to be followed by other groups and that has triggered a sort of revitalization of the tool, however, has come at the price of deviating from the original purpose of the question time, of the quality of the contents and of the style of debate, becoming more and more adversarial, though not for the sake of advancing and confronting sound arguments on a certain issue, but in many cases just to make captivating and effective statements.

Final Remarks

The last populist turn of the Italian political system has triggered significant developments in the Parliament, entailing—in continuity with the past—a further marginalization of this institution. In other words, it has worsened a trend that was already in place. Nevertheless, there are some issues in which the access to the Parliament or the transformation of populist parties has determined significant shifts.

A first shift, mainly led by the 5SM, has occurred in relation to the status of MPs. The anti-*casta* rhetoric this party has promoted has been linked to the idea of revising and limiting the 'privileges' of MPs, from their allowance and pension, to attacking the principle of free mandate, up to the reduction of the number of parliamentary seats or the provocation to resort to a lottery system for MPs' selection (Corso 2019). Taken together they devalue the status of MPs and, ultimately, the role of the Parliament in the constitutional system. While some of these claims are not new, the 5SM's discourse tends to oversimplify the *raison d'être* of century-old principles, like the free mandate, and to misinterpret the ratio-

[65] See, amongst many, Facebook Post, In diretta dalla Camera per il question time di FdI al Governo per dire NO al Global Compact, by Giorgia Meloni, 21 November 2018, https://www.facebook.com/giorgiameloni.paginaufficiale/videos/in-diretta-dalla-camera-per-il-question-time-di-fdi-al-governo-per-dire-no-al-gl/271315460194022/

nale of having certain parliamentary procedures or immunities, which rather than being individual privileges protect the functional autonomy of parliamentary institutions.

Another feature of the latest populist legacy affecting the Parliament, also linked to the aim to revise the status of MPs, is the claim to provide 'total transparency' of parliamentary procedures for the sake of enhancing democratic accountability. Such a vision of transparency, especially if coupled with the use and abuse of Internet tools and social media, can however distract the Parliament from its ordinary function to favour political negotiations and the achievement of compromises, offering avenues for accommodation to an extremely fragmented political landscape; a function which requires some level of informality and even the secrecy of parliamentary procedures to be fulfilled.

The 'spectacularization' of politics that populist groups, both in the majority, the 5SM and the Lega, and in opposition, like Fratelli d'Italia, endorse has led to the exploitation of some traditional instruments of parliamentary oversight, like committees of enquiry and parliamentary questions, as part of the strategy of political propaganda. If, on the one hand, this had led to a sort of 'revitalization' of parliamentary enquiries and of the question time, on the other, they have been diverted from their original purpose to allow the Parliament and, hence the citizens, to properly control government action. As the experience with the setting up of the enquiry committee on the banking and the financial system established during the 18th parliamentary term shows, there are clear risks in broadening the mandate of committee of enquiries and in overstretching their powers in that they can exercise a quasi-judicial function. By the same token, the increasing use of the question time and the fact that it has eventually become more 'entertaining', also using social media, like in the practice of Fratelli d'Italia, does not necessarily conclude that these developments improve the quality of parliamentary oversight as long as they only serve to echo the political strategy of a party without adding substantive contents to the scrutiny.

References

Bagehot, W. [1867] (2001). *The English Constitution*, M. Tylor (Ed.). Oxford: Oxford University Press.

Bargiacchi, S. (2017, January 31). Quando la lunghezza degli atti di sindacato ispettivo ne determina l'inammissibilità (Osservazioni al parere della Giunta per il Regolamento del 3 agosto 2016). *Amministrazioneincammino*, 1–16. Available at www.amministrazioneincammino.luiss.it

Biondi Dal Monte, F. (2017). Svelare il voto. La percezione del voto parlamentare tra comunicazione politica e rappresentanza. *Osservatorio sulle fonti online*, *2*, 1–31. Available at www.osservatoriosullefonti.it

Blokker, P., & Anselmi, M. (2019). Introduction. In P. Blokker & M. Anselmi (Eds.), *Multiple Populisms. Italy as a Democracy's Mirror* (pp. 1–14). London: Routledge.

Bobbio, N. (1984). *Il futuro della democrazia. Una difesa delle regole del gioco.* Torino: Einaudi.

Bull, M., & Rhodes, M. (1997). Between Crisis and Transition: Italian Politics in the 1990s. *West European Politics*, *20*(1), 1–13.

Carducci, M. (2018). Le dimensioni di interferenza del 'contratto' di governo e l'art. 67 Cost. *federalismi.it*, *13*, 1–12. Available at www.federalismi.it

Caretti, P., & Morisi, M. (Eds.). (2014). La pubblicità dei lavori parlamentari in prospettiva comparata. Speciale Seminario di studi e ricerche parlamentari 'Silvano Tosi.' *Osservatorio sulle fonti online*, *2*, 1–130. Available at www.osservatoriosullefonti.it

Caretti, P., Morisi, M., & Tarli Barbieri, G. (2019). Il divieto di mandato imperativo: un principio in discussione, Seminario di studi e ricerche parlamentari 'Silvano Tosi' – Ricerca 2019. *Osservatorio sulle fonti online*, *2*, 1–380. Available at www.osservatoriosullefonti.it

Caterina, E. (2016). Il giudice civile e l'ordinamento interno dei partiti: alcune considerazioni sulle recenti ordinanze dei tribunali di Napoli e di Roma. *Osservatorio sulle fonti online*, *3*, 1–19. Available at www.osservatoriosullefonti.it

Ceccanti, S., & Curreri, S. (2015). I partiti antisistema nell'esperienza italiana: il MoVimento 5 Stelle come partito personale autoescluso. *Diritto pubblico comparato ed europeo*, *3*, 799–832.

Celentano, M. (2016). L'istituto dell'inchiesta e le attività di vigilanza e controllo nel sistema bicamerale differenziato. *federalismi.it*, *22*, 1–30. Available at www.federalismi.it

Chessa, O. (2019). L'incerto monismo. Modello e prassi della forma di governo negli anni 1953–1970. *Quaderni costituzionali*, *1*, 31–54.

Ciaurro, L. (2006). *Art. 67*. In R. Bifulco, A. Celotto, & M. Olivetti (Eds.), *Commentario alla Costituzione* (pp. 1287–1297). Torino: Utet.

Conti, G. L. (2018). Sfera pubblica e sfera privata della rappresentanza. La giustiziabilità dell'art. 67, Cost. nella sua attuazione da parte dello statuto di un gruppo parlamentare. *federalismi.it*, *13*, 1–16. Available at www.federalismi.it

Corso, L. (2019). When Anti-Politics Becomes Political: What Can the Italian Five Star Movement Tell Us about the Relationship Between Populism and Legalism. *European Constitutional Law Review*, *15*(3), 462–487.

Curreri, S. (2004). *Democrazia e rappresentanza politica: dal divieto di mandato al mandato di partito*. Firenze: Firenze University Press.

Curreri, S. (2019, October 14). Gruppi in movimento. *Costituzione.info*. Available at http://www.lacostituzione.info/index.php/2019/10/14/banca-dati-sulla-mobilita-parlamentare/

De Fiores, C. (2017). Sulla rappresentazione della Nazione. Brevi note sul divieto di mandato imperativo. *Diritto e società, 1*, 19–41.

Della Porta, D., & Vannucci, A. (2007). Corruption and Anti-corruption: The Political Defeat of "Clean Hands" in Italy. *West European Politics, 30*(4), 830–853.

Di Palma, G. (1976). Institutional Rules and Legislative Outcomes in the Italian Parliament. *Legislative Studies Quarterly, 1*(2), 149–179.

Elia, L. (1970). Governo (forme di). In *Enciclopedia del diritto* (Vol. XIX). Milano: Giuffrè.

Erkkilä, T. (2012). *Government Transparency: Impact and Unintended Consequences*. Basingstoke: Palgrave.

Fasone, C., & Lupo, N. (2015). Transparency vs. Informality in Legislative Committees: Comparing the US House of Representatives, the Italian Chamber of Deputies and the European Parliament. *Journal of Legislative Studies, 21*, 342–359.

Filippetta, G. (1991). L'illusione ispettiva, le interrogazioni e le interpellanze parlamentari tra ricostruzioni dottrinali, rappresentanza politica e funzione di indirizzo. *Giurisprudenza costituzionale, 6*, 4203–4260.

Frosini, T. E. (2019). *Liberté Egalité Internet*. Napoli: ES.

Gianfrancesco, E. (2007). Il ruolo dei Presidenti delle Camere tra soggetti politici e arbitri imparziali. In E. Gianfrancesco & N. Lupo (Eds.), *Le regole del diritto parlamentare nella dialettica tra maggioranza e opposizione* (pp. 21–39). Rome: LUISS University Press.

Gianfrancesco, E. (2018). Chi esce paga: la 'penale' prevista dallo Statuto del MoVimento 5 Stelle della Camera. *Quaderni costituzionali, 2*, 484–486.

Gianniti, L., & Lupo, N. (2018). *Corso di diritto parlamentare*, (3rd ed.). Bologna: Il Mulino.

Grasso, G. (2017). La 'cifra democratica' del MoVimento 5 Stelle alla prova dell'art. 49 della Costituzione. *Quaderni costituzionali, 3*, 616–617.

Guarnieri, C. (1997). The Judiciary in the Italian Political Crisis. *West European Politics, 20*(1), 157–175.

Hibberd, M. (2007). Conflicts of Interest and Media Pluralism in Italian Broadcasting. *West European Politics, 30*(4), 881–902.

Höhmann, D., & Sieberer, U. (2019). Parliamentary Questions as a Control Mechanism in Coalition Governments. *West European Politics, 43*(1), 225–249.

Ibrido, R. (2015). *L'interpretazione del diritto parlamentare. Politica e diritto nel "processo" di risoluzione dei casi regolamentari*. Milano: Franco Angeli.

Ignazi, P. (2009). La crisi della politica in Italia. *XXI secolo, Enciclopedia Treccani online*. Available at http://www.treccani.it

Issacharoff, S. (2018). Democracy's Deficits. *The University of Chicago Law Review, 85*, 485–519.

Judge, D., & Leston-Bandeira, C. (2018). The Institutional Representation of Parliament. *Political Studies, 66*, 154–172.

Kelsen, H. [1924] (1982). Il problema del parlamentarismo. Id., *Il primato del parlamento*. Milano: Giuffrè.

Lauri, G. (2018). Le commissioni parlamentari di inchiesta nella XVII legislatura. Appunti e tendenze. *Osservatorio sulle fonti online*, *2*, 1–21. Available at www.osservatoriosullefonti.it

Lessig, L. (2009, October 9). Against Transparency. The Perils of Openness in Government. *The New Republic*. Available at newrepublic.com

Lippolis, V. (2008). L'innovazione attraverso i regolamenti parlamentari. Come migliorare il Parlamento del bipolarismo. *federalismi.it*, *9*, 1–7. Available at www.federalismi.it

Lippolis, V., & Pitruzzella, G. (2007). *Il bipolarismo conflittuale: il regime politico della seconda repubblica*. Soveria Mannelli: Rubbettino.

Lupo, N. (2018). La riforma del (solo) Regolamento del Senato alla fine della XVII legislatura. *Forum di Quaderni costituzionali*, *1*, 1–4. Available at http://www.forumcostituzionale.it

Lupo, N. (2019). 'Populismo legislativo'? Continuità e discontinuità nelle tendenze della legislazione italiana. *Ragion pratica*, 251–271.

Maestri, G. (2019, September 19). Il nuovo gruppo 'Psi-Italia viva' al Senato: le falle della riforma 'antiframmentazione' del Regolamento. *Costituzione.info*. Available at www.lacostituzione.info

Mair, P. (2013). *Ruling the Void: The Hollowing of Western Democracy*. London: Verso.

Malvicini, M., & Lauri, G. (2016). Le commissioni parlamentari di inchiesta: recenti sviluppi e osservazioni alla luce della prassi. *Osservatorio costituzionale*, *3*, 1–48. Available at www.osservatorioaic.it

Manin, B. (1996). *Principes du gouvernement représentatif*. Paris: Flammarion.

Manzella, A. (2003). *Il parlamento*. Bologna: Il Mulino.

McCubbins, M. D., & Schwartz, T. (1984). Congressional Oversight Overlooked: Police Patrols Versus Fire Alarm. *American Journal of Political Science, 28*, 165–179.

Morelli, A. (2018). *Rappresentanza politica e libertà del mandato parlamentare*. Napoli: ES.

Müller, J.-W. (2016). *What Is Populism?* Philadelphia: University of Pennsylvania Press.

Orrù, R. (2015). Divieto di mandato imperativo e anti-defection laws: spunti di diritto comparato. *Diritto pubblico comparato ed europeo, 4*, 1097–1116.

Orsina, G. (2017). Perfectionism Without Politics. Politicisation, Depoliticisation, and Political History. *Ricerche di storia politica*, (special issue), 75–86.

Pace, A. (1973). *Il potere di inchiesta delle assemblee legislative: Saggi*. Milano: Giuffrè.
Pace, A. (2011). Le commissioni parlamentari di inchiesta possono disporre sequestri preventivi di immobili? *Giurisprudenza costituzionale, 3*, 2669–2674.
Pelizzo, R., Stapenhurst, R., & Oslon, D. (2006). *Parliamentary Oversight for Government Accountability*. Washington, DC: World Bank Institute.
Piccione, D. (2011). Fuori o oltre la linea d'ombra? Ancora sul sequestro dei locali degli ospedali psichiatrici giudiziari, a tutela dei diritti costituzionali degli internati sottoposti a misure di sicurezza. *Giurisprudenza costituzionale, 4*, 3402–3416.
Pinelli, C. (2011). The Populist Challenge to Constitutional Democracy. *European Constitutional Law Review, 7*(1), 5–16.
Polsby, N. W. (1975). Legislatures. In F. I. Greenstein & N. W. Polsby (Eds.), *Handbook of Political Science* (Vol. 5, pp. 257–319). Reading: Addison-Wesley.
Ridola, P. (1994). La rappresentanza parlamentare fra unità politica e pluralismo. *Diritto e società, 4*, 709–727.
Rivosecchi, G. (2008). I poteri ispettivi e il controllo parlamentare a dieci anni dalla riforma del regolamento della Camera dei deputati. In *Il Parlamento del bipolarismo: un decennio di riforme dei regolamenti delle Camere* (pp. 201–242). Napoli: Jovene.
Saafeld, T. (2011). Parliamentary Questions as Instruments of Substantive Representation: Visible Minorities in the UK House of Commons, 2005–10. *Journal of Legislative Studies, 17*(3), 271–289.
Sartori, G. (1992). *Seconda Repubblica? Si, ma bene*. Milano: Rizzoli.
Scarciglia, R. (2005). *Il divieto di mandato imperativo. Contributo ad uno studio di diritto comparato*. Padova: Cedam.
Taggart, P. (2002). Populism and the Pathology of Representative Democracy. In Y. Mény & Y. Surel (Eds.), *Democracies and the Populist Challenge* (pp. 62–80). London: Palgrave.
Tarli Barbieri, G. (2018). *La legislazione elettorale nell'ordinamento italiano (1948–2017)*. Milano: Giuffrè.
Torre, A. (2001). *Il magistrato dell'assemblea. Saggio sui presidenti parlamentari*. Torino: Giappichelli.
Verzichelli, L., & Cotta, M. (2018). Shades of Technocracy: The Variable Use of Non-partisan Ministers in Italy. In A. C. Pinto, M. Cotta, & P. T. de Almeida (Eds.), *Technocratic Ministers and Political Leadership in European Democracies* (pp. 77–110). London: Palgrave.
Zanon, N. (1991). *Il libero mandato parlamentare. Saggio critico sull'art. 67 della Costituzione*. Milano: Giuffrè.

CHAPTER 4

Populism and Referendum: The Italian Debate from a Comparative Perspective

Giuseppe Martinico

The End of Representative Democracy?

Following an idea endorsed by Davide Casaleggio, the mastermind of the Rousseau platform,[1] former minister Riccardo Fraccaro[2] denounced the insufficiency of classic representative democracy and stressed the need for more direct democracy, especially with the advent of new technologies. Davide Casaleggio recently said that "the overcoming of representative democracy is inevitable".[3] These are vital considerations that deserve

[1] Rousseau is the Five Star Movement's platform, where the registered users of the Movement discuss and vote. It is understood as a tool of direct democracy. Davide Casaleggio is also son of Gianroberto Casaleggio, the late *guru* of the Five Star Movement.

[2] "Riccardo Fraccaro: meno onorevoli e più referendum. In cinque leggi il piano di riforme", https://www.lastampa.it/2018/09/11/italia/riccardo-fraccaro-meno-onorevoli-e-pi-referendum-in-cinque-leggi-il-piano-di-riforme-c8Au3U67EJO7cm2YbxJKvK/premium.html See "La democrazia integrale", https://ricerca.repubblica.it/repubblica/archivio/repubblica/2018/06/19/la-democrazia-integrale32.html

[3] "Davide Casaleggio: 'Il Parlamento? In futuro forse non sarà più necessario'", www.corriere.it

G. Martinico (✉)
Scuola Sant'Anna, Pisa, Italy
e-mail: giuseppe.martinico@santannapisa.it

G. Delledonne et al. (eds.), *Italian Populism and Constitutional Law*, Challenges to Democracy in the 21st Century,
https://doi.org/10.1007/978-3-030-37401-3_4

attention and should not necessarily be seen as populist. Nevertheless, starting from them one may express concerns, especially concerning the maximum dose of direct democracy that a system of representative democracy can tolerate. This chapter is not about the Five Star Movement's understanding of democracy, which will be examined in the chapter by Bassini, but it aims to offer an overview of how the Italian legal system deals with the political risks connected to the referendum.

The short (but intense) experience of government carried out by the Lega and the Five Star Movement was characterised by a constant reference to the need for change. It is not coincidental that the government declared itself as the "government of change"[4] (*il governo del cambiamento*). It is interesting to start this chapter with a look at the constitutional reforms proposed by the Conte I (to distinguish it from the Conte II executive[5]) government.[6]

Among others,[7] apart from the reduction of the number of parliamentarians (this is again a long-standing issue, see the failed Renzi Reform),[8] the most interesting proposals are those connected to the enhancement of direct democracy. In this sense, it is necessary to pay attention to the popular initiative[9] with the introduction of a type of legislative referendum (*referendum propositivo*) if Parliament does not deal with and approve said popular initiative within a reasonable term (18 months), provided that the Constitutional Court declares the referendum permissible.[10] These proposals

[4] See the "Summary of the contract for the government of change" signed by Five Star Movement and Lega: http://www.efdd-m5seuropa.com/imgblog/summary_of_the_contract_for_the_government_of_change_in_italy.pdf

[5] Supported by the Five Star Movement, the Democratic Party (PD), the Free and Equal Party (Leu) and the new political force created by Matteo Renzi, *Italia Viva*.

[6] I am not going to offer an overview of all of the constitutional reforms proposed as I shall focus on those proposed by exponents of the majority: http://www.camera.it/temiap/documentazione/temi/pdf/1104514.pdf. There is an entire section devoted to that in the "Nota di aggiornamento del DEF 2018", http://www.mef.gov.it/inevidenza/documenti/NADEF_2018.pdf

[7] Ibidem.

[8] A.S. n. 805 (Patuanelli et al.) http://www.senato.it/leg/18/BGT/Schede/Ddliter/50605.htm

[9] Currently, Art. 71 of the It. Const. reads: "Legislation may be introduced by the Government, by a Member of Parliament and by those entities and bodies so empowered by constitutional amendment law. The people may initiate legislation by proposing a bill drawn up in sections and signed by at least fifty-thousand voters".

[10] A. C. n. 1173 (D'Uva et al.) http://documenti.camera.it/leg18/pdl/pdf/leg.18.pdl.camera.1173.18PDL0028960.pdf

clearly look at Switzerland, in particular, the legislative referendum is inspired by Art. 139b of the Swiss Constitution, which provides for a simultaneous referendum on a popular initiative and its counter-proposal (Raible and Trueblood 2017). These potential reforms have been criticised since they would risk altering the equilibrium between direct and representative democracy by introducing a sort of "concurrent and alternative popular legislative power" (Morrone 2018). These words stress the antiparliamentary flavour that inspired this proposal. There are also a number of technical points that can be made in this regard: first of all, Art. 139b of the Swiss Constitution refers to a "popular initiative requesting a partial revision of the Federal Constitution in specific terms" (which is governed by Art. 139), while the proposal advanced in Italy concerns legislative proposals. Second, and this was the most problematic aspect of this sort of legislative referendum, is the fact that according to the original proposal, it was possible to activate a referendum even if Parliament had adopted a different text. Indeed, according to the original text, in cases of "non-merely formal changes" it was possible to have a ballot on the original proposal and the new text passed by Parliament. According to the initial draft, the people could be asked to decide on two different texts, and this would have inevitably rendered the referendum question heterogeneous. The most recent version of the text excludes such a ballot and now states that if the Chambers approve the popular proposal with amendments that are not merely formal, the referendum is called on the proposal presented, unless the promoters of the initiative decide to give up their original proposal. Here, the draft amendment refers to implementing legislation (to be passed by an absolute majority) to identify the actor in charge of controlling the nature of the changes introduced by the Houses. The proposal approved by the Chambers will be promulgated if the one subject to a referendum is not approved. Another important element of this proposal is represented by the turnout threshold, which was not mentioned in the original version; this responded to one of the *mottos* of the Five Star Movement: "Zero quorum, more democracy".[11] The new draft amendment states that the referendum shall be considered to have been carried out if a majority of valid votes has been

[11] "Referendum senza quorum: decide chi partecipa. Per riconquistare la sovranità servono cittadini attivi" https://www.riccardofraccaro.it/referendum-senza-quorum-decide-chi-partecipa-per-riconquistare-la-sovranita-servono-cittadini-attivi/

achieved "provided that it is higher than a quarter of those entitled to vote". The same quorum is also extended to abrogative referendums pursuant to Art. 75 Cost.

This chapter does not aim to offer an exhaustive analysis of this proposal, which is just the tip of the iceberg. Rather, I shall first recall how populists understand referendums. Second, I shall recall the comparative debate about referendums to comprehensively understand the advantages and disadvantages of this instrument. Third, I shall recall the constitutional frame characterising the Italian context and the critical role played by the Italian Constitutional Court to "rationalise" this instrument (Barbera and Morrone 2003: 63).

How Populists Understand the Referendum

The obsession of populist movements with the "politics of immediacy" (Corrias 2016: 12) inevitably results in questioning many of the instruments of representative democracy and in emphasising the importance of instruments of direct and participatory democracy. This explains the importance that referendums play in the populist agenda as they offer visibility to charismatic leaders that look for direct contact with "the people" (a concept frequently employed, but hardly developed, as Canovan pointed out in 2004[12]). Frequently, the attack on representative institutions and the emphasis on referendums are taken as two sides of the same coin, since they are both emanations of that lack of mediation that political scientists frequently portray as one of the pillars of populism (Mény and Surel 2004). As Canovan pointed out: "New Populists often call for issues of popular concern to be decided by referendum, by-passing professional politicians and leaving decisions to the people" (Canovan 2004: 242). Referendums also galvanise that dichotomous approach frequently endorsed by populists in the constant appeal to the people understood as

[12] "It seems astonishing that so little attention has been paid by political theorists to this term and its meanings. It is after all a key term not only within populist politics but in modern politics more generally. Unlike 'freedom', 'justice', or even 'nation', 'people' has attracted hardly any analysis, even by theorists of democracy. But is conceptual analysis actually the right way to approach it? 'People'—'the people', 'a people'—is extraordinarily open and variable in its significance. What the term signifies is perhaps not so much a concept as a series of discourses about political identity, discourses used by partisans of many different causes to fight many different political struggles" (Canovan 2004: 247).

a monolithic entity, in the sense that they tend to represent a part of the people as the people.[13]

References to the necessity of calling a referendum to amend the constitution were also present in the strategy endorsed by Ms. le Pen during the presidential electoral campaign in 2017 to restore the superiority of national law over the international obligations of France, especially with regard to the duties stemming from the EU (Patard 2017; Fournier 2019). A massive use of referendums and need for a grand constitutional reform are elements that have characterised the recent history of the *Front National* (later *Rassemblement national*), which also proposed a referendum to reintroduce the death penalty and other very sensitive issues (Fournier 2019: 9). However, referendums are also unpredictable, and the Hungarian case is very telling of that. Orbán called a referendum on the so-called EU migrant quotas which was held on 2 October 2016. This referendum was the apex of a long racist and anti-refugee campaign orchestrated by the media close to Orbán. On that occasion, Hungarian people were asked to answer the following (and very broad) question: "Do you want the European Union to be entitled to prescribe the mandatory settlement of non-Hungarian citizens in Hungary without the consent of parliament?". Those who voted rejected (with a percentage of 98%) the EU's quotas, but in spite of the declarations released after the referendum, the consultation did not reach the necessary turnout (50%). Nevertheless, as often happens with populists, Orbán presented the result as a great message sent to Brussels and announced possible reforms to "remove the necessity for 50% of the country's voters to participate in a referendum for it to be valid" (Culik 2016). It has been said that the real intent of Orbán was to influence domestic politics, and in that populists probably managed to achieve their goal (Halmai 2018). At the same time, the Hungarian context confirms how risky and unpredictable referendums are, as they can act as a boomerang against those who have supported their call.

It has been said that "referendums do not automatically improve the democratic process. Instead, they often function as a substitute for a comprehensive discussion on the merits of vital policy issues" (Topaloff 2017:

[13] "Brexiters, too, invoke the referendum as the 'will of the people', a phrase understood as a singular homogeneous monolith, conveniently ignoring that 62.5% of the electorate ('remainers', and those who abstained from participating) did not vote to leave the EU but are 'automatically' included in that will" (Freeden 2017: 7).

127). These lines say a lot about the constitutive ambiguity of referendums: on the one hand, they have entered the toolbox of post-totalitarian democracies; on the other hand, the idea that they represent a window of opportunity to discuss the merits of some fundamental political choices may introduce risks for the entire system. As political scientists and historians recall, referendums have been frequently employed by authoritarian leaders in the past,[14] which is why they are still seen today with suspicion and permitted with varying levels of freedom by different countries' constitutional provisions (Butler and Ranney 1994; Qvortrup 2002). Scholars have also identified the reasons why excessive use of this instrument may be problematic:

> Referendums are also poor tools for addressing complex questions that cannot be posed in a straightforward yes-or-no manner. The "Oxi" referendum, initiated by Greece's populist ruling party Syriza, contained 68 words and name-checked four international institutions. It also asked citizens to give their opinion on an EU and IMF proposal whose deadline had already passed by the time of the vote. In holding this referendum, Greece's leaders seemed to be interested more in rallying support that might aid them at the international negotiating table than in setting the actual policy options clearly and honestly before the voters. The 2016 Brexit referendum also failed to offer clear options [...] In fact, referendums are a highly problematic mechanism for channeling the people's voice in representative democratic systems. Referendums raise difficult questions concerning the nature of legitimacy within these systems. They also often fail to allow for adequate public debate, as the recent experiences of the "Oxi" and Brexit referendums have revealed. (Topaloff 2017: 138)

More recently, the possibility of distinguishing between referendums and plebiscites has seemed to become more problematic (Butler and Ranney 1994), although scholars keep on using this distinction by arguing that "plebiscite is a populist device through which the people are treated by a government as a manipulable mass rather than a reasoning public" (Hayward 1996).[15]

[14] "Here popular votes have—as the case of Napoleon Bonaparte shows—been used as a top-down device to acquire legitimacy for a decision made by a more or less autocratic ruler" (Qvortrup 2018: 10).

[15] "Two criteria allow us to identify which phenomenon we are facing. Who initiates the proposal on which the people vote and who phrases the question? What is the issue to be settled?" (Hayward 1996: 15).

Referendum and Constitutional Law: An Instrument to Handle with Care

Although the use of referendums is a relatively recent phenomenon,[16] this is a very long debate (Luciani 2005, 2008; Di Giovine 2005). Already Max Weber, for instance, recalled such risks and stressed how it can be used to deresponsibilise the political forces:

> The referendum does not know the compromise, upon which the majority of all laws is based in every mass state with strong regional, social, religious and other cleavages [...] Moreover, the plebiscitary principles weaken the autonomous role of the party leader and the responsibility of the civil servants. A disavowal of the leading officials through a plebiscite which rejects their proposals does not and cannot enforce their resignation, as does a vote of no-confidence in parliamentary states, for the negative vote does not identify its reasons and does not oblige the negatively voting mass, as it does a parliamentary majority voting against a government, to replace the disavowed officials with its own responsible leaders. (Weber 1922)

These are considerations that have inspired generations of social scientists and that are dramatically topical nowadays. New lifeblood to the debate on this noble and yet complex instrument of the referendum has been given by the British events connected to the Brexit vote held on 23 June 2016. There are different explanations for that: the crisis of traditional political parties, since referendums became increasingly called "at the time when the relationship between 'aggregators' and 'articulators' broke down; at the time when the frozen party system began to thaw, and at the time when the number of party-identifiers began to drop" (Qvortrup 2018: 14).[17] These considerations do not exclude the possibility that referen-

[16] "According to the Center for Research on Direct Democracy, a total of only fourteen national referendums took place worldwide between the years 1700 and 1800. All of these fourteen votes took place after 1792, and six of them occurred in France. In the course of the next century, this number went up to 140. In both the nineteenth and the twentieth centuries, the majority of referendums took place in a single country—Switzerland, which introduced the referendum as a national political institution with its 1848 constitution and has since held more nationwide referendums than all other countries combined" (Topaloff 2017: 128).

[17] "The decline in the ability of élite-directed organizations such as parties, trade unions, and churches to achieve mass mobilization has provided the political space for the emergence of élite-directing social movements that are disposed to use methods of political action other than voting for political representatives" (Hayward 1996: 22).

dums can also give an added value to representative democracy. Scholars have dealt extensively with this subject (Hayward 1996: 17) and there are also mature democracies that have inherited and to a certain extent constitutionalised some plebiscitary elements. Such is the case of the French Fifth Republic, for instance. Art. 3 of the French Constitution reads: "National sovereignty belongs to the people who shall exercise it through their representatives and by means of referendum". Tierney has dealt with this provision, showing how it responds to a certain constitutional tradition and idea of the constituent power developed during the revolutionary period.[18] The frequent use of the referendum during the presidency of General de Gaulle has induced some scholars to speak of "Bonapartism" (Mitterrand 1965: 27; Hazareesingh 2008: 3), an element which can be found even more recently in French history (Hewlett 2007).

Comparative lawyers have reflected at length on the complicated relationship between referendums and representative democracy (Carré de Malberg 1931; Mirkine Guetzévitch 1931; Butler and Ranney 1994; Qvortrup 2002; Uleri 2003; Tierney 2012; Lewis 2013). British lawyers have reclaimed the topic in light of the recent debate on Brexit, and EU law scholars have also developed a mass of literature on that, due to the several examples of consultations that have taken place on European issues, starting from the referendum conducted in 1975, for instance (Mendez et al. 2014, 2017; Özlem Atikcan 2015).

More recently, Morel has identified at least two research strands in the debate on referendums and argued:

[18] "This seems by one reading at least to embody a restatement of the radical pouvoir constituant of the French body politic, returning us to the age-old paradox—does the constitution become the only source for any legitimate exercise of popular constitutional power or does popular sovereignty in France contain its own source of legitimacy? In other words, does Art. 3 constitute mere recognition of popular sovereignty rather than legitimacy for it, acknowledging that a higher power vested in the people resides outside and above that of the constitution itself? But there is another element to the equation: the specific reference to the referendum in Art. 3. Since the constitution explicitly invokes the referendum as the mode of expression of this power, a further question is begged: even if this higher power of the people above and beyond the constitution does indeed survive constitutional instantiation of lawful authority, are expressions of this power only legitimate when exercised through a referendum? In other words, it may be that the constitution cannot contain (as in circumscribe) the sovereignty of the people, but can it contain (as in facilitate) the vehicle for the exercise of this sovereignty. And if so, how and by whom may such referendums be triggered?" (Tierney 2012: 133).

> Theoretical accounts on referendums belong either to the constitutional debate or to democratic theory. What distinguishes the two debates in a rather precise way is the set of questions raised: while the classical, constitutional, debate questions the issue of the compatibility of the referendum with representative democracy and the extent and modalities of its use, the democratic debate rather focuses on the democratic quality of the referendum and whether its extension could help to improve the quality of contemporary democracies. (Morel 2012: 502)

The ideal starting point of this debate is obviously the well-known exchange between Carré de Malberg and Mirkine Guetzévitch (Carré de Malberg 1931; Mirkine Guetzévitch 1931). According to the former, the referendum was compatible with parliamentary systems (see also Guarino 1947), especially if understood as a way of solving the conflicts occurring between parliament and government and of limiting the parliamentary almightiness (Carré de Malberg 1931: 272). According to the latter, the referendum implied a tension that could hardly be solved with the idea of rationalisation of parliamentarism (Mirkine Guetzévitch 1931: 334).[19] It is necessary to recall that Mirkine Guetzévitch partly changed his mind, as observed by Morel.[20] Actually, as Luciani pointed out, the two scholars started from different premises represented by the antiparliamentary flavour of the referendum (Luciani 2005: 33). This debate is partly connected to the qualification of the referendum as an instrument of direct democracy. This position is for instance quite widespread in the Italian debate, but there are important scholars who have rejected this view by understanding the referendum as a device of popular participation (Luciani 2008: 163) on the basis of an interesting historical excursus. It is the case of those, for instance, who stressed the necessary physical coexistence of people ("the assembled people", as Luciani wrote commenting on

[19] "The discussion of the Russian constitutionalist focused in particular on a new variety of referendums and popular initiatives aimed at solving conflicts between the executive and the legislative, which could lead to the dissolution of parliament or the revocation of the head of the state. Mirkine Guetzévitch regarded this as contradictory with the trend toward a 'rationalization' of parliamentarism, by means of a strengthening of executives, which he welcomed as the great novelty of these Constitutions" (Morel 2012: 504).

[20] "The author had, however, expressed a rather different position one year earlier, in *Les Constitutions de l'Europe nouvelle* (1930), where he wrote that 'the referendum is the logical conclusion of the process of rationalization of parliamentarism'" (Morel 2012, footnote n. 9).

Rousseau[21]) as an essential connotation of direct democracy. Similar considerations have been shared by political scientists who argued that direct democracy does not exist as a modern form of government and is a misleading category (Uleri 2003: 17), also in light of the continuity that exists between referendum and political competition. If comparative law offers a variety of typologies of referendum (constitutional, legislative, conventional, preventive, successive, mandatory, optional, advisory; Volpi 1997, 2016), such a variety does not impede the finding of common concerns and trends. This does not deny the analytical validity of the distinction between experiences in which the referendum initiative belongs to constitutional bodies only and experiences where the initiative is, so to speak, diffused (as opposed to centralised/institutionalised) in civil society. In these contexts, referendums have been seen as a "counter-power" (Fois 1978: 130) or a manifestation of the "right of resistance" (Volpe 1998).

How Constitutions Coordinate Referendums and Representative Democracy

In order to minimise the impact of the referendum on the life of the legal systems they govern, constitutions establish forms of limitation of the political risks connected to the referendum or strategies that have emerged over the years to challenge shared concerns. For instance, in an essay devoted to the Swiss and American experiences, Auer once recalled the fear of the American founding fathers towards "pure democracy" (Auer 1992: 64), and in light of that he went on to explain the lack of the referendum at federal level in the US. These remarks do not come as a surprise if it is true, as Elster argued, that constitutions are frequently the product of violence and fear (Elster 2012). Obviously, the British experience is very particular due to the only partially written nature of its constitutional sources (Bogdanor 1981: 75) and to the relatively recent practice of an instrument which has been, however, studied by eminent British lawyers such as Dicey (Dicey 1890). However, there have been attempts to extend to the British case some of the considerations made with regard to Continental Europe (Calamo Specchia 2012), and British constitutional lawyers have stressed that the UK peculiarity does not impede fruitful

[21] Luciani (2005: 11); Luciani (2008: 158). On that occasion, Luciani referred to J.J. Rousseau, *Il contratto sociale* (*The Social Contract*), 1762, L. III, chap. XII, available at: https://www.earlymoderntexts.com/assets/pdfs/rousseau1762.pdf

comparisons (Leyland 2013: 145). Indeed, even in the UK, concerns about the use of the referendum have not been absent. The report of the Select Committee on the Constitution of the House of Lords gave an important contribution to this debate. First, it offered an account of the pros[22] and cons[23] in the use of the referendum; second, it recalled some of the fundamental constitutional issues that would require the holding of a referendum (House of Lords 2010: 27). In the UK there is legislative discipline which governs the use of this tool,[24] although it is not easy to understand what the formula "constitutional matters" means. Indeed, although it is unquestioned that "referendums undoubtedly have a constitutional role to play" (Leyland 2013: 146), in this context, as Bogdanor said, "the problem is that in Britain constitutional issues can easily arise out of seemingly non-constitutional legislation" (Bogdanor 1981: 73). Not to mention that "without clear rules referendums can be manipulated politically" (Leyland 2013: 146). Another element of comparability is given by the common influence exercised by the EU.

There are, finally, two other considerations that make the referendum fascinating to comparative lawyers: the fact that eminent lawyers have changed their minds about this instrument (Mirkine Guetzévitch and Dicey), which confirms its very complex nature and, above all, the chameleonic nature of this instrument. The first consideration can be explained in light of the fact that it is always necessary to look at it from the systemic impact that it might have on the context of representative democracy.

[22] "That referendums enhance the democratic process"; "that referendums can be a 'weapon of entrenchment'"; "that referendums can 'settle" an issue'; "that referendums can be a 'protective device'; "that referendums enhance citizen engagement"; "that referendums promote voter education"; "that voters are able to make reasoned judgments"; "that referendums are popular with voters"; "that referendums complement representative democracy" (House of Lords 2010: 13).

[23] Among others: "That referendums are a tactical device"; "that referendums are dominated by elite groups"; "that referendums can have a damaging effect on minority groups"; "that referendums are a conservative device"; "that referendums do not 'settle' an issue"; "that referendums fail to deal with complex issues"; "that referendums tend not to be about the issue in question"; "that voters show little desire to participate in referendums"; "that referendums are costly"; "that referendums undermine representative democracy" (House of Lords 2010: 16).

[24] "The Election Commission is placed under a duty to advise on the intelligibility of any referendum questions and the legislation also establishes control over donations and expenses and many other issues. However, no clear rules have emerged to determine under what precise constitutional conditions referendums can be held" (Leyland, 2013: 145).

Many criticised Dicey for this change of mind; others have tried to find continuity in his thought by stressing the parliamentary disappointment that would have caused that (Weill 2003: 475). This was due to the 1911 *Parliament Act* which had removed, in Dicey's own words, "[the] last effective constitutional safeguard" (Dicey 1912: 81), by recognising the supremacy of the House of Commons over the House of Lords and creating a system where the majority of the Commons "can arrogate to itself that legislative omnipotence which of right belongs to the nation" (Dicey 1912: 91). In other words, according to Dicey, the referendums could compensate the new institutional scenario after the weakening of the House of Lords. Because of the fact that the British institutional equilibrium had changed, Dicey's point was necessary to involve the people in the "constitutional changes". The referendum has also had a chameleonic nature; it is sufficient here to notice what has happened in the UK, where in 1981 Bogdanor defined the referendum as a "conservative device" (Bogdanor 1981: 69). This explains why referendums "could serve to increase its [the government's] power", and it is no coincidence that over recent years the debate has been focusing on how to discipline it to avoid possible abuses. This intuition was confirmed in the 1990s when it was used as an instrument to enfranchise the leadership from the internal influences of the party and to create a direct connection with the people. This has led to forms of plebiscitary drift (Torre 2012: 73). These considerations also clarify why the referendum—once defined by Bogdanor as a "conservative device"—has become part of the reformist season (Carboni 2012: 401).

The Italian Constitutional Frame

Referendums have played an important role in Italian constitutional law; this can be argued even whilst looking at the genesis of the constitutional system, since it was through the so-called institutional referendum held in 1946 that Italy became a Republic. The Italian case is also interesting from a constitutional law perspective for several reasons. It responds to a long-standing debate in continental Europe about how to reconcile direct and representative democracy. It is sufficient to look at the discussion in the Constituent Assembly to confirm this, where Costantino Mortati—later justice of the Italian Constitutional Court and eminent constitutional lawyer—proposed to constitutionalise different types of referendums (advisory, binding, deliberative) to be triggered by different institutional actors and by the people. In his view, the referendum was a stimulus to keep the institutions in touch with their citizens (Mortati 1946; Rosa 2018: 117). However, in his view, there were three elements to be considered with care: (1) the turnout; (2) the deliberative quorum; and (3) the number of proponents necessary to trigger the procedure. Finally, he also warned of the necessity to inform the people in order to favour awareness and ensure that they were sufficiently educated to decide on the issue. This proposal has been only partly accepted by the rest of the Constituent Assembly. The Italian case is particularly interesting as—unlike in other countries—the Italian Constitution permits referendum at both the state and regional levels. Moreover, the abrogative referendum as disciplined by the Italian Constitution has been described as a *unicum* in comparative law (Rosa 2018: 116). The relevant constitutional provisions are the following: Arts. 75, 123, 132 and 138.[25] Art. 123 is about regional fundamental charters ("Statuti") and provides for the holding of a referendum on these "Statuti", "if one-fiftieth of the electors of the Region or one-fifth of the members of the Regional Council so request within three months from its publication" (Art. 123). Art. 132 examines a referendum on the possible "merger between existing Regions" or "the creation of new Regions having a minimum of one million inhabitants". The constitutional amendment procedure is governed by Art. 138, which provides for the possibility of submitting laws amending the Constitution or other constitutional laws "when, within three months of their publication, such request is made by one-fifth of the members of a House or five hundred thousand voters or five Regional Councils".

Art. 138 also clarifies that the "law submitted to referendum shall not be promulgated if not approved by a majority of valid votes. A referendum shall not be held if the law has been approved in the second voting by each of the Houses by a majority of two-thirds of the members". This is what Italian scholars call "constitutional referendums".

[25] See also Art. 87 about the power of the President of the Republic to call a general referendum in the cases provided for by the Constitution. Of special mention is the only EU-related referendum in Italy, which was held in 1989. It regarded the transformation of the European Communities into a European Union provided with a European Parliament entitled to draft a Constitution for Europe. The outcome was highly positive. This referendum is understood as special and advisory in nature. In this respect, a specific constitutional law was adopted (constitutional law 2/1989) since this kind of referendums was understood to be different from those governed by the Italian Constitution (Barbera and Morrone 2003: 102–103).

The recent attempts at reforming the Italian Constitution (Politi 2014: 43) have reserved a central role in the constitutional referendum; it is sufficient to mention here the referendum on Renzi's reform held in 2016. Unlike Salvini and Conte, Renzi has never defined himself as populist but, as suggested by Blokker, amongst others, his behaviour in the campaign for the referendum on the constitutional reform and his general conduct remind us of the populist rhetoric. This is particularly true if one thinks of the way in which Renzi tried to dichotomise "the vote between those that want to modernise Italy – a reform that will 'bring Italy into the future' – and the 'conservatives' that supposedly cling to a (corrupt) past" (Blokker 2016). However, as Faraguna deals with the constitutional amendment procedure in his chapter, I shall limit myself to some general considerations. The abrogative referendum is governed by Art. 75, which reads:

> A general referendum may be held to repeal, in whole or in part, a law or a measure having the force of law, when so requested by five hundred thousand voters or five Regional Councils. No referendum may be held on a law regulating taxes, the budget, amnesty or pardon, or a law ratifying an international treaty. Any citizen entitled to vote for the Chamber of Deputies has the right to vote in a referendum. The referendum shall be considered to have been carried if the majority of those eligible has voted and a majority of valid votes has been achieved.

Here, we have a fundamental difference between the constitutional and abrogative referendum: while Art. 75 provides for two types of *quorum*—a structural/participatory one and a deliberative one—Art. 138 only provides for a deliberative *quorum* without making the validity of the result conditional upon a minimum turnout. This has triggered an interesting debate, as Art. 138 was designed for micro-reforms but, since the 1990s, it has been used either to carry out[26] or to propose grand constitutional reforms and sometimes deviations from the procedure designed by Art. 138 have been established by constitutional laws. This is the case of constitutional law 1/1997, which established a bicameral parliamentary committee on constitutional reforms ("Bicamerale D'Alema"), in particular by transforming the constitutional referendum from a possible one—if requested according to the terms of Art. 138—into a necessary part of the procedure.

[26] This was the case of constitutional law 3/2001, which reshaped Title V of the second part of the Constitution.

According to some scholars (Romboli 2007), this would have altered the nature of the constitutional referendum, which would be understood by the Constitution as a means to preserve minorities (it would be "oppositive" in nature) and which would have been transformed by constitutional law 1/1997 into a "confirmative" referendum. The project drafted by the bicameral commission was later abandoned, and the new procedure designed by constitutional law 1/1997 was never implemented.

However, the use of Art. 138 in cases of grand reforms has inevitably had an impact on the homogeneity of the question submitted to the reform, since voters have been asked (in 2001, 2006 and 2016) to vote either 'yes' or 'no' on particularly heterogeneous and complex questions.

Concerning the participation in the constitutional referendums held so far, in 2001 the turnout was very low, that is, 34.05%, while it increased in both 2006 (52.46%) and 2016 (65.48%).

The constitutional frame, however, is not exhaustive; in fact, the first referendums were activated only after the entry into force of law 352/1970, which complements the constitutional picture by designing the procedure, the conditions and the temporal limitations by which requests for referendums can be presented.[27] Additionally, it gave the Central Office of the *Corte di Cassazione* the power to control compliance with the legislative requirements (i.e. validity and number of signatures).

Moreover, by means of constitutional law 1/1953 a new fundamental competence was given to the Italian Constitutional Court, which is charged with controlling the permissibility of referendums requested ex Art. 75. Originally, the *Corte costituzionale* understood its role within a narrow perspective by verifying whether the law subject to referendum belonged to exceptions mentioned by Art. 75. Later, however, it went beyond this duty by giving a fundamental contribution to the "rationalisation" of the referendum (Barbera and Morrone 2003: 63; Bettinelli 1978). For instance, in judgement 16/1978, the Constitutional Court referred to a number of further limitations that can be inferred from the principles governing the system and the very nature of the referendum.

[27] This law was passed by the Italian Parliament after a long period of reluctance. It is not coincidental that scholars wrote of an unwritten anti-referendum convention (*convenzione antireferendaria*) to describe this political attitude. See Bettinelli (1978) and Barbera and Morrone (2003).

In this way, the Corte costituzionale paved the way for a series of decisions that have insisted on the homogeneity and clarity of the question and on the need to limit the risk of destabilisation connected to the improper use of the instrument:

> For example, the Court has disallowed requests for referenda in which a single question incorporates several distinct items to be abrogated, thus precluding voters from independently exercising their judgment with respect to each component of the referendum. Likewise, the Court has blocked requests for referenda aimed at abrogating laws the content of which is in some way bound by the Constitution, or which cannot be amended without revising the Constitution itself. A referendum is not permitted if it amounts to an attempt to introduce new legal provisions by rewriting a legislative text rather than an attempt to simply eliminate existing provisions. Nor may a referendum seek to repeal laws required by international or Community obligations, to avoid giving rise to international responsibility on the part of the State without parliamentary approval (Italian Constitutional Court 2019: 38).

Thanks to this case law,[28] the Italian Constitutional Court has also contributed to guaranteeing the space reserved to political institutions[29] by minimising the risk of collisions between direct and representative democracy. As mentioned previously, referendums have always played an important role in Italian constitutional law, covering particularly sensitive issues (Santomauro 2019) that divided the country (the referendums of divorce and abortion held, respectively, in 1974 and 1981, for instance) and contributing to the reshaping of the institutional system. Here, the example is of course given by the referendum on the electoral system in 1993. This referendum contributed to a fundamental shift towards a majoritarian system which seemed to favour the emergence of elements of a political bipolar system in Italy before the start of a long reform period, in which different electoral systems have been approved by the Italian Parliament. Its impact over the institutional system has been due to the abrogative nature of referendums, according to Art. 75 and to the possibility of

[28] See also Corte costituzionale, decisions 30/1981, 31/1981, 8/1995, 27/1997, www.cortecostituzionale.it (Rosa 2018: 120).

[29] This can be found even with regard to other types of referendums, like consultative referendums held at the regional level. See Corte costituzionale, decision 118/2015, www.cortecostituzionale.it

partial abrogative referendums, that is, referendums on portions of laws. The latter may result in manipulative referendums, since they erase only part of the original provision. In this way, it is not only the letter of the provision that changes (as it can be partially cancelled, thanks to the abrogative force of the referendum) but also its content. This explains why abrogative referendums are generally considered as sources of law (provided with the same force of the laws that they repeal) by Italian constitutional scholars, since by their means it is possible to contribute to the law-making process. This also explains why referendums are risky.

It is not by coincidence that, in a pivotal book published in 2003, Barbera (current justice at the Italian Constitutional Court) and Morrone defined Italy as the *Republic of the referendums* (Barbera and Morrone 2003). These authors have identified different seasons in the history of the Italian Republic by showing the chameleonic nature of this instrument, which has sometimes served a crucial role in the fight for civil rights carried out by the *Partito Radicale*, while in other periods it has worked as a stimulus for Parliament or a form of contestation or counter-power, understood to question the establishment (Rosa 2018: 121). Constitutional scholars in Italy still debate on what happens to the legislation previously in force when a statute is repealed due to an abrogative referendum. Furthermore, in light of the Constitutional Court case law,[30] the automatic restoration of the legislation previously in force seems to be excluded. Another issue regards whether it is forbidden for the legislator to reintroduce the legislation repealed by a referendum. Since it is prohibited to repeat a referendum which has been rejected in the last five years (Art. 58 of law 352/1970), scholars have argued that a similar temporal limitation should be imposed on Parliament, but the issue is still debated (Luciani 2005: 680). Over the last 20 years, the meagre turnout has characterised rounds of consultations and triggered an interesting debate about whether to reform abrogative referendums. This also explains the changes proposed by the Five Star Movement and recalled at the beginning of this chapter, in particular, those concerning lowering the turnout in cases of "legislative referendums" and "abrogative referendums". Scholars have expressed concerns about this (Morrone 2018; Grasso 2019), and it is useful to recall that, originally, the proposal did not provide for a minimum turnout threshold. Another interesting element which acknowledges the important case law of the Italian Constitutional Court is the latest

[30] Corte costituzionale, sentenza 13/2012, www.cortecostituzionale.it

version of the draft amendment to Art. 71, which has incorporated some of the further limitations inferred by the Court in recent years and codified some implicit limits to the referendum.

It seems, thus, that the parliamentary arena has tamed the most controversial aspects of this reform, although many ambiguous points remain (Morrone 2018).

References

Atikcan, E. Ö. (2015). The Puzzle of Double Referendums in the European Union. *Journal of Common Market Studies, 53*(5), 937–956.

Auer, A. (1992). L'esperienza del referendum in Svizzera e negli Stati Uniti. In M. Luciani & M. Volpi (Eds.), *Referendum* (pp. 61–76). Roma/Bari: Laterza.

Barbera, A., & Morrone, A. (2003). *La Repubblica dei referendum.* Bologna: Il Mulino.

Bettinelli, E. (1978). Itinerari della razionalizzazione della convenzione antireferendaria. *Politica del diritto, 50*(5), 513–559.

Blokker, P. (2016). 'Vote Yes for a Safe Italy' or 'Vote No to Defend the Constitution': Italian Constitutional Politics Between Majoritarianism and Civil Resistance. *Verfassungsblog.* Available at https://verfassungsblog.de/italy-constitution-referendum-renzi-blokker/

Bogdanor, V. (1981). *The People and the Party System: The Referendum and Electoral Reform in British Politics.* Cambridge: Cambridge University Press.

Butler, D., & Ranney, A. (Eds.). (1994). *Referendums Around the World: The Growing Use of Direct Democracy.* Washington, DC: AEI press.

Calamo Specchia, M. (2012). Quale disciplina referendaria nel Regno Unito? Brevi note su di un approccio sistematico per un modello a-sistematico. In A. Torre & J. Frosini (Eds.), *Democrazia rappresentativa e referendum nel Regno Unito* (pp. 139–154). Rimini: Maggioli.

Canovan, M. (2004). Populism for Political Theorists? *Journal of Political Ideologies, 9*(3), 241–252.

Carboni, G. G. (2012). I referendum mai realizzati e ancora da realizzare. In A. Torre & J. Frosini (Eds.), *Democrazia rappresentativa e referendum nel Regno Unito* (pp. 399–426). Rimini: Maggioli.

Carré de Malberg, R. (1931). Considérations théoriques sur la question de la combinaison du referendum avec le parlementarisme. *Annuaire de l'Institut international de droit public, 2*, 272–284.

Corrias, L. (2016). Populism in a Constitutional Key: Constituent Power, Popular Sovereignty and Constitutional Identity. *European Constitutional Law Review, 12*(1), 6–26.

Culik, J. (2016). Hungary's Invalid Refugee Referendum Dents Viktor Orbán's Anti-EU 'Revolution.' *The Conversation*. Available at https://theconversation.com/hungarys-invalid-refugee-referendum-dents-viktor-orbans-anti-eu-revolution-66424

Di Giovine, A. (2005). Referendum e responsabilità politica. *Diritto Pubblico Comparato ed Europeo, 7*(2), 1214–1221.

Dicey, A. V. (1890). Ought the Referendum to Be Introduced into England? *Contemporary Review, 20*(3), 531–546.

Dicey, A. V. (1912). The Parliament Act 1911 and the Destruction of All Constitutional Safeguards. In W. R. Anson (Ed.), *Rights of Citizenship: A Survey of Safeguards for the People* (pp. 81–107). London: Frederick Warne.

Elster, J. (2012). Constitution-Making and Violence. *Journal of Legal Analysis, 4*(1), 7–39.

Fois, S. (1978). Il referendum come 'contropotere' e garanzia nel sistema costituzionale italiano. In E. Bettinelli & L. Boneschi (Eds.), *Referendum, ordine pubblico, Costituzione* (pp. 130–157). Milano: Bompiani.

Fournier, T. (2019). From Rhetoric to Action: A Constitutional Analysis of Populism. *German Law Journal, 20*(3), 362–381.

Freeden, M. (2017). After the Brexit Referendum: Revisiting Populism as an Ideology. *Journal of Political Ideologies, 22*(1), 1–11.

Grasso, G. (2019). La balestra di Guglielmo Tell e l'iniziativa legislativa popolare. Note minime a proposito del disegno di legge costituzionale in materia di iniziativa legislativa popolare e di referendum. *Osservatorio AIC, 7*(1–2), 245–250.

Guarino, G. (1947). Il referendum e la sua applicazione al regime parlamentare. *Rassegna di diritto pubblico, 2*(1), 30–57.

Halmai, G. (2018). The Coup against Constitutional Democracy: The Case of Hungary. In M. A. Graber, S. Levinson, & M. Tushnet (Eds.), *Constitutional Democracy in Crisis?* Oxford: Oxford University Press.

Hayward, J. (1996). The Populist Challenge to Élitist Democracy in Europe. In J. Hayward (Ed.), *Elitism, Populism, and European Politics* (pp. 10–32). Oxford: Oxford University Press.

Hazareesingh, S. (2008). De Gaulle, le mythe napoléonien, et la consécration de la tradition consulaire républicaine. *Cahiers Jaurès, 9*(3), 3–20.

Hewlett, N. (2007). Nicolas Sarkozy and the Legacy of Bonapartism: The French Presidential and Parliamentary Elections of 2007. *Modern & Contemporary France, 15*(4), 405–422.

House of Lords. Select Committee on the Constitution. (2010). 12th Report of Session 2009–10, Referendums in the United Kingdom. Report with Evidence. https://www.publications.parliament.uk/pa/ld200910/ldselect/ldconst/99/99.pdf

Italian Constitutional Court. (2019). The Italian Constitutional Court. https://www.cortecostituzionale.it/documenti/download/pdf/The_Italian_Constitutional_Court.pdf
Lewis, D. (2013). *Direct Democracy and Minority Rights: A Critical Assessment of the Tyranny of the Majority in the American States*. Abingdon: Routledge.
Leyland, P. (2013). Referendums, Popular Sovereignty, and the Territorial Constitution. In R. Rawlings, P. Leyland, & A. Young (Eds.), *Sovereignty and the Law* (pp. 145–164). Oxford: Oxford University Press.
Luciani, M. (2005). *Commentario della Costituzione. Art. 75 Referendum*. Bologna: Zanichelli.
Luciani, M. (2008). Il referendum: questioni teoriche e dell'esperienza italiana. *Revista catalana de dret públic, 24*(2), 157–182.
Mendez, F., Mendez, M., & Triga, V. (2014). *Referendums and the European Union: A Comparative Inquiry*. Cambridge: Cambridge University Press.
Mendez, F., Mendez, M., & Triga, V. (2017). *Referendums on EU Matters*. The Policy Department for Citizens' Rights and Constitutional Affairs, European Parliament's Committee on Constitutional Affairs. Available at http://www.europarl.europa.eu/RegData/etudes/STUD/2017/571402/IPOL_STU(2017)571402_EN.pdf
Mény, Y., & Surel, Y. (2004). *Populismo e democrazia*. Bologna: Il Mulino.
Mirkine Guetzévitch, B. (1931). Le référendum et le parlementarisme dans les nouvelles constitutions européennes. *Annuaire de l'Institut international de droit public, 2*, 285.
Mitterrand, F. (1965). *Le Coup D'etat Permanent*. Paris: Plon.
Morel, L. (2012). Referendum. In M. Rosenfeld & A. Sajó (Eds.), *The Oxford Handbook of Comparative Constitutional Law* (pp. 501–528). Oxford: Oxford University Press.
Morrone, A. (2018). L'iniziativa popolare propositiva: per una democrazia plebiscitaria contro la democrazia rappresentativa? *federalismi.it, 16* (23). Available at www.federalismi.it
Mortati, C. (1946, September 3). Relazione alla II Sottocommissione. *nasciatcostituzione.it*. Available at https://www.nascitacostituzione.it/05appendici/01generali/00/02/06-mortati.htm
Patard, J. (2017). Le référendum constitutionnel de Marine Le Pen: Moi présidente, je rétablirai la supériorité du droit national! Available at https://www.lepetitjuriste.fr/droit-constitutionnel/referendum-constitutionnel-de-marine-pen-moi-presidente-retablirai-superiorite-droit-national/
Politi, F. (2014). Il procedimento di revisione della Costituzione Repubblicana. La funzione di garanzia dell'art. 138 Cost. e il ricorso a procedimenti alternativi della forma di governo e tutela dei valori costituzionali. In V. Baldini (Ed.), *La Costituzione e la sua revisione* (pp. 43–86). Pisa: Pisa University Press.

Qvortrup, M. (2002). *A Comparative Study of Referendums: Government by the People.* Manchester: Manchester University Press.
Qvortrup, M. (2018). Introduction: Theory, Practice and History. In M. Qvortrup (Ed.), *Referendums Around the World* (pp. 1–18). London: Palgrave.
Raible, L., & Trueblood, L. (2017). The Swiss System of Referendums and the Impossibility of Direct Democracy. *UK Constitutional Law Association Blog.* Available at https://ukconstitutionallaw.org/2017/04/04/lea-raible-and-leah-trueblood-the-swiss-system-of-referendums-and-the-impossibility-of-direct-democracy/
Romboli, R. (2007). Il referendum costituzionale nell'esperienza repubblicana e nelle prospettive di riforma dell'art. 138 Cost. In A. Pisaneschi & L. Violini (Eds.), *Poteri, garanzie e diritti a sessanta anni dalla Costituzione: scritti per Giovanni Grottanelli de' Santi* (pp. 573–619). Milano: Giuffrè.
Rosa, F. (2018). Art. 75. In F. Clementi, L. Cuocolo, F. Rosa, & G. E. Vigevani (Eds.), *La Costituzione italiana* (Vol. II, pp. 116–121). Bologna: Il Mulino.
Santomauro, G. (2019). Referendum as an Instrument of "Policy Change" on a Crucial Bioethical Issue: A Comparative Case Study on Abortion in Italy and Ireland. *Nomos. Le attualità del diritto, 22*(1), 1–37. Available at www.nomos-leattualitaneldiritto.it
Tierney, S. (2012). *Constitutional Referendums: The Theory and Practice of Republican Deliberation.* Oxford: Oxford University Press.
Topaloff, L. (2017). The Rise of Referendums: Elite Strategy or Populist Weapon? *Journal of Democracy, 28*(3), 127–140.
Torre, A. (2012). Il referendum nel Regno Unito: radici sparse, pianta rigogliosa. In A. Torre & J. Frosini (Eds.), *Democrazia rappresentativa e referendum nel Regno Unito* (pp. 11–112). Rimini: Maggioli.
Uleri, P. V. (2003). *Referendum e democrazia. Una prospettiva comparata.* Bologna: Il Mulino.
Volpe, G. (1998). Referendum abrogativo e diritto di resistenza. In Corte costituzionale (Ed.), *Il giudizio di ammissibilità del referendum abrogativo* (pp. 281–286). Milano: Giuffrè.
Volpi, M. (1997). Referendum (dir. cost). In *Digesto delle discipline pubblicistiche, IV* (pp. 494–518). Torino: UTET.
Volpi, M. (2016). Referendum e iniziativa popolare. Quale riforma. *costituzionalismo.it.* Available at http://www.costituzionalismo.it/download/Costituzionalismo_201602_567.pdf
Weber, M. (1922). *Economy and Society.* Available at https://archive.org/stream/MaxWeberEconomyAndSociety/MaxWeberEconomyAndSociety_djvu.txt
Weill, R. (2003). Dicey Was Not Diceyan. *Cambridge Law Journal, 62*(2), 474–494.

CHAPTER 5

Populism and Constitutional Amendment

Pietro Faraguna

Introduction

Populism is a harshly debated and controversial concept. Only recently, it attracted growing attention from legal scholars, and from public law scholars in particular. In a relative short span of time, it has taken centre stage in the public law realm. Debates over constitutionalism and populism are flourishing all over the (western) world: doctoral theses are assigned on the topic, and workshops, seminars and conferences are being organized on this complex relationship. In addition, the relevant literature has grown exponentially in the last years. However, there is no other field where the disagreement reigns on the same identification of the research field. Not by chance, "What is populism?" (Müller 2016) is the title of one of the most quoted books that was recently published on the matter. A quantitative look into the table of contents of the many special issues and monographic volumes devoted to the topic reveals a disproportionately high attention for what populism is, compared to the attention ever devoted to the definition of "liberal constitutionalism" (Oklopcic 2019a, b). However, definitional challenges are always very ambitious, and in the present case, the field is already packed with prominent studies on a far

P. Faraguna (✉)
University of Trieste, Trieste, Italy
e-mail: pfaraguna@units.it

G. Delledonne et al. (eds.), *Italian Populism and Constitutional Law*, Challenges to Democracy in the 21st Century,
https://doi.org/10.1007/978-3-030-37401-3_5

from settled definition. Therefore, in the present chapter, we will not deal with such an ambitious definitional question: On the contrary, the chapter adopts the most commonly acknowledged definition of essential characters of populism, namely its anti-elitist and anti-pluralist polemic.

Starting from these definitions, we will explore a rather under-investigated relationship, namely between populism and constitutional amendment. First, we will provide a conceptual framework of this relationship, by analysing the use, misuse and abuse of constitutional amendment by populists. To do this, we will focus on a very specific species of the populist genre: that is—populism in power. In fact, constitutional amendment is a legal tool that is only available to populists in power. In fact, whatever procedures and machineries a specific constitution requires to be amended, all constitutions require one (or more) deliberation(s) from a parliamentary majority to start the constitutional amendment procedure. Therefore, we will focus on the most commonly acknowledged experiences of populism in power to analyse whether this species of populism makes use of constitutional amendment, and, if so, what are the recurrent patterns of the investigated use of constitutional amendments by populists in power. My chapter will argue that, if constitutional amendment is correctly understood, populists in power usually stay at large from constitutional amendments: they rather prefer to replace the Constitution or to disable it in concrete. In fact, populists tend to reject any distinction between "constitutional" and "ordinary" politics. This denial is central to our argument: populism tends to deny any distinction between ordinary legislation and constitutional legislation, as constitutional rigidity is a typical machinery inherited by liberal-democratic constitutionalism. However, we will argue that there are some cases where populists in power made (instrumental) use of constitutional amendments to occupy the state and mobilize the constitution around their own specific and partisan goals.

Then, we will explore possible constitutional remedies against the populist (ab)use of constitutional amendment: procedural mechanisms and doctrines of unconstitutional constitutional amendment. Within this picture, the chapter argues that constitutional machineries designed to slow down the process of constitutional amendments may be more effective than the doctrine of unconstitutional constitutional amendment. Subsequently, I will test the conceptual map designed in the first part of the chapter to the Italian case. Constitutional developments in the last 30 years in Italy have been characterized by a never-ending debate on overarching constitutional reforms. However, this debate has rarely led to the positive conclusion of any project of constitutional amendments. Nonetheless, this permanent mobilization of the constitutional amendment power has some resemblances with the populist approach to constitutional amendments. However, the identification of some disturbing resemblances with the populists' (ab)use of constitutional amendments only emerges if one adopts a purely methodological perspective. In fact, substantially, the most important attempts of overarching constitutional reforms in Italy did not share their most classic aims, such as the capture of counter-majoritarian institutions and the removal of the essential pluralist character of post–World War II constitutions. Finally, the chapter will argue that the procedure required by the Italian Constitution to be amended was able to disable populist impulses so far.

Setting the Scene: Populism, Anti-Pluralism and Contemporary Constitutionalism

The exploration of the relationship between populism and constitutional amendment requires, if not a proper definition, some approximate understanding about what we mean with the two terms: "populism" and "constitutional amendment". The definition of populism is one of the most controversial topics currently debated in a lively transnational scholarly debate (Müller 2016; Mudde and Rovira Kaltwasser 2017). Within this scholarly global conversation, disagreements probably outnumber agreements, and the concept remains indeterminate and vague. Populism is usually not considered a traditional ideology, but a strategy, a discourse, a style of political mobilization, a "thin-centered ideology" (Mudde 2004: 544), a meta-ideology, that considers society to be ultimately separated into two homogeneous and antagonistic groups: "the pure people versus the corrupt elite" (Mudde 2004: 543). As a meta-ideology, populism can accommodate many different substantive political projects. Observers have identified many variates of populism, which applies the above-mentioned division with specific set of economic policies, ideas of social justice and so on.

Separation between pure people and elite is one of the recurrent and characterizing elements of populism, along with another feature, namely its anti-pluralism. In reality, the anti-elitist and anti-pluralist characters of populism are tightly connected, as both stems from the specific understanding that populism adopts of the concept of the "people": the peoples are viewed not only as sovereign (in fact, popular sovereignty is one of the essential pillars of liberal-democratic constitutionalism), but also as "homogeneous, pure, and virtuous" (Akkerman et al. 2013: 1327). This specific understanding of the people mirrors the populist *pars-pro-toto* understanding of the majority (Arato 2016: 269; Blokker 2019: 544): the "good people" (Albertazzi and McDonnel 2008) as opposed to the corrupted elite, are the only morally legitimate representatives of the real people. Therefore, other representative claims are by definition illegitimate and not worth of respect.

Anti-pluralism[1] is, in its roots, following the populists' denial of any conflicts within the society. By definition, there might be no conflict within a homogenous people, and therefore social conflict is excluded by the populist discourse. This is a crucial point from the point of view of constitutional studies: in fact, the essential character of post–World War II constitutions, and the normative justification underpinning them, is the institutionalization, and precisely constitutionalization, of the social conflict. In fact, whereas the mainstream narrative identifies constitutional rigidity as one of the most distinctive features of post–World War II constitutionalism (vs. the flexible character of liberal constitutions), there is a far more profound distinction between the constitutions of the liberal period and the contemporary constitutions. While liberal constitutions kept social conflict outside of constitutional bodies by limiting franchise, post–World War II constitutions incorporate and regulate social conflict through constitutional bodies and laws (Bin 2007).

This is why post–World War II constitutions include diverging principles and values in their texts and only trace the field for political settlement of conflicts. Post–World War II constitutions, far from denying social conflict, constitutionalizes it by including possible diverging principles in the texts. The 1948 Constitution of Italy, for instance, simultaneously establishes the principle of formal (Art. 3.1 It. Const.) and substantial (Art. 3.2 It. Const.) equality; the liberal principle of protection of private ownership (Art. 42.1 It. Const.) and a social understanding of private ownership, admitting limitations to it if this aims at social purposes (Art. 42.2); freedom of enterprise (Art. 41 It. Const.) and public interventions in the economy (Art. 43 It. Const.).

[1] The anti-pluralist character of populism emerges in a particularly evident manner in forms of right-wing populism, as pointed out by Galston 2018.

Populism, by denying conflict, rejects the primary mission of post–World War II constitutionalism. This is the conceptual reason that explains why populism is usually credited as incompatible with constitutionalism.[2] In fact "[d]espite the great divergence of approaches to understanding populism, … many observers appear to agree on one point – namely, that whatever else it is, populism is inherently hostile to the mechanisms and ultimately, the values commonly associated with constitutionalism" (Müller 2016: 60). Even though Müller includes among these values constraints on the will of the majority, checks and balances, protections for minorities and even fundamental rights, the consideration of the social conflict seems the most privileged perspective to clarify the contrast between populism and post–World War II constitutionalism: while the first denies it, the second one constitutionalize it, by including potentially diverging principles in the text of the constitution, and by giving to ordinary politics the task of refining the composition of these diverging principles through ordinary legislation.

In other words, post–World War II constitutions are pluralistic and therefore consider social conflict as constitutionally physiological. On the contrary, populists "understand conflict as an inherently problematic phenomenon" (Blokker 2019: 544), incompatible in its roots with the populists' understanding of the people. A pure and homogeneous people tolerate no conflict: this denial implies the denial of the "distinction between ordinary politics (in which conflicts between different social forces play out) and foundational or constitutional politics" (Blokker 2019: 544), in which the rules of the game are fixed, or—to adopt another author's point of view—in which the boundaries of the social conflict are set (Bin 2007). As a consequence, populists attempt at giving an ultimate answer to a problem that post–World War II constitutionalism consciously leaves open, namely the locus of sovereignty. In fact, contemporary representative democracy consists of a process that reveals that power does not belong to anybody, neither to the representatives who exercise it in the name of the people, nor to the people in whose name power is exercised (Lefort 1988: 13 and ff.). Constitutional democracy makes sure that the

[2] Some notable exceptions are to be mentioned. Among recent defenders of populism, Laclau believed that populism fosters a democratization of democracy (Laclau 2007), while Rovira Kaltwasser problematizes the relationship between democracy and populism as ambivalent (Rovira Kaltwasser 2012). Within this picture, also Paul Blokker has repeatedly underlined how the relations between constitutionalism and populism are much more complex than their straight incompatibility (for further details, see his chapter in this volume).

will of the people "remain the permanent creation and recreation of the democratic process itself" (Urbinati 2017).

The Populist Denial of the Distinction Between Constitutional and Ordinary Politics

As largely explored by prominent studies in the field, the anti-elitist character of populism does not make "populism in power" impossible, wrongly assuming that populism is a primarily opposition movement, protesting against the government. On the contrary, when populists win elections and formally become the ruling elite, they still manage to identify new elites to be blamed, at home or abroad. Populists in power continue to behave like victims, even though they turned a parliamentary majority (Müller 2016: 42). While its anti-elitist character needs to adapt to the new situation (by easily finding "new elites" to fight against), its anti-pluralistic polemic remains untouched.

Populists in power, however, might use new legal tools from their ruling position. They can now mobilize law in the name of their collectivist project (this pragmatic approach characterizing populists in power was referred to as "instrumentalism" (Blokker 2019: 545). In particular, when populists in power gain enough power to amend the constitution, they do so, by mobilizing the constitution for merely instrumental aims. This is what happened in Hungary, where the conservative coalition led by Fidesz gained 52.7% of the votes in the general parliamentary elections in 2010. This electoral majority resulted in a two-third parliamentary majority due to the disproportionately majoritarian effects of the electoral system (Scheppele 2018). The two-third majority was enough to change the Constitution, which occurred 12 times in its first year in office (Scheppele 2015). A first set of controversial amendments concerned taxation, media and the reduction of the number of MPs. Another set of amendments shared a common rationale: removing most of the institutional checks that could have prevented the replacement of the Constitution. Above all, Art. 24(5) of the 1989 Constitution, establishing the four-fifth rule for constitutional amendment, was repealed, making a constitutional revision possible with a two-third majority.[3] The populist project of constitutional replacement succeeded, with the entry into force of a new Constitution on

[3] The constitutionality of the repeal of the four-fifth rule was far from uncontroversial: see Arato 2010: 40.

1 January 2012. Its text was drafted quickly, with an extremely limited (if at all) impact of opposition parties and civil society on its content (for this reason it was referred to as a "one-party constitution"; see Scheppele 2015: 112), an unprecedented compressed parliamentary debate (it took approximately one month to be completed), the promulgation by a president appointed by the same Fidesz parliamentary majority and no popular ratification via referendum. Additional amendments have also been enacted after the entry into force of the new Constitution in 2012. These amendments are characterized by the common denominator of including in the text of the Constitution day-to-day policy decisions,[4] making the Constitution a policy-oriented legal tool, rather than the legal framework where all political players may find support for their legitimate political objectives.

Within this picture, the constitution—that usually serves the role of setting a framework for politics—is treated as a purely partisan instrument to capture the polity. It turns, in one word, into a "partisan constitution" (Dani 2013). Some have referred to this process as "state occupation" (Müller 2016; Urbinati 2017) or (using Ackermanian categories) as a permanent mobilization of constitutional norms in daily politics (Blokker 2019: 545).

Populists in power aim at creating a constitution of its own and finally a democratic regime that reflects closely the characteristics of its representation of the people. The populist constitution "is an entrenched constitution, filled with policy points traditionally left to ordinary legislative processes. As such, the populist Constitution seeks to eliminate any distinction between constitutional and ordinary politics, so critical to the maintenance of a liberal democratic order" (Brodsky 2014). Paradoxically enough, populists in power end up to overconstitutionalize the political debate, in short by doing what the EU—one of their anti-elitist propaganda preferred target—is criticized for (Grimm 2015).

[4] To provide a specific example, we could mention the constitutional amendment to Article L of the (new) Hungarian Constitution. The amendment introduced the following text: "Article L) (1) Hungary shall protect the institution of marriage as the union of a man and a woman established by voluntary decision, and the family as the basis of the survival of the nation. Family ties shall be based on marriage or the relationship between parents and children". On this constitutional amendment, see Venice Commission 2013.

Constitutional Amendment, Constitutional Replacement and Constitutional Sabotage

Provided that populism in power is of course much more problematic in the perspective of liberal—democratic constitutionalism, as a populist majority may be in the position to make use of legal and constitutional means to realize its anti-pluralistic objectives. On this point, we should distinguish between different conceptual categories, and precisely between constitutional amendment, constitutional replacement and constitutional sabotage.

Constitutional amendments in a strict sense is a form of constitutional change that keeps the constitutional identity of a given constitutional system untouched (Schmitt 1928). This minimal definition of the notion of "constitutional amendment" is enough to raise very serious problems as for the topic discussed in the present chapter. In fact, populism aims at touching a polity's constitutional identity. As long as the understanding of the notion of constitutional identity stays within a liberal-democratic range, from a normative perspective it must include the essential characters of constitutionalism, namely the democratic principle, separation of powers, the rule of law and protection of fundamental rights. This is a common heritage of liberal-democratic constitutionalism. Any given constitutional system may add local specificities, but these need to be compatible with essential core values of constitutionalism—otherwise we would not deal with constitutional identities but with unconstitutional identities.[5] However, if a merely descriptive perspective is adopted, constitutional amendments may be (ab)used (and have been used) in violation of the essential pillars of liberal-democratic constitutionalism—characterizing a normatively preferred understanding of constitutional identity—with the aim of turning a "constitutional constitution" into an "unconstitutional-populist-constitution". On this point, we are persuaded by the idea that populist constitutionalism is a contradiction in terms,[6] while it is perfectly fine to conceive populist constitutions.

In the first case (populist constitutionalism), the noun "constitutionalism" refers to the normative idea of constitutionalism, that is the doctrine

[5] A growing abuse of the concept of constitutional identity is reported in the legal scholarship, for example, by Fabbrini and Sajó 2019.

[6] This point is harshly contested and I will not elaborate on further. A different, but finely motivated, perspective is offered in the chapter by Paul Blokker in this volume.

of legal limitations to political power. In the second case (populist constitutions), the noun refers to a descriptive idea of constitutions (i.e., the fact of having a constitution). Therefore, it is perfectly fine to conceive a populist constitution, but is an oxymoron to conceive populist constitutionalism (in the same sense, see Halmai 2018; for the opposite perspective, see Blokker 2019).

Nevertheless, constitutional amendments might be used to turn a liberal-democratic constitution into a populist one. In other terms, to turn a constitutional constitution into a populist one. Populist in power seek to not only perpetuate their power (and this is not a specific characteristics of populism, but is a fundamental rule of politics), but also perpetuate what they consider as the proper image of morally pure people (what has been called "the proper constitutional identity" (Müller 2016: 63), which we would rather call "a corrupted understanding of constitutional identity"). Populists in power seek to turn all constitutional institutions into their constitution. While this is easy (if not natural) for political "majoritarian" institutions, and does not need any constitutional amendment, it is not easy at all for counter-majoritarian ones. Consequently, populists in power have often mobilized the constitution against counter-majoritarian institutions, trying to disable them. The preferred targets of populist in power are the independence of the judiciary, constitutional courts and independent supervisory bodies. In short, populists in power will try to mobilize all available means (including constitutional amendments) to design a constitution that not only limit the power of political bodies in general (this would sound perfectly fine for a constitutional constitution), but also (and primarily) limits the power of non-populists.

This is what might happen in theory, and at times, in practice. However, this kind of state occupation rarely occurs through constitutional amendments. Populists in power usually stay away from constitutional amendment and tend to prefer constitutional replacement, or unilateral major constitutional changes, as in the cases of Venezuela, Ecuador and Turkey (Landau 2018: 527). Constitutional replacement may be preceded by specific amendments, removing any possible constitutional hurdles to the populist project of constitutional replacement. This was the case in Hungary. However, constitutional amendment is not always available as a constitutional tool (in the sense used by Blokker's "instrumentalism"; see Blokker 2019) serving populists' projects of constitution-making. This might depend on the specific rules governing constitutional amendments, in particular when they require very high super-majorities. In these cases, populists attack the Constitution without formal constitutional change, but through other available means leading a constitutional sabotage. This usually occurs mainly through an extremely partisan appointments of member of highest judicial and administrative authorities and through a general deconstruction of the administrative state.[7]

The populists' pragmatic preference for constitutional replacement is perfectly in line with the theoretical framework designed above. In fact, populist majorities tend to deny the distinction between ordinary and constitutional politics, and—when needed and possible—they tend to take on the role of constituent power.

Constitutional Remedies Against the Populist Attack on the Constitution

Most of constitutional and, more generally speaking, legal approaches to populism try to address the puzzling problem of possible remedies to the populist attack on liberal democracy. These approaches are, often, truly disappointing (see for this idea, and some alternative approach, Barberis 2020). They commonly conclude by affirming that the populist challenge spurs us to confront and response to the weaknesses in liberal democracy that give legitimacy to populist (un)constitutional projects (see, e.g., Landau 2018; Howse 2019). It is probably true but not enough to state that "populism is a mirror of democracy" (Panizza 2005) that currently reflects a rotten image of the health of our liberal-democratic institutions (Doyle et al. 2019).

It sounds reassuring to just claim for a truly liberal-democratic renaissance. Even though we might agree on the necessity of this renaissance, we think that as public law scholars who still believe in the values of liberal-democratic constitutionalism we are probably called to do more and to try to assess constitutional machineries that work better than others in face of the current populist challenge to liberal-democratic constitutionalism. Therefore, we think it is possible to identify four possible constitutional remedies to the use of constitutional amendment (and, more generally speaking, to constitutional change) by populists aiming at transforming a liberal-democratic constitution into a populist (un)conti-

[7] Poland is often reported as the brightest case study in this field (for a detailed overview of these techniques, see Sadurski 2019), but also the case of President Trump is sometimes included within this category see Landau 2018: 526.

tutional constitution: (a) eternity clauses; (b) speed bumps; (c) bicameralism; and (d) supranational constraints.

Eternity clauses and doctrines of unconstitutional constitutional amendments are the first and most obvious mechanisms to protect constitutional constitutions against unconstitutional amendments. These doctrines are flourishing and migrating from one constitutional system to another (Roznai 2017). However, eternity clauses risks being constitutional remedies for good times only. In fact, eternity clauses require a powerful constitutional court to be considered as an effective remedy against unconstitutional constitutional amendments. However, populists in power immediately learned the lesson that constitutional courts are the first institutions to be captured. Once constitutional courts are captured, it is rather unlikely that they might use the unconstitutional constitutional amendment doctrine to react to a populist transformation of the constitution.

More promising are procedural mechanisms aiming at slowing down processes of constitutional change (for a comprehensive overview of these procedural mechanisms see Albert 2019). Constitutional amendment mechanisms might prove successful in contrasting populist constitutional amendments when these mechanisms require a long time to pass to complete the constitutional amendment procedure, with long intervals between multiple rounds of voting. In fact, populists are "impatient with procedures" (Crick 2005: 626; Müller 2016: 60–61). And populists are impatient, as all of those who seek to realize a constitutional revolution, they need to fight against time (Ackerman 2019), as it is likely that after a certain period of time their legitimation will be eroded. Therefore, speed bumps may work, as time works against populists. The counterproof is that when populist succeed in staying in power for longer periods of time, they tend to introduce constitutional changes "increasingly and overtly opposed to liberal democracy" (Landau 2018: 523).

Similarly, bicameralism may efficiently play the role of a retarder of populist captures of the constitution, in particular, if the bicameral system is designed so to realize a significant differentiation of the composition in the two houses. In this sense, Upper Houses usually favour a balanced separation of powers through restraints of governmental powers and the perfection of the deliberative process (Russell 2001; Uhr 2008). Not by chance, Hungary is a unicameral system and the Fidesz supermajority derived from an election where Fidesz gained 53% of votes. The populist assault on the Hungarian Constitution could have encountered much more robust hurdles in a bicameral system, provided that both are required

Houses take part to the constitutional amendment process and that the legitimation and composition of the two Houses differs.

Finally, the fourth and final legal arrangement that might be opposed against a populist assault on the constitution by means of constitutional amendments are supranational constraints. Similarly, supranational constraints may work at least as retarder of populist (un)constitutional occupation (Landau 2018: 542). The Polish and Hungarian examples are often quoted as proofs of a limited efficiency of supranational constraints. Exploring this dimension in detail would lead us too far (Müller 2015). However, and as weak as counterfactual arguments always are in social sciences, we would exclude that the state of constitutionalism in Hungary and Poland would be in better shape if these countries would not be subject to the current set of (certainly) imperfect supranational constraints.

The Populist Impulses Accompanying the Never-Ending Italian Experience of Constitutional Reform

Populists in power exist and make an instrumental use of constitutional change. They might use constitutional amendments to reinforce their position and to try to turn a pluralistic constitution into their partisan constitution. They tend to deny any distinction between constituent power and day-to-day politics. In this chapter, we will explore whether this scenario applies to the stormy seasons of Constitution reforms taking place in Italy since 30 years.

The 1948 Constitution of Italy is a rigid constitution, requiring a single degree of rigidity: no distinction is drawn between partial and total revisions of the constitution.[8] To begin with, the mere collocation of the articles regulating the amendment process in the Italian Constitution may be extremely telling for the purpose of the present chapter. In fact, Art. 138, providing for the constitutional amendment rules, is included in a section (technically: a title) named: "constitutional guarantees". As mentioned above, populists are generally impatient with procedures, and particularly with procedures expressing constitutional guarantees (see Pinelli 2019: 33). Specifically, the constitutional amendment rules provide for a particularly complex procedure. The amendment process requires a dou-

[8] Some authors argued that the Italian constitution only allows for limited amendments on specific points, and precludes overarching constitutional reforms: see, for example, Bettinelli 1995 and Pace 2013.

ble round of voting in the bicameral system, with reinforced majorities and a possible referendum (for further details, see Fusaro 2011). In particular, Art. 138 of the Constitution requires both houses of the Parliament to vote on the same constitutional bill twice. In the first round of voting, the constitutional bill is open to amendments, and a simple majority is required in both houses. When both houses voted in favour of the identical text for a first time, a second round of voting is required. At this point, no amendments are admissible; the approved text needs to be confirmed as it stands or rejected as a whole. The second round of voting cannot take place earlier than three months after the first round of voting in the same house.

At this point of the procedure, there are three alternative paths: (a) if one house approves the bill with a simple majority, but does not reach the threshold of an absolute majority (i.e. half of the members of the house plus one, regardless of the number of MPs taking part in the vote), the constitutional bill is rejected; (b) if both houses approve the act by a two-third majority, the constitutional amendment is immediately passed to the head of state, who is called to sign it and transmit it for publication in the official journal and entry into force; and (c) if, in both houses, an absolute majority is reached, but in one or both houses no two-third majority is met, the bill is published for mere informative purposes. In this case, a popular referendum may be called, if asked by the subjects entitled to do so by the Constitution. These subjects are a parliamentary minority (at least one-fifth of the members of one House), a territorial minority (at least 5 out of the 20 regional legislative assemblies), or an electoral minority (at least 500,000 voters). Once the referendum is called, no structural quorum is required and the constitutional bill is deemed passed if a majority of those who vote approve it.

Even though the number of constitutional amendments successfully passed in the Italian constitutional experience is rather limited (if compared with similar constitutional experiences in a comparable span of time),[9] the debate over constitutional reforms has been one of the central issues in the last 30 years, both in the institutional debate and in the academic circles. Attention has been devoted to many specific points, but

[9] The procedure regulated by Art. 138 is provided both for acts modifying the text of the Constitution and for acts introducing new constitutional laws, not to be incorporated into the text of the Constitution, but entitled with the same legal force of the Constitution. If one only considers acts amending the text of the Constitution, the count is limited to 14 constitutional amendments (in a strict sense). For an overview of passed constitutional amendments, see Luther 2017: 12.

some of them are particularly relevant for the purposes of the present chapter.

First, a controversial issue concerns the implications that may be drawn by the regulation of the optional referendum within the constitutional amendment process. In some author's view, only homogenous and specific constitutional amendments should be admitted, in order to put the voter in the referendum in front of a homogenous and univocal question and to avoid the unease situation of a voter who is in favour of one part of the constitutional amendment and against another part of it. This point has taken centre stage in the last decade of (failed) attempts of overarching constitutional reforms. Nonetheless, this debate dates back to the more remote origins of the scholarly and institutional debate over constitutional reforms in Italy (Bartole 2004: 370). However, the text of the Constitution does not give univocal reasons in support of this idea, and the constitutional praxis has pushed in another direction, with multiple examples of comprehensive and sometimes inhomogeneous constitutional reforms submitted to the popular approval via referendum.

A second point of debate is once again linked to the referendum, and relates to its deepest nature in the constitutional architecture. In fact, even though the constitutional regulation only requires the impulse of a parliamentary, electoral or territorial minority to activate the referendum, recent developments led to a political transformation of the original understanding of this option. In fact, it already happened in three occasions that a constitutional referendum was called not only by those MPs and parties who fought against the parliamentary approval of the constitutional revision bill, but also by MPs and parties who voted in favour of it and campaigned in support of the constitutional bill. A constitutional tool seemingly designed in favour of minorities, was finally turned into a constitutional arrangement (also) in the hands of the majority. In this way, political actors tried to turn the oppositional nature of the referendum into a sort of plebiscite. The constitutionality of this transformation has been largely debated and contested, even though (here as before) no textual elements supported the unconstitutionality of this understanding (Bin 2001). However, in two out of the three cases where political majorities contributed to call the referendum, the popular vote finally rejected the constitutional reform bill, concretely reaffirming the main oppositional nature of the constitutional referendum.

A third point of debate relates the impact of the electoral legislation on the constitutional amendment process and on related guarantees of minorities. This aspect was particularly debated when the electoral legislation inaugurated an unruly transition towards a majoritarian electoral system (1993–2017). Within that picture, it was claimed that the constitutional amendment process implied proportional representation as an implicit condition and that the majoritarian turn in electoral legislation threatened the value of constitutional rigidity. In fact, the guaranteeing force of supermajorities changes its meaning under a majoritarian electoral legislation. Once again, this approach fell short of considering positive constitutional law: no constitutional provision requires proportional representation and, on the contrary, the Constituent Assembly explicitly rejected all proposals for the inclusion of provisions concerning the electoral system in the text of the Constitution. However, the incomplete transition from proportional representation to a majoritarian electoral system was recently abandoned, after the popular rejection of the latest attempt of an overarching constitutional reform in 2016 and the subsequent decision by the Constitutional Court to strike down the electoral legislation (politically, if not institutionally) linked to the rejected constitutional reform.[10]

Most successful constitutional revisions were passed with a very large majority. Until 1970 a large majority was the only option available, as the parliamentary act implementing the referendum was only approved in 1970. Previously, the unavailability of any implementing legislation of the referendum led to a prevailing (if not unanimous) interpretation of Art. 138 It. Const., in the sense it always required a two-third majority for a constitutional amendment to be passed. Even after the adoption of the referendum act, most constitutional revisions have been adopted by large majorities and only in three cases a constitutional referendum was called on a project of constitutional amendment. This happened in 2001, in 2006 and in 2016: only in 2001 a majority of voters approved the constitutional bill.

Since more than 30 years, it is widely acknowledged that the institutional architecture of Italy needs some robust modernization (Fusaro 2011, 2015). To this aim, many legislative terms were inaugurated under the ambiguous "self-definition" of "constituent legislative terms". This terminology referred not only to the ambitious project of modernizing the institutional architecture through overarching constitutional reforms, but also to the idea that constitutional reforms represented a central point in the government programme. This politicization of the constitutional

[10] Constitutional Court of Italy, Judgment 35/2017 (for further details, see Faraguna 2017).

amendment power is at odds with the genesis of the Italian Constitution. In fact, "according to standard studies in Italian constitutional history, and in spite of the dramatic national and international developments during those months, the Constituent Assembly and the Government of the day succeeded in preserving the distinction between, respectively, constitutional politics and day-to-day politics" (Delledonne and Martinico 2017: 59, drawing from Cheli 2008).

This process of political immersion of the discourse on constitutional reforms led to a growing involvement of the executive in the constitutional amendment process. Traditionally, constitutional bills were introduced by single members of the Parliament, keeping the Executive at large.[11] A significant shift in this praxis was inaugurated with the project of overarching constitutional reform introduced by the centre-right government led by President Silvio Berlusconi (Pinelli 2006). This project was introduced by initiative of the executive. It was finally approved by the Parliament in 2005, but rejected by a popular referendum in 2006. A similar path was followed by the project of constitutional reform introduced by the centre-left government led by President Matteo Renzi in more recent times. The latter was similarly introduced by initiative of the executive, approved by the Parliament in 2016 and eventually rejected through a popular referendum on 4 December 2016.

However, the inclusion of overarching constitutional amendments in the core of governmental programmes was even more evident in the experience of the government led by Enrico Letta (2013–2014). This is a highly significant example for the sake of our exploration of the relations between constitutional amendments and populism. In fact, the Letta government is largely conceived as one of the recent governmental experiences that are more distant to populism in Italy. On the contrary, his government was supported by a large coalition of traditionally political opponents and appointed many members of the so-called technocratic elite

[11] However, exemptions are not rare, as reported by Piccirilli, who points out that the main procedural novelty in the governmental approach to constitutional reform, is their inclusion within the National Reform Programme (PNR), a key document to be transmitted yearly to European Institutions. These documents detail the specific policies that EU Member States will implement to boost jobs and growth and prevent/correct imbalances, and their concrete plans to comply with the EU's country-specific recommendations and general fiscal rules. While the government led by Enrico Letta mentioned institutional reforms in the PNR, Renzi's government not only included these reforms in the PNR, but put them in the very first place (for further details, see Piccirilli 2016: 157).

among it ministers.[12] Nonetheless, as far as constitutional change is concerned, the government led by Enrico Letta approached constitutional amendment in a strikingly similar manner to the one usually adopted by populists in power. The government presided by Enrico Letta included constitutional reforms as the primary goal of its governmental action, making their realization as a *condicio sine qua non* to remain in office. To this end, the executive, following the praxis recently inaugurated by the Berlusconi government of playing a decisive role in the activation of the constitutional amendment process, introduced a new bill of constitutional law for an ad hoc procedure in derogation from Art. 138 and created a commission composed of constitutional lawyers that delivered a survey of the most relevant reform ideas.[13]

Two derogations were highly significant to our aims. First, the ad hoc procedure introduced a compulsory popular referendum at the end of the constitutional amendment procedure. Second, the agenda of the constitutional amendment process was slightly rescheduled, with the aim of reducing the total time needed to amend the constitution.[14] The project was eventually abandoned after the abrupt change of political conditions within the centre-left political spectrum that led to the resignation of President Enrico Letta and the subsequent appointment of Matteo Renzi as President of the Council of Ministers. This abandoned project of constitutional amendment in derogation of the constitutional procedure suggests that distinctive dimensions of populist instrumentalism "equally emerge in the discourse and actions of political actors, who are not normally or predominantly defined as populist" (Blokker, Forthcoming). This not only indicates a "potential *diffusion* of a populist-constitutional mindset into the political mainstream" (ibidem), but also suggests the risk of normalization of populist legal practices. This risk is rather limited as long

[12] The whole preparatory process was cumbersome and inspired to examples of "elite deliberation" rather than of civic participation, with an essential role played by ad hoc commissions of experts, before and after the formation of the Letta government. For further details of this "elitarian deliberative process", see Blokker 2017.

[13] Disegno di legge costituzionale 15 October 2012 no. 3520 "Disposizioni di revisione della Costituzione e altre disposizioni costituzionali in materia di autonomia regionale", available at http://www.senato.it/service/PDF/PDFServer/BGT/00680798.pdf (last visited 30 September 2019).

[14] Specifically, the constitutional amendment bill scheduled a maximum total time of 18 months for the whole process of constitutional amendment to be completed. To this aim, the constitutional bill aimed at introducing a shortened term of only one month between the two rounds of voting in each House.

as populist instruments are applied to non-populist objectives.[15] However, the risk would be multiplied in the moment the normalized populist mechanisms would finally be in the hands of sincere populist, aiming at subverting the pluralistic character of the post–World War II constitutionalism. However, as fare as the Italian constitutional experience is concerned, the combination of the constitutional architecture and the unruliness of the political system finally resulted in a striking stable and robust reaction of the constitutional system before any kind of (methodologically) populistic attack on the Constitution. In fact, all projects of overarching constitutional reform eventually failed,[16] some because of the sudden change of political conditions, some because of the negative outcome of the popular referendum, as designed by Art. 138 It. Const.

It goes without saying that this constitutional stability is mainly nominal and mirrors the difficulties in introducing any kind of constitutional reforms (with populist or non-populist methodologies, aiming at populist or non-populist aims). Constitutional conservatism both applies to populist impulses and those reforms that are—from the perspective of the author of this chapter—much needed to adapt, on the one side, the Italian Constitution to the unprecedented transformations occurred in Europe in the last 60 years, and to fix some of the original sins of the constitutional architecture as designed by the Constituent Assembly.

[15] The substantial assessment in terms of constitutional law of the failed constitutional reform projects rejected by popular referendums in 2006 and in 2016 is highly contested. While in the first case, legal scholarship generally opposed the project, in the second case the legal debate was subject to a strong polarization (for further details, see Delledonne and Martinico 2017). Some authors (Blokker 2017) tend to identify common threads in the two projects, with an emphasis put on governability and efficiency of the decision-making process. However, the two reform projects consisted of significantly different institutional arrangements: the 2005–2006 constitutional reform process aimed at the introduction of a sort of "absolute premiership", while the main focus of the 2016 constitutional reform project was put on the modification of the bicameral system.

[16] With the exception of the early 2000s constitutional reform of the state-region relations. However, even though the constitutional amendment touched many provisions of the Constitution, its scope is usually considered more specific and limited compared to the overarching constitutional reforms we are referring to.

References

Ackerman, B. (2019). *Revolutionary Constitutions: Charismatic Leadership and the Rule of Law*. Cambridge, MA: Belknap Press: An Imprint of Harvard University Press.

Akkerman, A., Mudde, C., & Zaslove, A. (2013). How Populist Are the People? Measuring Populist Attitudes in Voters. *Comparative Political Studies, 47*(9), 1324–1353.

Albert, R. (2019). *Constitutional Amendments: Making, Breaking, and Changing Constitutions*. Cambridge: Cambridge University Press.

Albertazzi, D., & McDonnel, D. (2008). Introduction: The Sceptre and the Spectre. In D. Albertazzi & D. McDonnel (Eds.), *Twenty-First Century Populism – The Spectre of Western European Democracy* (pp. 1–11). London: Palgrave Macmillan.

Arato, A. (2010). Post-Sovereign Constitution-Making in Hungary: After Success, Partial Failure, and Now What? *South Afr J Hum Rights, 26*, 19–44.

Arato, A. (2016). *Post Sovereign Constitution Making: Learning and Legitimacy*. Oxford: Oxford University Press.

Barberis, M. (2020). *Populismo digitale. Come internet sta uccidendo la democrazia*. Milano: Chiarelettere.

Bartole, S. (2004). *Interpretazioni e trasformazioni della Costituzione repubblicana*. Bologna: Il Mulino.

Bettinelli, E. (1995). Referendum e riforma 'organica' della Costituzione. In E. Ripepe & R. Romboli (Eds.), *Cambiare costituzione o modificare la Costituzione* (pp. 39–52). Torino: Giappichelli.

Bin, R. (2001). Riforme costituzionali "a colpi di maggioranza": perché no? *Quaderni costituzionali, 21*(2), 341–343.

Bin, R. (2007). Che cos'è la Costituzione? *Quaderni costituzionali, 27*(1), 11–52.

Blokker, P. (2017). The Grande Riforma of the Italian Constitution: Majoritarian Versus Participatory Democracy? *Contemporary Italian Politics, 9*(2), 124–141.

Blokker, P. (2019). Populism as a Constitutional Project. *International Journal of Constitutional Law, 17*(2), 536–553.

Blokker, P. (Forthcoming). Populism and Constitutional Change. In X. Contiades & A. Fotiadou (Eds.), *The Routledge Handbook on Constitutional Change*. Abingdon: Routledge.

Brodsky, C. (2014). *Some of the People: Populist Constitution-Making in Hungary*. Conference Paper "Interpretations of Democracy," Columbia University. Quoted in Urbinati 2017.

Cheli, E. (2008). *Il problema storico della Costituente*. Napoli: ES.

Crick, B. (2005). Populism, Politics and Democracy. *Democratization, 12*(5), 625–632.

Dani, M. (2013). The 'Partisan Constitution' and the Corrosion of European Constitutional Culture. *LSE Eur Quest Discuss Pap Ser.* Available at http://www.lse.ac.uk/europeanInstitute/LEQS%20Discussion%20Paper%20Series/LEQSPaper68.pdf

Delledonne, G., & Martinico, G. (2017). Yes or No? Mapping the Italian Academic Debate on the Constitutional Reform. *Italian Law Journal, 2*(Special Issue), 49–60.

Doyle, O., Longo, E., & Pin, A. (2019). Populism: A Health Check for Constitutional Democracy? *German Law Journal, 20*(3), 401–407.

Fabbrini, F., & Sajó, A. (2019). The Dangers of Constitutional Identity. *European Law Journal, 25*(4), 457–473.

Faraguna, P. (2017). 'Do You Ever Have One of Those Days When Everything Seems Unconstitutional?': The Italian Constitutional Court Strikes Down the Electoral Law Once Again: Italian Constitutional Court Judgment of 9 February 2017 No. 35. *European Constitutional Law Review, 13*(4), 778–792.

Fusaro, C. (2011). Italy. In D. Oliver & C. Fusaro (Eds.), *How Constitutions Change: A Comparative Study* (pp. 211–234). Oxford: Hart Publishing.

Fusaro, C. (2015). Per una storia delle riforme istituzionali (1948–2015). *Rivista Trimestrale di Diritto Pubblico, 65*(2), 431–556.

Galston, W. A. (2018). *Anti-Pluralism: The Populist Threat to Liberal Democracy.* New Haven: Yale University Press.

Grimm, D. (2015). The Democratic Costs of Constitutionalisation: The European Case. *European Law Journal, 21*(4), 460–473.

Halmai, G. (2018). Is There Such Thing as 'Populist Constitutionalism'? The Case of Hungary. *Fudan Journal of the Humanities and Social Sciences, 11*(3), 323–339.

Howse, R. (2019). Epilogue: In Defense of Disruptive Democracy—A Critique of Anti-Populism. *International Journal of Constitutional Law, 17*(2), 641–660.

Laclau, E. (2007). *On Populist Reason.* London/New York: Verso.

Landau, D. (2018). Populist Constitutions. *University of Chicago Law Review, 85*(2), 521–544.

Lefort, C. (1988). *Democracy and Political Theory.* Cambridge: Polity Press.

Luther, J. (2017). Learning Democracy from the History of Constitutional Reforms. *Italian Law Journal, 2*(Special Issue), 9–29.

Mudde, C. (2004). The Populist Zeitgeist. *Government and Opposition, 39*(4), 541–563.

Mudde, C., & Rovira Kaltwasser, C. (2017). *Populism: A Very Short Introduction.* New York: Oxford University Press.

Müller, J.-W. (2015). Should the EU Protect Democracy and the Rule of Law Inside Member States? *European Law Journal, 21*(2), 141–160.

Müller, J.-W. (2016). *What Is Populism?* Philadelphia: University of Pennsylvania Press.

Oklopcic, Z. (2019a). Imagined Ideologies: Populist Figures, Liberalist Projections, and the Horizons of Constitutionalism. *German Law Journal, 20*(2), 201–224.

Oklopcic, Z. (2019b). Beyond Populism: Liberalist Projections and Quotidian Constitutions. In Panel on *Liberalism, Authoritarianism and the Tasks of Constitutional Theory: Making Sovereignty Popular Again?*, Pontifica Universidad Catolica de Chile, Santiago.

Pace, A. (2013). Sulle revisioni costituzionali. *Diritto Pubblico, 18*(2), 465–480.

Panizza, F. (Ed.). (2005). *Populism and the Mirror of Democracy*. London: Verso.

Piccirilli, G. (2016). Strumenti tecnici al servizio dell'attuazione del programma di governo. L'esperienza del Governo Renzi. In G. Grasso (Ed.), *Il governo tra tecnica e politica. Atti del Seminario annuale (Como, 20 novembre 2015)* (pp. 153–166). Napoli: ES.

Pinelli, C. (2006). The 1948 Italian Constitution and the 2006 Referendum: Food for Thought. *European Constitutional Law Review, 2*(3), 329–341.

Pinelli, C. (2019). Populismo, diritto e società. Uno sguardo costituzionale. *Questione Giustizia, 2*(1), 29–35.

Rovira Kaltwasser, C. (2012). The Ambivalence of Populism: Threat and Corrective for Democracy. *Democratization, 19*(2), 184–208.

Roznai, Y. (2017). *Unconstitutional Constitutional Amendments: The Limits of Amendment Powers*. Oxford/New York: Oxford University Press.

Russell, M. (2001). What Are Second Chambers for? *Parliamentary Affairs, 54*(3), 442–458.

Sadurski, W. (2019). *Poland's Constitutional Breakdown*. Oxford: Oxford University Press.

Scheppele, K. L. (2015). Understanding Hungary's Constitutional Revolution. In A. von Bogdandy & P. Sonnevend (Eds.), *Constitutional Crisis in the European Constitutional Area: Theory, Law and Politics in Hungary and Romania* (pp. 111–124). Munich: Hart/Beck.

Scheppele, K. L. (2018). Autocratic Legalism. *University of Chicago Law Review, 85*(2), 545–583.

Schmitt, C. (1928). *Verfassungslehre*. Berlin: Duncker & Humblot GmbH.

Uhr, J. (2008). Bicameralism. In S. A. Binder, R. A. W. Rhodes, & B. A. Rockman (Eds.), *The Oxford Handbook of Political Institutions* (pp. 473–494). Oxford/ New York: Oxford University Press.

Urbinati, N. (2017). Populism and the Principle of Majority. In C. R. Kaltwasser, P. Taggart, P. O. Espejo, & P. Ostiguy (Eds.), *The Oxford Handbook of Populism*. Oxford/New York: Oxford University Press.

Venice Commission [European Commission for Democracy through Law]. (2013). Opinion on the Fourth Amendment to the Fundamental Law of Hungary, Opinion 720/2013. CDL-AD(2013)012, Adopted by the Venice Commission at its 95th Plenary Session (Venice, 14–15 June 2013). Available at https://www.venice.coe.int/webforms/documents/default.aspx?pdffile=CDL-AD(2013)012-e

CHAPTER 6

Populism and Law-Making Process

Fabio Pacini

Introduction

A few years post the beginning of the current Italian constitutional experience, a major study on the legislative procedure commenced in the following manner: "The juridical phenomenon of the legislative procedure, the fact of law which subjects the very moment of its formation to the constraint of its own rules, seems almost utopia [...]. And yet the right of our new order, which, based on a rigid constitution [...] intends to implement the postulates of the rule of law in every moment of the state action, has such a confidence in its possibilities and in its means that this is precisely this – almost magical – goal that it aspires to achieve" (Galeotti 1957: 1).[1]

This idea obviously aligns with the line of thought for which the "*volonté du peuple*", that is the "people's will", is justified not only because it is the "will" of the majority, but also because it fits into forms that guarantee the most reasonable and fair expression of this "will" (Mirkine-Guetzévich 1936: 9).

[1] All translations are made by the author, unless otherwise noted.

F. Pacini (✉)
Scuola Sant'Anna, Pisa, Italy
e-mail: fabio.pacini@sssup.it

G. Delledonne et al. (eds.), *Italian Populism and Constitutional Law*, Challenges to Democracy in the 21st Century,
https://doi.org/10.1007/978-3-030-37401-3_6

Although it is indisputable that the (democratic) legislative procedure is, as a whole, governed by the majority rule, it is evident that it becomes preferable to other modes of normative production only to the extent that it maintains and protects its main characteristics thereby ensuring the effective possibility of participation for all parliamentarians and guaranteeing a high rate of transparency in the negotiations (Lupo 2019: 265).

However, in the context of an analysis of the Italian experience, it has been recently pointed out that, "as Walter Bagehot [...] taught long ago, the centrality of parliament has, with the exception of the finance law, little to do with lawmaking. The power of parliament manifests itself in the formation (and in the transformation, termination and reconstruction) of the government; in the provision of space for the opposition; in negotiations aimed at reconciling the interests and preferences of parliamentarians and their parties representing the majority and the opposition(s)" (Pasquino 2019: 198).

Populism is, by definition, against everything that appears to make public decisions less "easy", thus making the law-making process as one of its natural targets.[2] In fact, the essence of the legislative procedure is not to make the decision instant but subject it to a series of intermediate steps. Hence, a populist movement clashes with it once it enters the parliament. However, it is necessary to distinguish between the two scenarios, and Italy has given interesting examples of both: when the populist movement is in opposition and when it is in majority. In the first case, the opposition (populist) movement tends to exacerbate the use of obstructionism and generally transforms the moment of decision into that of a performance, for instance the protests by the Five Star Movement in the XVII parliamentary term (2013–2018). That is nothing particularly new by itself (Pertici 2018): prior to that, in 1993 the Northern League showed a noose in the Chamber of Deputies (Tambini 2001), and there had already been the anti-political provocations of the Radical Party in the 1970s and 1980s. This goes back to the notorious "pioneering role" of the *qualunquismo* of Guglielmo Giannini in the late 1940s (Tarchi 2015). However, present times (from 2018) are even more interesting from an Italian perspective; hence, here we will focus on the legislative activity under the first Conte government, "something new in Western Europe:

[2] We use the expression "law-making process" in order to encompass a broader meaning as compared to "legislative procedure" (see Pizzorusso 1988; Zander 2015), including in particular, as far as it is relevant here, the initiative phase which takes place within the government.

the first government formed 'exclusively' by populist parties" (Bressanelli and Natali 2019: 211).

The Relevance of Legislative Procedure Facing the Populist Challenge

It would be impossible to trace here the doctrinal evolution of the theory of administrative procedure in Italy, also seen as "a privileged moment in juridical phenomenology" (Ruggeri 1977: 268; Giannini 1970: 813 and ff.; Calamandrei 1954: 25): it will suffice to mention that this conceptual framework in the twentieth century had a considerable and expansive force in administrative law (Sandulli 1940), reaching all the other branches of law including the highest level of decision-making, that is the *political* one (Galeotti 1957; Predieri 1974 and 1975; Fazzalari 1986; *contra* Forti 1931).

It is known that the debate on procedural guarantees went through a good part of the twentieth century. It passed from a rather skeptical attitude towards this model (Cammeo 1914) moving on to the progressive (but still contrasted) recognition of its centrality *entre-deux-guerres* (Sandulli 1940) and then to the unanimous recognition of its importance (Benvenuti 1952: 129 and ff.). Related to this is its instrumentality with respect to the "step forward" of the constitutional state in its most modern version, which is aimed at the effective and democratic involvement of all citizens in the management of public affairs (Giannini 1970: 822; see Chiti 2008), with a *vis expansiva* having the likelihood to invest even *political* and *legislative* decisions with very few exceptions, thus making it a task of unprecedented difficulty in societies that are extremely complex in terms of interests (Ruggeri 1977: 275).[3]

[3]This is obviously something that did not concern Italy alone. For example, what Jerry L. Mashaw calls "the idealist's vision": in this view, administrative processes are a "part of the general fabric of American public and constitutional law. The law of administrative procedure contributes, as does all such law, to the construction of an operationally effective and symbolically appropriate normative regime. To put the matter slightly differently, administrative procedural requirements embedded in law shape administrative decision-making in accordance with our fundamental (but perhaps malleable) images of the legitimacy of state action. That is administrative procedure's purpose and its explanation" (Mashaw 1990: 268; id. 1985).

Furthermore, it is well known that Niklas Luhmann from a sociological point of view stressed on "legitimization through process" (Luhmann 1983): "the link with democracy is

Within the context of a tough ***reductio ad unum*** of the formal and substantial aspects of a regime that can be defined as "democratic", Carlo Lavagna essentially identified "the problem of democracy [...] right here: in the choice of the most suitable means to legally regulate [...] the supreme activities of the State, preparing not their general content but rather the ways to exercise them" to facilitate or even impose the compromise, given the "impossibility of achieving satisfactory and effective substantial norms of political and legislative activities" (Lavagna 1956: 392 and ff.) or to reduce democracy to the mere majority rule (Bobbio 1983: 12 and ff.; Pizzorusso 1993).

This kind of transition is clearly evident on a smaller scale in parliamentary law, which passed from being the expression of a single social class to be the arena of a pluralism that powerfully entered the constitutional mechanisms (Mirkine-Guetzévich 1936; Manetti 1990).[4] The compromise is notoriously crucial in Weber's analysis of politics (Weber 1922), and the work of Kelsen himself is marked by his "enthusiastic defense of compromise", a conception forged "in the specific discursive context of the German interwar period, during which this notion acquired a strongly depreciative connotation, mainly by authors such as Carl Schmitt and Rudolf Smend", at a time when, not by chance, "the strongest critics of compromises or coalitions sometimes emerged from the same source that denounced the deleterious effects of parliamentarism and political parties" (Baume 2017: 74).

evident, because by acting in a democratic way, the authorities can improve their legitimization. According to [Luhmann's] opinion, proceedings and participation are also devices that build up confidence and trust in the decisions reached not only for achieving consensus, but also for absorbing the disagreement of the community" (Fracchia 2005: 591).

[4] The issues related to the "explosion" of a system of administrative independent authorities (Predieri 1997; Merusi 2000; Grasso 2006) remained outside this contribution. It goes without saying that they have been the subject of critical attention in the Italian debate (also, for further references, see Pantalone 2018; Titomanlio 2017) revolving around the legitimacy of their action and the impact of their acts on the system of sources of law (Pantalone, 2018; Giannelli 2018).

Likewise, the matters relating to the *due process of law* will not be addressed here (see Della Cananea 2016; Morrone 2012: 847 and ff.), as well as—given the focus on the national level—those relating to the search of legality on a global scale (Klabbers and Palombella 2019; Palombella 2012: 67 and ff.).

Essentially, each law, here seen as a ***parliamentary law***, is approved following a legislative procedure,[5] which creates balance between social pluralism and the unity of the legal system. Today, the formula of law as an expression of the general will is no longer useful in terms of content, but remains fundamental on a procedural level, if there is a functioning legislative procedure that allows the active participation of the generality of *political* subjects (Lupo 2019: 253).

Italy's political institutions during the period ranging from 1948 to the beginning of 1990s "have often been considered rather inefficient: this is because they were characterised by heterogeneous coalitions racked by internal strife, unstable cabinets, a cumbersome legislative process and a mass of legislation, consisting mainly of small-scale measures incapable of generating any incisive process of reform even when the country was up against an alarming level of growth in public debt, as was the case in the 1980s", featuring "a multiplicity of party-political and institutional veto players, variously distributed across both the centre and the outer fringes of the political arena, both in government and in parliament" (Vassallo 2007: 692).

Yet, one of the consequences of such a consensual system was the so-called centrality of parliament, "the place where governing parties conducted continuous negotiations, and where, in the 1970s in particular, attempts were made to include the PCI in the decision-making process" (Vassallo 2007: 694).

Since the 1980s, this style of government progressively lost legitimacy, with profound changes being made after the end of the Cold War and a huge bribery scandal. The party system was completely changed along with the electoral system (shifting to a majority system; see D'Andrea 2013). Everything began revolving around the polarising presence of Silvio Berlusconi (Pasquino 1997).[6]

[5] Given their importance in the recent Italian experience, the delegated legislation and the decree-law (***decreto-legge***) will also be dealt with here.

[6] By referring to one of the most influential analysis of Italian politics at the end of the 1980s (i.e. LaPalombara 1987), Gianfranco Pasquino recently underlined that "[LaPalombara] warned that the proposed reforms would destabilise the political system and negatively affect Italian politics. Though its performance was often unsatisfactory, thanks to its ability to engage in bargaining, logrolling, and muddling through, the Italian political class had achieved significant results", so that "changing the rules of the game might destabilise Italian politics in many unexpected and unpredictable ways" (Pasquino 2019: 199).

The establishment of a bipolar political system "saw the demise of a number of practices adopted during the First Republic, [...]. Each coalition has also been headed by a leader who is that coalition's chosen candidate for the premiership. Thus, elections have become decisive, and as a consequence certain features that are characteristic of majoritarian democracies have emerged both within parliament and in the workings of the cabinet. [...] Briefly speaking, the Prime Minister's position within the cabinet has been strengthened, an adversarial dynamic has emerged within parliament, and government has acquired greater agenda-setting powers" (Vassallo 2007: 694).

This generated "a profound transformation in Italy's main socio-political structures, as well as in public communication and debates", so that "more than twenty years after that historical phase, it is safe to say that Italian society and politics have taken a markedly populist direction, to the point where Italy today is perhaps the only country in the world where several populist forces compete with each other and where a widespread political communication characterized by populist tones and styles prevails" (Anselmi 2018: 66).

Laws tend to get too close to the immediate "popular" will, making an almost pure and "naked" expression of the desire and not so much of the *representatives* but rather those of the *represented*. Not restricted to their needs and their interests, but also over and above their immediate reactions and moods, for how they are caught with ever greater precision and timing by polls and social media, as they are interpreted and exploited by populist leaders (Lupo 2019: 253). Therefore, in this perspective, the priorities of the legislative agenda will be given on the basis of the news of the day, with a "spectacularized" use of legislative activity. Thus, the parliament is no longer able to represent a suitable point of equilibrium between the society and the state, between plurality and unity, and between majority and opposition. This means that the determination of the equilibrium point in question is entrusted to others, firstly to the judges. If the legislator becomes too populist, we are approaching plebiscitarism. Consequently, constitutionalism, by reaction, is led to depend significantly on the courts, and tends to see the legislator as an "enemy" of guaranteeing rights and constitutional principles (Lupo 2019: 254).

Tendencies of the Law-Making Process During the First Conte Government

The first Conte government gained the confidence vote 75 days after the commencement of the parliamentary term. The parliamentary committees were constituted 90 days after the beginning of the term itself. It must be considered that after the 2008 elections, post a clear electoral outcome (in favour of the lists close to Silvio Berlusconi), the government had gained the confidence vote just after 16 days with the committees starting their work just after 23 days.

From the perspective of different phases of the law-making process, the distinctive trait of the first Conte government is that of an overall continuity with respect to the pathologies that emerged in the immediately preceding parliamentary terms, registering some further degeneration (the so-called pursuit of the worst precedent; see Ibrido 2015).[7]

The present parliamentary term has so far been conflicting on the mass media as well as on social media. However, it has proven to be less contentious in Parliament during the first Conte government, when the two majority (populist) political forces had generally succeeded in finding a way of life based on exchanges and mediations and had carved out important spaces for their own initiatives "with a clear predominance of the Five stars Movement, suffering partner in terms of visibility" (Pasquino 2019: 197) which had found in Parliament a partial compensation, owing to its numerical strength (Di Porto and Piana 2019b).

The XVIII parliamentary term has so far created a number of laws almost identical to the previous one, in the same period: 70 in the first year of the last term (2013–2014) and 69 in this one, up to the time of the resignation of the first Conte government in August 2019.

Since the beginning of the XVIII parliamentary term (March 23, 2018), 30 decree-laws have been issued (4 deliberated by the Gentiloni government and 26 by the first Conte government) with 23 of these being turned into law.

In the first year of the XVIII parliamentary term there has been a strong increase in the approval of laws coming from a parliamentary initiative

[7] Provocatively, one might recall that fascism began its authoritarian path precisely by exploiting the potentially authoritarian degenerations already present in previous years (Cassese 2016).

(20), when compared to the first year of the previous legislature where there had been 12 (Di Porto and Piana 2019b).

Three-quarters of these laws were put across from the initiative of the MPs of the Five Star Movement, three from the League, and one from the right-wing *Fratelli d'Italia*. A single law of parliamentary initiative has seen the convergence of majority and opposition. It is the law establishing the Commission of inquiry on the phenomenon of the mafia, which emerges from the unified text of four bills. Two other laws came from the confluence of popular and parliamentary initiatives (Di Porto and Piana 2019b).

It is interesting to note the declining use of the most typical instrument, at the hands of the government to coerce the will of the Parliament, that is, the vote of confidence on a bill. The first Conte government has placed it 15 times. In the last parliamentary term, during the same period, it had been used 28 times.

This, however, can be inferred not as a form of "deference" to the Parliament, rather as a symptom of the greater compactness of the parliamentary forces within the populist parties as compared to those of the ruling parties of the past, despite the fact that it was a coalition government.[8]

As mentioned before, a detailed analysis shows heavy forcing. Initially, see the use of the decree-law. It is a common feature for the start of each parliamentary term to be marked by an "uninhibited" use of the decree-law by a government which is often anxious to mark its presence, along with its discontinuity in comparison to the previous one. Moreover, the decree-law is *de facto* the sole legislative instrument available until the permanent committees are formed (Di Porto and Piana 2019a: 2).

The first Conte government was no exception, largely using the decree-law for communicative purposes. A relevant example is the Legislative Decree no. 4/2019, containing a provision that lowers the retirement age for numerous workers (electoral promise of the League) and the so-called

[8] Unlike other countries with consensual political orders such as Belgium and Holland, Italy has always proved to have an underdeveloped system of coalition governance wherein "coalition agreements focused almost exclusively on the distribution of governmental posts, and as a result the debate over public policies, both between parliamentary groupings and within the cabinet itself, only took place once the government had been formed, and it was an ongoing process", so that coalitions "were often undermined by the prospect that one single party or party faction could in practice veto or oppose the government's position on any given question" (Vassallo 2007: 694–695).

income of citizenship (electoral promise of the Five Star Movement). In both the cases, the requirement of urgency clearly doesn't exist, yet the decree was used to signal the electorate of the two coalition parties. Furthermore, law no. 400/1988 (on the activity of the government and the organisation of the Presidency of the Council of Ministers), as well as established constitutional jurisprudence suggest that the decree-laws must be homogeneous, this not being the case.[9]

The phase of the law-making process in which the first Conte government performed worse is the endo-governmental one, also with regard to the past (about which see Marchetti 2016). In fact, the constant need to show signs of activism, combined with the diversity of the two coalition partners, has led to the worsening of the so-called *approvazione salvo intese* phenomenon, a sort of an oxymoron which literally means an approval of decree-laws and bill proposals by the Council of Ministers "subject to further agreements", while it is formally a final approval.

With this expression we refer to the hypotheses in which is reached a political understanding *in principle* among the Council of Ministers, yet not fully translated into regulatory provisions.

In recent years, this practice has reached an evolutionary stage with the approval of the so-called *provvedimenti copertina* (literally "cover-measures", since the first page is the only one which actually exists at the moment of approval). In such cases, the act lacks all the normative content and is a resolution "on nothing" (Di Chiara 2019).

It is tough to have accurate numbers because the minutes of the meetings of the Council of Ministers are not public. It is estimated that at least one decree-law out of four of the first Conte government has been approved in this manner (Marini and Paris 2019).

Obviously, this deviant practice generates political and technical problems. An example that made the headlines was that of the decree-law in fiscal matters approved by the Council of Ministers on October 15, 2018. Two days after the meeting, Luigi Di Maio, the Minister of Labour and Economic Development as well as the political leader of the Five Star Movement, stated during a television broadcast that a controversial tax amnesty had been included in the text by a "technical or political *manina* [little, gentle hand in an idiomatic, ironic sense]", suggesting that this had

[9] See also the problematic practice of inserting heterogeneous provisions when the decree is converted into law, as in the case of Legislative Decree no. 135/2018, which grew from 39 to 152 articles (Matarazzi 2019: 182 and ff.)

happened *after* receiving an approval from the Council of Ministers and announcing that he would report the incident to the judicial authorities.

In a short time, a declaration by the Presidency of the Republic appeared via social media, according to which the text of the entire decree had never been transmitted to the head of state for promulgation. A new meeting of the Council of Ministers was necessary to officially break the deadlock (Lauri and Malvicini 2018). The story of a decree-law on public procurement is even more striking. The political clash between Lega and the Five Star Movement was harsh. It had been approved by the Council of Ministers on March 20, 2019. Interestingly, after almost a month it had not yet been published, in spite of being an emergency decree! Hence, an unprecedented, complete re-approval was therefore necessary on April 18, 2019 also because of the pressure of the President of the Republic (Magri 2019).

As for the delegating provisions,[10] the budget of the first Conte government is meagre.[11] In 2018, from the beginning of the XVIII parliamentary term only two delegating provisions on minor aspects were adopted (law no. 128/2018 and no. 132/2018). In 2019, there were only two other delegating provisions, one aiming to the mere coordination of previously adopted texts (law no. 3/2019) and the other one only aimed at allowing the correction and integration of other texts (law no. 20/2019). This must be added to law no. 51/2019, containing provisions "to ensure the applicability of electoral laws regardless of the number of parliamentarians", which contains the delegation to the government to redraw the election districts for both Houses.

Certainly the situation would be different in the case of approval of the broad and multiple delegations "on the subject of simplification and codification", contained in several bills of government initiative introduced on

[10] As it was well summarized a few years ago, legislative decrees are "promulgated by government on the basis of prior authorisation from parliament, and they immediately come into force as laws, without any need for further parliamentary ratification. Pursuant to article 76 of the Constitution, in order to delegate to government the power to promulgate legislative decrees, parliament has to pass a law establishing the subject matter and the 'directive principles and criteria' of the act of delegation, as well as the time period available to the government in which to promulgate the decrees" (Vassallo 2007: 698).

[11] At least since the mid-1990s, "each parliamentary term is structured around large delegated procedures. When it is difficult to approve broad delegation laws, even the legislature is struggling to continue. The choices may be different [...], but the design of reforms through the construction of delegated laws appears to be an essential prerequisite for the tenure of a parliamentary term" (Di Porto and Piana 2019a: 9).

April 30, 2019. It's quite unlikely to happen because of the major changes between the first and the second Conte government, which seems to imply a sort of a "legislative fresh start" dating from September 2019.

As of September 18, 2019, from the beginning of the XVIII parliamentary term in March 2018, 55 legislative decrees (i.e. delegated legislation) were published in the Official Journal. But in the light of what has just been said, they were mainly "inherited" by the previous parliamentary term, when the corresponding delegating provisions had been enacted. Furthermore, in 32 cases these legislative decrees are just transposing European Union legislation.[12]

Moreover, the first Conte government largely used another technique designed to force parliament's hand, which is that of the "block (or maxi-) amendment". This technique "consists of a government amendment, whilst examination of a bill is about to be concluded, which completely replaces the bill in question, and also integrates it with provisions that have nothing to do with the original bill" (Vassallo 2007: 702). Arriving from the government, these amendments can also be covered by the confidence vote to ensure that their chances to be approved are even higher.

This is a questionable practice, as it comprehensively shifts the negotiation of important parts (if not the whole) of significant measures out of the Parliament (widely Pistorio 2018), negatively impacting the accountability as well as the quality of the legislation (Ceccanti 2014).

What has just been said was very serious with reference to the budget law for 2019, which led a group of senators to seize the Constitutional Court in defense of parliamentary prerogatives.

In a landmark decision (order no. 17/2019), the Court noted that "members of Parliament could theoretically have a standing to initiate a jurisdictional dispute, although this matter turned upon the specific circumstances of each case". However, "due to the broad margin of appreciation in the application of parliamentary rules, the Court's power of review must be limited to cases in which violations are evidently identifiable already within a summary consideration. The Court held that, on the facts, this exacting test was not met in this case, although reserved the

[12] Although it cannot be dealt with here, the way in which the European Union legislation is transposed to Italy via delegated legislation is a topic of great interest; see recently Moavero Milanesi and Piccirilli (2018).

right to review particularly manifest violations of the rights of parliamentarians in future".[13]

In the current parliamentary term, as opposed to the immediately preceding one (see Passaglia 2017), no importance has been given to wide-ranging constitutional reforms, while political actors are essentially focusing on two proposals: the decrease in the number of parliamentarians and innovations in the matter of referendum.

Obviously, they are issues that can relate to the legislative procedure, and they will not be discussed here (see Martinico in this volume). However, it is worth mentioning the sharp clash between the majority and the opposition following some decisions by the President of the Chamber of Deputies Roberto Fico and the President of the Constitutional Affairs Committee of the Chamber Giuseppe Brescia, both members of the Five Star Movement, on the admissibility of amendments to the proposal aiming to reduce the number of parliamentarians. This led to an official letter from the President of the Chamber on April 17, 2019, to explain his decision (which is something not often seen), but did not prevent the proposal from taking its course (Piccirilli 2019).

Concluding Remarks

As we have attempted to outline, there are a number of elements with substantial continuity between the first year of the XVIII parliamentary term and the characteristics of the last ones, from 1994 onwards, largely marked in terms of adhesion or opposition by the (now fading) presence of Silvio Berlusconi. The pathological phenomena visible in legislative production have evidently not stopped, but on the contrary they have been consolidated, ending up in more cases to take forms more and more clearly contrasting with the constitutional norms as well as with the requirements of an efficient legislative procedure capable of producing good quality legislation (Lupo 2019).

In this context, following the 2018 election "on the one hand, the yellow-green governing majority has been less than willing to open space for the opposition, and, on the other hand, the opposition has been less than capable of playing an incisive role. Moreover, the yellow-green

[13] As translated on the website of the Court, www.cortecostituzionale.it. On the "'flexibilization' of the constitutional distribution of lawmaking powers and the limited role of constitutional adjudication" in relation to it, see Barsotti et al. (2016: 116 and ff).

majority has exacerbated some of the malpractices indulged in by all governments since 1994" (Pasquino 2019: 198).

What can be expected in the future? Solutions "will certainly not come from Italian society as long as it remains fragmented and corporatist, and marred by interpersonal mistrust. But the weakest link is represented by the parties (most of which no longer even deserve this name) and by the deconstructed nature of the party system. Will Italy be the first political system to have a working democracy in a situation in which parties have practically disappeared?" (Pasquino 2019: 203).

Obviously this is not a desirable scenario, and it is hoped that the new phase inaugurated by the second Conte government will help Italian politics to re-enter the tracks of a functioning democracy (although some of the very first signs, such as the agreement on "cutting" parliamentarians, are not encouraging).

From a broader perspective, as it was recently noted, the "populist" legislator tends to overemphasize the *input* legitimacy, stressing the directly elective nature of the Parliament itself, and therefore a possible solution is to use also for the analysis of individual state systems the full potential of "throughput legitimacy" (Lupo 2019), "an 'umbrella concept' accompanying the other two umbrella concepts of input and output legitimacy, as criteria for dynamic and 'multi-centric' processes of policy formulation and implementation" (Schmidt and Wood 2019). Throughput legitimacy is "judged in terms of the efficacy, accountability and transparency" of governance processes, not in opposition but "along with their inclusiveness and openness to consultation *with* the people" (Schmidt 2013: 2), within "the space between the political input and the policy output, which has typically been left blank by political systems theorists" and focuses on the quality of the governance processes "as contributing to a different kind of normative legitimacy from both the performance-oriented legitimacy of output and the participation-oriented legitimacy of input" (Schmidt 2013: 6). Will it be enough?

References

Anselmi, M. (2018). *Populism. An Introduction.* London/New York: Routledge.

Barsotti, V., Carozza, P. G., Cartabia, M., & Simoncini, A. (Eds.). (2016). *Italian Constitutional Justice in Global Context.* Oxford/New York: Oxford University Press.

Baume, S. (2017). What Place Should Compromise Be Given in Democracy? A Reflection on Hans Kelsen's Contribution. *Négociations, 27*(1), 73–89.

Benvenuti, F. (1952). Funzione amministrativa, procedimento, processo. *Rivista trimestrale di diritto pubblico, 2*, 118–145.
Bobbio, N. (1983). La regola della maggioranza e i suoi limiti. In V. Dini (Ed.), *Soggetti e potere. Un dibattito su società civile e crisi della politica* (pp. 11–23). Napoli: Bibliopolis.
Bressanelli, E., & Natali, D. (2019). Introduction. *Contemporary Italian Politics, 11*(3), 208–219.
Calamandrei, P. (1954). *Processo e democrazia*. Padova: Cedam.
Cammeo, F. (1914). *Corso di diritto amministrativo*. Padova: Cedam.
Cassese, S. (2016). *Lo Stato fascista*. Bologna: il Mulino.
Ceccanti, S. (2014). Decreti obesi e crisi economica, ovvero la vittoria strisciante dell'assemblearismo. *Quaderni costituzionali, Rivista italiana di diritto costituzionale, 34*(1), 109–112.
Chiti, E. (2008). La dimensione funzionale del procedimento. In *Le amministrazioni pubbliche tra conservazione e riforme* (pp. 211–240). Milano: Giuffrè.
D'Andrea, A. (2013). The Structure of Parliament. In V. Onida et al. (Eds.), *Constitutional Law in Italy* (pp. 108–128). Alphen aan den Rijn: Wolters Kluwer.
Della Cananea, G. (2016). *Due Process of Law Beyond the State: Requirements of Administrative Procedure*. Oxford: Oxford University Press.
Di Chiara, A. (2019). Due prassi costituzionalmente discutibili: delibere del Governo 'salvo intese' e pubblicazione tardiva dei decreti legge. *Osservatorio sulle fonti, 12*(1), 1–28. Available at www.osservatoriosullefonti.it
Di Porto, V., & Piana, A. (2019a). Il primo anno delle legislature nella cosiddetta 'seconda Repubblica'. *Osservatorio sulle fonti, 1*, 1–17.
Di Porto, V., & Piana, A. (2019b, August 17). Governo Conte al capolinea: bilancio di 503 giorni in tonalità gialloverde. *il Dubbio*. Available at https://ildubbio.news/ildubbio/2019/08/17/governo-conte-al-capolinea-bilancio-di-503-giorni-in-tonalita-gialloverde/
Fazzalari, E. (1986). Procedimento e processo (teoria generale). In *Enciclopedia del Diritto* (Vol. XXXV, pp. 819–835). Milano: Giuffrè.
Forti, U. (1931). 'Atto' e 'procedimento' amministrativo (note critiche). In *Studi di diritto pubblico in onore di Oreste Ranelletti* (pp. 441–466). Padova: Cedam.
Fracchia, F. (2005). Administrative Procedures and Democracy: The Italian Experience. *Indiana Journal of Global Legal Studies, 12*(2), 589–598.
Galeotti, S. (1957). *Contributo alla teoria del procedimento legislativo*. Milano: Giuffrè.
Giannelli, V. (2018). Linee guida Anac e 'fuga' dall'Esecutivo. *Forum Quaderni costituzionali*, 1–17. Available at www.forumcostituzionale.it
Giannini, M. S. (1970). *Diritto amministrativo*. Milano: Giuffrè.
Grasso, G. (2006). *Le Autorità amministrative indipendenti della Repubblica. Tra legittimità costituzionale e legittimazione democratica*. Milano: Giuffrè.
Ibrido, R. (2015). *L'interpretazione del diritto parlamentare. Politica e diritto nel processo di risoluzione dei casi regolamentari*. Milano: Franco Angeli.

Klabbers, J., & Palombella, G. (Eds.). (2019). *The Challenge of Inter-Legality*. Cambridge: Cambridge University Press.

LaPalombara, J. (1987). *Democracy Italian-Style*. New Haven/London: Yale University Press.

Lauri, G., & Malvicini, M. (2018). Sulla via del Quirinale. I processi endo-governativi di trasmissione di decreti-legge alla Presidenza della Repubblica nella recentissima esperienza italiana. *Osservatorio sulle fonti, 11*(3), 1–9. Available at www.osservatoriosullefonti.it

Lavagna, C. (1956). Considerazioni sui caratteri degli ordinamenti democratici. *Rivista trimestrale di diritto pubblico, 6*, 392–422.

Luhmann, N. (1983). *Legitimation durch verfahren*. Frankfurt: Suhrkamp.

Lupo, N. (2019). «Populismo legislativo?»: continuità e discontinuità nelle tendenze della legislazione italiana. *Ragion pratica, 26*(1), 251–271.

Magri, U. (2019, April 17). No ai decreti-fantasma, l'ultimatum di Mattarella. *La Stampa*. Available at https://www.lastampa.it/topnews/primo-piano/2019/04/17/news/no-ai-decreti-fantasma-l-ultimatum-di-mattarella-1.33695904

Manetti, M. (1990). *La legittimazione del diritto parlamentare*. Milano: Giuffrè.

Marchetti, A. (2016). Il procedimento governativo di approvazione dei decreti-legge tra regole formali e prassi: il *requiem* della collegialità ministeriale. *Osservatorio sulle fonti, 9*(3), 1–37. Available at www.osservatoriosullefonti.it

Marini, A., & Paris, M. (2019, August 13). L'eredità del governo M5S-Lega: un decreto su 4 è 'salvo intese. *Il Sole 24 Ore*. Available at https://www.ilsole24ore.com/art/l-eredita-governo-m5s-lega-decreto-4-e-salvo-intese-ACUYnkd

Mashaw, J. L. (1985). *Due Process in the Administrative State*. New Haven/London: Yale University Press.

Mashaw, J. L. (1990). Explaining Administrative Process: Normative, Positive, and Critical Stories of Legal Development. *The Journal of Law, Economics, and Organization, 6*(Special Issue), 267–298.

Matarazzi, D. (2019). L'avvio della XVIII legislatura e la decretazione d'urgenza: nuovo governo, vecchie abitudini. *Rivista di Diritti Comparati, 2*(2), 161–188.

Merusi, F. (2000). *Democrazia e autorità indipendenti: un romanzo quasi giallo*. Bologna: il Mulino.

Mirkine-Guetzévich, B. (1936). *Les nouvelles tendances du droit constitutionnel*. Paris: LGDJ.

Moavero Milanesi, E., & Piccirilli, G. (Eds.). (2018). *Attuare il diritto dell'Unione europea in Italia: un bilancio a 5 anni dall'entrata in vigore della legge n. 234 del 2012*. Bari: Cacucci.

Morrone, A. (2012). Teologia economica v. Teologia politica? Appunti su sovranità dello Stato e 'diritto costituzionale globale'. *Quaderni costituzionali, 32*(4), 109–112.

Palombella, G. (2012). *È possibile una legalità globale? Il Rule of law e la governance del mondo*. Bologna: il Mulino.

Pantalone, P. (2018). *Autorità indipendenti e matrici di legalità*. Napoli: ES.
Pasquino, G. (1997). No Longer a 'Party State'? Institutions, Power and the Problems of Italian Reform. *West European Politics, 20*(1), 34–53.
Pasquino, G. (2019). The State of the Italian Republic. *Contemporary Italian Politics, 11*(2), 195–204.
Passaglia, P. (Ed.). (2017). The 2016 Italian Constitutional Referendum: Origins, Stakes, Outcome. *The Italian Law Journal, 2*(Special Issue), 1–156.
Pertici, A. (2018). La Costituzione italiana alla prova del populismo. In *Associazione Italiana dei Costituzionalisti, Democrazia, oggi. Atti del XXXII Convegno annuale* (pp. 621–637). Napoli: ES.
Piccirilli, G. (2019). È possibile delimitare l'ambito di una revisione costituzionale perimetrando l'ammissibilità degli emendamenti? *Quaderni costituzionali, 39*(3), 680–683.
Pistorio, G. (2018). *Maxi-emendamento e questione di fiducia: contributo allo studio di una prassi illegittima*. Napoli: ES.
Pizzorusso, A. (1988). The Law-Making Process as a Juridical and Political Activity. In A. Pizzorusso (Ed.), *Law in the Making. A Comparative Survey* (pp. 1–87). Berlin/Heidelberg/New York: Springer-Verlag.
Pizzorusso, A. (1993). *Minoranze e maggioranze*. Torino: Einaudi.
Predieri, A. (1974). Aspetti del processo legislativo in Italia. In *Studi in memoria di Carlo Esposito* (Vol. IV, pp. 2457–2529). Padova: Cedam.
Predieri, A. (1975). Mediazione e indirizzo politico nel parlamento italiano. *Rivista italiana di scienza politica, 5*(3), 407–441.
Predieri, A. (1997). *L'erompere delle autorità amministrative indipendenti*. Firenze: Passigli.
Ruggeri, A. (1977). *Gerarchia, competenza e qualità nel sistema costituzionale delle fonti*. Milano: Giuffrè.
Sandulli, A. M. (1940). *Il procedimento amministrativo*. Milano: Giuffrè.
Schmidt, V. (2013). Democracy and Legitimacy in the European Union Revisited: Input, Output, and Throughput. *Political Studies, 61*(1), 2–22.
Schmidt, V., & Wood, M. (2019). Conceptualizing Throughput Legitimacy: Procedural Mechanisms of Accountability, Transparency, Inclusiveness and Openness in EU Governance. *Public Administration, 97*(Forthcoming), 1–14.
Tambini, D. (2001). *Nationalism in Italian Politics*. London: Routledge.
Tarchi, M. (2015). Italy: The Promised Land of Populism? *Contemporary Italian Politics, 7*(3), 273–285.
Titomanlio, R. (2017). Riflessioni sul potere normativo delle Autorità amministrative indipendenti fra legalità 'sostanziale', legalità 'procedurale' e funzione di regolazione. *Nomos: le attualità nel diritto, 20*(1), 1–37.
Vassallo, S. (2007). Government Under Berlusconi: The Functioning of the Core Institutions in Italy. *West European Politics, 30*(4), 692–710.
Weber, M. (1921–1922). *Wirtschaft und Gesellschaft*. Tübingen: Mohr.
Zander, M. (2015). *The Law-Making Process*. London: Bloomsbury.

CHAPTER 7

Populism and Government: Continuity and Paradoxes in the Yellow-Green Experiment

Giacomo Delledonne

Introductory Remarks

This chapter aims to consider whether and how the Italian government has been affected by the rise of populist parties and movements or, more broadly, by populist arguments and discourse. In order to answer these research questions, a two-sided paradox has to be considered carefully. This paradox has to do with the relevance of the executive in the populist discourse and, conversely, with its relatively undefined status in the conceptual toolbox of constitutional law. On the one side, a strengthened constitutional role of the executive lies at the heart of the populist constitutional project or, less ambitiously, constitutional discourse. A crucial component of the constitutional strategy of populism is to emphasise the opposition between the executive as the main or sole representative of the popular will and the possible counterpowers, most notably the judiciary and independent agencies (Müller 2016: 66). Furthermore, the executive

G. Delledonne (✉)
Scuola Sant'Anna, Pisa, Italy
e-mail: giacomo.delledonne@santannapisa.it

G. Delledonne et al. (eds.), *Italian Populism and Constitutional Law*, Challenges to Democracy in the 21st Century,
https://doi.org/10.1007/978-3-030-37401-3_7

plays a key role in the populist constitutional project, as it is supposed to trigger and lead constitutional change unilaterally: "This form of constitutional executivism tends to be univocal, partisan, and monistic, and therefore to violate any idea of inclusive, broad-based constituent power" (Blokker 2019: 547; see also Walker 2019: 524–528). In this respect, the populist discourse is obviously interested in keeping a close eye on the constitutional role of the government and in strengthening it vis-à-vis the other branches.

At the same time, however, domestic and comparative constitutional analyses routinely describe the government as the least studied among the constitutional organs in the comparative scene as well as in the Italian constitutional system (Dogliani 2012: 45–50). This can be explained, first, by the relatively late emergence of government as something distinct from public administration (Lupo 2018: 151–152). Moreover, the relevant provisions in the Constitution of the Italian Republic are quite few in number and vague (Articles 92 to 96 It. Const.): their open texture is the product of a deliberate choice of the drafters of the Constitution, who wished to preserve a margin for different interpretations thereof (Paladin 1970: 676). In their laconic wording, these constitutional provisions have been deeply shaped by massive institutional transformation—all the more so because the implementing law mentioned in Article 95 was approved as late as 1988.[1] Moreover, the main triggering factor of formal and informal change affecting the executive is to be found not in the Constitution but, rather, in electoral reform—most notably, the demise of proportional representation—and European integration. These have led to affirm a stronger role for the government as well as for its head (*Presidente del Consiglio dei ministri*, hereinafter the Prime Minister) within the constitutional order.

This chapter will consider the populist approach to the Italian executive in the light of the relevant constitutional principles and the subsequent evolution. Indeed, three pertinent principles can be drawn from the text of the Constitution: the Prime Minister's leadership (*principio monocratico*), internal collegiality (*principio collegiale*), and the autonomy of each ministerial department (*principio della competenza ministeriale*). Since the entry into force of the Constitution, the balance between these principles has significantly changed under the influence of legal and non-legal factors: interestingly, the Italian experiment of a purely populist government

[1] Law no. 400 of 23 August 1988 (*Disciplina dell'attività di Governo e ordinamento della Presidenza del Consiglio dei ministri*).

at the beginning of the 18th parliamentary term was based on a peculiar understanding of the operational interplay of these constitutional principles.

Populism, the Executive, and Constitutional Law: A General Overview

At first sight, an obvious starting point is the link between the trend towards the presidentialisation of the executives—and, correspondingly, the personalisation of politics—and the institutional programmes of populism. Furthermore, this starting point makes it possible to shed light on the idea that populism has a parasitic attitude towards constitutional law. As argued by Fournier (2018: 1), this is particularly true of the foundations of constitutional democracy: "populism could not appear without the specific features of constitutional democracy and could not prosper if constitutional democracy itself does not develop". However, this is also the case with informal or weakly formalised institutional developments that are not necessarily connected with the populist project and discourse.

Having this in mind, a recurring argument in comparative analysis is that the growing interdependence between legal orders and the rise of supranational governance not only boosts the idea of open statehood but also emphasises the role of the executive within state borders and beyond. Governmental stability and the consistency of governmental action are red threads that have inspired constitutional and legislative reform in the West in the last three decades (Carrozza 2009: 906–908). A typical underlying idea is that strengthening the executive for the sake of more efficient decision-making processes should go hand in hand with the emergence of a different conception (and culture) of parliamentary oversight (see e.g. Curreri 2008; Rosa 2012: 211–228). Meanwhile, the decline of traditional political cultures and the transformations in political communication have been described as important factors in shaping the trend towards the presidentialisation of politics, by which is meant the concentration of power around political leaders in constitutional democracies (see Poguntke and Webb 2005).[2] In sum, modernisation and efficiency—with the need

[2] Mény and Surel (2004: 85–124), in turn, have identified three main factors that explain the populist flavour of contemporary democracies: the decline of traditional systems of political mediation, the personalisation of political power, and the novel entanglement of politics and the media.

for stronger checks and balances—can be described as the main features in this trend of constitutional innovation.

In Italy, reference should also be made to the growing dissatisfaction with the alleged oligarchic, self-serving attitudes of the political parties—the so-called particracy (*partitocrazia*)—in the final years of the first phase of the history of the Italian Republic. Among constitutional scholars, Costantino Mortati strongly highlighted the need to revive popular sovereignty, which he thought was undermined by party dominance and proportional representation, as the result of a stronger, more direct link between voters and the executive (see Mortati 1975; Barbera and Ceccanti 1995). According to subsequent analyses, attention should be drawn not so much to voters anointing a leader by means of a blank proxy as to a combination of this and the possibility of steering the policy course of the executive (Elia 2009: 371).

There is no necessary link between these trends and populism. This being the case, what do these trends have in common with it?

The underlying idea is that a strong executive leadership would recreate the imagined unity that lies at the heart of the populist discourse. Among the typical institutions of Western democracies, the executive is the best placed to embody the "*pars pro toto*" ambitions of the populist discourse and project (see Arato 2013; Urbinati 2017: 573). The ability of the head of government to develop a direct relationship with the public and to act decisively is often set against the fragmented composition of the legislature and its focus on procedures. Indeed, laws passed by the legislature as the result of a formalised procedure are a typical target of populism, as they represent, within constitutional democracies, an attempt to strike a balance "between social pluralism and the unity of the legal order" (Lupo 2019: 253). In factual terms, the decline of traditional forms of political mediation, that is, the political parties that had shaped the Italian political system since the end of World War II, also contributed to the development of a populist counternarrative.

In this respect, institutional evolution since the early 1990s seems to have responded to some populist claims (which however, are shared by other ideological strains). Populist attitudes have marked, to different degrees, the behaviour of Italian governments since the time of the Tangentopoli scandals and the end of the "Republic of the political parties" (as defined by Scoppola 1997). Interestingly, electoral reforms and attempted constitutional reforms have often tried to strengthen and entrench the position of the Prime Minister within the executive as well as within the general constitutional order. However, these developments are to some extent in line with the institutional evolution of other Western democracies: at best, the Italian case can be said to have served as a laboratory and a forerunner for populism.

Against this complex background, the Italian laboratory (see Tarchi 2003: 7–8) generated an interesting and virtually unprecedented experiment in populist government in the aftermath of the general election of 4 March 2018. The first purely populist government in Europe[3] apparently contradicted many of the arguments that have been presented and discussed in this paragraph. At the same time, it has revived some long-established characteristics of the Italian executive, which had been carefully described (and criticised) in a rich line of scholarship.

In a nutshell, the Italian government that was formed in 2018 was based on a "contract" signed by the leaders of the Five Star Movement and the League (formerly known as the Northern League), and to whose drafting Giuseppe Conte, who later went on to be appointed Prime Minister, was largely foreign.[4] In its first months of activity, the Conte government seems to have revived the old-fashioned "departmental" or "feudal" descriptions of the functioning of the Italian government, leaving limited room for unitary political direction (be that collegial or monocratic, or a combination of the two). However, the current situation is clearly different from the past state of affairs, as the unifying role of political parties has also largely vanished.

In the next paragraph, the formation of the first Conte government will be analysed: special emphasis will be put on the significance and the implications of the "Contract for Government" between the political leader of the Five Star Movement and the federal secretary of the League. After

[3] Scholars in law and political science have used more nuanced labels, for example, "techno-populist" (Castellani 2018) and "populist-technocratic" (Lupo 2019: 261).

[4] The first Conte government was sworn in by the President of the Republic on 1 June 2018. After the European election of 26 May 2019, the relationship between the Five Star Movement and the League increasingly deteriorated. At the beginning of August 2019, Matteo Salvini, Deputy Prime Minister and leader of the League, publicly stated that the government by that time was no longer able to act and, consequently, he would ask the President of the Republic to dissolve the legislature and to call a snap election. The League submitted a motion of no confidence in order to speed up the process; still, it withdrew the motion a few days later. Prime Minister Conte decided to put an end to political cooperation with the League and resigned. Meanwhile, the Five Star Movement and the main opposition party, the Democratic Party, were entering into talks to form a new government. These negotiations were successful, and the second Conte government was sworn in on 5 September 2019.

that, in turn, the focus will be on the internal structure of the Conte government. In both paragraphs, the more recent institutional evolution will be assessed in the light of constitutional provisions as well as long-established practice.

The Genesis of the First Conte Government: The "Contract for Government"

As for its agenda, the first Conte government was based on a "contract" between the leaders of the two political parties in the majority, that is, Luigi Di Maio and Matteo Salvini.[5] The idea of a contract is not entirely new, as Silvio Berlusconi had signed a "contract with the Italian people" (*contratto con gli italiani*) ahead of the general election in 2001. Furthermore, coalition agreements ***negotiated and drafted after elections*** have become standard practice in some Western democracies, for example, Germany (see Rizzoni 2014; Saalfeld et al. 2019) and the Low Countries (see Timmermans 2003), not to mention the coalition agreement that opened a tumultuous decade in British constitutional life (see Bogdanor 2011: 45–54).

In the aftermath of the inconclusive general election of March 2018, and after three failed rounds of talks led by the President of the Republic and two explorative missions entrusted to the President of the Chamber of Deputies and the President of the Senate, the contract was perceived as a plausible tool to overcome the multiple disagreements between the Five Star Movement and the League and to cement a durable ruling majority. Indeed, the League had just run in the election in a coalition with two other parties, Forza Italia and Brothers of Italy, while the Five Star Movement had always refused to be part of coalitions either before or after elections. In some respects, as mentioned above, it is possible to draw parallels between the course of action followed by Di Maio and Salvini and the coalition agreements negotiated in other European countries. However, the Contract for Government negotiated by the leaders of the

[5] An English summary of the "Contract for the Government of Change in Italy" is available on the website of the Five Star Movement's Members of the European Parliament: www.efdd-m5seuropa.com/imgblog/summary_of_the_contract_for_the_government_of_change_in_italy.pdf. An unabridged version of the Contract (in Italian) is available at download.repubblica.it/pdf/2018/politica/contratto_governo.pdf (both websites accessed 16 October 2019).

Five Star Movement and the League also has some distinctive features showing that it is based, at least to some extent, on the contestation of the mechanisms of representative democracy.

First, the extensive resort to private law jargon—the Contract refers to its "parties", and was signed before a notary public—hints at a deeply rooted mistrust of the traditional mechanisms of representative democracy, including the constitutional role of political parties. In spite of it being impossible to conceive of private law remedies for violations of the Contract, this kind of language was instrumental in defining a distance from "the deviant behaviour of corrupt political elites, indifferent to the needs of their constituencies" (Guarnier 2019: 14–15).

Second, after Di Maio and Salvini ended their negotiations, members of their parties[6] were called on to approve or reject the draft contract en bloc even before the parliamentary groups of the Movement and the League were given any chance to discuss it. The lack of any form of discussion of the contents of the agreement is revealing of the plebiscitarian flavour of this move.

Third, the person who would take office as Prime Minister was not really involved in the preparation of this document. The Contract was signed by Di Maio and Salvini in their respective capacities as political leader of the Movement and federal secretary of the League: they went on to become Deputy Prime Ministers, in charge of extensive policy sectors lying at the heart of the electoral manifestos of their respective parties. On the one hand, Salvini became Minister of the Interior and was seen as the main responsible for security and migration policies, whereas Di Maio took the portfolios of Industry, Employment, and Welfare. In this respect, the composition of the executive seemed to be based on a rigid division of labour, with each party (and its leader) focusing on its own policy priorities. Interestingly, the person who would be picked by Di Maio and Salvini to be the Prime Minister had no part in negotiating and drafting the Contract, and the future head of government is hardly mentioned throughout the text of the Contract itself. Giuseppe Conte, a lawyer and private law professor with no previous political background, was invited to serve as head of the yellow-green government, as it was labelled in the media, on the condition that he accept the contents of the Contract. Meanwhile, the Contract had been signed and approved by the parties' grassroots. In his capacity as Prime Minister designate, Conte acted as a

[6] In fact, the ratification vote organised by the League was open to all citizens.

fiduciary of the two parties to the Contract. As some scholars have argued, the purposeful exclusion of the Prime Minister designate from the decisive stages of government formation was unprecedented and was possibly at odds with the constitutionally entrenched role of the Prime Minister (see Catelani 2018).

Fourth, when Prime Minister Conte presented his programme before the Senate and the Chamber,[7] the parliamentary parties of the Five Star Movement and the League submitted two motions of confidence that were discussed and criticised because they had certain innovative features. Under well-established practice, the parliamentary leaders of the ruling majority submit motions of confidence that broadly refer to the Prime Minister's speech before each house. On the contrary, the two motions submitted by Senators Crimi and Candiani on 5 June 2018 referred to the Contract for Government and the Prime Minister's statement, insofar as the latter was fully in accordance with the former. In sum, the relationship between the executive and the legislature was made less flexible because of the emphasis put on the Contract and the related pledges rather than on the autonomy of the constitutional organs and their dialectic interaction (see Petrucco 2018: 9–11). In particular, the constitutional role of the Prime Minister, who "conducts and holds responsibility for the general policy of the Government" (Article 95(1) It. Const.), was all but wiped out (Manzella 2018: 670). Therefore, the government's role was assumed to be merely that of an agency implementing the Contract.

In the scholarly debate, some authors (e.g. D'Andrea 2018: 681–682) have invited not to overestimate the implications of the Contract, claiming that Di Maio and Salvini's actual goal was to bring to the table a persuasive propaganda tool, illustrating the innovative approach of the self-styled "government of change" (*Governo del cambiamento*). This feeling is somehow confirmed by the subsequent vicissitudes of the Contract. Because of the far-reaching differences between the respective agendas and voting constituencies of the Five Star Movement and the League, the Contract itself referred to a further agreement in which the composition and functioning of a "Conciliation Committee" would be regulated in detail.

[7] Under Article 94 of the Constitution, "The Government must receive the confidence of both Houses of Parliament. Each House grants or withdraws its confidence through *a reasoned motion* voted on by roll-call. Within ten days of its formation, the Government shall come before Parliament to obtain confidence" (emphasis added).

However, this agreement was never implemented; neither was any "Conciliation Committee" put in place.[8] This testifies to the very peculiar nature of the first purely populist government experiment in Western Europe.

The Structure and Operation of the First Conte Government

The role of European integration in affecting the constitutional role of the Italian government has already been cursorily mentioned. In particular, the internal structure of the Italian government has been strongly shaped by Italy's membership of the European Union and the Economic and Monetary Union. This has triggered a significant shift in the internal balance of power within the executive. Quite predictably, the Prime Minister has taken advantage of his membership of the European Council, which has also greatly strengthened his status in the domestic sphere. However, similar arguments also apply to the Minister of Economics and Finance (Cuniberti 2016: 54–55). On the one hand, the Ministry of Economics and Finance, resulting from the merger of the Ministries of Finance, the Treasury, and Budgetary and Economic Planning in 1999, is one of the most senior positions within the national executive. On the other hand, the Minister of the day plays a crucial role in defining the contents of the annual state budget laws: since the outbreak of the sovereign debt crisis in the Eurozone, this activity has gradually turned into a step-by-step negotiation between national governments and supranational institutions. Among the Member States of the European Union, the Italian case looks quite peculiar. Since the launch of the third stage of the Economic and Monetary Union in 1999, most of the Ministers of Economics and Finance have been independent experts and not professional politicians: it is sufficient to mention Carlo Azeglio Ciampi (1996–99), Domenico Siniscalco (2004–05), Tommaso Padoa-Schioppa (2006–2008), Mario Monti (2011–2012), Vittorio Grilli (2012–2013), Fabrizio Saccomanni (2013–2014), and Pier

[8] Interestingly, the Contract for Government did not even make reference to any sanctions for possible violations of the programmatic pledges of the yellow-green majority: this might have suggested that its value was merely symbolic. Still, the preparation of the Contract "significantly affected not only the procedure for putting an end to the governmental crisis but also the very powers of the Prime Minister-designate and his relations with the President of the Republic and the parliamentary parties" (Catelani 2018: 678).

Carlo Padoan (2014–2018). Incidentally, many of them had had distinguished careers at the Bank of Italy prior to serving as government ministers.

Interestingly, the first Conte government did not depart from this ingrained practice. Initially, Prime Minister designate Conte unsuccessfully proposed Paolo Savona, a former cabinet minister and academic economist with controversial Eurosceptic views, as the new Minister of Economics and Finance. In a controversial move, however, the President of the Republic refused to appoint Savona: in President Mattarella's words, "uncertainty over our positions on the euro has raised alarm among investors and savers, Italian and foreign who have invested in our Government bonds and in our companies".[9] After this failed attempt, Conte, who had even given up the task of forming a government, and the two leaders of the yellow-green coalition opted for another academic, Giovanni Tria, formerly President of the Scuola nazionale dell'amministrazione. Tria was supposed to embody a pro-European policy course and to be closer to moderate centre-right political parties than to either of the partners in the yellow-green coalition. How should Tria's appointment be interpreted? One possible explanation is that Tria, like other ministers with no party affiliation—for example, Foreign Minister Enzo Moaveri Milanesi, who had already served as Minister for European Affairs under Prime Ministers Monti and Letta—was supposed to ensure continuity in the traditional orientations of the Italian government, thereby "taming" the possible impact of the implementation of the yellow-green programme in some sensitive policy areas. In many respects, however, the decision to opt for a non-partisan expert as Minister of Economics and Finance convincingly exemplifies a typical feature of the populist attitude towards public finance and budgetary policy (see Boggero in this volume): a radical refusal to have budgetary constraints, which are often perceived as undemocratic, imposed by *external* institutions. Therefore, ministers affiliated to the League and the Five Star Movement pursued their policy goals, whether that was the citizens' income (*reddito di cittadinanza*) or the so-called flat tax, without really taking responsibility for their financial sustainability. In spite of frequent disagreements with the two Deputy Prime Ministers, Tria stayed in office until the resignation of the first Conte government. As signalled by D'Andrea (2019: 13), Minister Tria took advantage of its

[9] Declaration by the President of the Republic Sergio Mattarella at the end of consultations with Professor Giuseppe Conte, Rome, 27 May 2018, available at www.quirinale.it/elementi/1417

close links with the President of the Republic as well as with European institutions and could act more independently than the two leaders of the ruling majority wished. Therefore, the decision to appoint another independent expert as Minister of Economics and Finance also shows that the populist experiment in government was marked by a combination of continuity and more innovative features: a "contradictory style", as Cassese (2018) defined it.

As mentioned above, the operation of the Italian government is based on the interplay and the evolving balance between prime ministerial leadership, collegiality, and the autonomy of ministerial departments (see Capotosti 1989: 9–12): all these principles can be drawn from Article 95 of the Constitution, whose wording seems to allow for a number of possible interpretations.[10] The decade-long hegemony of Christian Democracy was instrumental in preserving the ambiguity of this provision and the flexibility of the system (Lupo 2018: 165–66). A frequent criticism was that the Italian government generally had a feudal structure, in which the individual ministers, particularly because of the existence of multiparty coalitions, dominated their own departments, with little need for significant coordination with their colleagues. Constitutional law scholars resorted to the idea of "multiple dissociated political direction" (*direzione plurima dissociata*) in order to describe the functioning of the Italian government (Cheli and Spaziante 1977: 49). Law no. 400/1988 implemented Article 95(4) of the Constitution and tried to shift the balance towards collegiality and a stronger role of the Prime Minister. It is no coincidence that this law was passed a few years before the final decline of Christian Democracy and its allies, as the previous understandings were becoming untenable. The simplification of the political system in the wake of the adoption of majoritarian electoral laws seemed to announce the decline of a feudal, strongly departmentalised executive (Cherchi 2015: 145).[11]

[10] Under Article 95 of the Constitution, "The Prime Minister (*Presidente del Consiglio*) conducts and holds responsibility for the general policy of the Government. The Prime Minister ensures the coherence of political and administrative policies, by promoting and co-ordinating the activity of the Ministers. The Ministers are collectively responsible for the acts of the Council of Ministers; they are individually responsible for the acts of their own ministries. The law establishes the organisation of the Prime Minister's Department (*Presidenza del Consiglio*), as well as the number, competence and organisation of the ministries".

[11] Today, according to recent analyses, "multiple dissociated direction" does not emerge along party lines but in a complex web of relations with national and European bureaucracies (Cuniberti 2016: 55).

Having this in mind, the first Conte government deserves careful scrutiny. Its collegial dimension seemed quite weak: the Council of Ministers met quite often, but the meetings were fairly brief, with an average duration of less than an hour (Cassese 2019; Guarnier 2019: 21). However, there is some continuity with a frequent complaint in constitutional law scholarship: even in the early years of the Republic, “the meetings of so fundamental an institution … as the Council of Ministers is supposed to be are clearly not enough for the unity of the Government to be constantly affirmed” (Paladin 1970: 709).

The Prime Minister acted as an arbitrator rather than elaborating on and pushing forward consistent policy lines. In turn, the two Deputy Prime Ministers quite often elaborated general policy guidelines and even impinged on powers and tasks lying within the competence of the Council of Ministers or of individual ministers (Troilo 2019: 20; see detailed analysis by Tarli Barbieri 2019). This was particularly evident in the frequent migration crises in which Interior Minister Salvini came to the forefront, frequently interfering with the competences of the Minister of Defence and the Minister of Infrastructure and Transport. Moreover, Salvini, Di Maio, and Conte, even in spite of their respective competences, all engaged in active dialogue with union and business leaders. An attempt to institutionalise this model of strong decentralised leadership can be detected in the so-called Second Security Decree, many of whose provisions strengthened the position of the Minister of the Interior vis-à-vis the other members of the government.[12] In sum, the government's action seemed to be directed by the two Deputy Prime Ministers and leaders of the yellow-green majority, with both being provided with a sort of veto right (D'Andrea 2019: 14).

One final point should be mentioned: the dominance of the executive in the law-making process has been defined as one of the decisive factors in the gradual strengthening of government within the constitutional order (Sciortino 2016: 15–19; Sobrino 2015: 103–106). Detailed analyses of the main trends in the law-making activity under the first Conte government have generally pointed to continuity with the past and the persistence of certain problems (see Lupo 2019: 260–264, and Pacini in this volume). Here, reference will only be made to trends that are relevant for analysing the constitutional position of the government. The most evident trend, of course, is the frequent resort to decree-laws in order to bring about important reforms and to implement the government's

[12] Decree-law no. 53 of 14 June 2019.

agenda: in the light of the crucial role of the executive in the constitutional discourse, extensive resort to decree-laws allows the executive to engage in direct dialogue with the public. Decree-laws enter into force immediately after being enacted by the executive. Interestingly, the most important decree-laws are generally known under a catchy label that illustrates the policy priorities of the government (or, better said, the priorities of the minister responsible for a specific department) in an elementary, easily accessible way: the Dignity Decree,[13] the Security Decree,[14] the 2nd Security Decree, and so on. The lack of internal cohesion in the government is also exemplified by the frequent approval of bills and decree-laws subject to further agreement (*salvo intese*) with other departments (see Pacini in this volume). These examples show that the Contract for Government did not lead to any significant harmonisation of the respective pledges and policy goals of the Five Star Movement and the League: rather, both parties continued to pursue their own agendas with just a few adjustments. The elaboration of the annual budgetary law represented the main obstacle to this scheme: since the budgetary law is a crucial planning instrument, the first Conte government resorted to it in order to regulate the financial profiles of the citizens' income and to carry out pension reform. The extreme difficulty of accommodating all the main policy objectives of the yellow-green majority in the self-styled "people's budget" (*manovra del popolo*) convincingly explains why the elaboration and approval of the budget led to a harsh negotiation with supranational institutions and a complaint lodged before the Constitutional Court.

Concluding Remarks

As is highlighted by other contributors to this collection of chapters, a number of constitutional tools and arguments are a familiar component of the populist discourse but are not exclusively related to it. This is all the more correct when it comes to the role and functions of the government within the Italian constitutional order. Indeed, strengthening the executive has been a leitmotiv since the very beginning of the apparently endless discussion about whether and how to amend the Second Part of the Constitution of 1948 (see Carrozza 2017). Meanwhile, the abovementioned factors of institutional change have all contributed to enhancing

[13] Decree-law no. 87 of 12 July 2018.
[14] Decree-law no. 113 of 4 October 2018.

the weight of the government within the constitutional order. Therefore, the need for a stronger executive, or a more efficient one, has been a recurring feature in the constitutional life of Italy in the last four decades.

Populism strongly emphasises the role of a strong executive leadership and its ability to reach out to the people. A good example of this is Matteo Salvini's request for a snap election in the Summer of 2018, which would have allowed the voting public to grant him full power. However, the impossibility of forming a one-party government in the aftermath of the 2018 general election led to a surprising experiment. Because of the mutual distrust between the Five Star Movement and the League, neither Di Maio nor Salvini could become the head of government. Instead, a hitherto unknown figure was asked to serve as Prime Minister and to supervise the implementation of the Contract for Government like an arbitrator.[15] Meanwhile, the executive leadership was, so to speak, split into two, with two broad policy poles revolving around the two Deputy Prime Ministers. In a way, the Contract revived some aspects of the idea of "multiple dissociated political direction": nevertheless, this happened in the absence of strong political parties or any serious attempt to reconcile the opposing claims of the two parties in the majority. Rather, the two poles within the "government of change" were both seeking the maximal implementation of their respective policy priorities. The refusal to establish effective reconciliation mechanisms was among the factors that hastened the premature end of the first Conte government. In conclusion, the yellow-green experiment does not seem to have been exempt from a "Platonic" inconvenience that Orsina (2014) has identified as a recurring trait in the political history of Italy, "what counts is *who* holds the power, not *how* power is organized, disciplined, and limited".

References

Arato, A. (2013). Political Theology and Populism. *Social Research, 80*(1), 143–172.

Barbera, A., & Ceccanti, S. (1995). La lenta conversione maggioritaria di Costantino Mortati. *Quaderni costituzionali, 25*(1), 67–94.

Blokker, P. (2019). Populism as a Constitutional Project. *International Journal of Constitutional Law, 17*(2), 535–553.

[15] The institutional advantages associated with the position of Prime Minister have gradually led Conte to increase his stature, inside as well as outside Italy: however, this development is unrelated to the earliest scheme of the contract and, consequently, lies outside the scope of this chapter.

Bogdanor, V. (2011). *The Coalition and the Constitution*. Oxford: Hart Publishing.

Capotosti, P. A. (1989). Governo. In *Enciclopedia giuridica* (Vol. 19). Roma: Istituto dell'Enciclopedia italiana.

Carrozza, P. (2009). Governo e amministrazione. In P. Carrozza, A. Di Giovine, & G. F. Ferrari (Eds.), *Diritto costituzionale comparato* (pp. 853–920). Laterza: Roma-Bari.

Carrozza, P. (2017). The Paradoxes of Constitutional Reform. *The Italian Law Journal*, (Special Issue), 91–103. Available at www.theitalianlawjournal.it

Cassese, S. (2018, June 15). Due facce dello stesso Governo. *Corriere della Sera*.

Cassese, S. (2019, May 19). La verità dei numeri, il governo un anno dopo. *Corriere della Sera*.

Castellani, L. (2018, June 22). L'era del tecno-populismo: trasformazione o fine della politica liberal-democratica?. *Luiss Open*. Available at open.luiss.it/2018/06/22/lera-del-tecno-populismo-trasformazione-o-fine-della-politica-liberal-democratica/

Catelani, E. (2018). Il Presidente del Consiglio incaricato, individuazione e ruolo nel procedimento di formazione del Governo. *Quaderni costituzionali, 38*(3), 677–681.

Cheli, E., & Vincenzo, S. (1977). Il Consiglio dei ministri e la sua presidenza: dal disegno alla prassi. In S. Ristuccia (Ed.), *L'istituzione governo* (pp. 41–61). Comunità, Milano: Analisi e prospettive.

Cherchi, R. (2015). L'esecutivo tra effettività costituzionale e revisione costituzionale: verso la 'presidenzializzazione' del Governo? *Costituzionalismo.it, 13*(3), 135–172. Available at www.costituzionalismo.it

Cuniberti, M. (2016). L'organizzazione del Governo tra tecnica e politica. In G. Grasso (Ed.), *Il Governo tra tecnica e politica* (pp. 45–80). Napoli: Editoriale Scientifica.

Curreri, S. (2008). Riforme regolamentari e futuro del Parlamento. *Quaderni costituzionali, 28*(4), 763–788.

D'Andrea, A. (2018). Del ridimensionamento *per contratto* del ruolo del Presidente del Consiglio (e di altre forzature imposte dai capipartito). *Quaderni costituzionali, 38*(3), 681–685.

D'Andrea, A. (2019). La pervasiva vischiosità della politica italiana: la contraddizione costituzionale del governo del 'cambiamento' e il suo superamento. *Costituzionalismo.it, 17*(2). Available at www.costituzionalismo.it

Dogliani, M. (2012). Procedimenti, controlli costituzionali e conflitti nell'attività di governo. In Associazione italiana dei costituzionalisti (Ed.), *Decisione conflitti controlli. Procedure costituzionali e sistema politico* (pp. 45–80). Napoli: Jovene.

Elia, L. (2009). Per una democrazia di investitura e di indirizzo. Proposta per un riordino istituzionale possibile. (1988), Republished in Marco Olivetti (Ed.), *Costituzione, partiti, istituzioni* (pp. 363–382). Bologna: il Mulino.

Fournier, T. (2018). *From Rhetoric to Action – A Constitutional Analysis of Populism*. EUI Working Paper LAW 2018/08.
Guarnier, T. (2019). *'Contratto di Governo', Azione Governativa e Rapporto Fiduciario*. Paper Presented at the Annual Conference of the Gruppo di Pisa Association, Naples, 14–15 June 2019. Available at www.gruppodipisa.it/images/convegni/2019_Convegno_Napoli/Tatiana_Guarnier_-_Contratto_di_governo_azione_governativa_e_rapporto_fiduciario.pdf
Lupo, N. (2018). Il Governo italiano, settanta anni dopo. Rivista AIC, *9*(3), 150–200. Available at www.rivistaaic.it
Lupo, N. (2019). 'Populismo legislativo?': continuità e discontinuità nelle tendenze della legislazione italiana. *Ragion pratica, 26*(1), 251–271.
Manzella, A. (2018). Centralità proclamata ma difficile senza rispetto per opposizione e minoranze. *Quaderni costituzionali, 38*(3), 667–671.
Mény, Y., & Surel, Y. (2004). *Populismo e democrazia* (Andrea De Ritis, Trans.). Bologna: il Mulino.
Mortati, C. (1975). Articolo 1. In G. Branca (Ed.), *Commentario della Costituzione, Principii fondamentali* (pp. 1–50). Bologna/Roma: Zanichelli/Foro italiano.
Müller, J.-W. (2016). *What Is Populism?* Philadelphia: University of Pennsylvania Press.
Orsina, G. (2014). *Berlusconism and Italy: A Historical Interpretation*. London: Palgrave.
Paladin, L. (1970). Governo italiano. In *Enciclopedia del diritto* (Vol. 19, pp. 675–711). Milano: Giuffrè.
Petrucco, N. (2018). Le mozioni di fiducia al Governo Conte: rottura o continuità?. *Osservatorio sulle fonti, 11*(2). Available at www.osservatoriosullefonti.it
Poguntke, T., & Webb, P. (2005). The Presidentialization of Politics in Democratic Societies: A Framework for Analysis. In T. Poguntke & P. Webb (Eds.), *The Presidentialization of Politics: A Comparative Study of Modern Democracies* (pp. 1–25). Oxford: Oxford University Press.
Rizzoni, G. (2014). I contratti di coalizione nella Repubblica federale tedesca fra politica e diritto. *Rivista AIC, 5*(1). Available at www.rivistaaic.it
Rosa, F. (2012). *Il controllo parlamentare sul Governo nel Regno Unito. Un contributo allo studio del parlamentarismo britannico*. Milano: Giuffrè.
Saalfeld, T., Bahr, M., & Seifert, O. (2019). Contractual Arrangements, Formal Institutions and Personalised Crisis Management: Coalition Governance Under Chancellor Merkel. *German Politics, 28*(3), 371–391.
Sciortino, A. (2016). Il Governo tra tecnica e politica: le funzioni. In G. Grasso (Ed.), *Il Governo tra tecnica e politica* (pp. 9–44). Napoli: Editoriale Scientifica.
Scoppola, P. (1997). *La Repubblica dei partiti. Evoluzione e crisi di un sistema politico 1945–1996*. Bologna: il Mulino.
Sobrino, G. (2015). La forma di governo. In S. Sicardi, M. Cavino, & L. Imarisio (Eds.), *Vent'anni di Costituzione (1993–2013). Dibattiti e riforme nell'Italia tra due secoli* (pp. 63–160). Bologna: il Mulino.

Tarchi, M. (2003). *L'Italia populista. Dal qualunquismo ai girotondi*. Bologna: il Mulino.

Tarli Barbieri, G. (2019). Vicepresidenti o Co-presidenti del Consiglio? Alcune notazioni sparse su una carica controversa. *Rassegna parlamentare, 61*(2), 369–412.

Timmermans, A. I. (2003). *High Politics in the Low Countries: An Empirical Study of Coalition Agreements in Belgium and the Netherlands*. Abingdon: Routledge.

Troilo, S. (2019). La struttura del Governo. *Osservatorio sulle fonti, 12*(1). Available at www.osservatoriosullefonti.it

Urbinati, N. (2017). Populism and the Principle of Majority. In C. R. Kaltwasser, P. Taggart, P. O. Espejo, & P. Ostiguy (Eds.), *The Oxford Handbook of Populism* (pp. 571–589). Oxford: Oxford University Press.

Walker, N. (2019). Populism and Constitutional Tension. *International Journal of Constitutional Law, 17*(2), 515–535.

CHAPTER 8

"Kicking the Can Down the Road" Deferring Fiscal Adjustment as a Premise for Italian Budgetary Populism

Giovanni Boggero

Introduction: The Budget Role for a Populist Constitutional Project

The diverse composition of revenues and expenditures within the state budget is crucial to the realization of any political project, including the populist one, to build or implement a new social order aimed at promoting the common good of ordinary people against the partial interests of corrupt élites. In particular, populist leaders in power conceive the state budget as an instrument to shape the national economy towards certain political and social realignments, namely, to reduce the divergence between a purported general will of the people and the will of the élites. While somewhat akin to the democratic constitutional idea, whereby the budget law is a legislative tool enabling citizens through their own elective representatives to control how much taxes are raised and how resources are spent, the populist constitutional narrative rejects several distinctive

G. Boggero (✉)
Dipartimento di Giurisprudenza, Università degli Studi di Torino, Turin, Italy
e-mail: giovanni.boggero@unito.it

G. Delledonne et al. (eds.), *Italian Populism and Constitutional Law*, Challenges to Democracy in the 21st Century,
https://doi.org/10.1007/978-3-030-37401-3_8

features of the liberal constitutional understanding of the budgetary process. In this respect, the populist approach in budgetary matters is characterized by a radical denial of the usefulness of constraints, which are considered being imposed mostly by non-democratic supranational institutions such as the European Union or the International Monetary Fund, whereas the abidance by them is portrayed as an illegitimate impediment to expansionary fiscal and social policies. Budgeting, therefore, is not regarded as a legal process under which the executive branch is limited in determining the allocation of resources among competing claims by the attainment of annual or multiannual financial objectives. By contrast, it is regarded as a mere political instrument in the hands of a ruling majority, which has free rein to design policies for the people who have been marginalized by a set of ruthless and self-dealing élites. Consequently, economic and social policies ought not to be subject to any test of rationality or feasibility by independent and technical bodies or ministerial bureaucrats; that is, they might also end up being contradictory to one another, thus making economic and financial planning more unpredictable and arbitrary. The permanent electoral campaign, in which populist regimes are immersed, therefore, makes variations or adjustments to the budget more frequent and unexpected, as in fact populists in power tend to react tactically to what the public opinion from time to time arguably regards as sensitive issues in order to guarantee their own re-election (on the functioning of democracy according to public choice theory see Buchanan and Wagner 1977: 98, 161–161, 183 and ff.).

Against this background, populists in power frequently adopt and overestimate the impact of measures having a short-term stimulus effect in order to keep together social groups at different levels of society and, conversely, often deny the possible adverse effects of more public spending and/or lower taxes in terms of a growing public debt or inflation (see Ifo Institute 2017: 53–54; Dornbusch and Edwards 1991: 8–11). For the same reason, they abstain from properly delivering a spending review for every area of expenditures, as across-the-board spending reductions (*tagli lineari*), if anything, are by far a less demanding task than a strategic reallocation of resources. This means a populist constitutional regime rejects the idea of a proper budgetary planning, as it generally would be the case in a traditional multiparty democracy, in which the ruling majority accepts interferences by technical bodies, as they are expected to bring in relevant elements of rationality.

For the enactment into law of their economic and social policies, populist leaders believe, in fact, that the people's majority just ought to regard them as politically urgent. The inherent disregard of budget constraints, therefore, goes hand in hand with a distorted conception of representative democracy, whereby the ruling majority should get rid of any sort of institutional checks and balances, since it represents homogeneous and self-evident interests of a unified people, whose indivisible will by no means can be limited by formalistic legal rules. This critical attitude towards liberal democracy and, in particular, division of powers results in a disruption of the relationship between the executive and the legislative branch, the latter no longer being expected to control the former, but, on the contrary, the former being designed to expand its decision-making power with no need of authorization or evaluation by the latter. The structural alteration of the separation of powers' doctrine has a serious impact on the budgeting process as a whole, since it restrains the work of independent fiscal councils and weakens oppositional as well as minority prerogative powers, which end up being severely curtailed. The populist deliberate attempt to blur the difference between the executive and the legislature and to do away with an allegedly faceless bureaucratic financial supervision is meant to allow the state to be captured from within in the name of achieving the ultimate goals of the people. This phenomenon inevitably produces "legal resentment" by populist leaders towards those laws and procedures enjoying a higher rank than ordinary laws, that is, constitutional and quasi-constitutional prescriptions, including supranational laws. Once the distinction between constitutional and ordinary provisions has also been removed, a constitutional or a supreme court might be the very last institution required to address the unavoidable question of the limits to legislative discretion, thus becoming essential to the survival of a liberal-democratic understanding of the Constitution as a whole.

This chapter will draw on these theoretical assumptions to show that Italy finds itself "and not since yesterday" in a political situation in which populism risks to prevail also in budgetary matters. Budget constraints in fact have been long considered as an obstacle to the legitimate realization of fiscal and social policies by leaders who claimed to truly act in the name of a unified will of the people. This attitude harks back to how questions of public finance have been dealt with by both right- and left-wing cabinets over the last 40 years (Paragraph 1). An attempt to reverse the weakening of the financial constitutional framework caused by a bipartisan populist course of action has been made with a number of reforms passed between 2009 and 2012, which aimed to strengthen the entrenchment of the Italian normative framework into the European one. However, this attempt backfired, as it appears that the parliamentary budgetary process still lacks faithful abidance by constitutional and EU legal prescriptions (Paragraph 2). Therefore, the Constitutional Court has been most recently unleashed to act as the "last bastion" against the typical populist approach towards the Constitution, whereby if the latter supports populists' views, it will be revered as sacred, but if it does not, it will be demonized or, at most, ignored (Paragraph 3).

The Deep Roots of a Bipartisan Populist Approach in the Italian Budgeting Process

Manifestations of populist constitutionalism do not come out of the blue, but are a tangible sign of a deep popular distrust towards certain institutions of liberal democracy or sometimes even of a precarious societal embedment thereof. Fiscal discipline in Italy is an example of this kind, since it was never well rooted in the social Constitution of the country. During the constitutional history of the Italian Republic, legal constraints on the budget have been strained and misinterpreted, while judicial review of legislation for a long time barely played a role in implementing them. Besides, the entrenchment of budget constraints is, still nowadays, all but accepted in the academic legal community, since some authors consider them to call into question the neutrality of the Constitution *vis-à-vis* different economic thoughts and, in particular, lean it towards a modern form of authoritarian constitutionalism (see *inter alia* Alvar Garcia 2019: 37–56).

As the Italian Constituent Assembly enshrined Article 81 into the text of the new Constitution in 1946–1947, the primary concern of the Founding Fathers and among them, especially, of the future Finance and Budget Minister, Ezio Vanoni and the future second President of the Republic, the economist Luigi Einaudi, was to restrict the parliamentary spending initiative, since an expanded role of the legislature, that is, its capacity to amend budget decisions, appeared as a potential source of deficit finance (Santagostino 2017: 44–48; Einaudi 1956: 205). What the Founding Fathers had before their eyes, in fact, was the early twentieth-century degeneration of parliamentary powers, when political majorities were prompted to loosen the public purse strings in order to meet the multifarious interests of their constituencies. In their view, therefore, an effective constitutional provision should have prevented the Parliament from amending the executive's budget proposals (Gianniti 2011). On the contrary, once the executive had submitted the draft budget, the Parliament should have been vested with the power to hold it accountable by examining the bill and ultimately approving or rejecting it. Yet, the power of amendment by members of Parliament was eventually preserved, but severely restricted by the final text of Article 81 (4) IC, which stipulated that "any [...] law involving new or increased expenditures shall detail the means therefor". The original idea behind this clause was to hamper Parliament in its attempt to increase public spending, at the same time by embedding a strict balanced budget rule. However, those MPs who believed that in a multiparty system the Parliament should have been entrusted with the power to fully expose citizens' needs—while the government should have been in charge of providing the corresponding financial resources—did not share this final institutional settlement (cf. Mostacci 2016: 178–183). Therefore, one can claim that Article 81 was born on shaky premises, thus being an ideal breeding ground for its opportunistic interpretation (see also: Delledonne 2014: 188–189; Tanzi 2018: 269).

In fact, the idea of a strict balanced budget rule was gradually discarded and superseded during the 1960s by a new understanding of the budget, even though all through the 1950s the balanced budget rule was generally, albeit spontaneously, complied with by the cabinets then in power. This thriving new conception drew on the Keynesian doctrine, whereby the budget is primarily an instrument of fiscal policy aimed at steering and stabilizing the economy, even if the short-run effect was to disrupt the balanced budget. Yet, not only did the Italian Constitution not provide for an explicit balanced budget rule, but it also designed the budget as a mere law in a formal sense, which means that the budget "may not introduce new taxes and new expenditures", as Article 81 (3) IC originally stipulated.[1] It could only provide for the authorization to collect the revenues and release the expenditures as established by other laws. On this basis, the fiercest critics of this provision lamented that a government could hardly put forward a comprehensive project of fiscal and social policy and was not able to respond to changing circumstances at any time. Widespread social pressure to regard the balanced budget as a mere principle and not as a rule and to make the budget law a fully fledged financial planning act of

[1] Italian Constitutional Court, *inter alia* see: Judgments No. 9/1958, No. 7/1959 and 16/1961.

the executive branch paved the way for a gradual circumvention of the principles laid down in Article 81 IC.

Legal theories developed by prominent constitutional lawyers helped in achieving this outcome (see Onida 1969: 442–443). In particular, they advocated a literal interpretation according to which a balanced budget rule had never been enshrined explicitly into the Constitution, whereas Article 81 IC only prohibited a comprehensive reappraisal of all existing revenue and expenditures legislation by means of the budget law; yet, this provision did not rule out the enactment of new legislation mandating the expenditure of special funds on various entitlement programmes. These further expenditures did not need to be equalized by new revenues, thus allowing for a government policy of deficit expansion. Even the Italian Constitutional Court (*Corte costituzionale*) conceded that expenditures could exceed revenues in a single fiscal year, being the balanced budget, a principle merely supporting a general tendency to be complied with over a prolonged period of time (Judgment No. 1/1966).[2]

In the 1970s, when state revenues were insufficient to cover expenditures, Italian governments started to struggle with accumulated deficits. Yet, this course of action was not seen as fiscally irresponsible by either the political class then in power or by the electorate, since the executive branch resorted to monetary financing of gaping fiscal deficits through the Italian Central Bank (*Banca d'Italia*). No constitutional rule existed, in fact, as to whether and how expenditures should be equalized, so that large-scale government borrowing began to grow, leading to high levels of inflation. Given the long-standing Italian tradition of deficit spending, this radical departure from the guiding principles of the Founding Fathers was disguised as a naked necessity due to their blatant lack of sociopolitical embedment. Moreover, according to its critics, a balanced budget rule would have no longer been up to date at the time, as it would have prioritized, so to say, a rigid accounting target over a fluctuating ceiling supporting the legitimate desire of a ruling majority to meet the people's true expectations. In short, both right- and left-wing governments progressively deprived constitutional limits on budgetary policy of their effectiveness, because of their alleged loss of legitimacy within Italian society. All of

[2] Italian Constitutional Court, Judgment No. 1/1966, according to which the Constitution does not require "a fiscal policy based upon an automatic balanced budget rule, but on the contrary mandates the achievement of an overall budgetary equilibrium [...] which therefore does not rule out a budget deficit" (translation by the author).

the attempts by academics and minority politicians to reverse this constitutional trend failed miserably (Bognetti 1995: 113 and ff.), including the embedment into legislation of a mandatory requirement for the legislature to fix a government-borrowing ceiling every year. Enacted in 1978, it ended up being highly ineffective, since the executive branch used to circumvent it by raising the ceiling according to expenditure needs. Only after the decision made by the Italian Republic to join the Economic and Monetary Union (EMU) in 1992, fiscal policy started being bound by more stringent limits, laid down in the 1997 Stability and Growth Pact (SGP). This set of rules aimed at preventing cross-border spillover effects, which were expected to arise from a single monetary policy. As known, these rules envisaged *inter alia* a 3 per cent of deficit/GDP threshold and a debt-to-GDP ratio of 60 per cent, whereas a country-specific medium-term budgetary objective (MTO) further complemented the SGP in 2005. This new fiscal rulebook affected the Italian constitutional framework on budgetary matters insofar as it altered national procedures and the corresponding deadlines, yet without any prior constitutional amendment being introduced in Parliament. In fact, Article 11 IC empowers the Italian Republic on equal footing with other states to hand over or, as someone would critically appraise, "surrender" (Bartole 2004: 298 and ff., 442; Modugno 1979: 926) sovereign powers to international organizations fulfilling peace and justice objectives without any textual constitutional amendment being required (cf. Italian Constitutional Court, Judgment No. 14/1964).

The Impact of Budgetary Populism on the EU and Italian Constitutional Framework

A revival of budget upper limits to counter excessive deficits and reduce public debt was crucial to Italy's recovery from the early 1990s financial crisis and for its subsequent accession to the EMU. Yet, this revival was not a result of an unconventional popular bottom-up campaign to re-establish fiscal discipline, but rather a consequence of the increasing Europeanization of public finance. The entrenchment of substantial limitations to the budgeting process through the backdoor was initially heralded as a success, as in the opinion of many only an "external constraint" (*vincolo esterno*) could contribute to the country's prosperity (see Carli 1996). Most recently, this positive connotation turned into its opposite, as

Italian politicians and media started epitomizing these limits as an irrational set of constraints imposed by foreign governments and supranational organizations with no democratic legitimacy (cf. Begg and Featherstone 2018). This narrative caught on during the so-called European sovereign debt-crisis, especially when the Cabinet led by Prime Minister, Silvio Berlusconi, first and then the one led by Mario Monti, backed a constitutional amendment meant to enshrine eventually into the Constitution a structural balanced budget rule, a debt sustainability clause and an explicit limit on public borrowing. The Italian commitment to stricter fiscal requirements built on the Euro-Plus Pact as well as on the legal obligations entrenched in the so-called *Fiscal Compact*, an international treaty negotiated among many member states of the EU.[3] At the same time, further reforms of the SGP were enacted in 2011 and in 2013 (Six-Pack and Two-Pack regulations) in order to have an expenditure benchmark and more stringent budgetary rules at a domestic level. Yet, the 2012 amendment of Articles 81, 97 and 119 of the Italian Constitution triggered a new wave of widespread distrust and dissatisfaction against the ruling class and especially against supranational technocratic bodies, including the European Central Bank (ECB), as they were accused of dismantling the cardinal constitutional principle "no taxation without representation" by pushing through Parliament both the constitutional reform and the ensuing austerity measures enacted between 2011 and 2013.

Thereinafter, the populist approach towards the budgeting process emphasized the need for a sovereign country like Italy of doing away with constitutional rules and foreign institutions charged with the task of assessing their compliance and vested with a sanctioning power. A normative framework preventing the Italian Republic to run larger deficits would be per se antidemocratic, as well as highly ineffective in sorting out the country's socio-economic problems, which would instead require expansionary fiscal policies, regardless of the economic cycle. In this respect, it cannot be forgotten that the former Prime Minister Silvio Berlusconi urged Enrico Letta's cabinet in 2013 to not comply with the financial commitments undertaken with the European Commission, because nobody

[3]Article 3, para. 2 of the Treaty on Stability, Coordination and Governance (TSCG), in particular, mandated that the rule limiting the structural budget deficit to 0.5 per cent GDP took effect in the national law "through provisions of binding force and permanent character, preferably constitutional, or otherwise guaranteed to be fully respected and adhered to throughout the national budget process".

would have ever dared to kick Italy out of the EU or of the Eurozone, it being too big a member state to allow to pull out and/or fail (see Boggero and Annicchino 2014). Threatening their own European counterparts to exceed the budget's deficit, as spelled out in the SGP as well as in the Fiscal Compact, has become one of the distinctive features of a number of Italian cabinets, even though these limitations are no longer formally "external", since they are fully incorporated into the Italian constitutional framework.[4] It is, therefore, no wonder that most recently some populist parties, such as, for instance, the right-wing Brothers of Italy (*Fratelli d'Italia*), have been insistently pleading for a constitutional amendment reinstating ordinary domestic law as a higher source of law than both EU and international treaty law (see Bartolucci 2018).[5]

This argumentative pattern based on threat towards supranational powers enabled populist leaders to set up a confrontational approach with EU bodies, whenever the Italian draft budget was subject to their in-depth review within the European Semester. Yet, the legal resentment against constraints still perceived as external mounted not only within self-proclaimed populist cabinets as the one uniting right- and left-wing populists under the leadership of Giuseppe Conte (2018–2019) but also within governments regarded by the wider public as pro-European and closer to the establishment, including the cabinets led by Matteo Renzi (2014–2016) and Paolo Gentiloni (2016–2018). This bipartisan attitude towards budgetary constraints testifies to the potential dissemination of a populist mindset also into the traditional party mainstream (Blokker 2017; Mudde 2004: 550–551). Yet, while right-wing populist leaders such as the former League (*Lega*) leader and Minister of the Interior, Matteo Salvini, as well as some prominent members of the Five Star Movement (*Movimento 5 Stelle*) have been flirting with the idea of a so-called Italexit (Miglio 2019), Democratic Party MPs have been always reiterating their full support for both the single currency and the EU. In turn, the European Commission

[4] Cf. Article 3, para. 2 of Law No. 243/2012 (implementing new Article 81 (6) IC), which stipulates that "*the balancing of budgets corresponds to the medium-term objective (MTO)*", which in turn is defined by Article 2, para. 1, lett. e) as "the value of the structural balance determined using the criteria established in EU Law".

[5] See the draft proposal No. 291 submitted to the Chamber of Deputies (*Camera dei Deputati*) and the draft proposal No. 321 submitted to the Senate of the Republic (*Senato della Repubblica*) during the current parliamentary term. Both bills are aimed at repealing Articles 11, 97, 117, para. 1 and 119 IC insofar as they mandate the supremacy of EU Law and international treaty law over domestic law.

has shown greater willingness to grant budgetary flexibility to address unusual critical events towards governments formed by pro-EU parties, whereas the one led by Giuseppe Conte (2018–2019) underwent an unprecedented preliminary rejection of the draft budget law and, by means of Law-Decree No. 61/2019, was later on forced to pass a budget variation to stave off an excessive deficit and debt procedure (EDP). This friendly attitude by the European Commission depending on the interlocutors reinforced the populist narrative of the EU as a supranational organization dominated by partisan and technocratic élites, profoundly detached from the everyday concerns of the common people.

Nonetheless, a shared populist attitude towards budgetary procedures can be detected throughout the Italian political spectrum, the consequences of this behaviour being evident at both a domestic and EU level. At a domestic level, the dominance of the executive in the budgetary process has been progressively steered from acting as a constitutionally embedded matter of principle to a tool endangering institutional checks and balances. The executive dominance swept away parliamentary debate, making the budget dependent upon the sole will of the Economy and Finance Ministry. In this regard, a practice has consolidated over the last decade whereby the draft budget law, as amended by Parliament, ends up being significantly redesigned or even completely replaced by a final single government correction bill (*maxi-emendamento*), an item of business on which the cabinet tables a confidence motion at short notice (*questione di fiducia*). This tool implies outright rejection of the parliamentary amendments submitted so far, thus squeezing the amount of time available for discussion and, therefore, impairing parliament's scrutiny and oversight functions (Bergonzini 2014: 77 and ff.). In addition, from a substantive point of view, budgetary laws are passed with no primary concern for debt repayment, as light-hearted and provocative statements on the budget by government members routinely provoke market interests' rates of Italian sovereign bonds to spike, thereby causing borrowing costs to increase. At the same time, recurrent budget items like "spending review" or "fighting taxing evasion" seek to act as fictitious revenue justifications for enabling the government to raise current expenditures. It is not by accident that ad hoc recommendations by the cabinet's commissioner for spending review, the economist Carlo Cottarelli, have never been acted upon and the commissioner himself resigned from his post in 2014 shortly after submitting his proposals to the then Prime Minister, Matteo Renzi.

The majoritarian populist grip on the Constitution extended itself further over the functioning of technical bodies entrusted with the task either of assessing the adequacy of funding for any draft law implying a public expense (such as the *Ragioneria Generale dello Stato*, the State General Accounting Office) or analysing and evaluating government fiscal policy and its sustainability (such as the *Ufficio parlamentare di bilancio*, the Parliamentary Budget Office). While the former has been accused by government members of political infiltrations by technocratic élites disguising political motives as matters of technical nature (cf. De Filio and Vicchiarello 2018), the Italian fiscal council's functioning has been hampered by the fact that it depends on the Economy and Finance Ministry for data collection, so that it currently enjoys no forceful power to support the legislature's control action within the budget session (Francaviglia 2019: 196–197; Vernata 2017). In the background, a well-nurtured rhetoric stands out directed at non-partisan government bodies for their being non-democratically legitimized, as if one needed to be directly elected by the people to be entitled to evaluate political choices (cf. Bilancia 2018: 3–4).

The open mockery of experts heading up the figures goes hand in hand with the steady attempt by different ruling majorities of resorting to loopholes and legislative safeguard clauses to postpone fiscal consolidation, thereby burdening future generations and passing the buck to the following cabinet. This attitude by a ruling majority of "kicking the can down the road", that is, of buying time while shifting the blame on somebody else's political action, marks the attraction of the Italian fiscal constitutional framework to an area of perpetual blurring between the executive and the legislature, in which the former is no longer to be held accountable by the latter. Despite Article 67 IC depicting the Nation as represented by members of Parliament, the legislature has been diminished to a rubber stamp for government legislation, while the executive branch entrusts itself with the power of addressing all popular social problems, thereby routinely making and unmaking rules, stretching their meaning to secure a favourable interpretation or, if necessary, lobbying EU bodies for their reform (see Camera dei Deputati ed. 2019).

In this latter respect, the political quarrel put forward by former Economy and Finance Minister, Pier Carlo Padoan, and by the current Chair of the Budget Committee in the Senate, Alberto Bagnai, is of some interest and revolves around the need for a more reliable methodology for calculating the output gap,[6] an economic measure of the difference between the actual GDP and its potential. Under current EU law, medium-term budgetary objectives (MTO) relate to a country-specific structural, that is, cyclically adjusted deficit, the calculation thereof depends on the size of the output gap. Consequently, if output gap estimates are too low, a large part of the fiscal deficit will be considered as being structural and, therefore, to be countered by the member state in question with proper fiscal consolidation efforts. On this basis, all Italian political parties have been lashing out at the high political discretionality and statistical uncertainty by which budget balances are calculated at an EU level, therefore promising to their own electorate to fight to change them at an EU level. In June 2019, for instance, a majority resolution passed by the Italian Senate called the European Commission for "the exclusion of productive investments, including those in human capital" from deficit calculations and "the revision of reference to the structural balance". The Italian political struggle to do away with the output gap intertwines in fact with a more generic proposal of excluding investment expenditures from the calculations on the deficit ceiling, that is, of supporting the "golden rule" as a form of deficit financing which arguably increases future revenues and prevents negative effects on growth potential (see Blanchard and Giavazzi 2004). Finally, Italian cabinets of the recent past joined other southern European member states in putting pressure and calling on the German government to boost public investment spending on grounds of the solidity of its federal budget balances, thus suggesting German selfishness being at the origin of the current crisis. The newly sworn in Italian cabinet, bringing together the Five Star Movement and the Democratic Party (*Partito Democratico*), makes no exception, as it appears to share the same policy intentions of previous executives, with the coalition agreement between the two parties supporting the idea of overcoming the excessive rigidity of EU limits on member states' budget policies, while using them as a scapegoat for their own inaction. Even the President of the Republic, Sergio Mattarella, who is institutionally required to keep himself out of the political spotlight, publicly pledged for a revision of the Stability and

[6] *Italy accuses Brussels of "shaky" accounting*, in: www.ft.com, November 20, 2014, and *The EU must rationalise its rules on national deficits*, in: www.ft.com, June 6, 2019 (last accessed on September 30, 2019).

Growth Pact (SGP), thus making this goal almost a constitutional priority of the state beyond political affiliations.[7]

The move by the Head of State to officially promote a rethinking of EU fiscal policymaking is not a matter of pure chance, but fits within a strategy of rendering populist parties harmless by taking over themes from their political agenda and making them mainstream. This strategy could be deemed constitutionally anchored insofar as Article 87 (1) IC entrusts the President of the Republic with the guardianship of national unity, a task on the basis of which the Head of State can try to reinvigorate the Constitution as a tool capable of reproducing a community's collective identity based—as it shows in the case at hand—on an ever-closer European integration. Yet, the pledge for a more agile fiscal rulebook bears the risk of backfiring, since co-opting populist assumptions might contribute to feeding their agenda rather than to eradicating them from the political arena. If bowing to rather than sidestepping populist pressure, pro-EU parties might help propagate policies based on higher deficit levels financing current expenditures rather than on an active fiscal policy, envisioning a plan of public capital investments and on a centralized Eurozone budget with the aim of performing macroeconomic stability, as some asset management companies instead suggest (Algebris Policy & Research 2019).[8] The current EU fiscal framework already foresees a broad flexibility clause affording a provisional deviation from the country-specific MTO on grounds of either structural reforms, investments or unusual events. Yet, Italy has rarely made the best use of this clause, since it has benefitted from numerous allowances over the past years with the purpose of avoiding VAT hikes and financing further current expenditures.[9]

To conclude, ruling majority parties in the Italian domestic legal order have been constantly attempting to avoid budgetary controls by watchdog institutions, trying instead to use accounting tricks to defer fiscal

[7] See the message sent by the Italian President of the Republic, Sergio Mattarella, to the 45th edition of The European House—Ambrosetti Forum in Villa d'Este on Lake Como, available at: https://www.quirinale.it/elementi/35612 (last accessed on September 30, 2019).

[8] In this respect, see also the proposal to protect investments linked to climate action made by the new Minister of Economy and Finance, Roberto Gualtieri, and put forward before the Eurogroup convening in Helsinki on September 13, 2019. Originally, the European Fiscal Board (EFB), in its assessment on the EU fiscal rules published on September 11, 2019, available at: www.ec.europa.eu, only vaguely suggested that in well-defined areas a "golden rule" could apply, yet under a strict monitoring system involving EU bodies. Cf. Bartolucci (2019).

[9] In this respect see the critical appraisal of the German Council of Economic Experts—Setting the Right Course for Economic Policy—Annual Report 2018/2019, in: www.sachverstaendigenrat-wirtschaft.de, 7 November 2018, 36–38.

consolidation and putting the blame on foreign states and EU institutions for their own meagre economic results. This practice hinges on a widespread populist justification, that is, meeting people's social and economic needs without surrendering to technocratic drifts or financial markets demands. Yet, populist policy-making in budget matters comes at the price of undermining the fiscal constitutional framework to the extent to hollow out its content or even to turn it into its very opposite. In this respect also, the 2012 constitutional amendment does not appear to have triggered a profound change in the Italian constitutional culture of budget constraints. The well-established narrative whereby fiscal rules are either not useful or they need to change every once in a while has, on the contrary, put not only general budgetary rules and principles as enshrined in Articles 81, 97 and 119 of the Constitution under an area of tension, but also the very idea of a non-arbitrary government under a Constitution.

What Remedies Against Constitutional Budgetary Populism?

The absence of a strong culture of constitutional resilience within Italian society, together with a significant resurgence of political constitutionalism, is a key factor in understanding the Italian populist challenge in general, and in budgetary matters in particular. The very political constitutionalist idea that the imperfections of democracy cannot be perfected by judicial review, but ought to be resolved within the same democratic procedures, has legitimized a widespread attitude of distrust by MPs and government members not only towards the constitutional fundamental rights of the individual, but also towards the same constitutional arrangements that political constitutionalists believe are the only viable means to work through the social disagreements on the common good and to come to enforceable collective decisions (see Bellamy 2007: 15–51).

In a nutshell, the "circumstances of politics" ended up offsetting the very idea of constitutionalism as one of preventing arbitrary rule, while, on the contrary, allowing rulers systematically not to be responsive to the ruled. When this happens, that is to say, when all self-policing and self-correcting mechanisms fail, a remedy should be granted, if necessary, this being also of a judicial nature. From a "thick" legal constitutional point of view, it remains therefore to be seen whether any mechanism exists in the Italian constitutional design that may bring about a trend reversion or, at least, minimize the populist detrimental effects to the country's liberal-democratic stability. In other words, insofar as there is little consensus within Italian society around a comprehensive conception of shared values as embodied by the Constitution, including, and most importantly, those of a procedural nature related to the law-making process, one should ask oneself whether there is any other method of establishing a deeper connection between its fundamental principles and society itself. Even though the basic structure of the Italian Constitution is not beyond politics and there is no solid identity (Portinaro 2018: 4–5; Dickie 2001: 17–33; Putnam 1993), or critical and distinctive mass of constitutional identity, one can argue, in fact, there is at least some political foundation of power relations, and the constitutional design provides the infrastructure for a politics of bounded, partisan, pluralist contestation, which can avoid a collapse of the constitutional order (cf. Choudhry 2018). Yet, this constitutional infrastructure, albeit existing, appears not to be able to self-enforce alone, therefore needing to be implemented by legal constitutional steps involving the Constitutional Court (see Sajò and Uitz 2017: 302 and ff.).

The Italian Constitutional Court has long refused to scrutinize budgetary questions, insofar as they represented discretionary political choices of resource allocation, upon which even a supreme judge would not enjoy the necessary expertise and/or legitimacy to adjudicate, for instance, as to whether funding was adequate or a correct assessment of coverage of expenditures took place. After the entering into force of the 2012 constitutional amendment, however, things abruptly changed. While some constitutional law scholars still doubted whether the new provisions were justiciable or not (see: Scaccia 2012), the Court started checking regional budgetary legislation challenged by the state against the coverage clause of the new Article 81 (3) IC. For the first time, the Court declared this provision as being the logic and necessary premise to achieve a balanced budget, as now stipulated by Article 81 (1) IC (Italian Constitutional Court, Judgments No. 70 and 115/2012). Against this background, the Court showed its readiness to declare single budgetary legal provisions null and void, insofar as they entailed spending or tax revenues without complying with a number of procedural requirements set out by the Law on Public Sector Accounting and Public Finance No. 196/2009. This Law substantially altered the conception of the budget law without a constitutional amendment yet being adopted by Parliament, thereby shifting the focus from the budget as a mere accounting document with no autonomous legislative content to the budget as a legislative planning instrument aimed at enabling both executive and legislature to evaluate how resources are being used and what socio-economic objectives should be achieved. At the same time, this piece of legislation envisaged multiple legal criteria to assess the correct quantification of financial resources when drawing up legislative measures implying new or increased expenditures or providing for the collection of new or increased taxes. These mandatory procedural requirements forced both regional and state governments to justify their own budgetary choices on the allocation of resources in order for them to be responsive to their own legislature bodies in the first place and, ultimately, also to the people.

A justification of budgetary items by the government, in fact, requires the striking of a transparent and reasonable balance between different constitutional interests at stake: ensuring a balanced budget or at least an adjustment towards the MTO, as routinely agreed with the European Commission; practising a loyal cooperation between state and territorial authorities, which avoids passing on the financial burden to the latter without their involvement; and, finally, making budgetary decisions dependent on the guarantee of the fundamental human rights' minimum core. Reconciling this sheer number of interests is, in the first place, a task of both the legislature and the executive when negotiating on a new multi-year budget and the Court cannot but remind them of their constitutional duty to do so. Yet, as a sort of guardian of Parliament's authority, the Court went a bit further and embraced a truly innovative constitutional narrative, according to which the budget is a "public good", whereby the people should be able to check for themselves how many resources have been collected and how they have been spent over the course of a parliamentary term.[10] If budgetary legislation embodies a number of unclear items, which can hardly be used to cover new expenditures or employs accounting technicalities to circumvent borrowing constraints, the people would purely and simply be deprived of their own right to a democratic representation as resulting from Article 1 (2) IC, insofar as incomplete and

[10] This idea has been first explicitly endorsed by the Italian Constitutional Court in its Judgment No. 184/2016, according to which "the budget is a 'public good' aimed at summarizing and providing certainty to the choices made by a territorial authority with regard both to the collection of revenues and to the implementation of public policies. Those carrying out an electoral mandate are in fact under the imperative duty of undergoing an assessment comparing what is promised with what is achieved" (translation by the author). This principle has been upheld and further elaborated by the Court in the subsequent Judgments, No. 228/2017, 247/2017 and No. 49/2018.

even false information by constitutional organs undermine voters' ability to assess and evaluate public policies. Therefore, the Constitutional Court should be able to adjudicate whether the use of legislative discretion in budgetary questions fulfils constitutional ends, and whenever this is not the case, restore the proper functioning of democratic constitutional procedures. Moreover, as long as such an interest in a democratic process in financial matters lacks a formal holder and is instead attributable to all individuals pertaining to a certain territorial community (*interessi adespoti*), the Constitutional Court also entrusted the Court of Auditors (*Corte dei conti*) with the power of raising the question of constitutionality, thus making budgetary constraints easier to be justiciable. The Court of Auditors judges, while reviewing the conformity of territorial entities and state budgets with legal accounting standards, are deemed to be better placed than other judges to evaluate to what extent single financial provisions avoid or defer fiscal consolidation in a detrimental way both to the functioning of democratic mechanisms, as well as to the interests of future generations (so, for instance, Judgment No. 18/2019).

Nonetheless, the yet to be explored function of the Court of Auditors as a gatekeeper to the constitutional judicial review of legislation in budgetary matters should not leave without notice that the Italian Constitutional Court still currently applies a certain self-restraint when confronted with fiscal questions, especially when directly related to the interpretation of the Parliament's internal rules of procedures (*regolamenti parlamentari*) on the relationship between legislature and executive. In this respect, it might be worth referring to Order No. 17/2019, by means of which the Court rejected to consider the challenge lodged by the Democratic Party parliamentary group in the Upper House of Parliament against the adoption of the yearly budget law, which the government had proudly renamed "people's budget" (*manovra del popolo*).[11] The claimants argued that the budget for the year 2019 was unlawfully rammed through the Italian Parliament. In fact, the cabinet sought a

[11] Quite ironically, this term was coined by the British Prime Minister David Lloyd George to refer to the budgetary draft law proposed by his liberal government with the aim of bringing about substantial wealth redistribution in the country and "eliminating poverty", a statement which also Italian Minister of Labour, Luigi di Maio, dared to make in 2018. The draft law was passed by the House of Commons in 1909, but was firmly rejected by the unelected House of Lords in 1910, thus causing a deep parliamentary crisis. The crisis was overcome in 1911 with the restriction of the Lords' powers and the reaffirmation of the Common's supremacy. (M. Russell, 2013: 27).

confidence vote (*questione di fiducia*) in Parliament after the former had replaced almost entirely the draft budget with its own amendment bill (*maxi-emendamento*). This tool entailed the outright rejection of all so far submitted parliamentary amendments, thus squeezing the amount of time available for discussion and forcing MPs to give their blank consent to the budget as enhanced by the government, unless they did not want the cabinet to resign and a government shutdown to occur as of January 1, 2019. Yet, the Court dismissed the appeal as inadmissible because the encroachment upon minorities' prerogative powers did not reach the threshold of evidence required by constitutional law to allow for a judicial review of legislation on grounds of a procedural defect. When it comes to applying the Houses' internal rules of procedure, in fact, the Parliament retains a high margin of appreciation, which means that the ruling majority has the power to make its own interpretation prevail. The well-established practice of replacing the draft budget under discussion with another text while at the same time resorting to a confidence vote has been acknowledged by the Court as being a standard practice of the ruling majority (Pistorio 2018; Di Porto 2017: 103 and ff.; De Lungo 2013). Even though this practice might at some point lead to a violation of MPs' prerogative powers, in the case at hand, it did not ultimately frustrate the ability of Parliament to carry out its constitutional functions, as at least some of the amendments put forward by MPs were included in the final correction bill rammed through the two Houses. Even aside from that, the parliamentary budgetary process was shortened on the grounds of a number of reasonable justifications, including the long exchange of views on the draft budget the cabinet had with the European Commission, which resulted in a full recalculation of the balances at an advanced stage of the parliamentary scrutiny. In addition, a recent amendment of the Upper House's internal rules of procedure and its first application to the budgetary process at hand might have, paradoxically (cf. Curreri 2019; Sorrentino 2019; Morrone 2019), contributed to restricting parliamentary prerogatives, thus explaining a provisional deviation from the correct parliamentary process. This deviation, if reiterated in the future, might not yet be further tolerated by the Court.

To conclude, the Italian Constitutional Court has become one of the last bastions against budgetary inconsistencies, which a populist understanding of public life has been fuelling over the last decades. The Court, however, has been balancing "idealism" and "realism" while exercising its review on government action and parliamentary legislation in budgetary matters. This means that in principle the Court feels bound to vindicate Parliament's core duties of scrutiny and oversight[12] whenever the government/parliamentary majority continuum attempts to overthrow the fundamentals of the Constitution, such as the division of powers and, more specifically, the normative machinery, which allows the Parliament to hold the government to account. In other words, the Court sees in political constitutionalism a doctrine potentially evolving in forms of populist-democratic politics and therefore opposes to it legal constitutional solutions aimed at restoring the sovereignty of the people, yet in the forms and within the limits of the Constitution, as Article 1 (2) IC stipulates.

On the other hand, the Court is cautious enough to restrain its consideration to the sole questions that are less political and thus less controversial than others. Therefore, even though it decided to grant remedies against accounting tricks leading to more deficit financing as well as against legislation disregarding budgetary constraints as a whole—remedies, which were unthinkable only a decade ago— –the Court, nonetheless, did not go so far as to doing away systematically with majority-led decisions in order for the Constitution to remain liberal (see Vermeule 2019). On the contrary, as also Order No. 17/2019 suggests, the Court fully acknowledged allegiance to the government and to the ruling majority power of adopting the budget and enacting the implementing law decrees, whereas at the same time it has been attempting to strengthen the procedural tools for genuine democratic participation. In particular, the Court eschews from arrogating to itself the power to replace the Parliament's will with its own, as it is perfectly aware that, by acting plainly in a counter-majoritarian way, it could exacerbate the populist backlash against non-directly elected bodies. Therefore, either it resorts to the instrument of deferring and postponing decisions in order to let the Parliament amend the unlawful situation or it declares legislation unlawful, it being then up to the Parliament to fill the void and restore an order in conformity with the Constitution. In this respect, the Court seeks to enable Parliament to better discharge its own constitutional duties, if necessary, even defending its prerogatives from their own misuse by the same legislature, as the Parliament sometimes appears prone to give up its task to hold the government to account (Lupo 2019: 255).

[12] Italian Constitutional Court, Judgment No. 165/1963, whereby "[former] Article 81 (1) IC accorded constitutional legal force to a normative accounting standard of the Italian pre-republican legal order, according to which the two Houses of Parliament are entrusted with the primary power to authorise the collection of taxes from the citizens as well as with that of controlling over public expenditures" (translation by the author).

References

Algebris Policy & Research Forum (Ed.). (2019, September). *Budgeting for Uncertainty. Time for Eurozone Fiscal Risk Sharing*, Issue 3. Available at: www.media.algrebris.com

Alvar Garcia, H. (2019). Neoliberalism as a Form of Authoritarian Constitutionalism. In G. Frankenberg & H. A. Garcia (Eds.), *Authoritarian Constitutionalism. Comparative Analysis and Critique* (pp. 37–56). Elgar: Cheltenham/Northampton.

Bartole, S. (2004). *Interpretazioni e trasformazioni della Costituzione repubblicana*. Bologna: Il Mulino.

Bartolucci, L. (2018). Sugli effetti di una ipotizzata rimozione delle "clausole europee" dalla Costituzione. *Osservatorio sulle Fonti, 3*, 1–14. Available at https://www.osservatoriosullefonti.it.

Bartolucci, L. (2019). *La riforma delle regole fiscali europee: la proposta dello European Fiscal Board*. Forum di Quaderni costituzionali (10), pp. 1–18. Available at: https://www.forumcostituzionale.it

Begg, I., & Featherstone, K. (2018). *From 'Vincolo Esterno' to 'Nemico Esterno': The Disturbing New Demonisation of the EU*. LSE Blogs. Available at: https://www.blogs.lse.ac.uk

Bellamy, R. (2007). *Political Constitutionalism*. Oxford: Oxford University Press.

Bergonzini, C. (2014). *Parlamento e decisioni di bilancio*. Milano: Giuffrè.

Bilancia, F. (2018). *The Italian Constitutional Conundrum and the Rise of Populism*. The Foundation for Law, Justice and Society, pp. 2–7. Available at: https://www.fljs.org

Blanchard, O., & Giavazzi, F. (2004). *Improving the SGP Through a Proper Accounting of Public Investment*. Centre for Economic Policy Research, Discussion Paper No. 4220.

Blokker, P. (2017). *Populist Constitutionalism*. I·CONnect. Available at: https://www.iconnectblog.com

Boggero, G., & Annicchino, P. (2014). Who Will Ever Kick Us Out? Italy, the Balanced Budget Rule and the Implementation of the Fiscal Compact. *European Public Law, 20*(2), 247–261.

Bognetti, G. (1995). *La Costituzione economica italiana*. Milano: Giuffrè.

Buchanan, J. M., & Wagner, R. E. (1977/2000). Democracy in Deficit: The Political Legacy of Lord Keynes. In H. G. Brennan, H. Kliemt, & R. D. Tollison (Eds.), *The Collected Works of James M. Buchanan* (Vol. 8). Indianapolis: Liberty Fund.

Camera dei Deputati (Ed.). (2019). *Osservatorio sulla legislazione, Rapporto 2017–2018*. Available at: www.camera.it

Carli, G. (1996). *Cinquant'anni di vita italiana*. Bari: Laterza.

Choudhry, S. (2018). *Constitutional Resilience to Populism: Four Theses*. Verfassungsblog.de, Available at: https://www.verfassungsblog.de

Curreri, S. (2019). *L'occasione persa (prime note sull'ordinanza n. 17/2019 della Corte costituzionale)*. Federalismi.it, 4, pp. 1–9. Available at: https://www.federalismi.it

De Filio, G., & Vicchiarello, P. (2018). *La strettoia. La copertura finanziaria come strumento di contenimento dell'attività legislativa di iniziativa parlamentare.* Napoli: Jovene.

De Lungo, D. (2013). *Tendenze e prospettive evolutive del maxiemendamento nell'esperienza della XV e della XVI legislatura.* Rivista AIC, *3*, pp. 1–13. Available at: https://www.rivistaaic.it

Delledonne, G. (2014). A Legalization of Financial Constitutions in the EU? Reflections on the German, Italian, Spanish and French Experience. In M. Adams, F. Fabbrini, & S. Larouche (Eds.), *The Constitutionalization of European Budgetary Constraints* (pp. 181–204). Oxford/Portland: Hart Publishing.

Di Porto, V. (2017). La problematica prassi dei maxiemendamenti dei maxiemendamenti e il dialogo a distanza tra Corte costituzionale e Comitato per la legislazione. In V. Lippolis & N. Lupo (Eds.), *Il Parlamento dopo il referendum costituzionale (Il Filangieri. Quaderno 2015–2016)* (pp. 103–115). Jovene: Napoli.

Dickie, J. (2001). The Notion of Italy. In Z. G. Baranski & R. J. West (Eds.), *The Cambridge Companion to Modern Italian Culture* (pp. 17–33). Cambridge: Cambridge University Press.

Dornbusch, R., & Edwards, S. (1991). *The Macroeconomics of Populism in Latin America*. Chicago: Chicago University Press.

Einaudi, L. (1956). *Lo Scrittoio del Presidente.* Torino: Einaudi.

Francaviglia, M. (2019). Populismo, Costituzione e decisione di spesa pubblica: c'è spazio per le future generazioni? In G. Allegri, A. Sterpa, & N. Viceconte (Eds.), *Questioni costituzionali al tempo del populismo e del sovranismo* (p. 2019). Napoli: Jovene.

Gianniti, L. (2011). *Il pareggio di bilancio nei lavori della Costituente.* Astrid Rassegna. Available at: https://www.astrid-online.it

Ifo Institute (Ed.). (2017). *Economic Policy and the Rise of Populism – It's Not So Simple.* The EEAG Report on the European Economy, Munich. Available at: www.cesifo-group.de

Lupo, N. (2019). Populismo legislativo?: continuità e discontinuità nelle tendenze della legislazione italiana. *Ragion Pratica, 52*, 251–271.

Miglio, A. (2019). *Le incertezze dell'Italexit tra regole costituzionali interne e diritto dell'Unione europea.* Federalismi.it, 12, pp. 1–30. Available at: https://www.federalismi.it

Modugno, F. (1979). È illegittimo l'art. 189 del Trattato di Roma nella interpretazione della Corte di giustizia delle Comunità europee? *Giurisprudenza costituzionale, 24*(1), 916–938.

Morrone, A. (2019). *Lucciole per lanterne. La n. 17/2019 e la terra promessa di quote di potere per il singolo parlamentare.* Federalismi.it, 4, pp. 1–9. Available at: https://www.federalismi.it

Mostacci, E. (2016). From the Ideological Neutrality to the Neoclassical Inspiration: The Evolution of the Italian Constitutional Law of Debt and Deficit. In F. L. Morrison (Ed.), *Fiscal Rules – Limits on Governmental Deficits and Debt* (pp. 173–204). Cham: Springer International.

Mudde, C. (2004). The Populist Zeitgeist. *Government and Opposition, 39*(4), 541–563.

Onida, V. (1969). *Le leggi di spesa nella Costituzione*. Milano: Giuffrè.

Pistorio, G. (2018). *Maxi-emendamento e questione di fiducia*. Napoli: ES.

Portinaro, P. (2018). *Le mani su Machiavelli. Critica dell'Italian Theory*. Roma: Donzelli.

Putnam, R. (1993). *Making Democracy Work. Civic Traditions in Modern Italy*. Princeton: Princeton University Press.

Russell, M. (2013). *The Contemporary House of Lords: Westminster Bicameralism Revived*. Oxford: Oxford University Press.

Sajò, A., & Uitz, R. (2017). *The Constitution of Freedom. An Introduction to Legal Constitutionalism*. Oxford: Oxford University Press.

Santagostino, A. (2017). *Luigi Einaudi, the Father of the Fathers of Europe*. Cambridge: Cambridge Scholars Publishing.

Scaccia, G. (2012). La giustiziabilità della regola del pareggio di bilancio. In V. Lippolis, N. Lupo, G. Salerno, & G. Scaccia (Eds.), *Costituzione e pareggio di bilancio (Il Filangieri. Quaderno 2011)* (pp. 211–248). Jovene: Napoli.

Sorrentino, F. (2019). *La legge di bilancio tra Governo e Corte costituzionale: il Parlamento approva a scatola chiusa*. Federalismi.it, 4, pp. 1–6. Available at: https://www.federalismi.it

Tanzi, V. (2018). *Termites of the State: Why Complexity Leads to Inequality*. Cambridge: Cambridge University Press.

Vernata, A. (2017). L'Ufficio parlamentare di bilancio. *Diritto pubblico, 23*(2), 469–514.

Vermeule, A. (2019). All Human Conflict Is Ultimately Theological. *Church Life Journal – University of Notre Dame*. Available at: https://www.churchlife-journal.nd.eu

PART II

CHAPTER 9

Italian Populism and Fake News on the Internet: A New Political Weapon in the Public Discourse

Matteo Monti

Introduction

Scholars acknowledge the fundamental contribution of the press in informing and shaping public opinion, as well as ensuring the accountability of government (Norris 2008: 186–187). The press is "the bible of democracy, the book out of which a people determines its conduct" (Lippmann 1920: 47). Western constitutionalism has developed this concept of the press within two different models: the European one and the US one. The two models are heralds of two opposite paradigms when it comes to freedom of information, that is, the *species* of the *genus* of freedom of expression that describes the activity of news diffusion. The

M. Monti (✉)
Scuola Sant'Anna, Pisa, Italy
e-mail: matteo.monti@sssup.it

G. Delledonne et al. (eds.), *Italian Populism and Constitutional Law*, Challenges to Democracy in the 21st Century,
https://doi.org/10.1007/978-3-030-37401-3_9

European systems[1] have codified the right to be informed[2] and the need to respect the truth.[3] By contrast, older constitutional systems, such as that of the United States of America, formulated this idea without the use of legal tools.[4] In the range of European systems, the Italian model could be considered, using Hirschl's categorisation (Hirschl 2014: 256 and ff.), as a prototype case regarding both the freedom of information paradigm and the massive use of fake news by populist movements.

The aim of this chapter is to explore the instruments and possible solutions available in Italian constitutional law to combat the populist use of fake news.

As a preliminary, it is necessary to frame the fake news problem and its use by populist movements. For the purposes of this chapter, fake news is a piece of news—*id est*, an output of journalism—that is invented and false—*id est*, it is based on invented or non-existent facts or events—.[5] As an example of fake news, one could recall the false scandal regarding the presence of members of the Italian government and the Democratic Party at the funeral of the Mafia leader Toto Riina (Il Fatto Quotidiano 2017). The current spread of fake news seems to be connected with two

[1] *Ex pluribus* "Whilst the First Amendment addresses mainly the active dimension to the right to express freely one's own thoughts, Article 10 of the European Convention (but also Article 11 of the Charter of Fundamental Rights of the European Union) emphasises the passive dimension to the right to be pluralistically informed. In this respect, it could be argued that fake news is not constitutionally covered by the European vision of free speech" (Pollicino 2017: 25).

[2] See Article 5 of the German Basic Law. Regarding the Italian legal system, see *ex pluribus*, *Corte costituzionale*, judgments no. 348/1990 and 1/1981.

[3] See, *ex pluribus*, Art. 20 of the Spanish Constitution, which explicitly refers to: "the right to freely communicate or receive *truthful* information by any means of dissemination whatsoever" (my italics).

[4] So-called objective journalism—in which 'objective' does not mean impartial or with an absence of bias (Cf. American Press Institute, *The lost meaning of 'objectivity'*, available at https://www.americanpressinstitute.org/journalism-essentials/bias-objectivity/lost-meaning-objectivity/)—was born in the US with Adolph S. Ochs at the end of the nineteenth century and became dominant during the twentieth century (see Mindich 1998 and cf. Bennett 2016: 161).

[5] This is a very simple definition and a minimalistic one (cf. Wardle 2017), but methodologically speaking, it seems to be the only acceptable definition of fake news, and can accommodate the most modern theory of the narration of facts (cf. *ex pluribus* Foucault 1970). Of course, this definition of fake news applies just to the particular category of *news* and not, for example, to satirical speech, which is protected in Italy (Bevere and Cerri 2006: 265) even if false, or to political ideologies, which cannot be defined as either true or false.

correlated phenomena: the new 'mediated populism' (Mazzoleni 2008) and the role assumed by Internet platforms in the news ecosystem. In a framework where traditional media have lost credibility and it is possible to create fake news through Internet platforms, populist movements have exploited sensational and viral fake news to gain a consensus and a substantial increase in their voting shares. The aforementioned phenomena seem, at least in part, to be mutually correlated. On the one hand, fake news has always existed, but the advent of the Internet has facilitated its widespread diffusion, given the lack of ethical rules of journalism on Internet platforms and the absence of control over news diffusion. On the other hand, the use of fake news as a political weapon by populist movements seems to be the main reason for its widespread diffusion: from this point of view, it is likely that the fake news issue would be less dangerous if it arose solely for economic motives or reasons. Populist fake news concerns some of the issues covered in the other chapters of this book (science and democracy, the public use of religious discourse, migration, criminal law).

This chapter is structured as follows. The first section will explore the constitutional framework of freedom of information in the Italian legal system, with particular regard to new Internet media. The second section will study the problem of the use of fake news by populist movements. In the third section, a number of possible solutions will be proposed.

Fake News and the Paradigm of Freedom of Information in Italy: The Advent of Internet Platforms

The phenomenon of populist fake news on the Internet will be explored through the analysis of the fundamental principles of freedom of information and media freedom as enshrined in the Italian constitutional system (for a more in-depth analysis, written in English, of media freedom in Italy, see Casarosa and Brogi 2014; Monti 2017).

The Italian system is characterised by a pervasive regulation of the media that aims to ensure the pluralism of the system even under conditions of monopoly, and substantive rules concerning the products of journalism and the press: it is "a 'constitutional imperative' that 'the freedom of information', guaranteed by Article 21 of the Constitution, should be qualified and characterised, inter alia, by the pluralism of the sources (...)

and by the objectivity and impartiality of the provided data, and finally by the completeness, correctness and continuity of the information activity" (*Corte costituzionale*, judgment no. 155/2002, my translation).[6] This because the mass media "have to be considered in our legal system (...) as a public service or at least as a public interest service" (*Corte costituzionale*, judgment no. 94/1977, my translation).[7]

From the substantive point of view, the Constitutional Court has claimed on many occasions that freedom of information is 'essential' to the system of freedoms guaranteed by the Constitution and to democracy (*ex pluribus*, *Corte costituzionale*, judgments no. 348/1990 and 1/1981). Furthermore, freedom of information is built on both an active feature and a passive one: the active feature is the freedom to inform, while the passive one is the right to be informed (*ex pluribus*, see what is stressed in the very clear judgment of the *Corte costituzionale*, judgment no. 112/1993). From this perspective, it can be affirmed that the passive feature—the right to be informed—is strongly connected to the necessity of observing the truth of facts or the rectification of falsehoods.[8] The correlation between the spread of news and the banning of fake news was stated by the Italian Constitutional Court in an *obiter dictum*: "the right to obtain, to publish and to submit news to public opinion must be compliant with the (substantial) truth of the facts" (*Corte costituzionale*, judgment no. 16/1981, my translation). From this perspective, it has to be stressed that the Court has also affirmed that the criminal sanction for fake news, as provided by Article 656 of the Italian Criminal Code, is consistent with the Constitution.[9] Italian schol-

[6] Additionally, "[T]he information, in its passive and active features, expresses not only a subject, but rather a "precondition" or an "irrepressible requirement" for the implementation at any level, central or local, of the correct features of a democratic state". *Corte costituzionale*, judgment no. 29/1996 (translated by Casarosa and Brogi 2014: 103).

[7] "Quite importantly, the CC has also acknowledged that the freedom of expression and media freedom enjoy an equal position as constitutional values, though the latter must be interpreted as instrumental to the former" (Casarosa and Brogi 2014: 105). The authors cited the *Corte costituzionale* judgment no. 48/1969.

[8] The correction process—see below—is linked with human fundamental rights and with the public interest in the objectivity of news, as claimed by the *Corte costituzionale*, judgment no. 133/1974.

[9] *Corte costituzionale*, judgments no. 19/1962, 199/1972 and 210/1976. However, it has to be emphasised that the Court has upheld the lawfulness of the *criminal censorship* of fake news only when there is a risk to public order.

arship, independently of the adhesion to an individualistic theory of free speech (i.e., a sort of American vision) or a functionalist theory of free speech (a vision more similar to the German idea), seems to have considered subjectively false statements not to be guaranteed by Article 21 of the Constitution (see and cf. Barile 1953: 121; Esposito 1958: 37; Fois 1957: 210–211; Pace 2006: 89). Looking at the case law of the Constitutional Court, this seems quite clear so far as concerns falsehoods in the news field.

In the Italian legal system, the way to affirm fact-based information and to avoid the diffusion of fake news is complicated, and is based on different factors: the presence of a Journalists' Association (*Ordine dei giornalisti*) and journalists' adherence to the Journalist Code of Ethics enshrined in law; criminal and civil sanctions and fines for the diffusion of fake news; and legal tools to 'correct' fake news that has already been diffused. The Journalists' Association—which the Constitutional Court has decided is compatible with the Constitution (*Corte costituzionale*, judgments no. 11/1968 and 98/1968)—has its own rules, which include respect for the truth (with the possibility of imposing sanctions on journalists spreading fake news and an obligation to correct fake news).[10] The civil and criminal sanctions for fake news in the news field are contained in Article 656 of the Criminal Code (diffusion of fake news), Article 595 of the Criminal Code (defamation) and Articles 185 and 186 of the consolidated law on financial intermediation (*Testo unico in materia di intermediazione finanziaria*). [11] In this matter, the case law of ordinary courts has argued that the limit of the truth of facts is directly related to the main outputs of journalism (*right of chronicle*, *right of critique*—right to criticise—and *investiga-*

[10]Article 2 of law no. 69/1963 (the Journalists' Code of Ethics) requires respect for the truth: journalists working for news broadcasters, newspapers, and so on must scrupulously endeavour to report the truth and rectify falsehoods. As stressed by the Supreme Criminal Court: "the correction of false news is, for the journalist, mandatory" (*Cassazione penale*, judgment no. 16323/2006).

[11]Of course, it has to be remembered that a journalist cannot be convicted of a crime if he or she has checked his or her sources of information (unless there is negligence).

tive reports).[12] Finally, the instrument of rectification,[13] both on television and in newspapers, has opened the possibility of correcting *ex post* the diffusion of fake news by allowing the audience that has read or watched the fake news to receive a correction. The legal discipline of the rectification of fake news is complex (see Monti 2018: 19 and ff.), and it can be applied under three different circumstances: rectification as the duty of a journalist imposed by Article 2 of law no. 69/1963 (the Journalists' Code of Ethics), correction as a consequence of a judicial decision, and correction in the media at the request of an individual. The last of these was originally applicable to broadcasting pursuant to law no. 223/1990[14] and to newspapers pursuant to law no. 47/1948 (see Article 8 of law no. 47/1948). The rectification must be made in the same *locus* as that in which the fake news was diffused, so that it can be read or watched by the same audience. Thus, it must be made in the same newspaper's pages or the same broadcasted programme.

Against this background, the utilisation of fake news as a political weapon was almost impossible before the advent of the Internet: the creation of fake news was complicated, because traditional media rarely spread it, and although populist movements could try to diffuse it, there was a

[12] See the ordinary court's categorisation of the *right of chronicle*, the *right of critique* (right to criticise) and *investigative reports*. The first of these is the simple right to report facts as news, and it requires a check on the sources of information in order for the reporter not to be prosecuted if the news is fake news (for defamation matters, see: *Cassazione penale*, judgment of 7 July 1987; for the application of a fake news criminal provision see: Tribunal of Milano decision of 16 May 2011). The *right of critique* is the freedom to criticise an idea, event, news item, and so forth, and in judicial applications this requires minor attention to the truthfulness of the event that is commented on and critiqued, but the use of fake news is prohibited (*ex pluribus*, *Cassazione penale*, judgment no. 15236/2005. Concerning the need to check the facts, see: *Cassazione penale*, judgment of 16 March 1993). Finally, *investigative reports* are expositions of theories about incomplete and unverifiable facts; in judicial applications a check on the sources of information is less necessary, and the utilisation of a doubting tone in the article is sufficient to avoid fines and sanctions (*ex pluribus*, *Cassazione penale*, judgment no. 9337/2012).

[13] In order to translate this very particular legal instrument into English, the same terminology is used as in Article 16 of Regulation (EU) 2016/679, which seems to be aimed at achieving a very similar purpose.

[14] See Art. 10 of law no. 223/1990. The individual has the right to ask for the correction of reported falsehoods. If the television channel or news broadcaster does not correct the falsehood, the individual has the right to appeal to the Communications Authority, which can require the correction of the falsehood.

serious risk that it would be detected and debunked by the press:[15] "While the mass media adhere to professional norms and news values, social media serve as direct linkage to the people and allow the populists to circumvent the journalistic gatekeepers. In this way, social media provide the populists with the freedom to uncontestably articulate their ideology and spread their messages" (Engesser et al. 2016: 1110). Indeed, with the advent of Internet media and their associated platforms, there has been a dramatic change in the media landscape,[16] and this has changed the rules of communication.[17] "As the role of information gatekeeper starts to pass from journalists at legacy news organizations to engineers, coders, and designers, the very nature of the Fourth Estate and the news it produces is changing. While their aspirations may be sweeping, platform executives have not indicated a desire to be a Fourth Estate" (Carroll 2017: 71). With traditional media having been bypassed, traditional tools of control over the truth of information have disappeared (cf. Floridi 1996): the lack of ethical rules and legal standards in relation to the news being diffused has made the massive spread of fake news possible.

Regarding this topic, it has to be stressed how Internet platforms (search engines and social networks) have acquired a vitally important role in the world of information and news diffusion: more than one Italian in three uses search engines and social networks to find news (AgCom 2018: 42). The lack of regulation of Internet platforms (on the general problem concerning the issue of freedom of information, see Monti 2017) and the absence of rules of journalism on them (on the form of the 'production' and distribution of news and the media logic of Internet platforms, see Klinger and Svensson 2015: 1246 and ff.) has allowed populist movements to distort the 'rules' of the freedom of information and to distribute fake news, contaminating the public discourse. This is an innovative challenge for the Italian constitutional model of freedom of information.

[15] In the past, the only way in which populist movements were able to win the battle against the media was by conquering their power and creating forms of authoritarian control over them, as the Latin American populist phenomena have shown (Waisbord 2018: 25).

[16] "Our news ecosystem has changed more dramatically in the past five years than perhaps at any time in the past five hundred" (Bell 2016).

[17] "[T]he communication environment that has been developing with the expansion of the Internet and of digital technology has impressively changed the rules of the game and has made available to political actors an unprecedented abundance of communication tools: new platforms, new outlets, social media with potentially huge publics" (Mazzoleni and Bracciale 2018: 3).

Indeed, "those with an economic and/or political interest in the dissemination of false news are now far better equipped than in the past to deliver their content to those they most desire to reach. Targeting exclusively right- or left-leaning news consumers (or other, more specific political traits) with false news or information has never been easier" (Napoli 2018: 75). There are numerous new phenomena that are having an impact on these unregulated media and thus contributing to the spread of fake news; these include the influence of 'prior convictions' (Sunstein 2014: 75 and ff.), 'virality' (Howell 2013; Vis 2014; Bessi et al. 2015), the so-called social cascade (Sunstein 2014: 40, 48), echo chambers (Sunstein 2007; Nikolov et al. 2015), or filter bubbles (Pariser 2011; Flaxman et al. 2016: 298 and ff.) and a general 'collective credulity' that seems to operate on the Internet (Mocanu et al. 2015). All these phenomena are at the heart of the success of the political weapon of fake news as used by populist movements. To date, search engines and social networks have not developed efficient solutions to counter the spread of fake news (Monti 2018).

Fake News and Populism: Between Political Propaganda and Media Regulation

The connection between populism and Internet platforms could be framed in the definition of 'mediated populism' (Mazzoleni 2008), meaning a sort of 'new logic of political communication' (Chakravartty and Roy 2015). The use of fake news by populist movements will be studied below in the wider scenario of the relationship between the Internet and political communication, in which it appears that populist movements have been able to exploit these new media better than 'traditional' political actors (Kalia et al. 2018). From this starting point, it is necessary to underline the fact that the paradigm of the freedom of information seems to have been deeply distorted by the advent of the mix between the unregulated new media (Internet platforms) and the rise of populism. Indeed, "[p]opulism embraces the notion that truth does not exist as a common good. Truth as a collective enterprise is dismissed as a pure ideological illusion of liberalism (...). Truth is divided, partisan, and ideological; it is anchored in particular social interests. Truth-seeking politics is about reaffirming 'popular' truths against 'élite' lies" (Waisbord 2018: 29).

In Italy, this assumption has led to the spread of fake news by populist movements. According to some commentators, the Five Star Movement

(Movimento 5 Stelle) made substantial use of the weapon of fake news, gaining advantages from this.[18] Indeed, BuzzFeed's investigative reports (Nardelli and Silverman 2016, 2017) underlined the point that there may be websites that are politically close to the Movement (and to Lega Nord) that have diffused fake news against immigrants and the establishment. In addition, through the social network accounts of its supporters and sometimes of its members, the Movement shared (perhaps in good faith, but perhaps not) fake news that strongly influenced many electoral campaigns, including the most recent one for the national elections. For example, before the constitutional referendum, the most frequently shared news on Facebook was the fake news that half a million ballot papers had been faked to enable the side voting in favour of the constitutional amendment—the Democratic Party's side—to win (Pagella Politica 2016). Also, in the last general election, the role of fake news seems to have favoured the populist movements (Trevisan 2018). Finally, in May 2019, Facebook erased some Facebook pages spreading fake news; according to the press, more than half of these were pages that supported the Italian populist government, which was composed of the Five Star Movement and Lega (Amabile 2019).

The reaction of the Five Star Movement to the BuzzFeed and *New York Times* reports (Horowitz 2017) was to accuse its opponents of spreading fake news about the Movement (Phelan 2017). Mr. Grillo, the founder of the Movement, has repeatedly attacked the traditional press[19] and its role (one of the main topics addressed by the Movement is the media: Manucci and Amsler 2018). In addition, as regards the attempts made by the Italian parliament to enact a law that would have regulated the news on the web, and the declarations of the president of the Italian competition authority (*Autorità Garante della Concorrenza e del Mercato*—AGCM) about fake

[18] There were also other reasons: "Several factors have contributed to the rise and consolidation of populist parties and movements in Europe and other countries. Among others, the spread of fake news on the Internet, the educational divide, the adverse effects of financial crisis, and more recently, the emergence of international terrorism are often ranked among the causes for the populist surge" (Bassini 2019: 316).

[19] "The other 'caste' targeted by Grillo is that of journalists, daily newspapers, and television companies. His criticism of the news media mirrors that of the parties: they are accused of being in cahoots with big political and economic interests, of hiding the truth and of dulling the consciousness of citizens" (Bordignon and Ceccarini 2013: 433). See the video posted by the newspaper *Corriere della sera*: http://video.corriere.it/beppe-grillo-contro-giornalisti-vi-mangerei-il-gusto-vomitarvi/be9643fc-9d2f-11e7-bc32-abadbc125b15

news, the reaction of the Five Star Movement was highly disappointing. Mr. Grillo commented that elites were trying to act as "the new inquisitors of the web", and that they wanted to create "a court to control and condemn [those] who disgrace them" (Ansa 2016, my translation), which showed that he did not believe that fake news was a problem in the public debate.

From this point of view, a distinction has to be made between news and political propaganda. As previously stressed, the lack of interest by populist movements in truth-seeking in political communication (Waisbord 2018) is not of relevance for constitutional law, but what is relevant is the fact that their own lack of interest is contaminating the paradigm of the freedom of information. It is true that political lies, and even the use of fake news by politicians, are—subject to the limits of defamation—protected expressions under Article 21 of the Constitution, according to the principle of the marketplace of ideas in political issues.[20] Trying to censor a political actor for the fake news that he or she has diffused would be an infringement of the freedom of expression that is guaranteed by Article 21 of the Constitution: a politician who affirms, for instance, that there is a new European tax or that immigrants have destroyed a police car (which were two very well-known fake news stories in Italy) cannot be censured. It is the role of the press to detect these claims and debunk them as fake news. However, the issue changes when looking at the 'sources of production' of these fake news pieces, independently from their production by a party's newspaper, a website or other media. Indeed, as has been said, the production of news as an output of the freedom of information is connected with the duty of respecting the truth or, more properly, the duty not to use actual malice to create fake news; the news has a particular role in the Italian legal system since it is connected to the traditional role of the press in informing public opinion and holding governments accountable.

Consequently, it is possible to speculate about how to deal with sources of fake news on the Internet (that is, with websites and accounts creating and diffusing fake news) that simulate to be a newspaper or a journalist that has the responsibility of informing the audience (following the ethical rules of narrating the facts of what has happened). Indeed, because there are unregulated and innovative media such as Internet platforms, populist

[20] The principle of the so-called marketplace of ideas in the political field within the European framework finds its sole limit in the prohibition of racist hate speech (Stradella 2008).

movements have created a new form of political communication—the use of fake news—that can rank as news despite being false, given the difficulty of discrediting it. Thus, fake news is handed out as fact, and it influences public opinion and public debate by introducing false information and non-existent events: sharing a fake journalism article describing an invented fact from a false newspaper, or a counterfeit video, or a report by a fake journalist who has created the news, is a disruptive way to pollute public discourse.

The Internet's unregulated market of news is the perfect habitat for populist movements intending to use fake news as a political weapon to destroy the reputations of their opponents or to orient the public debate towards their major political points.

Constitutional Challenges and Possible Solutions

Nowadays, populist movements are exploiting Internet platforms to improve their propaganda, and are taking advantage of the fake news created by their supporters, foreign propaganda entities, or simply people who want to gain money from click-baiting.

The problem with this phenomenon is the way in which it is transforming the constitutional model of the freedom of information as the cornerstone of liberal democracy. The idea of the press as the watchdog of democracy may disappear because of the populist use of fake news. The role of the press as a tool to inform public opinion of facts and to hold governments accountable using descriptions of events has been deeply distorted by the advent of unregulated Internet media and the utilisation of these media by populist movements. Given the fact that the solutions developed by social networks and search engines have not worked very well (Monti 2018), and that the marketplace of ideas seems to be unable to react independently to the spread of fake news on the Internet (Pitruzzella 2018: 36; Napoli 2018), it is necessary to regulate these new media and to develop solutions that could help to prevent the spread of fake news on the Internet, particularly in the results from search engines and on social networks. In this perspective, it could be useful to remember that in its case law the Constitutional Court has stated that there is a need to regulate, in a more timely and complete manner, mass media that are pervasive and 'influential' for public discourse. "The acknowledgment of the peculiar diffusion and pervasiveness of the television message (...) is well-known and has been consistently affirmed in the case law of this

Court, so as to justify the adoption, targeting only broadcasting stations, of a rigorous discipline capable of preventing any inappropriate conditioning in the formation of the will of the voters" (*Corte costituzionale*, judgment no. 155/2002, my translation).

In this prescriptive and normative section, some workable solutions are proposed that are consistent with the paradigm of the freedom of information and could help the constitutional system to react to the challenges of populism in the field of the free press (for a broader analysis of the proposed solution, see Monti 2018: 18 and ff.). As previously stated, in the Italian context the only practicable and permissible regulatory solution is to act on the sources of information and on the media that are creating and spreading fake news (that is, Internet media). To fulfil the constitutional principles concerning freedom of information and to respect the right to be informed, an applicable (co)regulation is desirable (regarding the necessity for the general regulation of Internet platforms, see Monti 2017). Against this background, a discipline similar to that of *rectification* could be used to correct fake news on Internet platforms, with this tool obviously being adapted to the new Internet media and with due regard being paid to the fact that these new media are not managed by journalists, and, consequently, are not bound by the deontological code.

Regarding search engines, the Internet corporations could be forced to develop tools for de-indexing fake news websites once their nature has been checked by independent authorities or fact-checking and bipartisan agencies. This solution seems to be quite similar to that proposed by the former president of the Italian competition authority (Politi 2016; Pitruzzella 2018), but it is also what search engine companies are trying to do when they de-index fake news websites (as reported by Ansa 2017) or websites without an identification of their location (La Repubblica 2017), or when they use some type of 'fact checked' tag in order to describe websites after they have undergone scrutiny by fact-checking agencies (Betti 2017). In addition, it could be possible to prevent fake news websites from receiving advertising income in order to make the generation of fake news websites uneconomic (High Level Group on fake news and online disinformation 2018: 15). In the case of a website part of whose content is fake news, it may be possible to apply an instrument of rectification aimed solely at requiring the website to correct the fake news by posting articles with the same visibility, and giving those articles adequate publicity. The main problem with this solution is linked to 'collateral censorship' (Wu 2011): who makes sure that search engines are not removing partisan websites along with fake news websites? And more importantly, what are the precise characteristics of fake news websites? Starting with the definition given in this paper, fake news websites should be identified as websites that, with *actual malice*, produce a large amount of fake news. It is clear that without the participation of an impartial actor in the checking process, the risk posed to political thought and speech is high. For this reason, it would be necessary to create a private–public process with the participation of an independent authority (as suggested by Pitruzzella 2018: 25), as is the case for the process of rectification originally developed for broadcasters. This process would be founded on so-called *objective truth*, that is, on verifying that contested facts are actually fake, with the possibility of an appeal to the Communications Authority (Autorità per le Garanzie nelle Comunicazioni—AgCom) to check the authenticity of the news in the case of broadcasting media who refuse to correct a particular fake news item. In Italy, there are many tools for removing and de-indexing a website from a page ranking (Pretelli 2016: 359–385), and a law could require search engines to de-index fake news websites after they have been evaluated by a third-party and impartial arbiter (which could be the Ordine dei giornalisti, a court, or an independent agency, such as the Communications Authority) with the possibility of an appeal. Ultimately, the solution of de-indexing fake news websites could work well, both to prevent the phenomenon of the spread of fake news and to transform the search engines into media corporations.

Concerning the role of social networks in the spreading of fake news, one can claim that the solutions developed by Facebook[21] seem to have failed in the task of fighting fake news. Facebook's so-called *Fact-check partnership* (Isaac 2016; Mosseri 2016; cf. Pennycook et al. 2017; Ananny 2018)[22] and its questions testing the credibility of sources of news (Kantrowitz 2018) have not worked very well. Again, a good solution for the spread of fake news on Facebook could be derived from the Italian law regarding the rectification/correction of fake news. A similar mechanism to that developed for the broadcasting media could be applied, requiring

[21] The choice to focus on Facebook and not on other social networks has been made because Mark Zuckerberg's social network is the most popular social network in Italy. See, for the Italian scenario, the data reported here: https://vincos.it/2018/10/22/censis-i-consumi-mediali-degli-italiani-nel-2018/

[22] The solution has had problems with, inter alia, sluggish 'virality' and the ability to reach every user who has received the fake news.

that the correction be posted in the same place as the original fake news after a check by an independent authority has confirmed its falsity. The mechanism should be changed slightly so that it is equal to the challenges posed by the new media environment: indeed, merely correcting the sources of fake news (which are, in many cases, websites) will not affect the sharing of the fake news on social networks. Thus, in addition to a correction on the original website, a law could require Facebook to advertise the correction to users who had interacted with the fake news by sharing, commenting on, or liking it. After a warning by users, a law could require Facebook to redirect the news to an independent authority, a bipartisan agency or some other agency (e.g., the *Ordine dei giornalisti*, a court, or an independent agency, such as the Communications Authority), which could determine its truth or falsity (in a very similar way to the current methods used by the fact-checking partnership). In the case of a 'go ahead', the fake news could be marked as fake news, so that future readers on social networks could be informed. In addition, a notification of the rectification of the fake news (something like 'dear user, be aware that you have recently read fake news') could be sent to users, by posting the rectification in the misinformed user's newsfeed or wall or in place of Facebook's 'good morning' at the top of the newsfeed. In this way, all users who had interacted with the fake news would be informed of its rectification.[23] Furthermore, a law could require Facebook to ban the pages used to spread fake news, or to force pages that only occasionally disseminate fake news to rectify falsehoods with another post 'promoting' the rectification. The first solution seems to have been followed recently by Facebook, which has censored some Facebook pages that only spread fake news (Amabile 2019). This action was probably taken to follow the guidelines of the EU *Code of Practice on Disinformation*. The problem with this type of action, as with the actions encouraged by the Code of Practice, is that collateral censorship or, to put it better, the privatisation of censorship, without an independent check such as a check by an independent authority, risks undermining political speech and free speech (for reasons of space this problem cannot be analysed here, but see Monti 2019).

[23] It should be noted that even where robots operate, for example on Twitter, it seems to have been proved that the reason for the diffusion of fake news is linked to human users (see Vosoughi et al. 2018).

Looking at public actions, given the attempts that have failed in parliament,[24] a system called the 'Red Button Project' seems to have become active in informing the Polizia Postale (the police department responsible for addressing crimes linked to the Internet)[25] about possible fake news: The police will check fake news, and, in case of falsehoods, will obscure/block the news, rectify it with their websites or transfer the matter to a prosecutor. The legal basis for this procedure seems to be uncertain and its actual and current mode of operation and current operability are not clear. Without checks being made by an independent authority (a judge or another impartial actor), this solution does not seem desirable either, given the risk of government censorship that it could involve.

While the actions developed by Facebook and the Polizia Postale raise concerns about respect for free speech, the solutions proposed here would be consistent with Article 21 of the Italian Constitution. On the one hand, they would protect the right to be informed, without using criminal law to accomplish this aim,[26] and on the other, they would bring into the procedure independent and impartial actors, avoiding censorship power being conferred on the police, the government, or private corporations. Finally, it must be stressed that both the solutions proposed (the removal from the page ranking/Facebook and the rectification) could be useful and effective from a sociological point of view as well, because, as claimed (Sunstein 2014: 75, 80), the "credibility of the source of the correction" (an independent agency, etc.) could be the only method of facilitating the debunking of fake news.[27] In addition, as suggested by some scholars (Gonzalez and Schulz 2017: 317), a "nongovernmental accreditation system" could be developed to "identify and promote the spread of truthful information".

[24] Two legal proposals against fake news were presented in the previous legislature in the Italian parliament: Ddl S. 2688 – Senato della Repubblica, XVII Legislatura and Ddl S. 3001 – Senato della Repubblica, XVII Legislatura.

[25] See the statement on the Ministry of the Interior website: http://www.interno.gov.it/it/notizie/progetto-red-button-contro-fake-news

[26] Concerning the criminal provision regarding the 'publication or spread of fake news' (article 656 of the Italian Criminal Code), the Constitutional Court declared this provision to be constitutionally legitimate, although with some specifications (i.e., the presence of an actual danger). See Constitutional Court, judgment no. 19/1962, no. 199/1972, and no. 210/1976.

[27] A recent poll in Italy has said that 40% of the population does not recognise fake news (poll available at: https://www.termometropolitico.it/1287990_sondaggi-politici-fake-news.html). According to the XIV Rapporto Censis-Ucsi (2017), 52.7% of Italians have sometimes believed fake news.

Final Remarks

As has been underlined, the problem of fake news has emerged with the rise of the Internet and mediated populism. Populist fake news is a real challenge for constitutionalism and it is having an impact on one of the most important components of democratic theory: freedom of information. The regulatory solutions proposed here could help to regenerate the paradigm of the press as a tool of accountability, and transform the new Internet media into a watchdog with democratic responsibilities.[28] Obviously, in order to solve the fake news problem, 'Internet education'—which has been one of the most commonly publicised solutions—will also be necessary,[29] and could help individuals to be aware of the insidious dangers of the Web. Regarding 'Internet education', it is highly probable that in the future we will smile about our worries about the spread of fake news on social media, because fake news will be easily recognisable by people and will not be a problem. Currently, however, this is not the case.

Ultimately, the important and only conclusion that can be reached is that it is necessary to try to prepare new tools for the Internet platforms and to (co)regulate them in accordance with the old paradigm of freedom of information as enshrined in the Constitution, although it should not be taken for granted that this will work.

References

AgCom. (2018). *Rapporto sul consumo di informazione*. Available at https://www.agcom.it/documents/10179/9629936/Studio-Ricerca+19-02-2018/72cf58fc-77fc-44ae-b0a6-1d174ac2054f?version=1.0

Amabile, F. (2019, May 13). Facebook chiude 23 pagine: 'Fake news a favore del governo'. *La Stampa*. Available at https://www.lastampa.it/politica/2019/05/13/news/facebook-chiude-23-pagine-fake-news-a-favore-del-governo-1.33701617

[28] "If Facebook is going to function as the new social arbiter of trust, replacing a role journalism has, however imperfectly, long served, then they will need to both counter the spread of misinformation and encourage the spread of journalism based in fact. They will simply need to begin making editorial decisions" (Bell and Owen 2017: 77).

[29] As proposed by some participants of the report entitled *Fighting Fake News* hosted by The Information Society Project (Floyd Abrams Institute for Freedom of Expression), available at https://law.yale.edu/system/files/area/center/isp/documents/fighting_fake_news_-_workshop_report.pdf, p. 9. Or by the High Level Group on fake news and online disinformation (2018: 26).

Ananny, M. (2018, April 4). Checking in with the Facebook Fact-Checking Partnership. *Columbia Journalism Review*. Available at https://www.cjr.org/tow_center/facebook-fact-checking-partnerships.php

Ansa. (2016, December 31). Antitrust, stop alle bufale sul web. Grillo: 'Volete l'inquisizione'. *Ansa*. Available at http://www.ansa.it/sito/notizie/politica/2016/12/30/antitrust-stop-bufale-web.-grillovolete-inquisizione_66ed11a3-67df-4714-b96b-882e14d4f7d8.html

Ansa. (2017, April 26). Google, nuovo algoritmo contro le fake news. *Ansa*. Available at http://www.ansa.it/sito/notizie/tecnologia/internet_social/2017/04/25/google-nuovo-algoritmo-contro-fake-news_f648a676-0fea-45bd-887c-6e758ad28138.html

Barile, P. (1953). *Il soggetto privato nella Costituzione Italiana*. Padova: Cedam.

Bassini, M. (2019). Rise of Populism and the Five Star Movement Model: An Italian Case Study. *Italian Journal of Public Law, 11*(1), 302–333.

Bell, E. (2016, March 7). Facebook is Eating the World. *Columbia Journalism Review*. Available at https://www.cjr.org

Bell, E., & Owen, T. (2017, March 29). The Platform Press: How Silicon Valley Reengineered Journalism. *Tow Center for Digital Journalism, 9*. Available at www.cjr.org

Bennett, W. L. (2016). *News: The Politics of Illusion*. New York: University of Chicago Press.

Bessi, A., Petroni, F., Del Vicario, M., Zollo, F., Anagnostopoulos, A., Scala, A., Caldarelli, G., & Quattrociocchi, W. (2015). Viral Misinformation: The Role of Homophily and Polarization. In *Proceedings of the 24th International Conference on World Wide Web* (pp. 355–356). New York: ACM.

Betti, I. (2017, April 7). Google contro le fake news: arriva l'etichetta "fact check" per verificare notizie vere e false. *Huffpost*. Available at https://www.huffingtonpost.it/2017/04/07/google-contro-le-fake-news-arriva-letichetta-fact-check-per_a_22029937/

Bevere, A., & Cerri, A. (2006). *Il diritto di informazione e i diritti della persona. Il conflitto della libertà di pensiero con l'onore, la riservatezza, l'identità personale*. Giuffrè: Milano.

Bordignon, F., & Ceccarini, L. (2013). Five Stars and a Cricket. Beppe Grillo Shakes Italian Politics. *South European Society & Politics, 18*(4), 427–449.

Carroll, C. E. (2017). Making News: Balancing Newsworthiness and Privacy in the Age of Algorithms. *Georgetown Law Faculty Publications and Other Works, 2017*, 69–114.

Casarosa, F., & Brogi, E. (2014). The Role of Courts in Protecting the Freedom of Expression in Italy. In E. Psychogiopoulou (Ed.), *Media Policies Revisited* (pp. 101–114). London: Palgrave.

Chakravartty, P., & Roy, S. (2015). Mr Modi Goes to Delhi: Mediated Populism and the 2014 Indian Elections. *Television and New Media, 16*(4), 1–12.

Engesser, S., Ernst, N., Esser, F., & Büchel, F. (2016). Populism and Social Media: How Politicians Spread a Fragmented Ideology. *Information, Communication & Society, 20*(8), 1109–1126.

Esposito, C. (1958). *La libertà di manifestazione del pensiero nell'ordinamento italiano*. Milano: Giuffrè.

Flaxman, S., Goel, S., & Rao, J. (2016). Filter Bubbles, Echo Chambers, and Online News Consumption. *Public Opinion Quarterly, 80*, 298–320.

Floridi, L. (1996). Brave.Net.World: The Internet as a Disinformation Superhighway? *The Electronic Library, 14*(6), 509–514.

Fois, S. (1957). *Principi costituzionali e libera manifestazione del pensiero*. Milano: Giuffrè.

Foucault, M. (1970). *L'ordre du discours*. Paris: Gallimard.

Gonzalez, A., & Schulz, D. (2017). Helping Truth with Its Boots: Accreditation as an Antidote to Fake News. *Yale L.J. F.*, 315–366.

High Level Group on Fake News and Online Disinformation. (2018). *A Multi-Dimensional Approach to Disinformation*. Available at https://ec.europa.eu/digital-single-market/en/news/final-report-high-level-expert-group-fake-news-and-online-disinformation

Hirschl, R. (2014). *Comparative Matters: The Renaissance of Comparative Constitutional Law*. Oxford: Oxford University Press.

Horowitz, J. (2017, November 24). Italy, Bracing for Electoral Season of Fake News, Demands Facebook's Help. *The New York Times*. Available at https://www.nytimes.com/2017/11/24/world/europe/italy-election-fake-news.html

Howell, W. L. (2013). Digital Wildfires in a Hyperconnected World. *Report Global Risks 2013*.

Il Fatto Quotidiano. (2017, November 22). 'Boschi e Boldrini ai funerali di Riina'. La sottosegretaria: 'Fake news, passato il limite'. Il M5s prende le distanze. *ilfattoquotidiano.it*. Available at: https://www.ilfattoquotidiano.it/2017/11/22/boschi-e-boldrini-ai-funerali-di-riina-la-sottosegretaria-fake-news-passato-il-limite-il-m5s-prende-le-distanze/3995358/

Isaac, M. (2016, December 15). How Facebook's Fact-Checking Partnership Will Work. *The New York Times*. Available at https://www.nytimes.com/2016/12/15/technology/facebook-fact-checking-fake-news.html?partner=IFTTT

Kalia, A., Barr, C., & Giuffrida, A. (2018, December 17). Revealed: How Italy's Populists Used Facebook to Win Power. *The Guardian*. Available at https://www.theguardian.com/world/2018/dec/17/revealed-how-italy-populists-used-facebook-win-election-matteo-salvini-luigi-di-maio

Kantrowitz, A. (2018, January 23). This Is Facebook's News Survey. *Buzzfeed*. Available at https://www.buzzfeed.com/alexkantrowitz/this-is-facebooks-news-survey?utm_term=.la0RkwLNY2#.kiG5kb2B0p

Klinger, U., & Svensson, J. (2015). The Emergence of Network Media Logic in Political Communication: A Theoretical Approach. *New Media & Society, 17*(8), 1241–1257.

La Repubblica. (2017, December 18). Google contro le fake news, stop a siti che nascondono l'origine. *La Repubblica*. Available at http://www.repubblica.it/tecnologia/2017/12/18/news/google_contro_fake_news_stop_a_siti_che_nascondono_origine-184488662/

Lippmann, W. (1920). *Liberty and the News*. New York: Harcourt, Brace and Howe.

Manucci, L., & Amsler, M. (2018). Where the Wind Blows: Five Star Movement's Populism, Direct Democracy and Ideological Flexibility. *Italian Political Science Review, 48*(1), 109–132.

Mazzoleni, G. (2008). Mediated Populism. In W. Donsbach (Ed.), *The International Encyclopedia of Communication*. Oxford: Blackwell Publishing.

Mazzoleni, G., & Bracciale, R. (2018). Socially Mediated Populism: The Communicative Strategies of Political Leaders on Facebook. *Palgrave Communications, 4*, 1–10.

Mindich, D. T. Z. (1998). *Just the Facts: How Objectivity Came to Define American Journalism*. New York: New York University Press.

Mocanu, D., Rossi, L., Zhang, Q., Karsai, M., & Quattrociocchi, W. (2015). Collective Attention in the Age of (Mis)Information. *Computers in Human Behavior, 51*, 1198–1204.

Monti, M. (2017). Perspectives on the Regulation of Search Engine Algorithms and Social Networks: The Necessity of Protecting the Freedom of Information. *Opinio Juris In Comparatione, 1*(1), 71–96.

Monti, M. (2018). The New Populism and Fake News on the Internet: How Populism Along with Internet New Media Is Transforming the Fourth Estate. *Stals Research Paper, 4*, 1–27.

Monti, M. (2019). Privatizzazione della censura e Internet platforms: la libertà d'espressione e i nuovi censori dell'agorà digitale. *Rivista italiana di informatica e diritto, 1*, 35–51.

Mosseri, A. (2016, December 15). News Feed FYI: Addressing Hoaxes and Fake News. *Newsroom, Facebook*. Available at http://newsroom.fb.com/news/2016/12/news-feed-fyi-addressinghoaxes-and-fake-news/

Napoli, P. (2018). What if More Speech Is No Longer the Solution: First Amendment Theory Meets Fake News and the Filter Bubble. *Federal Communications Law Journal, 70*, 55–104.

Nardelli, A., & Silverman, C. (2016, November 29). Italy's Most Popular Political Party Is Leading Europe in Fake News and Kremlin Propaganda. *Buzzfeed*. Available at https://www.buzzfeed.com/albertonardelli/italys-most-popular-political-party-is-leading-europe-in-fak?utm_term=.aibKgJZrY9#.bdga16njeM

Nardelli, A., & Silverman, C. (2017, November 21). One of the Biggest Alternative Media Networks in Italy Is Spreading Anti-Immigrant News and Misinformation on Facebook. *Buzzfeed*. Available at https://www.buzzfeed.com/albertonardelli/one-of-the-biggest-alternative-media-networks-in-italy-is?utm_term=.ourQWLr0n1#.ohZvMkYzAy

Nikolov, D., Oliveira, D. F. M., Flammini, A., & Menczer, F. (2015). Measuring Online Social Bubbles. *PeerJ Computer Science, 1*, e38.

Norris, P. (2008). *Driving Democracy: Do Power-Sharing Institutions Work?* Cambridge: Cambridge University Press.

Pace, A. (2006). *Commentario della Costituzione. Art. 21*. Bologna-Roma: Zanichelli.

Pagella Politica. (2016, December 2). La notizia più condivisa sul referendum? È una bufala. *pagellapolitica.it*. Available at https://pagellapolitica.it/blog/show/148/la-notizia-più-condivisa-sul-referendum-è-una-bufala

Pariser, E. (2011). *The Filter Bubble: How the New Personalized Web is Changing What We Read and How We Think*. New York: Penguin Books Limited.

Pennycook, G., Cannon, T. D., & Rand, D. G. (2017, April 30). Prior Exposure Increases Perceived Accuracy of Fake News. *ssrn*. Available at SSRN: https://ssrn.com/abstract=2958246

Phelan, J. (2017, November 27). Italy's Five Star Movement Hits Italy's Five Star Movement Hits Out at New York Times and Buzzfeed Over 'Fake News'. *The Local*. Available at https://www.thelocal.it/20171127/italy-five-star-movement-new-york-times-buzzfeed-fake-news

Pitruzzella, G. (2018). La libertà di informazione nell'era di Internet. *MediaLaws, 1*, 19–47.

Politi, J. (2016, December 30). Italy Antitrust Chief Urges EU to Help Beat Fake News. *Financial Times*. Available at https://www.ft.com/content/e7280576-cddc-11e6-864f-20dcb35cede2

Pollicino, O. (2017). Fake News, Internet and Metaphors (to Be Handled Carefully). *MediaLaws, 1*, 23–25.

Pretelli, I. (2016). Comparative Study on Blocking Filtering and Take-Down of Illegal Internet Content – Italy, in Vv. Aa., *Comparative Study on Blocking, Filtering and Take-Down of Illegal Internet Content* (pp. 359–385). Lausanne: Swiss Institute of Comparative Law.

Stradella, E. (2008). Hate Speech in the Background of the Security Dilemma. *German Law Journal, 9*(1), 59–88.

Sunstein, C. (2007). *Republic.com 2.0*. Princeton: Princeton University Press.

Sunstein, C. (2014). *On Rumors: How Falsehoods Spread, Why We Believe Them, and What Can Be Done*. Princeton: Princeton University Press.

Trevisan, F. (2018, March 5). In Italy, Fake News Helps Populists and Far-Right Triumph. *The Conversation*. Available at https://theconversation.com/in-italy-fake-news-helps-populists-and-far-right-triumph-92271

Vis, F. (2014). The Rapid Spread of Misinformation Online. *Outlook on the Global Agenda 2014.*

Vosoughi, S., Roy, D., & Aral, S. (2018). The Spread of True and False News Online. *Science, 359*, 1146–1151.

Waisbord, S. (2018). Why Populism Is Troubling for Democratic Communication. *Communication, Culture and Critique, 11*(1), 21–34.

Wardle, C. (2017). *Fake News: It's Complicated.* First Draft. Available at: https://medium.com/1st-draft/fake-news-its-complicated-d0f773766c79

Wu, F. T. (2011). Collateral Censorship and the Limits of Intermediary Immunity. *Notre Dame L. Rev, 87*, 293–349.

CHAPTER 10

Rise of Populism and the Five Star Movement Model: An Italian Case Study

Marco Bassini

Introduction

It is well known among scholars that working out a widely accepted definition of populism is very difficult and, in any way, problematic. This holds especially true in the field of legal research, where the concept of populism seems to be borrowed from the language of political science (for instance, Müller 2016: 2–3; see also Canovan 1999).

For the purposes of this chapter, I will particularly focus on those populist expressions that call into question the well-established, constitutional law category of representative democracy and, accordingly, the role and responsibilities of traditional political parties (Pinelli 2011). There is, in fact, a natural tension between constitutionalism and the emergence of populist movements,[1] which challenges the foundations of representative democracies. As noted by some authors (Grasso 2017a: 209–210), such

[1] For an overview on the current debate regarding populist constitutionalism, and generally populism and public law, see, among others, Blokker (2017), Scheppele (2017), Müller (2015).

M. Bassini (✉)
Bocconi University, Milan, Italy
e-mail: marco.bassini@unibocconi.it

G. Delledonne et al. (eds.), *Italian Populism and Constitutional Law*, Challenges to Democracy in the 21st Century,
https://doi.org/10.1007/978-3-030-37401-3_10

an approach would dispute the very aim of constitutionalism, that is, to protect individuals from abuses of power. But at the same time, populism can be the last resort when the functioning of representative democracy disregards people's will or even contradicts the interests of the people (Grasso 2017a: 209–210).

In this chapter, I will focus, in particular, on movements and parties that stand out among anti-party or so-called antiestablishment parties. In this respect, the advent of new political actors has been fostered—according to a pretty rhetorical utterance—by a desire to disrupt long-standing dominant elites and let people's voices be heard (Mény and Surel 2002; see Lanzone 2014). I will argue that the spread of populist movements constitutes a reaction to the decline of traditional parties and the crisis of representative democracy. This chapter will particularly explore the rise of the Five Star Movement (in Italian, 'Movimento Cinque Stelle') in Italy and will focus on the challenges that it poses from the perspective of constitutional law. In such a model, the use of the Internet as a channel for bridging the gap between voters and 'political establishment' has played a pivotal role. Unlike other parties which likewise have largely resorted to social media as a campaigning tool, the Five Star Movement has seen from the very origin the Internet as a means to reshape the essence of political representation in that of delegation and to allow direct democracy to flourish. The Five Star Movement has relied so much on the use of online consultations with voters to give rise to some debate on the possible de facto revision of certain constitutional institutions.[2]

I will move from the constitutional background, exploring the status of political parties as well as anti-party and antiestablishment parties. I will then highlight some critical points of the Movement model and speculate on its compatibility with the Italian Constitution in the *pars destruens*. Finally, in the *pars construens*, I will explore measures that may be taken to respond to the populist surge by revitalizing representative democracy, most notably in light of the Five Star Movement's model strengths and weaknesses with regard to the use of the Internet. I will conclude that, given the tolerant attitude of the Italian Constitution vis-à-vis

[2] For instance, the Five Star Movement made it conditional the constitution of a new cabinet led by them and the Democratic Party upon the approval of the majority of voters in an ad hoc online consultation after President Mattarella reappointed as Prime Minister Giuseppe Conte, who had already headed the previous cabinet, supported by the Five Star Movement and the League.

antiestablishment and anti-party parties, this phenomenon can be marginalized, but is unlikely to be defeated.

The reason why this chapter focuses on the Five Star Movement instead of other populist movements that arose in Italy at different times (like the League) lies with the unprecedented constitutional challenges that this organization has brought about in the realm of political representation.

Political Parties in the Italian Constitution

Before introducing the recent developments in Italy regarding the rise of populist movements, it is of utmost importance to explore the constitutional framework concerning political parties (see generally, among others in this regard: Ridola 1982; Predieri 1950; Ferri 1950). A full understanding of the most critical challenges posed by the rise of anti-party and anti-establishment parties, in fact, requires taking into account the relevant constitutional paradigm and the way political parties affect the Italian form of government (in this respect see Staiano 2014, 2015; Giuffrè 2016; Prisco 2018). It is against this background that the Internet stands out as a genuinely unprecedented means for supporting political representation.

Article 49 of the Italian Constitution reads as follows: *'Any citizen has the right to freely establish parties to contribute to determining national policies through democratic processes.'*

While granting citizens the right to assembly for political purposes, this provision does actually refer to a particular dimension of the freedom of association, which is protected, in general and broader terms, by Article 18, irrespective of the underlying purposes.

The Italian Constitution does not treat political parties as institutions or—better said—as parts of the frame of government. Rather, they are considered as bodies through which the several interests of political nature are represented (see Italian Constitutional Court, order no. 79/2006). As noted by prominent scholars (Ridola 1982: 72), the option to frame the constitutional coverage for political parties in terms of freedom of political assembly was very ambiguous and discussed at the origins. Article 49, in fact, compromised two different dimensions: on the one hand, this provision is included in the section concerning political rights (Title IV) and not in the part of the Constitution regarding the organization of the Republic; on the other hand, however, this provision emphasizes the role of political parties as institutional intermediaries between the State and society.

In the light of this inherent connection with the freedom of association,[3] political parties are immune from the State's ideological influence. Freedom of assembly for political purposes is thus subject to the same limitations imposed by the Constitution to the freedom of assembly as such. Accordingly, even anti-party and antiestablishment movements enjoy full constitutional protection.[4] This is witnessed by the fact that even members of monarchist parties (pursuing the restoration of the Monarchy, in spite of Article 139 of the Constitution) sat in the Parliament in the aftermath of establishing the Republic. The Twelfth Transitional and Final Provision places a specific limit on political parties, by prohibiting reorganization '*under any form whatsoever,* [of] *the dissolved Fascist party*'. The existence of this restriction does not per se deprive the Italian Constitution of its tolerant nature or include the Italian constitutional order within the scope of 'protected democracies' (like the German one and the Spanish Constitution; see Bonfiglio 2013). The Italian Constitutional Court, in fact, held that the pursuit of radical changes of the constitutional order is compatible with the Constitution as long as it is realized through a democratic process and without using violence (see Italian Constitutional Court, order no. 114/1967). The prohibition entrenched in the Twelfth Transitional and Final Provision, thus, is far from constituting an 'abuse clause' to exclude antiestablishment forces from the enjoyment of the right to political assembly. Rather, this provision clarifies the essence of the founding covenant of the Republic, that is, rejection of the Fascist regime, which would be a priori incompatible with the Constitution. This is the only exception to the pluralistic principle regarding political parties, in addition to the limits generally placed by Article 18 on the freedom of association.[5] As pointed out by Paolo Ridola, Article 49 of the Constitution

[3] Despite this framing, the provision does not contain any specific reference to the democratic nature of parties. As noted by Ridola, some members to the Constituent Assembly made a proposal (the so-called amendment 'Mortati-Ruggiero') to require that political parties could ensure the democratic organization of the State; however, this amendment was later withdrawn (Ridola 1982: 73). Some scholars directed some criticism towards the option of regulating political parties, as noted by Ridola (1982: 78), whereas the critic against 'particracy' emerged only some years later: see Maranini (1958).

[4] For a specific focus on the attitude of the Italian Constitution toward anti-establishment parties, see Nicotra (2008). Generally, on political parties in the Italian Constitution see Gambino (1977), Crisafulli (1967), Esposito (1954), and, *passim*, Martines (1957). Among the most recent works, see Gianfrancesco (2017), Marsocci (2012).

[5] As noted by Ridola (1982: 113), the significance of this provision has been widely debated.

is then derogated from the Twelfth Transitional and Final Provision, and the origins of this compromise date back to the founding covenant of the Constitution in 1947. On the one hand, the goal of the latter provision was to avoid that the new constitutional order could be indifferent to the variety of possible political actors: this way, the Twelfth Transitional and Final Provision encapsulates a specific evaluation made a priori by the Constituent Fathers to reject, by discriminating it in the political arena, the Fascist Party. On the other hand, the Twelfth Transitional and Final Provision aims at avoiding the reestablishment of the Fascist Party based on the overall consideration of its ideology rather than because of the threat that it represents for the democratic attitude of the State.

Against this background, another crucial provision, namely, Article 67 of the Italian Constitution, prohibits subjecting members of the Parliament (hereafter, MPs) to a binding mandate (for more details on this, see: Zanon 1991: 288–289; Azzariti 2008; Rinaldi 2017). Even though the Constitution does not draw any qualified connection between political parties and MPs, it goes without saying that the constitutional framework relating to political parties is intertwined with this cornerstone of representative democracy.

By requiring the MPs to be free from any binding mandate, the Constitution has taken the option to protect their freedom of action vis-à-vis both their voters and the relevant political parties, with a view to sheltering them from the liability caused by any decision diverging from the original political address. In the words of the Italian Constitutional Court, every MP is free to vote in accordance with his/her political view and the party's address to which he/she belongs and also, not to adhere to the same.[6] This way, the Constitution shields the MPs from any legislative or statutory provisions that may impose legal consequence as a result of 'disobedience' to their respective parties and constituents. This prohibition, therefore, assumes that the functioning of the parliamentary mandate does not aim at representing sectorial interests, rather at compromising the various societal interests mirrored by political parties. Against this background, measures like the *recall* or dismissal of MPs would be contrary

[6] See Italian Constitutional Court, judgment no. 14/1964. As pointed out by Zanon (1991), this judgment took the view that, despite the apparent contradiction between the principle underlying Articles 49 and 67, the latter placed a limit preventing too much extreme implications of the democratic principle enshrined to the former, such as recall or loss of the seat as a consequence of exclusion or resignation from a party.

to Article 67. However, as noted by Justice Zanon, the relevant scholarly debate includes a variety of views on the theoretical and practical effects of this ban. First of all, the ban may merely exclude that a mandate, whether given from the voters or from a party, has any relevance and effect. According to this construction, agreements and instructions for MPs are still possible, but deprived of any legal guarantee: thus, they are not enforceable and MPs can depart from the instructions received. From a different perspective, the ban enshrined in Article 67 may constitute an actual prohibition, forbidding in any case agreements and instructions aimed at conditioning MPs. However, the critical point of this option lies with determining the consequences of a possible mandate: instructions and agreements could be considered 'void' (and not merely unenforceable) but from a practical standpoint this would make only a little difference compared to the aforesaid alternative interpretation.[7]

Regardless of the specific understanding and the consequences of the ban in question, the ultimate goal thereof is to avoid a degradation of political representation where instead of a competition among ideas and political programs a compromise between sectoral interests would take place (Zanon 1991: 299). As I will specify more in detail below, this cornerstone, common to many constitutions, is confronted by the rise of parties, such as the Five Star Movement, that call for a return to direct democracy, including by making the Internet a privileged channel for voters to take part in the political process.

The prohibition of binding mandate embodied in the Italian Constitution is then a pivotal factor to bear in mind while considering the transformations in the recent political scenario, notably the rise of the Five Star Movement.[8] The Italian Constitution adheres to a liberal view of representation, where although representatives are chosen by voters, they remain free to take any steps for the pursuit of general interest.[9] On the contrary, according to the democratic theory of representation (inspired by Rousseau), representatives act in accordance with a specific mandate received from voters to bring into the parliamentary assembly the specific

[7] As Zanon (1991: 291) observed, these alternative options for interpreting Article 67 rely on different views on the concept of political representation and the legal status of MPs.

[8] Article 67 has been interpreted not as a general and absolute prohibition for every member of the Parliament to receive any instructions, but as the freedom to act without being bound by the same, that can be either disregarded or taken into account.

[9] See the famous *Speech to the electors of Bristol* by Edmund Burke given on 3 November 1774: 'Parliament is not a *congress* of ambassadors from different and hostile interests (…)".

interests of the latter. As I will discuss more in detail, this is exactly the view of the Five Star Movement and its constituency, whose online platform for consultation with voters is by no coincidence named 'Rousseau'.

How the Five Star Movement Entered the Political Arena: The Internet as Enabling Factor for *the People* to Contrast *Elites*

Probably, the most distinguishing and telling feature of the Five Star Movement is that it grew out of its founder's blog—the former comedian Mr. Beppe Grillo.[10] Started in 2005,[11] the blog quickly became a virtual agora, where the posts, reflecting Grillo's political opinion and ideology, generated thousands of interactions. Given the massive success, a mixture of contemporary outbreak of financial crisis and some controversies concerning traditional political parties made Mr. Grillo's blog the backbone of an organized structure with political purposes. This way, the Five Star Movement came into being in 2009 as a political actor and took part in the local and regional elections in 2010, 2011 and 2012. Eventually, the Movement was able to elect a couple of majors; in the 2013 general election, it became the most-voted party, one of the 'big three minorities' that came up (Diamanti 2013). In the 2016 municipal elections, Ms. Virginia Raggi from the Five Star Movement became Rome's new major. In the 2018 general election, the Five Star Movement was again the most-voted party, gaining 32% of the vote, while the right-wing coalition captured the largest share of the vote, that is, 35%.

In the 2018 general election, since no majority premium was provided under the election law, known as 'Rosatellum', neither the Five Star Movement nor the right-wing coalition obtained the absolute majority of seats, while the Democratic Party reached a historical low (18%). However, as the very turning point of the election, League, led by Matteo Salvini, became the first party in the right-wing coalition (17%), overtaking Berlusconi's Forward Italy (14%). It is not by coincidence that 88 days after the general election and the failure of the Senate and Lower House speakers (Casellati Alberti and Fico) to reach a compromise between

[10] See www.beppegrillo.it

[11] For a general introduction on the rise of the Five Star Movement, see Diamanti (2014), Tronconi (2015), Corbetta and Gualmini (2013) and Tarchi (2015). See also Mueller (2008).

different political parties and coalitions in their 'exploratory mandate', the Five Star Movement and League formed a new government headed by Giuseppe Conte (an independent supported by the Five Star Movement) where Matteo Salvini and Luigi Di Maio (the respective parties' leaders) served as deputy prime ministers. The advent of the Conte Cabinet was possible because the two parties managed to reach an agreement on a government program (for a critical overview on the aftermath of the 2018 general election, see Martinico 2018; Torre 2018; Clementi 2018). They symbolically entered into a contract[12] and this way made the life of the Cabinet conditional upon the pursuit of the compromised program (including the most sensitive matters for the respective constituencies).[13] Such outcome, as I will point out more in detail below, contradicts one of the main claims made against traditional political parties by the Five Star Movement, that is, the establishment of cross-movement coalitions blurring the lines of boundaries and differences. However, such an outcome is not unprecedented, as the Letta, Renzi and Gentiloni Cabinets demonstrate. But the most emblematic example of the abandonment of such attitude by the Five Star Movement comes from the events which followed in August 2019, where Matteo Salvini decided to withdraw League's support to Giuseppe Conte and the Five Star Movement entered into another government coalition with the Democratic Party to sustain the second (so-called Conte-bis) Conte Cabinet.

Which factors permitted the Five Star Movement to become the most-voted party in the 2013 and 2018 general elections? Several factors are said to have contributed to the rise and consolidation of populist parties and movements in Europe and other countries. Among others, the spread of fake news on the Internet,[14] the educational divide, the adverse effects of a financial crisis and, more recently, the emergence of international terrorism are often ranked among the causes for the populist surge. Most of these circumstances definitely had an impact. However, from the perspective of constitutional law, they fail to explain properly why Grillo's party has obtained such widespread support in Italy.

[12] See Di Marzio (2018). As to the constitutional law issues raised by the choice of a 'contract' to define the political agenda of the Conte Cabinet, see Carducci (2018).

[13] The 'contract' is available at this url: http://download.repubblica.it/pdf/2018/politica/contratto_governo.pdf

[14] In this respect see the chapter authored by M. Monti in this volume.

The use of the Internet has allowed the Five Star Movement to obtain broad consensus (facilitating the spread of populist counter-narratives) and supported the creation of an organization that is quite similar to political parties, notwithstanding Grillo's opposite (and not very reliable) claim (see, more in detail, Falletti 2014; Bordignon and Ceccarini 2015).

The most remarkable characteristic of the Five Star Movement is that, while its political view reflects a distinctively antiestablishment attitude, it also emerges as an anti-party movement seeking emancipation from the model of traditional parties. Traditional parties are deemed as the enemy, the symbol of 'old politics' that led Italy to the brink of economic disaster. To highlight the distance marked from political parties, the Movement called itself a 'non-party' and its statute as 'non-statute'. Setting aside this rhetorical self-understanding that actually corresponds more to 'food for voters' than to an accurate description of the movement, it is worth noting that the Five Star Movement model calls for a disintermediation of political representation from political parties (see Urbinati 2015). In Grillo's view, the use of the Internet is supposed to allow voters to directly participate in the political process, according to the model of e-democracy, and thus increase transparency and political accountability. The MPs are considered to be mere spokesmen bound by the will of their constituents, as debated on Grillo's blog, open to all registered users of the same.

A recent comparative study on anti-party parties in Italy and Germany by Andrea De Petris and Thomas Poguntke (De Petris and Poguntke 2015) has focused on some distinguishing features of the Five Star Movement. De Petris (De Petris 2015), in particular, explored the following characteristics, that I find worth quoting:

(a) The Five Star Movement is a personified party; this characteristic depends on the strict relationship that the Movement's voters/supporters entered into with Grillo ('a link of mutual interdependence,' according to De Petris) mainly through his extremely popular blog.
(b) The Five Star Movement is a 'non-association' with a 'non-statute': This character is an expression of 'a systematic refuse to adopt definitions and the lexicon in use by political parties'.
(c) The mechanism for the creation of 'certified lists' and the selection procedures of candidates for national elections: The Five Star Movement has adopted a very detailed mechanism to allow citizens wishing to contest in the local elections to create their own lists of

candidates. Once each list is created, it must undergo a certification process controlled by the Movement itself, and it must comply with a set of strict requirements. Likewise, the Movement has launched online primary elections for the selection of candidates at the general election held in 2013.

(d) It is a political program 'under permanent construction' that is consistent with the understanding of the Five Star Movement as an open platform working according to a 'fluid' approach.

From a speculative point of view, one may wonder now whether this model is compatible with the Italian Constitution. As specified above, Article 49 does not place any limit to the freedom of association for political purposes, except for the dissolution of the Fascist party. Antiestablishment and anti-party parties are therefore protected as such by the Constitution and entitled to take part in the democratic political activities. The very crucial point, however, does not relate to the qualification of the Five Star Movement as an antiestablishment and anti-party movement. It rather lies with the compatibility of the Movement's views with the Constitution, regarding direct and participatory democracy and the role of political parties (Sartori 2013).

Pars Destruens: Some Critical Remarks on the Five Star Movement

The model of political representation proposed by the Five Star Movement has been described as a hybrid between direct democracy and participatory democracy (Falletti 2014: 5).

Actually, different aspects in the structure and functioning of the Movement reflect these underlying principles—the possibility of a certain number of voters to require introducing a bill to the Parliament; the extensive use of online consultations both for the selection of candidates and for debating the approval or repeal of bills (or again, for deciding whether an MP must be excluded from the Movement); and the direct involvement of the constituents in a range of activities.

If one places these developments against the background of the decline of political parties, increasingly depicted as closed oligarchies, they look promising in respect of the reduction of the divide between citizens and political actors or, in the eyes of the populists' categories, the (only) *people* and the *elites*.

However, far from entering into the merits of the controversial results of the Five Star Movement from a political standpoint, the impact of these novelties needs to be revisited.

In particular, more than the specific forms of direct and participatory democracy, it is the general attitude of the Five Star Movement toward the representative system that appears unlikely to be reconciled with the constitutional framework.

In the view of the Movement, political parties would no longer act as the 'center' where different views are compromised, and the will of the people is 'filtered'. The exercise of representation is supposed to be emancipated from the intermediation of political parties, whose representative attitude is weakened because of the Internet's potential. New media, in fact, allow citizens to 'speak aloud', participating in the political process without any filter or intermediary (see, among others, Orofino 2017).

I feel that this construction of the relationship between the use of media and the lack of parties' intermediation is too simplistic. When it comes to debating the state of health of political representation, a fully disenchanted view is indeed necessary.

Norberto Bobbio, one of the most enlightened authors, wrote in 1994 that the claim to realize a 'computercracy', allowing a direct democracy, was purely childish (Bobbio 1984). This scenario would have brought an excess of democracy—an even more dangerous option.

The rationale behind the Five Star Movement is that MPs are merely spokesmen, while the determination of political stances rests in the hands of voters, who have the power to bind the MPs' actions in Parliament. As such, the MPs are subject to a binding mandate, in fair contrast with the Constitution. More recently, criticism has been expressed (Grasso 2017b) with respect to the code of conduct adopted by the Five Star Movement that applies to the respective members of the European Parliament (MEPs). The code expressly provides voters with the power to recall a member of the European Parliament if a 'serious infringement' occurs.[15]

[15] The recall of the MEP can be requested, in case of serious infringement, by at least 500 registered members of the Five Star Movement residing in the electoral district from where the MEP was elected. Alternatively, a proposal of recall can, in any case, be approved with the vote of majority of the registered members of the Five Stars residing in the electoral college where the MEP was elected.

Furthermore, it establishes that a penalty of 250,000.00 euros must be paid to the Five Star Movement in case the concerned member of Parliament refuses to resign.

These internal rules are definitely incompatible with the prohibition of a binding mandate. Apart from Article 67 of the Italian Constitution (that would not be enforceable in this specific case), both the Statute for Members of the European Parliament and the Rules of Procedure of the European Parliament do prohibit MEPs to receive a binding mandate or be bound by any instructions.[16] Then, in case an MEP failed to resign after having committed a 'serious infringement' of the code of conduct, the obligation to pay a fine would be most likely unenforceable.

A very similar provision applies to the MPs who belong to the Five Star Movement Parliamentary Group in the Chamber of Deputies and Senate of the Republic. Article 21, para. 5, of the relevant statute approved on 27 March 2018, in fact, provides that '[a]ny MP who leaves the parliamentary group because of either his/her exclusion or voluntary withdrawal or resignation based on political disagreement shall pay a fine amounting to Euro 100,000.00 to the Five Star Movement by ten days'. Also the wording of the 'contract' between the Five Star Movement and the League encapsulates suggests a normative claim to make binding the political mandate on MPs with a view to contrasting party-switching.[17] This claim was common to many documents with no legal effects, most notably codes of ethics and codes of conduct[18] applying to Five Star Movement

[16] Rule 2 reads as follows: '*Members of the European Parliament shall exercise their mandate independently. They shall not be bound by any instructions and shall not receive a binding mandate.*'

[17] See p. 35 of the 'contract' under para. 20.

[18] See Scuto (2018a: 3–5). The Author notes that codes of ethics and codes of conduct aim at ensuring the respect of Article 54 of the Constitution, requiring citizens to whom public functions are entrusted to fulfill the same with 'discipline and honor', in addition to a general duty of loyalty to the Republic. Then, the adoption of said codes is up to the parties in the exercise of the organizational autonomy that they enjoy pursuant to Article 18 and Article 49 of the Constitution. These rules of conduct may have the effect of preventing members of a given party to run for election or other party offices but cannot in any case determine restrictions that are unconstitutional because either they contrast with the prohibition on binding mandate pursuant to Article 67 of the Constitution or are not compatible with the democratic standard for internal organization required by Article 49 thereof.

candidates and activists; now, it is enshrined to the statute of the parliamentary group, which is supposed to have also legal effects.[19]

Notwithstanding the Five Star Movement's calls for the repeal of Article 67 of the Constitution, the prohibition of binding mandate does make sense[20] still as a cornerstone[21] of representative democracy.[22]

The Italian experience, moreover, constitutes a litmus test of some difficulties that are related to the implementation of mechanisms of direct and participatory democracy (Sbailò 2018).

First, these mechanisms have failed to convey a significant participation of voters in the political decision-making process. When the Five Star Movement launched (apparently) open consultations in order to give the floor to their constituents (e.g. on the selection of candidates or on the decision to exclude or not certain members from the Movement), just a very limited number of voters actually took part in the voting procedures. Were a political entity bound to bring to the Parliament the views that only a few voters had contributed to form, the content of the relevant political decision would be, by definition, nondemocratic. In such a scenario, the promise of an actual representation of the will of people through disintermediation from political parties would be an empty one. This holds even truer in light of the larger and larger resort to online consultations with voters also for decisions which may have truly constitutional effects and impact, such as in the recent case of the survey launched to get

[19] The insertion of this clause into the statute of the Five Star Movement parliamentary group has given rise to a broad debate among constitutional law scholars on the nature of the clause and the legal remedies to challenge the imposition of the fine. See in particular Di Maria (2018: 4–8), Curreri (2018), Cerri (2018), Martinelli (2018); see also Marsocci (2018).

[20] According to a different interpretation (articulated by Grasso 2018), Article 67 of the Constitution does guarantee the free exercise of the mandate by MPs, but subject to the condition that such exercise is compatible with the Constitution, most notably with the duty of loyalty to the Constitution pursuant to Article 54. To a certain degree, in the view of Grasso, Article 21, para. 5, of the Statute of the Five Star Movement parliamentary group may play a role in securing MPs' accountability by ensuring that MPs act in accordance with a general political line (without prejudice to political dissent) and avoiding party-switching. Without prejudice to the above, the introduction of a penalty is considered in any case illegal.

[21] See, among others, Pinelli (2018), Demuro (2018), Ciancio (2018). For an overview of the possible effects of the claims regarding Article 67, see the chapter by C. Fasone in this volume.

[22] Some authors, however, argue that introducing some elements of direct democracy could be the sound remedy to revitalize representative democracy: see Ainis (2017).

the voters' approval of the new government coalition with the Democratic Party. What if the voters (better said: those who are 'registered users' and are therefore entitled to take part in online consultations) rejected such a deal? Such scenario would have likely triggered consequences difficult to reconcile with the constitutional framework, given the Five Star Movement's attitude that deem such instructions binding.

Additionally, since all the relevant decisions are taken on the basis of consultations held on a website, in order for such a model of direct and participatory democracy to work, access to the Internet platform should be universal (i.e. granted to the citizens of all generations and all areas of the country). The digital divide, however, is still a serious problem in Italy, like in Europe and in the US.

Finally, quis custodiet ipsos custodes? Examining the Five Star Movement, most of their relevant resolutions are not adopted by the voters, rather by a restricted group of individuals who determine the political line without any legitimacy. This leads to a general lack of transparency that affects the credibility of the Five Star Movement vis-à-vis the citizens. Furthermore, who guarantees that the outcome of the consultations carried out on the blog is correct and not subject to any alteration or manipulation?

The Five Star Movement, then, cannot escape reality and should confront the existing limits of the project of reaching a direct and participatory democracy through a 'non-party'.

In this respect, some courts have handed down interesting judgments that have lent doubts about the compatibility of the Five Star Movement with the legal order of certain internal mechanisms. A first decision was handed down in July 2016 by the Court of Naples.[23] The lawsuit originated from the exclusion of some members from the Movement. The plaintiffs were accused of having infringed the rules of the Movement (named '*non-statuto*', 'non-statute', with a view to emphasizing difference from the traditional parties) for having joined a Facebook secret group, facilitating the exchange of various political views. The exclusion from the Five Star Movement was communicated to the plaintiffs via email by an ill-defined 'Staff of Beppe Grillo', a body that had no grounds in the (non) statute. As a consequence of the exclusion, the plaintiffs could not take part (in their capacity both as voters and as candidates) in the primaries

[23] Court of Naples, order of 14 July 2016, affirmed by Court of Naples, 18 April 2018, no. 3773.

launched on the website for the 2016 municipal elections. The Court of Naples suspended the exclusion and found that notwithstanding the choice of the name and organizational structure, the Five Star Movement does amount to a political party whose members enjoy freedom of political association. Accordingly, membership to the Five Star Movement is governed by the same rules provided by the Italian Civil Code for associations. Pursuant to the relevant provisions of the Civil Code, measures such as exclusion from an association may be taken upon a duly approved resolution of the assembly, unless otherwise provided by a statute of the association.[24] The very interesting point in the decision of the Court lies with the acknowledgment that even the Five Star Movement falls within the category of political parties and is accordingly subject to the (few) relevant statutory provisions that are applicable to the same.

Another remarkable judgment was delivered in April 2017, prior to the municipal elections in Genoa.[25] The local court suspended the resolution by which Beppe Grillo, in his capacity as 'guarantor' of the Movement, had invalidated the results of the primary elections held on the website, won by the list headed by Ms. Marika Cassimatis, in order to replace her with another candidate. The Court noted that the power to exclude some candidates granted to the guarantor was limited by the (non)statute to special circumstances and did not amount to a generic veto power (or the 'last say') by the leader of the Movement. Also in this case, the Court found that the adoption of these types of resolutions is regulated by the relevant provisions of the Civil Code, unless otherwise established by the (non)statute. Not even the 'ratification' of the exclusion of Ms. Cassimatis through an online vote among the members of the Movement was found to constitute a sound basis to remedy the infringement of the statute and keep the resolution immune from any possible claim.

[24] Precisely, the Five Star Movement argued that the power to exclude members from the association was stipulated in the Regulation published on the blog of Beppe Grillo. However, the Court of Naples noted that such a Regulation may not overrule the biding statutory provisions applying to private associations, unless a specific amendment to the statute of the association is approved to introduce such a power of exclusion.

[25] Court of Genoa, order of 10 April 2017.

Pars Construens: Making Political Parties Democratic Again?

I have argued that populism has flourished in Italy also because of the deep crisis of the traditional political parties (according to the similar line that led, in the 1990s, to the rise of antiestablishment parties, such as the League, in reaction to the 'Tangentopoli' scandal). The Five Star Movement, for instance, has emerged as a genuinely anti-*elites* force, as a reaction to the claimed inability of left-wing and right-wing parties to capture citizens' needs and expectations. This is why the Internet has played such a pivotal role, to the extent its use allowed those who no longer felt represented to be voiced again in the political arena. The Five Star Movement so captured the sense of frustration felt by voters and channeled it into a critique of the model of representative democracy. I have outlined some factors that had an impact on the rise of the Movement from a constitutional-law standpoint. Some of these elements (e.g. the electoral system) directly relate to the form of government, whereas others (e.g. the advent of personalist parties) refer to how the form of government actually works. Both types of factors show that while antiestablishment and anti-party parties are not per se incompatible with the Constitution, there is, nevertheless, room to control the spread of populism by reinforcing representative democracy. Since the Constitution places no limits (except for reconstitution of the Fascist party) on the freedom of political association, some measures may be necessary, not to reject populism as such, but to strengthen the role of political parties and reduce the gap between them and the people. Evidently, the existing alternatives to representative democracy, such as the Five Star Movement model of direct and participatory democracy, may prove unsatisfactory and even raise constitutional law issues.

But how is it possible to reverse the trend of distrust of the mainstream political parties?

First and foremost, the approval of an electoral law to guarantee political stability was essential before the general election of 2018. After the Italian Constitutional Court struck down the electoral law in 2014, a new law named 'Italicum' was passed in 2015. However, on 9 February 2017, the Constitutional Court ruled that some crucial provisions of the Italicum Law were unconstitutional (Italian Constitutional Court, judgment no. 35/2017. See Caruso and Goldoni 2017; Delledonne and Boggero 2017). But this decision turned out to be even more disruptive in light of the failure of the constitutional referendum held, meanwhile, in December 2016 (Schefold 2017). In fact, the scope of the Italicum Law was limited to the election of members of the Chamber of Deputies, as the Senate of the Republic was supposed to be reformed and converted to an assembly composed of representatives of the Regions and Municipalities who were not elected by voters.[26] Yet, the constitutional referendum failed and the election to the chambers of the Parliament was governed by two sets of completely different rules[27]—an almost insurmountable obstacle to political stability—until the approval, on 3 November 2017, of a new law named 'Rosatellum'. This law was estimated to make it difficult for Five Star Movement to win the general election of 2018, by allocating one-third of the seats via a 'first-past-the-post' system based on single-member electoral districts and two-thirds thereof proportionally without any chance for voters to pick their candidates. Contrary to all expectations, the Five Star Movement won most of the seats, especially in singe-member electoral districts.

So, in the age of the crisis of representative democracy, giving voters the power to indicate their preference among candidates seems a sound way to reduce the gap between parties and citizens. Despite the existence of a pressing need to bridge this divide, the Parliament has taken another road.

A second proposal aims at introducing legislation regulating the sole aspect of functioning of political parties that reflect on their representative functions. The (limited) legal framework applying to political parties in Italy mainly concerns financing of the same (Biondi 2012). Italian Parliament passed a few provisions first in 2012[28] and then in 2014[29] with a view to ensuring 'transparency and democracy of political parties' in the

[26] The Five Star Movement campaigned against the reform focusing particularly on this profile, as the constitutional reform was supposed to deprive voters of the power to elect senators by replacing them with an assembly of 100 representatives of local authorities nominated by regional councils and municipalities.

[27] Namely, by the Italicum law, as amended by the judgment of the Constitutional Court no. 35/2017 as to the Chamber of Deputies and by the so-called Consultellum, that is, the electoral law of 2005 as amended by the judgment of the Constitutional Court no. 1/2014 as to the Senate of the Republic.

[28] Law 6 July 2012, no. 96 ('Provisions governing the reduction of public financing of political parties and movements and measures to ensure transparency and accountability').

[29] See Law 21 February 2014, no. 13 ('Passing into law Law-Decree 28 December 2013, no. 149, repealing public financing of political parties, regulating parties' transparency and democracy and governing voluntary and indirect contribution to political parties').

context of the reform of party funding.[30] These provisions turned out to have a limited impact (see Calvano 2018: 7–9; Scuto 2018b, 2017), as they merely introduce formal requirements concerning the content of the statutes of political parties. Respect of these requirements is a prerequisite for parties to be eligible for indirect public contribution. First, Article 5 of Law no. 96/2012 requires that the statutes of political parties must be compatible 'with democratic principles in the internal organization, most notably with regard to the selection of candidates, the respect of internal minorities and the protection of the rights of party members'. Article 3 of Law no. 13/2014, in turn (included in a specific section on 'Internal democracy, accountability and transparency'), provides a comprehensive description of the content of party statutes, including: rights and duties of party members; modalities of participation in the party's political activities; criteria to ensure the representation of minorities in nonexecutive bodies; disciplinary measures applicable to party members; criteria for the selection of candidates running for European, general and local elections. In light of this limited legal background, the implementation of the democratic principle enshrined in Article 49 of the Constitution seems to be only on paper. As noted by some scholars (Calvano 2018: 8–9), the Five Star Movement could easily circumvent the application of these requirements, by simply avoiding applying for public indirect contribution.

In the age of the crisis of political parties, where there is an increasing use—among others—of primary elections, the relationship between citizens and parties could probably benefit from the approval of a specific (and long-awaited[31]) piece of legislation on political parties to ensure more directly and effectively the respect of the democratic principle.[32] As suggested by some scholars, the content of a possible law regulating political parties should be as minimal as possible, in order not to undermine the freedom that is guaranteed by Article 49 of the Constitution. But the specific mission of these kinds of association may justify (if not require) some form of regulation with a view to making political parties more democratic. If more internal-party democracy is secured, traditional political

[30] On the 'changing landscape of structure and financing' of political parties, see Allegri et al. (2018).

[31] Time is probably ripe for a law on political parties to answer the question posed by Elia (2009)

[32] See Brunelli (2016), Lanzafame (2017). See also Amato (2012) and Barbera (2009).

parties will be able to compete more with the only apparently democratic model of the new populist movements.

Now, a question that may lead to speculating on other possible remedies: Is there room for any form of accountability of the MPs that does not challenge the prohibition of a binding mandate? Article 67 of the Italian Constitution is a cornerstone of representative democracy that should not be revisited at all. Yet, I am wondering whether, for instance, an extremely widespread practice of party-switching—one of the most serious threats to the stability of governments in Italy—would actually be compatible with the Constitution from a perspective other than that of Article 67. But this is probably a very demanding question.

Finally, to get back to the specific subject of this contribution, one may wonder whether it would be wrong to 'throw the baby out with the bathwater' and consider the Five Star Movement model as the root of all evils. Indeed, some elements of this model may be implemented to bridge the gap between voters and parties, but only on the assumption that the relevant forms of direct and participatory democracy can complement, but never replace, representative democracy as such. The Internet can definitely serve the purpose to reduce the existing divide, but only to the extent resort to it is made within the boundaries set by the Constitution.

References

Ainis, M. (2017, April 28). Come salvare il Parlamento. *Repubblica*. Available at: https://www.repubblica.it

Allegri, M. R., Diletti, M., & Marsocci, P. (2018). *Political Parties and Political Foundations in Italy*. Milan: Franco Angeli.

Amato, G. (2012). Nota su una legge sui partiti in attuazione dell'art. 49 della Costituzione. *Rassegna Parlamentare, 4*, 1–13.

Azzariti, G. (2008). Cittadini, partiti e gruppi parlamentari: esiste ancora il divieto di mandato imperativo?. *Costituzionalismo.it, 3*, 1–38. Available at www.costituzionalismo.it

Barbera, A. (2009). La democrazia "dei" e "nei" partiti, tra rappresentanza e governabilità. In S. Merlini (Ed.), *La democrazia dei partiti e la democrazia nei partiti* (pp. 231–252). Firenze: Passigli Editore.

Biondi, F. (2012). *Il finanziamento pubblico dei partiti politici. Profili costituzionali*. Milano: Giuffrè.

Blokker, P. (2017, May 4). Populist Constitutionalism. *VerfBlog*. Available at: https://www.verfassungsblog.de

Bobbio, N. (1984). *Il futuro della democrazia*. Torino: Einaudi.

Bonfiglio, S. (2013). *I partiti e la democrazia. Per una rilettura dell'art. 49 della Costituzione*. Bologna: Il Mulino.
Bordignon, F., & Ceccarini, L. (2015). The Five-Star Movement: A Catch-All Anti-Party Party. In A. De Petris & T. Poguntke (Eds.), *Anti-Party Parties in Germany and Italy* (pp. 17–44). Rome: Luiss University Press.
Brunelli, G. (2016). Partiti politici e dimensione costituzionale della libertà associativa. In F. Biondi, G. Brunelli, & M. Revelli (Eds.), *I partiti politici nella organizzazione costituzionale* (pp. 7–35). Napoli: Editoriale Scientifica.
Calvano, R. (2018). La democrazia interna, il libero mandato parlamentare e il dottor Stranamore. *federalismi.it, 13*, 1–13. Available at www.federalismi.it
Canovan, M. (1999). Trust the People! Populism and the Two Faces of Democracy. *Political Studies, Political Studies Association, 47*(1), 2–16.
Carducci, M. (2018). Le dimensioni di interferenza del 'contratto' di governo e l'art. 67 Cost. *federalismi.it, 13*, 1–12. Available at www.federalismi.it.
Caruso, C., & Goldoni, M. (2017, February 28). Halving the "Italicum": The Italian Constitutional Court and the Reform of the Electoral System. *VerfBlog*. Available at https://www.verfassungsblog.de
Cerri, A. (2018). Osservazioni sulla libertà del mandato parlamentare. *federalismi.it, 13*, 1–9. Available at www.federalismi.it
Ciancio, A. (2018). Disciplina di gruppo e tutela del parlamentare dissenziente. *federalismi.it, 13*, 1–23. Available at www.federalismi.it
Clementi, F. (2018, August 15). I-CONnect Symposium–The Aftermath of the Italian General Election of March 4, 2018–The Italian Political Elections: A Definitive Back to the Past?. *International Journal of Constitutional Law Blog*. Available at: https://www.iconnectblog.com
Corbetta, P., & Gualmini, E. (2013). *Il partito di Grillo*. Bologna: Il Mulino.
Crisafulli, V. (1967). Partiti, parlamento, governo. In P. L. Zampetti (Ed.), *La funzionalità dei partiti nello stato democratico* (pp. 93–119). Milano: La Nuova Europa.
Curreri, S. (2018). Costituzione, regolamenti parlamentari e statuti dei gruppi politici: un rapporto da ripensare. *federalismi.it, 13*, 1–24. Available at www.federalismi.it
De Petris, A. (2015). Programs, Strategies and Electoral Campaigns of the Five Stars Movement in Italy. A Brand New Party Model or an "Anti-Party" State of Mind? In A. De Petris & T. Poguntke (Eds.), *Anti-Party Parties in Germany and Italy* (pp. 125–142). Rome: Luiss University Press.
De Petris, A., & Poguntke, T. (Eds.). (2015). *Anti-Party Parties in Germany and Italy*. Rome: Luiss University Press.
Delledonne, G., & Boggero, G. (2017, February 8). The Italian Constitutional Court Rules on Electoral System. *International Journal of Constitutional Law Blog*. Available at: https://www.iconnectblog.com

Demuro, G. (2018). Il diritto individuale al libero mandato parlamentare. *federalismi.it, 13*, 1–4. Available at www.federalismi.it

Di Maria, R. (2018). Una "clausola vessatoria" in bilico fra la democrazia rappresentativa e la tutela giursidizionale dei diritti. *federalismi.it, 13*, 1–10. Available at www.federalismi.it

Di Marzio, F. (2018). *La politica e il contratto.* Rome: Donzelli.

Diamanti, I. (2013). Introduzione. 2013: il Paese delle minoranze in-comunicanti. In I. Diamanti, F. Bordignon, & L. Ceccarini (Eds.), *Un salto nel voto. Ritratto politico dell'Italia di oggi* (pp. IX–XXVIII). Laterza: Rome-Bari.

Diamanti, I. (2014). The Five-Star Movement: A New Political Actor on the Web, in the Streets and on Stage. *Contemporary Italian Politics Journal, 6*(1), 4–15.

Elia, L. (2009). A quanto una legge sui partiti? In S. Merlini (Ed.), *La democrazia dei partiti e la democrazia nei partiti* (pp. 51–58). Firenze: Passigli Editore.

Esposito, C. (1954). I partiti nella Costituzione italiana. In Id., *La Costituzione italiana* (pp. 215–243), Padova: Cedam.

Falletti, E. (2014, June). *Direct Democracy and the Prohibition of the Binding Mandate: The Italian Debate.* Paper Presented at the World Congress of Constitutional Law, Oslo, pp. 1–14.

Ferri, G. (1950). *Studi sui partiti politici.* Roma: Edizioni dell'Ateneo.

Gambino, S. (1977). *Partiti politici e forma di governo.* Napoli: Liguori.

Gianfrancesco, E. (2017). I partiti politici e l'art. 49 della Costituzione. *Forum di Quaderni Costituzionali*, 1–23. Available at https://www.forumcostituzionale.it

Giuffrè, F. (2016). Crisi dei partiti, trasformazione della politica ed evoluzione della forma di governo. *federalismi.it, 23*, 1–19. Available at www.federalismi.it

Grasso, G. (2017a). Le "Mouvement 5 étoiles" et les défis de la démocratie représentative: à la recherche d'une notion constitutionnelle de populisme? *Percorsi Costituzionali, 1*, 205–226.

Grasso, G. (2017b). Mandato imperativo e mandato di partito: il caso del MoVimento 5 Stelle. *Osservatorio costituzionale, 2*, 1–7. Available at www.osservatorioaic.it

Grasso, G. (2018). Qualche riflessione su statuti e regolamenti dei Gruppi parlamentari, tra articolo 49 e articolo 67 della Costituzione. *federalismi.it, 13*, 1–6. Available at www.federalismi.it

Lanzafame, A. (2017). Sui livelli essenziali di democrazia nei partiti. *Rivista AIC, 1*, 1–21. Available at www.rivistaaic.it

Lanzone, M. E. (2014). The 'Post-Modern' Populism in Italy: The Case of the Five Stars Movement. In D. D. Woods & B. Wejnert (Eds.), *The Many Faces of Populism: Current Perspectives* (pp. 53–78). Bingley: Emerald.

Maranini, G. (1958). *Governo parlamentare e partitocrazia.* In Id (Ed.), *Miti e realtà della democrazia* (pp. 39–63). Milano: Ed. di Comunità.

Marsocci, P. (2012). *Sulla funzione costituzionale dei partiti e delle altre formazioni politiche.* Napoli: Editoriale Scientifica.

Marsocci, P. (2018). Lo status dei parlamentari osservato con la lente della disciplina interna dei gruppi. Gli argini (necessari) a difesa dell'art. 67. *federalismi.it, 13*, 1–6. Available at www.federalismi.it

Martinelli, C. (2018). Libero mandato e rappresentanza nazionale come fondamenti della modernità costituzionale. *federalismi.it, 13*, 1–8. Available at www.federalismi.it

Martines, T. (1957). *Contributo ad una teoria giuridica delle forze politiche*. Milano: Giuffrè.

Martinico, G. (2018, August 17). I-CONnect Symposium-the Aftermath of the Italian General Election of March 4, 2018–Populism Versus Constitutionalism 101: What Can We Learn from the Italian Scenario?. *International Journal of Constitutional Law Blog*. Available at https://www.iconnectblog.com

Mény, Y., & Surel, Y. (2002). The Constitutive Ambiguity of Populism. In Id (Ed.), *Democracy and the Populist Challenges* (pp. 1–21). London: Palgrave Macmillan.

Mueller, T. (2008, February 4). Beppe's Inferno. *The New Yorker*. Available at https://www.newyorker.com

Müller, J.-W. (2015). *Populist Constitutionalism: A Contradiction in Terms?*. Unpublished Paper. Available at https://www.law.nyu.edu

Müller, J.-W. (2016). *What Is Populism?* Philadelphia: University of Pennsylvania Press.

Nicotra, I. (2008). *Democrazia "convenzionale" e partiti antisistema*. Torino: Giappichelli.

Orofino, M. (2017, November 17). The Web 2.0 and Its Impact on Relations Between Citizens and Political Representatives. *MediaLaws*. Available at https://www.medialaws.eu

Pinelli, C. (2011). The Populist Challenge to Constitutional Democracy. *European Constitutional Law Review, 7*, 5–16.

Pinelli, C. (2018). Libertà di mandato dei parlamentari e rimedi contro il transfughismo. *federalismi.it, 13*, 1–5. Available at www.federalismi.it

Predieri, A. (1950). I partiti politici. In P. Calamandrei & A. Levi (Eds.), *Commentario sistematico alla Costituzione italiana, I* (pp. 171–215). Firenze: Barbera.

Prisco, S. (2018), Elogio della mediazione. Statuti dei gruppi parlamentari e libertà di mandato politico nelle democrazie rappresentative. Brevi annotazioni. *federalismi.it, 13*, 1–25. Available at www.federalismi.it

Ridola, P. (1982). Partiti politici. In *Enciclopedia del diritto* (pp. 66–126, Vol. XXXII). Milano: Giuffrè.

Rinaldi, E. (2017). Divieto di mandato imperativo e disciplina dei gruppi parlamentari. *Costituzionalismo.it, 2*, 133–186. Available at www.costituzionalismo.it

Sartori, G. (2013, November 6). Una violazione macroscopica. *Corriere della Sera*. Available at: https://www.corriere.it

Sbailò, C. (2018). Presidenzialismo contro populismo: col mandato imperativo si dissolve la democrazia costituzionale, ma non basta dire 'no'. *federalismi.it, 13*, 1–12. Available at www.federalismi.it

Schefold, D. (2017). Constitutional Reform and Constitutional Unity. Reflections on the Constitutional Referendum of 4 December 2016 and on the Judgment of the Constitutional Court No 35/2017. *Italian L.J*, (Special Issue), 147–156.

Scheppele, K. L. (2017, November 16). Autocratic Legalism. *blogs.eui.eu*. Available at https://blogs.eui.eu/constitutionalism-politics-working-group

Scuto, F. (2017). Democrazia rappresentativa e partiti politici: la rilevanza dell'organizzazione interna ed il suo impatto sulla rappresentanza politica. *federalismi.it, 1*, 1–20. Available at www.federalismi.it

Scuto, F. (2018a). I pericoli derivanti da uno svuotamento dell'art. 67 Cost. unito ad un "irrigidimento" dell'art. 49 Cost. Alcune considerazioni a partire dalla vicenda dello Statuto del Gruppo parlamentare 'Movimento 5 Stelle'. *federalismi.it, 13*, 1–13. Available at www.federalismi.it

Scuto, F. (2018b). *La democrazia interna dei partiti: profili costituzionali di una transizione*. Torino: Giappichelli.

Staiano, S. (Ed.). (2014). *Nella rete dei partiti. Trasformazione politica, forma di governo, network analysis*. Naples: Jovene.

Staiano, S. (2015). Trasformazioni dei partiti e forma di governo. *federalismi.it, 19*, 1–14. Available at www.federalismi.it

Tarchi, M. (2015). *Italia populista. Dal qualunquismo a Beppe Grillo*. Bologna: Il Mulino.

Torre, A. (2018, August 16). I-CONnect Symposium–The Aftermath of the Italian General Election of March 4, 2018–Taming the Crisis. *International Journal of Constitutional Law Blog*. Available at: https://www.iconnectblog.com

Tronconi, F. (Ed.). (2015). *Beppe Grillo's Five Star Movement: Organisation, Communication and Ideology*. London/New York: Routledge.

Urbinati, N. (2015). A Revolt Against Intermediary Bodies. *Constellations, 22*(4), 477–485.

Zanon, N. (1991). *Il libero mandato parlamentare*. Milano: Giuffrè.

CHAPTER 11

Populism, Science and the Italian Democracy

Marta Tomasi

Introduction

Although there is still no commonly accepted definition of populism, and scholars disagree on how best to categorize it, or to distinguish the boundaries between its different manifestations (Caiani and Graziano 2016), consensus can probably be found on some of its features: mistrust of elites, deemed corrupt or morally inferior, is arguably the most distinctive trait of populist rhetoric (Müller 2016; Mudde and Rovira Kaltwasser 2017). One of the many problematic declinations of this trait relates to scientific and health-related issues, where scepticism and suspicion risk compromising the relationship between political institutions and the scientific community, and could eventually endanger fundamental rights. Allowing policymakers to treat scientific advice grounded in a well-established, transparent scientific process as just another special interest opinion may well jeopardize policymakers' capacity to make sound decisions, and, consequently, everyone's health and quality of life (Rosenberg et al. 2013). Italy, which has been described as a "laboratory of populism" (Tarchi 2015), offers some paradigmatic examples of how, when expert and popular knowledge stand in opposition, the political discourse can be contaminated, generating

M. Tomasi (✉)
Free University of Bozen-Bolzano, Bolzano, Italy
e-mail: marta.tomasi@unibz.it

G. Delledonne et al. (eds.), *Italian Populism and Constitutional Law*, Challenges to Democracy in the 21st Century,
https://doi.org/10.1007/978-3-030-37401-3_11

problematic impasses and making good policy outcomes significantly less likely.

Science, Policymaking, and the Populist Discourse

Public health policies are commonly assumed to be rooted in the available scientific evidence, strong and effective communication processes, and the competence of policymakers to evaluate any evidence presented to them (Camargo and Grant 2015). This expectation leads—in most national legal systems—to the key role of technical-scientific evaluations in the processes of defining and implementing regulatory contents and the consideration of scientific soundness and expertise as a condition for the constitutional legitimacy of regulatory choices (Penasa 2015).

It must, however, be recognized that, despite the strong emphasis placed on science, on no level can policy be dictated by science alone. Policy choices are inevitably and necessarily informed by values, and science-based arguments do not always enjoy strong credibility in public debate. On the contrary, in fact, the public sphere is very often dominated by emotion and ideology rather than scientific soundness (Camargo and Grant 2015).

It is therefore important to monitor whether, how, and to what extent current populist trends are affecting—and challenging—the role of science in policymaking, and to investigate the consequences for democracy and the constitutional rule of law.

The equation of politics with the mere expression of the *volonté générale* (Mudde and Rovira Kaltwasser 2017: 6), and the anti-elitist and anti-expert ideology that accompanies this equation, combined with the dissemination of misinformation through the media, can be shown to marginalize science and scientific advice in public policy debates. Mistrust of science can make it less likely for sound policy to arise from public debate; it also inevitably widens the troubling current disconnect between scientific elites and general populations. This is happening around the world, in many different situations, with regard to natural resource use, environmental impacts, public health and safety, and more (Rosenberg et al. 2013).

In Italy, where UFO and chemtrail theories have actually been proposed for discussion in the national Parliament, the tradition of pseudoscience is long and well-established, dating back to well before the rise of the contemporary "populist tide". Nonetheless, recent examples prove how far this tendency can go, when the law renounces its role of controlling and selecting individual (health-related) demands that the legal system can be expected to take into account, and allows (health) policies to become the immediate conduit of a non-technical popular will.

Vaccine Scepticism and the Protection of Public Health

The safety and effectiveness of vaccines are subject to constant investigation and, so far, the vast majority of studies have shown today's vaccines to be safe and effective, and serious side effects to be rare (Maglione et al. 2014, and many others). Nonetheless, the debate around mandatory vaccinations has never ceased to be coloured by scepticism and hesitation, leading to reduced vaccination uptake becoming a recurrent story in recent decades (Smith 2017).

Italy is no exception. Its story—centred around four compulsory vaccinations, the strength of which has steadily been decreased over the years—is convoluted and painful (Tomasi 2017). The obligation to vaccinate children against tetanus, diphtheria, polio, and hepatitis B, introduced between 1939 and 1991, was originally accompanied by the provision of criminal sanctions (then turned into administrative fines). A further, although indirect, incentive for complying with the vaccination regime derived from the stipulation that children be vaccinated before admission to (any level of) compulsory education. This requirement was removed in 1999,[1] and in fact, a law passed five years before had made it impossible to actually enforce the legal obligation.[2]

Public pressure meant that the statutory obligation to vaccinate—although not taken off the books—yielded, in practice, to a more flexible and tolerant path towards forms of voluntary acceptance.

Although higher courts upheld the constitutionality of the vaccination mandate,[3] its standing was substantially weakened by the national Vaccinations Plan 2005–2007, in which the Ministry of Health, stressing the importance of information policies, advocated that the regions be

[1] Decree of the President of the Italian Republic no. 355, 26 January 1999.

[2] Law decree no. 273, 6 May 1994.

[3] See, for examples, Court of Cassation, I sez. civ., judgment no. 14384, 8 July 2005 and, analogously, Court of Cassation, I sez. civ., judgment no. 11226, 18 July 2003 and Constitutional Court, judgment no. 262, 8–22 July 2004.

empowered to embark on an experimental path towards the suspension of the national mandatory vaccinations. This recognition of regional autonomy allowed some regions to suspend the administrative fines for not complying with the vaccination mandate.[4] And the Veneto Region, with the introduction of regional Law 7/2007, suspended, at the local level, all obligatory childhood vaccination. The legal obligation was replaced by the proactive offer of all vaccines recognized as safe and effective (without charge), and the experiment was carefully monitored to prevent any decline in compliance.

This national strategy to promote voluntary vaccination proved unsuccessful[5] and a new law, which increased Italy's obligatory vaccines from the original four to ten, was introduced in 2017.[6] The mandate led to large-scale protests across the country.

The constitutionality of the new legislation was challenged (by the Veneto Region), but upheld by the Constitutional Court. The former's claim was that the state's intervention was too sweeping and disproportionate. In the Court's view, although the role of the regions in the field of healthcare is crucial, the national interest in uniformly protecting health, offering essential health services, managing international prophylaxis, and regulating the right to education prevails. The Court also held that, given the epidemiological situation, the new law could not be deemed either non-rational or disproportionate (Ciaccio 2018).[7]

The success of the Lega in the 2018 general election and the subsequent formation (in coalition with the populist Five Star Movement) of a "Government of change" (Vampa 2018) once again threw the issue of obligatory vaccination into question. In their electoral campaigns, both parties had trenchantly opposed the vaccination policy, repeatedly raising

[4] See, for example, the decision of the regional authorities in Piedmont (no. 63/2598, 10 April 2006).

[5] It has to be acknowledged that there has, in the past, been no proof of a direct link between obligatory vaccinations and increased immunization rates, or vice versa.

[6] Law of 31 July 2017 n. 119, converting law decree 7 June 2017, n.73/2017, in the Official Gazette of the Italian Republic, n. 182, 5 August 2017. The new law required that parents vaccinate children under 16 against diphtheria, *Haemophilus influenzae* type B, hepatitis B, measles, mumps, pertussis, polio, rubella, tetanus, and varicella before enrolling them in school, with only medical exemptions allowed and fines imposed on non-compliant parents (for children aged 6–16, the only sanction is fines; children under 6 may not attend school).

[7] Constitutional Court, decision n. 5/2018, in the Official Gazette of the Italian Republic, n. 4, 24 January 2018.

pseudoscientific objections, to MMR (measles, mumps, and rubella) injections in particular (Wheaton and Zampano 2018).

The ability of powerful populist parties, whose political momentum partly derives from their criticism of scientific orthodoxy, to discredit scientific knowledge, threaten legal certainty, and even compromise public health will be demonstrated by example below.

Some months after the election, Minister Giulia Grillo, a member of the Five Star Movement, announced that parents did not need to provide official immunization records for the school year 2018–2019. The decision to temporarily allow "self-certification"—a parental declaration that their child has been immunized—to substitute ratified medical proof[8] is not, admittedly, anti-vaccine; nevertheless, it clearly undermines the 2017 policy to require vaccination by law (Morelli et al. 2017).

Another attempt to dilute the contents of the mandate was made in August. The upper house of the Italian Parliament passed an amendment postponing (until the 2019/2020 school year) the exclusion from school of children under 6. The final version of the bill, modified by the lower chamber, did not postpone the sanction of school exclusion but, backing the act adopted by the executive in July, extended the validity of self-certifications to 10 March 2019.[9] This was a significant step, in particular because it allowed the "hierarchical" objection to be overcome: according to some commentators, the ministerial act did not have the necessary authority to modify the mandatory vaccination law.

The final intention was to adopt comprehensive legislation to either repeal or weaken the law: in early October 2018, the Senate began to discuss a new Five Star Movement proposal. The bill, designed to repeal the 2017 mandate legislation, stressed the importance of a National vaccine registry, encouraged vaccination and citizens' voluntary informed compliance, and reinforced the surveillance system. There was provision for the (re)introduction of obligation in emergencies and/or if a semestral report (which would also be provided for) indicated that herd immunity was being compromised. Failure to comply could incur an administrative fine of between 100 and 500€. In the above circumstances, a child who had

[8] Memo circulated by the Ministry of Health and the Ministry of Education, Universities and Research, concerning obligatory vaccines for the 2018/2019 school year, available at: http://www.trovanorme.salute.gov.it/norme/renderNormsanPdf?anno=2018&codLeg=64928&parte=1%20&serie=null, (last visited September 26, 2019).

[9] Article 6, 3-quarter, law decree 25 July 2018, n. 91 as converted by Law 21 September 2018, n. 108, in the Official Gazette of the Italian Republic, n. 220, 21 September 2018.

not had the requisite vaccine(s) might lawfully be (temporarily) excluded from school, in order to protect immunodeficient children.[10] This approach was referred to as "flexible duty".

During its short tenure, the Lega–Five Star government made several U-turns, in a tense relationship with the scientific community: vocal criticism of vaccine safety and/or efficacy; the indulgence of 'anti-vaxxer' claims to individual self-determination; support for four compulsory vaccinations only; regional initiatives aimed at removing obligation at the local level;[11] Beppe Grillo's decision to sign, together with other politicians, a "pact for science" launched by virologist Roberto Burioni which supported vaccination; and, finally, the discussion about the curiously termed "flexible duty", which would come into force only during an epidemic (despite the fact that this would seem to defeat the point of vaccinations).

A widespread lack of clarity naturally confused parents and schools alike: both scientific consistency and legal certainty were at stake. In August 2018, the northern Italian province of Bozen-Bolzano, in the light of the incoherent national policy, took matters into its own hands and adopted an administrative act which postponed (until January 31, 2019) the deadline for presenting immunization records.[12] Although the province enjoys greater autonomy than most Italian regions,[13] the legal basis for its measure is possibly open to question. A month later, two parents (in Piedmont) took the school authorities to court for having excluded their unvaccinated child from kindergarten. The 2017 mandatory

[10] Article 5, Senate bill, n. 770.

[11] This proposed law, which was controversial not only outside but also within the Five Star Movement, not only didn't provide for any obligation, but also required that a child be in "optimal psychological and physical health" at the time of any vaccination, and that the physician had to "authorize", under his/her own responsibility, the vaccination. It calls for the titre testing of all children before vaccination, and originally suggested that health authorities quarantine children receiving attenuated virus vaccines for four to six weeks after vaccination to protect their classmates from shedding (in the second version of the proposal quarantine was merely recommended). The draft bill proposes that nutrition be used to prevent disease and that single vaccines (gradually) replace combination vaccines. See Regional Council of Lazio, Legislative Proposal no. 52, 17 July 2018, available at: http://www.quotidianosanita.it/allegati/allegato9859338.pdf (last visited 26 September 2019).

[12] Provincial council of Bozen-Bolzano, 28 August 2018, n. 853.

[13] The Italian Constitution provides for special conditions of autonomy for five regions (Sicily, Sardinia, Friuli Venezia Giulia, Trentino Alto-Adige, and Valle d'Aosta) and two autonomous provinces (Trento and Bolzano).

vaccination law requires that when a child is enrolled in a school, the immunization records of children aged 0–6, or, alternatively, either a medical exemption certificate or a formal request to the local health authority that your child be vaccinated, be presented. In this case, the parents had merely demonstrated to the school that they had requested a meeting with the local health authorities. The Administrative Tribunal of Piedmont upheld the school's decision and clarified that [simply] having requested a meeting did not meet the legal requirements.[14]

Although policymakers did not clearly state their opposition to vaccines in general, their all too frequent ambivalence intensified a debate the basis of which is rarely scientific argument, and helped to legitimize positions grounded in controversial science.

The relationship between politics and scientific trust also seems to have been highlighted by other recent findings. According to a study by Queen Mary University of London (Kennedy 2019), there is a substantial association between the increase in European populism and levels of mistrust in science and corresponding vaccine resistance. The study, published in the *European Journal of Public Health*, looked at national-level data from 14 European countries. The data included the percentage of people in a country who voted for a populist party in the 2014 European Parliament elections, and the percentage who believed that vaccines are not important, safe, and/or effective, according to data from the 2015 Vaccine Confidence Project.

A highly significant positive association between the percentage of people in a country who voted for a populist party and the percentage who believed that vaccines were not important and not effective was found.

Although further empirical investigation is needed, according to the author, "it seems likely that scientific populism is driven by similar feelings to political populism, for example, a profound distrust of elites and experts by disenfranchised and marginalised parts of the population". In the article, Italy is cited as a prominent example of the suggested connection between the rise of populist politicians and political movements in Western Europe and increasing levels of vaccine hesitancy. In 2017, a *New York Times* editorial entitled "Populism, Politics and Measles" noted that The Five Star Movement had raised concerns about vaccine safety and the link between MMR and autism and that these concerns might have contributed

[14] Regional Administrative Tribunale, Piedmont, decision n. 1034/2018, 19 September 2018.

to the MMR vaccination coverage decline from 90% in 2013 to 85% in 2016, and resulted in an increase in measles cases from 840 in 2016 to 5000 in 2017 (New York Times 2017).

Similarly, in December 2018, a *Guardian* investigation "showed growing concern about the impact of populism on public confidence in vaccines, revealing that measles cases in Europe were at a 20-year high, with 60,000 cases and 72 deaths" (The Guardian 2018, 2019).

These studies highlight the circular relationship between two forms of populism: on the one hand, political populism, born out of a deep distrust of traditional politics, may have extended to influence people's attitudes to the scientific and medical community; and, on the other—in Italy, at least—distrust in science and "technological populism" (which denies scientific experts any role in public policy debates (Collins and Evans 2008)) may have been one of the factors that led to the rise of populist parties. Scepticism about vaccinations and distrust of institutions seem to feed off one another, and both fit perfectly within the populist discourse.

Unvalidated Therapies: The Italian "Stamina" Case

A non-rigorous approach to science can also lead into the field of non-validated therapies, which often overlap with "miracle cures". The Italian case that exemplifies the harms that populist trends can cause to fundamental rights has come to be known as the "Stamina case". Although these events did not occur when populists were in government,[15] they nonetheless highlight the risks involved when the instruments of law and democracy are deformed by emotional discourse and popular pressure.

In 2013, some of the Italian media were engaged in an emotive campaign that called for people with degenerative diseases to be given access to an untested and controversial stem cell therapy, which was promoted by the Stamina Foundation's president, a psychologist who claimed it could work miracles. These treatments, initially administered in a public hospital (Spedali Civili di Brescia), had been blocked by the Italian Medicines Agency (AIFA) for reasons of safety and transparency, following an inspection of the laboratories in the hospital where the infusions were performed. The story resonated throughout Italy and beyond, and was covered—frequently and critically—by international scientific journals such as *Nature* (Abbott 2013, 2016; Bianco et al. 2014).

[15] For the main manifestations of Italian populism, see Blokker and Anselmi (2019).

Following the media campaign, the parents of severely ill children filed several petitions before a number of different courts, seeking authorization to access, or to continue, contentious stem cell treatments offered by the Stamina Foundation.

Initially, the legal basis for these treatments was found in a Health Ministry decree on the use of gene therapy and human somatic cell therapies,[16] according to which such treatments were to be allowed (outside clinical trials) only where no alternative therapy was possible, and patients were in life-threatening situations. Further requirements included approval from an ethics committee, the patient's consent, the existence of relevant publications in international scientific reviews and journals, and compliance with specific safety procedures during the infusions.

The interpretations of these requirements, and the subsequent diverging adjudications, created an ambiguous situation and generated uncertainty. In an attempt to deal with the question, and in response to public pressure, the Italian government decided to modify the normative framework and to address the issue with a specific law decree ("decreto legge").[17] The new regulation requires (i) to begin a formal clinical trial of the Stamina treatments and (ii) allows the National health service to administer the treatments offered by the Stamina Foundation only to people who have already received authorization from the judiciary, or have already had one or more infusions. All of this happened despite the fact that the vast majority of the scientific community had never believed the treatments to be effective and, indeed, had, from the very beginning, warned of their possible harm. In a letter to the Ministry, many Italian stem cell scientists described the decision to permit the use of an untested treatment as providing "a dangerous short circuit between patients' hopes and [the] lucrative commercial practices" of organizations operating without the "scientific and moral foundations" of medicine.[18]

[16] Ministry Decree 5 December 2006, Official Journal of the Italian Republic, no.57, 9 March 2007.

[17] Law decree 25 March 2013, n. 24, converted into law 23 May 2013, n. 57 (Italian Official Gazette 25 May 2013, n. 121).

[18] According to Italian scientists "The decision seems to be dictated by emotions raised by public opinion rather than by scientifically based reasons. (…) The freedom of any citizen to adopt any personal health decision, including the wish to refuse any cure, does not imply that the Government is obliged to authorize all medical procedures that anyone may suggest as appropriate. (…) It is not the Government's role to respond to pressure from patients to

The decisions of many judges (made under both of the above normative frameworks) in favour of access to the treatments offered by the Stamina Foundation, show the pitfalls of judicial intervention in health policy: many judges proved to be heavily influenced by the tragic aspects of some of the cases, and/or often influenced by expert witnesses unrepresentative of mainstream public health opinion and, moreover, often focused on individual interests at the expense of the community's claim to public health protection (Gostin 2008: 84–85). In the Stamina case, the borders of the concept of health were expanded beyond acceptable, rational limits: among the many decisions delivered by several judges,[19] some detach the concept of health from even the most basic scientific rationale.[20]

While this outcome, although highly problematic, is, to some extent, understandable—given the urgency of the claims presented to the judges, and the limited (to each individual case) efficacy of the decisions—the attitude of the legislature is much more open to criticism.

The Italian legal system is not unprepared to deal with the pressing nature of health-related needs: like many other national frameworks, it provides for treatment strategies that can—if deemed appropriate—circumvent the time-consuming procedures of clinical trials. A case in the 1990s, for example, led the Italian Constitutional Court to state that, faced with acute therapeutic need, where no alternative cure is available, the right to health can be extended to cover expectations prompted by ongoing clinical trials[21] (Benelli 2003: 179–186; Fattore 1999: 123–142). This ruling provides for the compassionate use of experimental therapies under specific circumstances.[22] The aforementioned decree of 2006 further extends this approach, making it possible to access non-validated treatments, even outside clinical trials.

translate an individual choice into a therapeutic option for ready use in any health structure" (translation provided by EuroStemCell, at: www.eurostemcell.org)

[19] Original texts of several judgments have been collected on the website www.biodiritto.org

[20] See, for example, the judgment by the Tribunal in Asti (12 November 2013) stating that the legal requirement of a minimum degree of scientificity of new experimental treatments and the requisite of the approval by an ethics committee are to be considered unconstitutional.

[21] See Constitutional Court judgment n. 185/1998 concerning the so-called Di Bella therapy, a supposedly revolutionary alternative cure for cancer.

[22] See also Art. 83 of Regulation (EC) N° 726/2004 concerning compassionate use programmes.

Despite the granting of these options, the Italian government decided to further intervene (at a time when the scientific truths on the issue were still under construction),[23] adopting a new policy which professes trust in the treatments offered by the Stamina Foundation, and consequently paves the way for extremely unrealistic demands for health. The government, driven by emotional rather than rational concerns, enacted law decree n. 24/2013. According to Art. 77 of the Italian Constitution, the Government can, in extraordinary cases of necessity and emergency, adopt law decrees independently of the legislature; such acts subsequently have to be converted into law by the Parliament. The documents accompanying the law decree stated that the authorization to continue, or to begin, a treatment previously authorized by a judge is necessary to alleviate the profound distress of people who hope to obtain benefits from Stamina stem cell treatments which cannot be achieved by any other means. Moreover, the first version of the decree approved by the Government allowed the continuation of therapies which had already been started, even if these had been prepared in laboratories which did not comply with European pharmaceutical manufacturing standards.[24] Similar provisions, subsequently amended by the Parliament to conform to European legislation, show how the law, when in thrall to unfounded claims, can dramatically contribute to widening the gap between the scientific community and a country's institutions.

The recognition of such demands, detached from basic scientific standards and defined in Italy as the "right to hope" (which largely corresponds to the "right to try" in the US), led to the law decree n. 24/2013, which challenged the Italian constitution:[25] the decree, in fact, allowed certain individuals to access new unproven treatments, while excluding others. The former were identified solely on the basis of having obtained

[23] Two different ad hoc scientific committees were set up, tasked with giving an opinion about the safety and efficacy of the Stamina treatments. Both committees concluded by clearly expressing a negative judgment, recommending that clinical trials, given the lack of scientific prerequisites, should not be allowed to begin (September 2013 and October 2014).

[24] See art. 2.2 of law decree 24/2013, stating, in the Italian wording, that treatments should not be discontinued: "anche se preparati presso laboratori non conformi ai principi delle norme europee di buona fabbricazione dei medicinali e in difformità delle disposizioni del decreto del Ministro della salute 5 dicembre 2006".

[25] Constitutional Court, judgment n. 274, 1 December 2014, Italian Official Gazette n. 51, 10 December 2014.

either judicial authorization (although, as we saw before, judicial opinion was far from unanimous on this issue), or a previous infusion before the date upon which the decree had come into force: seriously ill patients would thus have been discriminated against purely on the basis of when they had asked to access the therapies.[26] Despite apparently upholding the decree, the Court (which could not rule on the government's decision to authorize the prosecution of therapies, which had not been challenged) said something fundamental about the identification of the right to be protected. If the legal intervention—which derogated from the general rules governing the administration of new drugs—had really been intended to protect patients' right to health, it would have been unreasonable to exclude patients (whose state of health was as grave as the people whose right to avail of the treatment had been protected) from accessing the same treatment solely on the above mentioned chronological basis. The Constitutional Court found that the decree had intervened within an "abnormal context",[27] with the aim of privileging principles of therapeutic continuity and the need not to interfere with the authority of the judiciary. It would therefore be unreasonable to extend such a time-limited derogation to other patients, to whom the peculiar and exceptional circumstances which animated the legislator do not apply.[28]

The Court, implicitly excluding that the rationale of the legislative provision could be found in the direct protection of the fundamental right to health, referred to a recent decision by the European Court of Human Rights, on the treatments offered by the Stamina Foundation[29]

[26] The constitutional challenge was raised by the Taranto Tribunal, judgment n. 4960, 24 September 2013.

[27] Determined by the fact that the treatments proposed by the Stamina Foundation took place under the auspices of the national health service (outside clinical trials, despite their experimental nature) and by the fact that some infusions were authorized by judges as a matter of urgency.

[28] It might be relevant to note that the Court was not asked (and was consequently not allowed to take a position) about the constitutionality of the choice to allow ill-founded treatments for some patients, but only about the constitutionality of the choice to discriminate between claims.

[29] The reference is to the European Court of Human Rights' decision in the case of *Durisotto v. Italy* (application no. 62804/13). The Court had (by a majority) declared inadmissible the application of a father alleging that there had been a violation of his daughter's right to life and health on account of the fact that the Italian courts had refused to allow her to obtain the compassionate therapy known as "Stamina" under law decree no. 24/2013. The ECHR held that the prohibition to access this therapy, imposed by the Italian court in

(Rial-Sebbag and Blasimme 2014: 39–43). In its judgment, the European Court of Human Rights stated that, in view of the fact that knowledge in the field of stem cell treatment is still far from comprehensive, the judge's decision to restrict patient access to Stamina treatments lawfully pursues the scope of protecting their health, being proportionate to that aim. Since it was not in a position to judge the constitutionality of the legislature's decision (which had not been challenged) to listen to the demands of (only) certain citizens, the Court found that, for other patients, the more general principle of caution in the validation and administering of drugs should prevail.

The decision by the Constitutional Court sets limits to the individual choices the legal system can be expected to take into account, restating that not even the broadest concept of health can disregard, in its realization, the temporary, progressive and incomplete acquisitions of science.

Populism, Science, and Democracy

The cases involving vaccines and non-validated therapies in Italy exemplify the challenges posed by populist trends to effectively informing government policy by objective scientific information and advice.

Since it is seems to be impossible to find a consensus on any definition of populism, it is difficult to unequivocally link the incidents described above with populist trends; nonetheless, what has happened is, without question, closely connected to some of the most common aspects of current understandings of "populism": they are characterized by the emergence of an anti-elitist ideology, the spread of "highly emotional" rhetoric, and an "opportunistic use of policies" to gain the support of voters (Mudde 2004).

An analysis of these identifiers allows us to draw some conclusions concerning the relationship between populist attitudes and the respect for science, and the consequences of this dynamic on a democratic society.

First, as said before, scientific and technological populism, understood as disaffection with, and criticism of, scientific knowledge and expertise (Collins and Evans 2008), seem to be strongly related to populist political trends. On the one hand, populist thinking in the field of science and

applying law decree no. 24/2013, pursued the legitimate aim of protecting health and was proportionate to that aim. The national court's decision had not been arbitrary, since the therapeutic value of the "Stamina" method had not, to date, been proven scientifically.

medicine contributes to creating subcultures and a climate of scepticism that allows political populism to flourish, thereby also affecting other institutions, such as technical bodies. It seems highly unlikely that the storm around the Stamina case and the decrease in confidence in vaccines coincided by chance; both arose from a profound discontent with the Italian health service's decisions and policies. On the other hand, political populism can, by adopting questionable and unorthodox decision-making processes, contribute to tarnishing the image of science. Whether in dealing with the issue of vaccination, or that of stem cell therapies, the law cannot be held primarily responsible for scientific difficulties, since the media played a key role in disseminating distorted or misinterpreted truths. Moreover, politics can act as an echo chamber for pseudo-science: an ambiguous message is conveyed when sanctions for non-compliance with laws on vaccination are weakened; alternatives to obligatory vaccination are promoted without due surveillance; unproven treatments are permitted to continue—all of which clearly casts doubt on the solidity of scientific knowledge and expert authority.

Science and the law need reciprocal legitimation. In many fields, regulatory choices, to be deemed adequate and constitutionally sound, have to take solid scientific arguments into due consideration, while science, when disregarded by institutional authorities, risks losing its coherence and persuasive force.

The second issue is related to the emotional basis of populist policies. How much room can the law allow to individual convictions about health and treatments? The reported cases deal with individual notions of health, which result in demands for treatments of dubious, or no, efficacy or, on the other hand, to sceptical attitudes or open aversion to well-established medical practices. The multiplicity of individual interests challenges the workability of the pluralist principle, the rejection of which is, by many scholars and with good reason, considered to lie at the heart of populism (Müller 2016). In the area of health, pluralism is sometimes distorted and exaggerated. Ultimately, both sagas prove that democratic pluralism, when it entails divergent visions of health, based on misinformation, emotional involvement, or distrust, can only be tolerated up to a certain point; that is, it cannot diverge too far from generally recognized levels of scientific reasonableness, and should not affect the health of others. Thus, non-validated therapies can be administered as long as proxies for efficacy and safety exist, and a small percentage of non-vaccinated people can be tolerated in society, without jeopardizing public health. Beyond that limit, the norms of scientific soundness must prevail.

One last consideration addresses the relationship between science and democracy. Philosophical and historical analyses have suggested that the former provides both the basis of, and a method for, the latter; democracy is best achieved and flourishes in reliance on science (Edel 1944; Sigerist 1938). Given this interconnection, populist attitudes to science, and the populist movements' use of science in policymaking, seem all too likely to directly affect the democratic process itself.

As we have shown, the denial of scientific truths may endanger fundamental rights. Of course, the intention is not to suggest that scientific evidence can simply be translated "verbatim" into policymaking. Populism, however, by challenging the role of science as a critical tool of informed policymaking, has moulded political decision-making processes to impulse and individual demands driven by pseudo- or anti-scientific theories.

The problem is that scientific issues, for as long as they are perceived as top-down, absolute truths, will always be vulnerable to populist attack. Science, of course, is not, and can never be, democratic in its content. To prevent mistrust of scientists from being used as an ideology for political purposes, it is therefore necessary to remember that science and democracy ultimately share the same values. Democratic societies are founded on open debate, the free flow of information, mutual respect, and the critical role of inquiry and evidence—all values that are also fundamental to the scientific method (Branscomb and Rosenberg 2012).

It is much more difficult to correctly assess scientific findings than was once believed and they cannot lead straight to political conclusions. Nevertheless, there is no inherent contradiction between expertise and democracy, as long as politicians and the public maintain a critical stance with regard to expert opinion (Turner 2001). Scientists (and, above all, science communicators), in turn, if they wish to persuade, should adopt Aristotle's three elements of good rhetoric: their arguments should be based on sound theory and data ("logos"), but also give the impression that they are speaking in the interest of the listener ("ethos") whom they need to touch on an emotional level ("pathos") (Pigliucci 2018). Science has to be made accessible, comprehensible, and usable for everybody (especially when its findings are related to human health); moreover, its production processes can be inclusive and participatory.[30] Conversely, with regard to its content, personal opinions and views have to give way to empirically based theories. And while error is undoubtedly an inevitable feature of science, the attempt to build trust around mistaken theories—including through public policy—strengthens pseudo-science, which has been described as a perpetration of mistakes (Pigliucci and Boudry 2013). Today, science and democracy share, not a majoritarian vocation, but the constitutional nature of being governed by accepted limits and methods.

References

Abbott, A. (2013, July 2). Italian Stem-Cell Trial Based on Flawed Data. Scientists Raise Serious Concerns about a Patent that Forms the Basis of a Controversial Stem-Cell Therapy. *Nature. News*. Available at https://www.nature.com/news/italian-stem-cell-trial-based-on-flawed-data-1.13329

Abbott, A. (2016). Stem-Cell Scandal Gets Fresh Scrutiny. *Nature, 539*, 340.

Benelli, E. (2003). The Role of the Media in Steering Public Opinion on Healthcare Issues. *Health Policy, 63*(2), 179–186.

Bianco, P., Cattaneo, E., De Luca, M., & Pani, L. (2014). Stamina Therapies: Let the Record Stand. *Nature, 506*(7489), 434–434.

Blokker, P., & Anselmi, M. (2019). *Multiple Populisms: Italy as Democracy's Mirror*. New York: Routledge.

Branscomb, L. M., & Rosenberg, A. A. (2012, October). Science and Democracy. *The Scientist*. Available at https://www.the-scientist.com/critic-at-large/science-and-democracy-40425

Bucchi, M. (2009). *Beyond Technocracy: Science, Politics and Citizens* (A. Belton, Trans.). Dordrecht: Springer.

Caiani, M., & Graziano, P. R. (2016). Varieties of Populism: Insights from the Italian Case. *Rivista Italiana di Scienza Politica, 46*(S2), 243–267.

Camargo, K. J., & Grant, R. (2015). Public Health, Science, and Policy Debate: Being Right Is Not Enough. *American Journal of Public Health, 105*(2), 232–235.

Ciaccio, V. (2018). I vaccini obbligatori al vaglio di costituzionalità. Riflessioni a margine di Corte Cost., sent. n. 5 del 2018. *Giurisprudenza costituzionale, 18*(1), 451–468.

[30] In particular, of key importance is the effort to involve laypeople in decision-making on socio-technical controversies. On this, see Bucchi (2009), Kleinman (2000). More generally, on the multifaceted issue of participatory efforts to "democratize" science, see Jasanoff (2003: 223–244).

Collins, H. M., & Evans, R. (2008). *Rethinking Expertise*. Chicago: University of Chicago Press.

Edel, A. (1944). The Relations of Science and Democracy. *The Journal of Philosophy, 41*(26), 701–710.

Fattore, G. (1999). Clarifying the Scope of Italian NHS Coverage. Is It Feasible? Is It Desirable? *Health Policy, 50*(1–2), 123–142.

Gostin, L. O. (2008). *Public Health Law. Power, Duty, Restraint*. Berkeley: University of California Press.

Jasanoff, S. (2003). Technologies of Humility: Citizen Participation in Governing Science. *Minerva, 41*(3), 223–244.

Kennedy, J. (2019). Populist politics and vaccine hesitancy in Western Europe: An Analysis of National-Level Data. *European Journal of Public Health, 29*(3), 512–516.

Kleinman, D. L. (2000). *Science, Technology, and Democracy*. Albany: State University of New York Press.

Maglione, M. A., Das, L., Raaen, L., Smith, A., Chari, R., Newberry, S., Shanman, R., Perry, T., Bidwell Goetz, M., & Gidengil, C. (2014). Safety of Vaccines Used for Routine Immunization of U.S. Children: A Systematic Review. *Pediatrics, 134*(2), 325–337.

Morelli, A., Pizzetti, F. G., Risicato, L., Ruggeri, A., Spadaro, A., Curreri, S., Sorrenti, G., Salazar, C., Maestri, G., Agosta, S., Falzea, P., & D'Andrea, L. (2017). *Forum: vaccini obbligatori: le questioni aperte. BioLaw Journal – Rivista di BioDiritto, 2*, 15–50.

Mudde, C. (2004). The Populist Zeitgeist. *Government and Opposition, 39*(4), 541–563.

Mudde, C., & Rovira Kaltwasser, C. (2017). *Populism: A Very Short Introduction*. New York: Oxford University Press.

Müller, J.-W. (2016). *What Is Populism*. Philadelphia: University of Pennsylvania Press.

New York Times. (2017, May 2). *Populism, Politics and Measles*. Available at: https://www.nytimes.com/2017/05/02/opinion/vaccination-populism-politics-and-measles.html

Penasa, S. (2015). *La legge della scienza: nuovi paradigmi di disciplina dell'attività medico-scientifica. Uno studio comparato in materia di procreazione medicalmente assistita*. Trento: Università degli Studi di Trento.

Pigliucci, M. (2018). *Nonsense on Stilts. How to Tell Science from Bunk*. Chicago: University of Chicago Press.

Pigliucci, M., & Boudry, M. (Eds.). (2013). *Philosophy of Pseudoscience: Reconsidering the Demarcation Problem*. Chicago: University of Chicago Press.

Rial-Sebbag, E., & Blasimme, A. (2014). The European Court of Human Rights' Ruling on Unproven Stem Cell Therapies: A Missed Opportunity? *Stem Cells and Development, 23*(S1), 39–43.

Rosenberg, A. A., Halpern, M., Shulman, S., Wexler, C., & Phartiyal, P. (2013). Reinvigorating the Role of Science in Democracy. *PLoS Biology, 11*(5). Available at https://www.ncbi.nlm.nih.gov/pmc/articles/PMC3646724/.

Sigerist, H. E. (1938). Science and Democracy. *Science & Society, 2*(3), 291–299.

Smith, T. C. (2017). Vaccine Rejection and Hesitancy: A Review and Call to Action. *Open Forum Infectious Diseases, 4*(3). Available at https://www.ncbi.nlm.nih.gov/pmc/articles/PMC5597904/

Tarchi, M. (2015). *Italia populista. Dal qualunquismo a Beppe Grillo* (2nd ed.). Bologna: Il Mulino.

The Guardian. (2018, December 21). *Rightwing Populists Ride Wave of Mistrust of Vaccine Science.* Available at https://www.theguardian.com/world/2018/dec/21/rightwing-populists-ride-wave-of-mistrust-of-vaccine-science

The Guardian. (2019, February 25). *Vaccine Scepticism Grows in Line with Rise of Populism – Study.* Available at https://www.theguardian.com/world/2019/feb/25/vaccine-scepticism-rises-in-line-with-votes-for-populists-study-finds

Tomasi, M. (2017). Politiche sanitarie vaccinali fra diritto, scienza e cultura. *Quaderni costituzionali, 17*(4), 903–905.

Turner, S. (2001). What Is the Problem with Experts? *Social Studies of Science, 31*(1), 123–149.

Vampa, D. (2018). Il centrodestra a guida leghista. In M. Valbruzzi & R. Vignati (Eds.), *Il vicolo cieco. Le elezioni del 4 marzo 2018* (pp. 57–77). Bologna: Il Mulino.

Wheaton, S., & Zampano, G. (2018, February 14). Vaccine Debate Gives Italian Election Campaign a Shot in the Arm. *Politico.* Available at: https://www.politico.eu/article/vaccine-debate-gives-italian-election-campaign-a-shot-in-the-arm/

CHAPTER 12

"Le cose sono un po' più complesse": Constitutional Law and Religion in Italy and the Populist Challenge

Pasquale Annicchino

Introduction

Populism represents a challenge to constitutional democracy (Pinelli 2011: 5–16), and legal scholars in many parts of the world are reflecting on the difficulties that populist movements introduce in established constitutional frameworks (Allegri et al. 2019; Blokker 2019; Halmai 2019). In part II, I will outline the general framework of constitutional relationships between religions and the State in Italy. Part III will introduce the reader to populism in the Italian constitutional and political context. Part IV will analyze the relationships between populism and religion in Italy, particularly through the experience of the first Italian populist government between the League and the Five Stars Movement. In the conclusion I argue that the collapse of the coalition government between the Five Stars Movement and the League has not terminated the Italian popu-

P. Annicchino (✉)
Centre for Religious Studies, Bruno Kessler Foundation, Trento, Italy

Cambridge Institute on Religion and International Studies,
Cambridge, UK
e-mail: Pasquale.Annicchino@eui.eu

G. Delledonne et al. (eds.), *Italian Populism and Constitutional Law*, Challenges to Democracy in the 21st Century,
https://doi.org/10.1007/978-3-030-37401-3_12

list experience. Tensions and challenges for the Italian constitutional framework are here to stay, especially thanks to the black-box character of the Five Stars Movement (Manucci and Amsler 2018). The very delicate field of the regulation of the relationships between religions and the State will not be exempted.

Constitutional Law and Religion in Italy

Over the years, debates on the relationships between religions and the State have been a topic of political and social controversy in Italy. Legal scholars have produced an impressive amount of scientific contributions on the topic (Fattori 2018). If we look at the recent period of Italian history, we witness the transition from a Catholic State and society to a pluralistic society and a non-Catholic State, at least as far as its official institutions are concerned. In fact, according to article 1 of the Statuto Albertino[1]: "Catholic, Apostolic and Roman Religion is the only religion of the State. Other existing denominations are tolerated, according to law". With the introduction of the 1948 Constitution, the regulation of religion was included in the constitutional project with the presence of several different articles in the text of the Constitution. The Italian Constitution includes at least five articles, which, directly or indirectly, have an impact on the regulation of religion. The importance of the Constitution moreover lies not only in the article that, directly or indirectly, affects the regulation of religion. As Marco Ventura has argued, the Constitution marked a major break with the Fascist past:

> The Constitution of 1948 opened a new era based on democracy, equality and fundamental rights. The Constitution marked a significant change of direction, but could not avoid some contradictions. The State, which emerged from the alliance between the left (Socialists and Communists), the Christian Democrats and the *laici* (representatives of those political parties, which were neither on the left not Christian democratic), was not a Catholic one. The proposal to mention the Holy Trinity or to include some other form of invocation of God was rejected. (Ventura 2013: 45)

[1] The Statuto Albertino was the Constitution that Charles Albert of Sardinia conceded to the Kingdom of Sardinia in Italy on 4 March 1848. It later became the Constitution of the unified Kingdom of Italy and remained formally in force until 1948.

As we have mentioned before, the 1948 Constitution includes several articles which impact religion. Article 3 prescribes equality on different grounds, religion being one among them.[2] Article 8, based on the principle of "equal freedom"[3] among different religious groups, has served as the cornerstone provision for many *intese*[4] among the Italian State and non-Catholic religious groups. Article 19 proclaimed the constitutional principle of religious freedom[5] and article 7 provided for regulation of the relationships between the State and the Catholic Church as two "independent and sovereign" entities. It is also worth pointing out article 20, prohibiting discrimination against religious organizations on the basis of their religious nature.[6] Over the years the judiciary, and especially the Constitutional Court, contributed to the shaping of the boundaries between religion and politics in the new constitutional order, particularly in decisions adopted at the end of the 1980s. In 1988 the Constitutional Court drew a clear line between the sociological reality of having a country which was Catholic in the majority of its population and legal consequences stemming from that fact; according to the Court: "any discrimination based on the fact that a majority or minority of people belong to a given denomination is unacceptable".[7] In 1989 the Court declared the principle of *laicità*, one of the supreme principles of the constitutional order, "one of the aspects of the form of State outlined by the Constitution"[8] which represented "the State's guarantee that religious freedom will be safeguarded, in a framework of denominational and cultural pluralism".[9] As Marco Ventura has underlined: "in 1989 the

[2] Article 3, Para. 1: "All citizens have equal social dignity and are equal before the law, without distinction of sex, race, language, religion, political opinion, personal and social condition". The translation of the articles of the Italian Constitution is taken from the work done by Casonato and Woelk (Casonato and Woelk 2013).

[3] Article 8, Para. 1: "All religious confessions are equally free before the law".

[4] In the Italian constitutional order *intese* are public law agreements between the State and religious groups.

[5] Article 19: "All have the right to profess freely their own religious faith in whatever form, individual or collective, to propagate it and exercise it in a private or public cult, provided that the rites are not contrary to public morals".

[6] Article 20: "The ecclesiastical nature and purpose of religion or worship of an association or institution may not be a cause for special limitations in law, nor for special fiscal impositions in its establishment, legal capacity or any of its activities".

[7] See *Corte Costituzionale*, 8 July 1988, judgment no. 925 (1989).

[8] See *Corte Costituzionale*, 11 April 1989, judgment no. 203 (1990).

[9] Ibid.

Constitutional Court made explicit for the first time that the Constitution had shaped Italy as a *Stato laico* (in this specific sense a secular State), devoted to a positive understanding of religion conducive to religious freedom, as well as denominational and cultural pluralism. This seemed to be the ultimate achievement of forty years of Republican and Constitutional experience" (Ventura 2013: 50; see also Albisetti 2014). Thirty years after the decision 203/1989, Italy is probably in a position to evaluate its experiment of becoming a truly plural country (at least from the point of view of religious demography), and how the legal tools available to the legislator, and to the judiciary, have been able to handle this societal pluralism.[10] In the context of this evaluation, one should take into consideration also the recent populist political earthquakes which have contributed to a dramatic change of the Italian political landscape and that might also have an impact on the relationships between religions and the Italian State.

The Italian Populist Experiment

The March 2018 elections were the defining moment for the populist transformation of the Italian political landscape (D'Alimonte 2019; Allegri et al. 2019). The election was seen largely as a backlash against the establishment, saw the Five Stars and the League becoming, respectively, the first and the third largest parties represented in Parliament.[11] However, the result of the election was a hung Parliament. Although the Five Stars Movement was the party with the largest number of votes and parliamentary seats, the center-right coalition, dominated by the League, was the main political force with a plurality of seats in both the Senate and the Chamber of Deputies. This political deadlock was broken only after weeks of consultations, with the appointment of the Five Stars-designated Giuseppe Conte as prime minister, supported by a coalition composed of the Five Stars Movement and the League. Many scholars and commentators have referred to this government as a "populist government". There is no agreement on the definition of populism and, therefore, it might be useful to provide some definitions, which could also help the reader to

[10] As Pietro Faraguna has argued, for a real understanding of the Italian constitutional framework on the regulation of religion one must go beyond the formal constitution and consider also the "living constitution" (Faraguna 2019: 31–56).

[11] The Five Stars Movement obtained 32.22% of the votes; the Democratic Party 18.9%, the League 17.69%, Forza Italia 13.94%, Fratelli d'Italia 4.35% (both Forza Italia and Fratelli d'Italia were part with the League of the Centre-right coalition).

understand the political context of this contribution. A working definition of populism is offered by Cas Mudde, according to which populism can be seen as "an ideology that considers society to be ultimately separated into two homogeneous and antagonistic groups, 'the pure people' versus 'the corrupt elite', and which argues that politics should be an expression of the *volonté générale* (general will) of the people" (Mudde 2004: 543).[12] In general, and for the sake of this contribution, which does not aim to contribute to the debate on the definition of populism, we can accept some basic general considerations, according to which movements associated with populism are inclined to be particularly impatient with certain features of liberal democracy, such as the respect of pluralism of political positions, societal pluralism, the mediation of different interest through Parliament and, therefore, the acceptance of parliamentary democracy and the role of independent institutions. Jan-Werner Müller has also argued that populists claim the moral monopoly on political representation of "the people" (Müller 2016; see also Canovan 1999). Some of these key characteristics can be found in both the Five Stars Movement and the League. The Five Stars Movement is a peculiarity of the Italian political context, as it is almost impossible to find a similar party in other European countries. It was built on a clear antiestablishment platform which challenged traditional political parties in the name of disintermediation of traditional political parties and refusal to use definition and language commonly used by such parties. It was founded in 2009 by the comedian Beppe Grillo, who worked very closely with the internet strategist Gianroberto Casaleggio. According to a typical populist framework, the Five Stars Movement developed through protest demonstrations against the Italian political class, which was defined, according to a book published by two Italian journalists, "*The caste*" (Stella and Rizzo 2008). The Five Star Movement called repeatedly for a direct democracy based on law-making through popular referendums and the use of the internet. The League, originally known as the Northern League, was revitalized under the leadership of Matteo Salvini and rebranded as an anti-immigration and anti-EU party (Passarelli and Tuorto 2018). It is also important that the League signed a coopera-

[12] The same claim is made by Eric Posner (Posner 2017: 2), according to which the common theme among many populist movements "is a challenge to the 'establishment' or 'elites' by outsiders on behalf of the common people or, in some cases, by insiders who claim a mandate from the common people. [...] The populist leader argues that the establishment is 'corrupt', meaning that it either enriches itself at the expenses of the people, or shows greater concern for foreigners or minorities than for the common citizen".

tion agreement with Putin's United Russia party in 2017. It is in this political context that Giuseppe Conte was designated as prime minister after the elections. Giuseppe Conte can offer some useful insights for a better understanding of the nature of Italian populism. He spoke before the UN General Assembly in September 2018. During the first months of the new government there was widespread skepticism on the real commitment of the populist government toward international institutions. During his speech Conte reaffirmed the Italian commitment to the UN, but also felt the need to defend its government against some critiques. He did so in a very particular way by affirming that:

> [w]hen some accuse us of souverainism or populism, I always enjoy pointing out that Article 1 of the Italian Constitution cites sovereignty and the people, and it is precisely through that provision that I interpret the concept of sovereignty and the exercise of sovereignty by the people. This approach does not modify the traditional position of Italy within the international community and consequently toward the United Nations. (Conte 2018)

Conte used the terms of "souverainism"[13] and "populism" as synonyms. This is probably not correct from a purely scientific point of view, and would need further investigation by political scientists, which is outside the scope of this chapter. We will use them as synonyms. What we can say is that, in the Italian legal context, there has been substantial reflection and scholarly production on both terms. What Conte seemed to forget in his speech was a proper understanding of article 1 of the Italian Constitution, according to which: "Italy is a democratic Republic founded on labor. Sovereignty belongs to the people and is exercised by the people in the forms and within the limits of the Constitution". Article 1, as is clear from its wording, provides for explicit limits to the exercise of sovereignty which must always respect the boundaries established by the Constitution. The theoretical question we are called to ask in this scenario is: to which extent a populist government can respect these boundaries? In the Italian case we should also take into account the specific norms that the Constitution provides for political parties. Within the Italian Constitutional context political parties play a key role. According to article 49 of the Constitution: "Any citizen has the right to freely establish parties to contribute to determining national policies through democratic processes". As it has been underlined by Marco Bassini:

[13] In Italian "sovranismo".

> even anti-party or anti establishment movements enjoy full constitutional protection. This is witnessed by the fact that even members of monarchist parties (pursuing the restoration of Monarchy, in spite of Article 139 of the Constitution) sat in Parliament in the aftermath of establishing the Republic. (Bassini 2017: 6)[14]

As we can see, there is not much room for maneuvering, as is the case in other countries with some borderline political movements, to declare radical parties unconstitutional. Taking into consideration this political and institutional context, we should now analyze how the Italian populist government has contributed to the advancement of the debate on the relationships between religions and the State and, eventually, which legislative measures have been enacted.

Populism and Religion in the Italian Constitutional Context

As we have mentioned in our introduction, there are natural tensions between constitutionalism and populism; this is particularly relevant in the very delicate field of religion. Often populism's incorporation of national identity impacts religious freedom for minorities in countries, like Italy, with an overwhelming majority religion.[15] This is also reflected in some theoretical reflections of scholars which have tried to defend a populist approach. In the case of "*sovranismo*" one significant account is given by Giuseppe Valditara, who, besides being a legal scholar, has also served in relevant positions in the Ministry of Education during the coalition government between the League and the Five Stars Movement. According to Valditara, identities are at the core of sovereignty.[16] Paolo Becchi also specifically refers to the theme of national identity (Becchi 2017: 103 and ff.). As one can immediately notice, the particular relevance given to identitarian issues easily clashes with a pluralist constitutional framework. In the Italian case, Catholicism, in this perspective, would play the role of

[14] Even the Constitutional Court, with the decision 114/1967, held that: "the pursuit of radical changes of the constitutional order is compatible with the Constitution as long as it is realized through a democratic process and without using violence".

[15] Many thanks to Fred Gedicks for the discussion on this point.

[16] Giuseppe Valditara also underlines how at the core of populism and souvranism is the battle between the establishment and "the people": "In realtà alla base del 'sovranismo' vi è l'eterno conflitto fra chiusure oligarchice e istanze democratiche; fra élites, e i loro clienti, da una parte e i ceti popolari, dall'altra" (Valditara 2017: 23).

civil religion.[17] From a populist perspective, religion, and in this case Catholicism, is transformed into a quasi-ideology used to create a shared political identity. This position raises many issues at the pure theological level,[18] but also at the political and, considering its full implications, at the legal level. In the case of the coalition government composed by the Five Stars movement and the League, we have witnessed several instances of these tensions. The nature of the two political movements is very different, with the League more inclined to take clear identitarian positions on religion. There is one document from which to start in order to analyze what has been the position of the Italian populist government on the regulation of religion. Very concretely, we can analyze the legislative measures foreseen in the founding document of the Italian populist government: the so-called government contract between the Five Stars and the League (Morelli 2018; Cavino 2019). This contract was aimed at laying down agreement on specific issues to be later implemented through legislation and the action of Parliament. In the text of the contract, we can find some specific wording referring to religious issues. Under section 12, devoted to immigration and titled: "*Immigration: repatriations and stop to the business*", specific measures are foreseen for the regulation of religion, specifically Islam. It is already telling that we find specific measures on religion under the chapter devoted to immigration, as if the problems of minorities were only a concern of foreigners and not of Italian citizens. It is specified in the text of the contract that new measures will be introduced

[17] According to Pacillo: "[…] in una prospettiva sovranista, il cattolicesimo può senz'altro essere considerato non nella prospettiva dogmatica e soteriologica, ma secondo una chiave di lettura storica e filosofico-politica: esso può essere considerato come la principale sorgente di quei valori pregiuridici e prepolitici che scorrono come un fiume carsico all'interno della società e costituiscono il fondamento ideale dei principi inderogabili su cui si fonda il nostro Stato. Secondo questa chiave di lettura, il cattolicesimo potrebbe essere visto non tanto nella prospettiva della religione-di-Chiesa (prospettiva che ovviamente i fedeli sono liberi di adottare nel rispetto della libertà religiosa di ciascuno), quanto in quella di una religione civica, di un set di valori de-teologizzati ma fortemente legati alla cultura nazionale europea, tanto da costituire in senso unitivo una parte significativa dell'identità del popolo italiano" (see Pacillo 2019: 184).

[18] Pacillo highlights how, from a theological point of view, this position may not be able to be defended: "In una recente intervista, Julian Carròn, Presidente della Fraternità di Comunione e Liberazione, ha messo in evidenza come la separazione dei valori del cristianesimo dal fatto storico che li ha generati, ossia l'incarnazione di Gesù Cristo, trasforma la religione in ideologia, con la conseguenza che pian piano tali valori finiscono per perdere forza ed attrattività a seguito della dialettica e dei cambiamenti d'epoca che attraversano le società umane" (Pacillo 2019: 186).

to prevent "terrorist infiltrations" and measures are listed with the main goal of combating terrorism. This is already an important indication of the framework under which the regulation of religion is understood by Italian populists. The background is in fact to be understood in the post-9/11 scenario (Ferrari 2004) and the fear of Islam, which is typical in the League position, but it is also widespread within the Five Stars Movement (Annicchino 2018). The specific measures foreseen in the government contract echo this framework: creation of a registry of imams, and transparency and traceability of funding donated to the construction of mosques and, according to the text of the contract, of cultural centers also used for religious worship. It also foresaw the immediate closure of all the radical Islamic associations, mosques and other places of worship which would violate the law.[19] This increased centralized control on places of Islamic worship is part of the contract general framework on immigration, which also included, among other things, a pledge to establish repatriation centers across the country and accelerated asylum procedures aimed at removing rejected applicants from Italy within 18 months of arrival. An earlier proposal that imams would have mandated imams to preach only in Italian was deleted from the final version. The approval of this proposal would have resulted in a facial violation of article 8.2 of the Constitution. Parliamentarians of the League also introduced a proposal for a new law which would have made the display of the crucifix mandatory in all the schools and in all offices of public administration.[20] None of these proposals

[19] According to the text of the government contract: "[...] è necessario adottare una normativa ad hoc che preveda l'istituzione di un registro dei ministri di culto e la tracciabilità dei finanziamenti per la costruzione delle moschee e, in generale, dei luoghi di culto, anche se diversamente denominati. Inoltre, occorre disporre di strumenti adeguati per consentire il controllo e la chiusura immediata di tutte le associazioni islamiche radicali nonché di moschee e di luoghi di culto, comunque denominati, che risultino irregolari. A tale riguardo, onde garantire un'azione efficace e uniforme su tutto il territorio nazionale è necessario adottare una specifica legge quadro sulle moschee e luoghi di culto, che preveda anche il coinvolgimento delle comunità locali", the text is available at: http://download.repubblica.it/pdf/2018/politica/contratto_governo.pdf

[20] Proposta di legge n. 387 submitted by Saltamartini, Fedriga, Castiello, Grimoldi and Guidesi titled: "*Disposizioni concernenti l'esposizione del Crocifisso nelle scuole e negli uffici delle pubbliche amministrazioni*" and published on 26 March 2018. In the text of the proposal the crucifix is described as a fundamental element of the historical and civic-cultural Italian heritage. According to art. 1 of the proposal: "Il Crocifisso, emblema di valore universale della civiltà e della cultura cristiana, è riconosciuto quale elemento essenziale e costitutivo e perciò irrinunciabile del patrimonio storico e civico-culturale dell'Italia, indipendentemente da una specifica confessione religiosa".

was realized and enacted into law by Parliament, but all contributed to shape the political narrative (Fournier 2019) of the government. The relationship between the two partners of the governing coalition rapidly collapsed and Giuseppe Conte announced his resignation on 20 August 2019, averting a no-confidence vote promoted by his coalition partner, the League. Since the *Tangentopoli* bribery scandal, the Italian political and institutional system has lived through a never-ending transition which, in its last chapter, has brought a populist government which briefly collapsed after less than one year and half. This has been the result not only of a change in Italian political cultures but also, and especially, of the impact of the global showdown of 2008–09, the ensuing sovereign debt crisis and the following recession, which has strongly affected Italians. In the final days of the fallen governing coalition there are other significant elements that we can find as far as the relationships between religions and the State are concerned, in fact during his resignation speech Giuseppe Conte explicitly criticized Matteo Salvini for using religious symbols during his political rallies,[21] as this behavior was also a violation of the constitutional principle of *laicità*.[22]

Conclusion

The first government that Giuseppe Conte led showed all the difficulties the populist parties face when in government. As one famous quote, attributed to former Italian Prime Minister Giulio Andreotti, ironically highlights: "*le cose sono un po' più complesse*",[23] when in government, even populist parties begin to realize that the oversimplification of the political permanent campaign narrative cannot hold. In the Italian case this has been particularly true for decisions in the economic realm.[24] But it is also true for many of the position that the parties in government, and espe-

[21] Matteo Salvini had repeatedly used the crucifix during his rallies.

[22] According to Conte: "Chi ha compiti di responsabilità dovrebbe evitare, durante i comizi, di accostare agli slogan politici i simboli religiosi. Matteo, nella mia valutazione questi comportamenti non hanno nulla a che vedere con il principio di libertà di coscienza religiosa, piuttosto sono episodi di incoscienza religiosa, che rischiano di offendere il sentimento dei credenti e nello stesso tempo, vedi, di oscurare il principio di laicità, tratto fondamentale dello Stato moderno" (Conte 2019).

[23] "Things are a little bit more complex".

[24] This is true especially for the Italian exit from the Eurozone that both the League and the Five Stars Movement had supported in the past and campaigned for.

cially the League, have taken over the years. While one can agree or not with the proposals advanced within the framework of the "government contract" or with other legislative proposals made by the League with the Five Stars Movement, one thing on which we can, and should, all agree is that even populist parties must respect basic constitutional principles that the Italian constitutional tradition has developed over the years.[25] Among them is the "supreme principle" of *laicità* as defined by the Constitutional Court. Without the respect of such basic principles there is no possible democracy. Besides that, we will also lose years of juridical experiments which have led Italy to create a form of secularism that has been capable over the years of being quite respectful of the plurality of the Italian religious landscape and that, without being perfect, has been able to adjust and evolve. The trial and error process must continue without the rejection of the pluralism which is typical of most populist movements and parties. What we can register after the fall of the coalition government between the League and the Five Stars Movements is that, as with many other governments before, the regulation of the relationships between religions and the State has not been a priority area of governmental action but mainly narrative used to frame political positioning.[26] In this case, that has not necessarily been a bad thing.

[25] The importance of this point is highlighted by Pacillo: "Come è noto, lo Stato-ordinamento delle democrazie occidentali garantisce a tutti, cittadini o stranieri, un set di diritti fondamentali: per quanto di nostro interesse, oltre alla libertà di professione religiosa, di propaganda confessionale e di culto, viene in rilievo il diritto di essere se stessi, ovvero il diritto alla estrinsecazione della propria identità religiosa o irreligiosa che non è comprimibile nemmeno dalla più ampia maggioranza parlamentare, a meno che esso si risolva in comportamenti capaci di pregiudicare diritti fondamentali altrui ovvero principi costituzionali inderogabili" (see Pacillo 2019: 188).

[26] This general consideration has been made by Roberto Mazzola as being one on the central aspects of the Italian action in this field: "[...]Essa continua, con generale disinteresse a convivere con una idea avvizzita di libertà religiosa basata sulla convinzione che il destino di essa dipenda esclusivamente dalla regolarizzazione formale di alcune procedure o aspetti di diritto pubblico o privato sostanziale. Manca da sempre nella Italia post-unitaria un ampio dibattito e una consapevolezza intorno alla cultura religiosa, conservandosi una frattura profonda fra coscienza popolare e esperienze religiose più mature di natura spirituale [...] Se uno spazio ci sarà in futuro per una riforma morale e politica del modo di concepire e governare i rapporti fra Stato e religioni, il tempo di tale cambiamento non è certamente quello attuale, visto che, nel Contratto di Governo, i termini: religione, laicità, pluralismo, spirito, spirituale, libertà religiosa, Chiesa cattolica, simboli religiosi o altre espressioni verbali che in qualche modo, sottolinea Casuscelli, richiamino i temi cui la Costituzione dedica gli artt. 7, 8, 19, 20, sono completamente assenti, né l'esperienza del religioso è stata fatta

The collapse of the coalition between the Five Stars Movement and the League has been the result of many factors, which cannot be detailed here. One thing that might surprise non-Italian readers is that this collapse has completely shifted the Italian political landscape from one of the most conservative governments in the Italian republican history to one of the most progressive, while keeping the same prime minister and one of the two members of the governing coalition. The return to the government of the Democratic Party will probably determine the definitive deletion of the immigration proposal that the Five Stars Movement had agreed with the League on the "government contract". Populism, however, seems still at the core of the Italian government. As in many other fields, also on the relationships between religions and the State, the Five Stars Movement is a black box which has basically never taken a clear position on the topic. It has sided with the League-proposed measures and, in several instances, has shown an anti-pluralist attitude which seems to collide with the requirements of a constitutional democracy.[27]

References

Albisetti, A. (2014). *Il diritto ecclesiastico nella giurisprudenza della Corte Costituzionale*. Milano: Giuffrè.

Allegri, G., Sterpa, A., & Viceconte, N. (2019). *Questioni costituzionali al tempo del populismo e del sovranismo*. Napoli: Editoriale Scientifica.

Annicchino, P. (2018, May 17). Anche su islam e religione il contratto Lega-M5s non tiene conto di realtà e Costituzione. *Il Foglio*. Available at https://www.ilfoglio.it/politica/2018/05/17/news/anche-su-islam-e-religione-il-contratto-lega-m5s-non-tiene-conto-di-realta-e-costituzione-195429/

rientrare tra i bisogni profondi del Paese. Dunque, lunga vita alla 1159! E così sia" (Mazzola 2019: 60).

[27] According to Nicola Colaianni, the Five Stars Movement's anti-pluralism is also a consequence of its stress on the principle of direct democracy: "Il costituzionalismo democratico, riconoscendo le differenze interne al popolo, esclude che le scelte politiche possano promanare direttamente e immediatamente da un inesistente popolo unitario e indifferenziato. Nell'organizzazione sociale narrata dal populismo, invece, non occorrono corpi intermedi, come le formazioni sociali in cui l'individuo svolge la sua personalità, con differenti interessi, valori, origini (gli stessi partiti sono 'comitati elettorali da montare e smontare') […] A risentirne sono le minoranze che non vogliono o non possono integrarsi e perciò diventano gruppi di non appartenenza al 'vero' popolo, i cui interessi possono essere legittimamente ignorati" (Colaianni 2019: 3).

Bassini, M. (2017, April 17). *Rise of Populism and the Five Star Movement Model: An Italian Case Study*. Jean Monnet Working Paper. Available at https://jeanmonnetprogram.org/wp-content/uploads/JMWP-04-Marco-Bassini-1.pdf

Becchi, P. (2017). Che cos'è il sovranismo? *Trasgressioni, 60*, 103–112.

Blokker, P. (2019). Varieties of Populist Constitutionalism: The Transnational Dimension. *German Law Journal, 20*(3), 332–350.

Canovan, M. (1999). Trust the People! Populism and the Two Faces of Democracy. *Political Studies, 47*(1), 2–16.

Casonato, C., & Woelk, J. (Eds.). (2013). *Costituzione della Repubblica italiana/ The Constitution of the Italian Republic*. Lavis: Alcione.

Cavino, M. (2019). The Manchurian Candidate. Il Presidente del Consiglio garante del contratto di governo. *Federalismi, 3*, 231–239.

Colaianni, N. (2019). Populismo, religioni, diritto. *Questione Giustizia, 1*, 151–161.

Conte, G. (2018, September 26). *Remarks to the 73rd Session of the United Nations General Assembly*. Available at http://webtv.un.org/watch/italy-president-of-council-of-ministers-addresses-general-debate-73rd-session/5840556728001/

Conte, G. (2019, August 20). Resignation Speech. *Il Messaggero*. Available at https://www.ilmessaggero.it/politica/crisi_di_governo_giuseppe_conte_discorso_completo_senato-4685616.html

D'Alimonte, R. (2019). How the Populist Won Italy. *Journal of Democracy, 30*(1), 114–127.

Faraguna, P. (2019). Regulating Religion in Italy. Constitution Does (Not) Matter. *Journal of Law, Religion and State, 7*, 31–56.

Fattori, G. (2018). *Diritto costituzionale della religione. Repertorio della manualistica e analisi dei percorsi*. Torino: Giappichelli.

Ferrari, S. (2004). Individual Religious Freedom and National Security in Europe After September 11. *BYU Law Review, 2*, 357–384.

Fournier, T. (2019). From Rethoric to Action, a Constitutional Analysis of Populism. *German Law Journal, 20*(3), 362–381.

Halmai, G. (2019). Populism, Authoritarianism and Constitutionalism. *German Law Journal, 20*(3), 296–313.

Manucci, L., & Amsler, M. (2018). Where the Wind Blows: Five Star Movement's Populism, Direct Democracy and Ideological Flexibility. *Italian Political Science Review/Rivista Italiana di Scienza Politica, 48*(1), 109–132.

Mazzola, R. (2019). La politica delle fonti di diritto in Italia in materia di libertà religiosa e di coscienza a settant'anni dalla entrata in vigore della Costituzione. In P. Consorti (Ed.), *Costituzione, religione e cambiamenti nel diritto e nella società* (pp. 33–54). Pisa: Pisa University Press.

Morelli, A. (Ed.). (2018). *Dal "contratto di governo" alla formazione del Governo Conte. Analisi di una crisi istituzionale senza precedenti*. Napoli: Editoriale Scientifica.

Mudde, C. (2004). The Populist Zeitgeist. *Government & Opposition, 39*(4), 541–563.

Müller, J. W. (2016). *What Is Populism?* Philadelphia: University of Pennsylvania Press.

Pacillo, V. (2019). Sovranismo e libertà religiosa individuale. In P. Consorti (Ed.), *Costituzione, religione e cambiamenti nel diritto e nella società* (pp. 173–190). Pisa: Pisa University Press.

Passarelli, G., & Tuorto, D. (2018). *La Lega di Salvini. Estrema destra di governo.* Bologna: Il Mulino.

Pinelli, C. (2011). The Populist Challenge to Constitutional Democracy. *European Constitutional Law Review, 7*(1), 5–16.

Posner, E. (2017). *Liberal Internationalism and the Populist Backlash.* Public Law and Legal Theory Working Papers, University of Chicago Law School. Available at https://chicagounbound.uchicago.edu/

Stella, G. A., & Rizzo, S. (2008). *La casta. Così i politici italiani sono diventati intoccabili.* Milano: Rizzoli.

Valditara, G. (2017). *Sovranismo. Una speranza per la democrazia.* Milano: Book Time.

Ventura, M. (2013). *Religion and Law in Italy.* Alphen aan den Rijn: Wolters Kluwer.

CHAPTER 13

The Italian Way to Migration: Was It 'True' Populism? Populist Policies as Constitutional Antigens

Simone Penasa

The Migration-Populist 'Connection': Always Incompatible with Constitutionalism?

Migration as a global, European and national phenomenon undoubtedly represents a privileged context where populism may find expression. The management of migration flows involves legal concepts which are traditionally related to populist trends: national security, border defence, national identity. By referring to the need to 'protect' national values, migration policies may be oriented towards securitarian approaches, which must be assessed in the light of their consistency with constitutional principles and rights at stake.

The analysis will be driven along two axes—populism and migration—which will be interconnected through the reference to the constitutional dimension: assessment of the 'constitutional sustainability' of populist

S. Penasa (✉)
University of Trento, Trento, Italy
e-mail: simone.penasa@unitn.it

G. Delledonne et al. (eds.), *Italian Populism and Constitutional Law*, Challenges to Democracy in the 21st Century,
https://doi.org/10.1007/978-3-030-37401-3_13

policies implemented in the context of migration within the Italian legal system shall be performed.

While it is not possible to analyse the vast literature on populism in depth, it is nonetheless necessary to clarify two preliminary assumptions which will drive the present analysis: on the one hand, populism in its 'pure' expression is incompatible with constitutionalism (Blokker 2018; Tushnet 2019); on the other hand, migration does not constitute the reason for the rise of populism within the European context, but more precisely plays the role of 'carrier' for populist policies. With regard to the former statement, within the comparison of different theories and doctrines related to the compatibility between populism and constitutionalism (Doyle et al. 2019), the incompatibility of the two seems to be the more satisfactory approach, as '[v]alues such as political pluralism, transnational solidarity and protection of minorities renders constitutional democracy incompatible with populism' (Fournier 2018: 23). Reference is made to a 'pure' version of populism, meaning a political and legal will which is 'inherently hostile to mechanisms and, ultimately, values, commonly associated with constitutionalism: constraints on the will of the majority, checks and balances, protections for minorities, or, for that matter, fundamental rights as such' (Mueller 2017: 590).

Therefore, if populist constitutionalism must be considered as an intrinsic oxymoron (Halmai 2018), a different stance can be adopted with regard to popular constitutionalism (Kaidatzis 2018; Alterio 2019). On the one hand, the former expresses a populist rhetoric which is outside and against the narrative traditionally linked to constitutionalism as a doctrine, essentially based on pluralism, protection of minorities and limitation of powers (thus also of the concrete exercise of popular sovereignty): the 'Us-Others' and 'In-Out' mechanisms (Blokker 2019), which are typical of 'pure' (Bugaric 2019: 11) populism, are inherently incompatible with the genetics of constitutionalism, of which the inclusion of social conflict into the institutional and legal structure (principle of pluralism) and the primacy of the individual over the State (principle of personalism) are constituent elements (Bin 2007). On the other hand, popular constitutionalism is placed inside the constitutional(ist) discourse: its ambition is not to gradually modify the ecosystem of constitutional democracy (Fournier 2018: 10), but rather to achieve—by activating proper constitutional tools—an alternative balancing between powers, functions and interests to the one achieved by 'liberal constitutionalism' (Blokker et al. 2019).

Thus, some degree of populism can be assimilated by constitutionalism, as long as the former adheres to the fundamentals of the latter and takes part fairly in the social, political and legal competition for concrete implementation of the constitutional project. Consistently, a populist attitude can also be considered as legitimate expression of constitutional pluralism, at least until it alters the foundations of constitutionalism. Thus, the populism-constitutionalism combination may alternatively produce an oxymoron or a paradox: depending on the degree, aims and 'quality' of the populist agenda, its association with constitutionalism can be qualified alternatively in terms of insurmountable incompatibility or sustainable coexistence, insofar as the former is an expression of the struggle for inclusion, which is typical of constitutionalism and does not aim to block what has been called 'chain of claim-making for inclusion' (Mueller 2017: 601).

The duality of the populism-constitutionalism connection also applies to the context of migration, where there is neither 'one right answer' nor 'one constitutionally compatible approach': the individuation of the concrete balancing between effective rights' protection and efficient management of migratory fluxes is reserved mainly to the political margin of appreciation of democratically legitimated bodies; in this context, counter-majoritarian bodies—such as constitutional and supranational courts (Baer 2018: 358 and ff.)—enjoy a reduced margin of appreciation for assessing political choices. Accordingly, parliamentary acts, which are referable to a populist attitude from a cultural and political perspective, may be declared legitimate from a constitutional one: in cases like these, the populist origin of the act is traced back to the 'open-texture' of constitution by linking it to the legitimate aim of guaranteeing constitutionally relevant public interests, such as national security or public order. Still, how do we determine the sustainable level of populist policies within a constitutional legal order?

The triangle is complete: migration represents a paradigmatic context in which the relationship between populism and constitutionalism achieves the highest level of complexity and relevance. As anticipated, migration must be considered a preferential 'carrier' of expression, rather than a constituent factor for populism (Taggart 2017). The (mis)use of migration as a context of expression and strengthening for populism is favoured by the convergence between features traditionally associated with populism, on the one hand, and migration management, on the other.

The foundations of populism perfectly fit some of the characters of current trends in migration management. The polarisation between 'Us' and the 'Others', which can also find an explicit constitutionalisation, as occurred in Hungary (Halmai 2018); a theory of Nation based on the paradigm of 'ethnos'—the building and protection of 'one ethnically defined nation' (Blokker 2019: 340; Stoyanova 2018)—instead of 'demos'; generally speaking, the dominance of an exclusivist paradigm, instead of an inclusive one, when there is the need to frame the conceptual and constitutional meaning of 'The People' (for the immigration issues, the emphasis is on 'the people as a homogeneous entity' Taggart 2017: 250), thus explicitly (Hungary) or implicitly (Italy) orienting the approach to migrants in the direction of a contraposition between 'Us' and 'The Others'. Once we have metabolised this inner association, the path towards securitisation of migratory policies is open and direct: it can be further strengthened when combined with a logic of 'perpetual state of emergency', able to justify and even compel exceptional legislative or administrative means, and an intense and systematic use of criminal law, which inevitably leads to 'crimmigration' (Stumpf 2006).[1]

Once we have detected the 'irresistible' fascination linking populist fundamentals and migration management, it is worth disentangling three different dimensions, in which this attraction may materialise.

Populism and Migration: Three Degrees of Attraction

Cultural Rhetoric, Political Narrative and Legal Action

Firstly, it can occur at a social and cultural level, thus in a pre-juridical phase of the construction of the rhetoric on migration, or rather, against migrants. At this level, social and political communication becomes essential in order to orient society towards a predetermined perception of the migratory phenomenon and—more importantly—of the detrimental impact that

[1] Within this trend, it is necessary to recall the role played, according to the populist rhetoric, by the systematic call to the connection between uncontrolled immigration and risks for European societies linked to the terrorist threat. This link is often used in order to justify, and in a certain way impose, very restrictive migration policies based on dissuasion, control and, eventually, real contrast of the phenomenon as a whole. In this sense, the confusion between supposed different 'types' of migrations (see further below) favours the gradual but inexorable transition from the fight against terrorism also in the context of migration, to the struggle to irregular immigration up to the fight against immigration *tout court* (Castelli Gattinara 2017; Armillei 2017: 154).

migrants—especially those seeking international protection and coming to the national borders—have on the cultural, economic and even ethnic condition of citizens. At this stage, the People, to whom sovereignty belongs, slowly becomes—or is pictured as—a monolith in social, religious, cultural and ethnic terms: the narrative of migrants as 'invaders' illegitimately coming to national soil, even when they belong to the most vulnerable groups of people, such as asylum seekers or victims of trafficking, is functional to progressively provoking the feeling of needing to resist against an undetermined group of 'enemies'. This feeling can eventually lead to the logic of the existence of a People, which legitimately expresses national sovereignty through the democratic and representative circuit, in opposition to a mass of individuals—'the Others'—who must be kept 'outside'.

In this mindset, which becomes the cultural prerequisite for a populist utilisation of power, migrants become 'symbolic figurants' of the main target of populist rhetoric: the elite. Migrants' flow is thus imagined as part of a cultural and political project of the 'corrupt elite', where core constitutional principles such as pluralism, solidarity and fundamental rights' protection are redesigned by a populist rhetoric, becoming negative factors which are instrumental to the realisation of the elite's cultural and political programmes, such as the building of a multicultural society and, ultimately, the disintegration of the 'pure people' (Mudde 2017).

Functional to the above is a political discourse—and this is the second level of relevance, the political level—which is focused on the reinforcement of a twisted perception of migration as a concrete phenomenon in terms of both numbers and effective impact on the economic and social condition of citizens. Italy paradigmatically expresses this trend, in that an increasing detachment between social perception and the real dimension of the phenomenon has become a constant feature of the political discourse. It must be acknowledged that objective elements have decisively contributed to this. Trends of migrants coming to the Italian borders, especially in the period between 2014 and 2016, objectively constituted an unexpected and unusual—even exceptional—phenomenon, when compared to the traditional migratory fluxes, which characterise Italy in ordinary times. Limiting the analysis to arrivals by sea in the last five years, official statistics[2] (Ministry of the Interior) documented a peak of arrivals

[2] Ministry of Interior, Cruscotto statistico giornaliero (http://www.libertaciviliimmigrazione.dlci.interno.gov.it/it/documentazione/statistica/cruscotto-statistico-giornaliero. Last accessed: 13 October 2019).

in the aforesaid period (2014–2016), which was followed by a slow but constant decrease in the last three years. With regard to Italy, it is possible to enucleate at least two 'seasons' of sea arrivals in the last five years. The events that occurred in the Southern part of the Mediterranean Sea and in Syria can undoubtedly be seen as the historical trigger for the 'migration crisis'; at the same time, these events are also strictly linked with the political and the legislative reaction of the Italian governments in power during this period, which was characterised—as we shall see later—by a systematic implementation of emergency measures (legislative decree; administrative act) and by a process of 'externalisation' of national borders by concluding operational Memoranda with transit countries for migrants, such as Libya (Savino 2019; Moreno-Lax and Lemberg-Pedersen 2019). The first season started in 2014, when 170,100 arrivals took place, and ended in 2017, when Italy experienced a decrease of 34.24% in arrivals compared with those of 2016 (181,436 arrivals). The second season is characterised by a significant decrease of arrivals by sea, which brought arrivals to the figure of 7521 in 2019 (data referring to the end of September): this trend means an astonishing 92.87% reduction compared to 2017 and 64.23% compared to 2018. Therefore, if it is indubitable that the 2014–2016 seasons experienced a massive and in some way—at least initially—exceptional and unexpected escalation of sea arrivals (Campesi 2017), the 2017–2019 season was characterised by an opposite trend, which has indisputably normalised the phenomenon of arrivals by sea.

At this stage, we limit the analysis to 'mere' statistics, with the aim of objectively describing the events and highlighting the split between empirical data and social perception of migration. We shall only mention that, while the first season found its trigger in contextual and historical reasons outside Italy—contingent factors—the second season derives from political and normative dynamics—structural factors—which find legitimisation directly in a narrative of migration flows based on obsessive reference to polarising concepts, such as emergency crisis, national security, public order, citizens' welfare. Narratives on migration conveyed by both politics and the media, combined with the—temporally defined—mass arrivals of migrants in the 2014–2016 seasons, have been driven by a systematic use of the keywords previously evoked. This contributed to consolidating within society a twisted perception of the phenomenon, which represents the cultural cornerstone on which securitisation of migration policies has recently been built.

National and European opinion polls starkly depict this trend (Chetail 2019: 2; Trimikliniotis 2019). According to the Special Eurobarometer on 'Integration of immigrants in the European Union',[3] only 16% of Italian citizens believe that the percentage of immigrants staying legally in their country is higher than the percentage of those staying illegally, while 47% of those polled think that there are more immigrants staying illegally than there are immigrants staying legally, and a further 25% believes that there is about the same number of the two categories of migrants. The data refer to surveys conducted during April 2017, when official statistics on sea arrivals started to decrease significantly; at the same time, the Report suggests that it is likely that this is influenced by the sharp increase since 2014 in the number of arrivals of people seeking protection in the EU, with Greece and Italy as the primary countries of entry. Further striking information is represented by the margin of error between the real number of foreign citizens living in Italy and the number effectively perceived by Italian society. According to the same Report, the percentage of immigrants in the total population perceived in Italy is 24.6%, when official data indicate 7% of the total population as the portion of non-citizens living in Italy: significantly, the error of perception—the misrepresentation of reality—by Italian citizens is the highest of all European Union countries (+17.4 percentage points).[4]

Even if it is not possible to infer from these data a direct connection between a populist trend characterising the Italian political environment and the cultural misrepresentation of the effective impact of migration on Italian society, the consolidation of a social perception, which seems to recall some of the features of 'pure' populism cannot be denied. This is not enough to qualify Italy as a populist environment, when dealing with migration. Regardless of this, data from the polls contribute to define a cultural environment which is ready to accept legislative and administrative reforms which can be defined—expressly or indirectly—as a manifestation of a populist trend at political level.

This leads to the third level of relevance, which follows the cultural and political construction of a narrative based essentially on a distorted social

[3] European Commission, 'Integration of immigrants in the European Union', Special Eurobarometer, 2018, no. 469.

[4] Istituto Cattaneo, Immigrazione in Italia: tra realtà e percezione, 2018 (https://www.cattaneo.org/2018/08/27/immigrazione-in-italia-tra-realta-e-percezione/). It links this error of perception not only to lack of information but also to the existence of deep-rooted prejudices against immigrants, which could bias voters' perception.

perception of both the dimension and characteristics of migratory flows, namely, normative relevance. What is the reaction of representative bodies vested with legislative and regulatory powers, when facing a declared 'emergency' pertaining to migration? As stated above, if we look at the last decade, Italian legislation on migration is characterised by a number of connotative elements shared by parliamentary majorities and governments very different for political culture, ideology and party.

Limiting our analysis to the last two legislatures, if we apply the essential characteristics traditionally associated with a populist political experience to the coalitional governments, which brought together left-wing and centre-right parties (the Letta, Renzi and Gentiloni governments) and then the 'yellow-green' coalition (Lega with Salvini and the Five Star Movement), the 'genetic' diversity between them appears to be self-evident.

In very broad terms, the 'yellow-green' coalition, which entered into an irremediable crisis last August, brought together the two political movements that at European level represent the paradigm of populism 'in power' and vividly expressed the complexity and multidimensionality of the populist phenomenon (Martinico 2019: 73; Mény and Surel 2002). On the contrary, previous coalition governments represented, when evaluated through populist lenses, the epiphenomenon of everything populist movements aim to defeat: the 'corrupt elites', who constitute, in the populist rhetoric, the enemy of the 'true people' (Mudde 2017: 32).

Even with this irreconcilable cultural and ideological background, the two coalitional experiences based their political agendas on partially common premises, which deal respectively with the nature of the phenomenon, the nature of the legal sources employed to regulate it and the legal status of people arriving at state borders.

The migratory phenomenon has been constantly qualified by rule-makers as an 'endless emergency', thus requiring extraordinary measures to react efficiently and promptly. The mechanism is perfect in its simplicity: the 'emergency' narrative, progressively inoculated at social level, justifies, and even requires, extraordinary reactions at legislative level.

The emergency paradigm has led to the systematic activation of emergency *sources*, such as decree-laws, adopted without distinction by all the governments in power, thus limiting the role of Parliament even in the event of the approval of structural reforms related to asylum procedure and status.[5] It also allows a broad interpretation of legislative clauses, which provides for the activation of emergency organisational *solutions* in the context of the reception of asylum seekers. In this case, the ordinary reception system (SPRAR-Refugee and Asylum Seekers Protection System, see Section 14 of Legislative Decree no. 142/2015; Penasa and Pretto 2016) has been de facto replaced by the extraordinary reception system (CAS – Extraordinary Reception Centres, Section 10 of the same legislative decree): this inevitably leads to lower standards of protection for asylum seekers' fundamental rights and of integration into the host society. The emergency approach to migration is the reason also for the implementation of unconventional *methods* for the management of arrivals at the national borders: the 'hotspot' approach has been required of some Member States (among which, Italy) by the European authorities in order to efficiently and promptly react to massive arrivals of migrants, with the aim of guaranteeing 'first reception' and the pre-qualification of migrants as asylum seekers or, alternatively, as irregular migrants (Casolari 2016; Savino 2016). By derogating from general rules (and guarantees) on reception and asylum procedures set forth at European and national levels and performed in the absence of any formal legal ground (only soft law and non-binding acts have been introduced by the Italian government in order to regulate the concrete implementation of this procedure: see the Standard Operation Procedure), the pre-qualification of migrants decisively orients the attribution of the status and consequently the legal regime applicable to them (access to the reception system and asylum procedure; administrative detention in ad hoc centres awaiting return to the country of origin; Campesi 2018).

This praxis contributes to increase the lack of legal certainty regarding the effective implementation of substantive and procedural guarantees linked with the specific status attributed to each migrant. If migrant's rights, which are functional to the effective access to the asylum procedure—such as the right to officially apply for asylum and to legal aid and linguistic and social support—are not effectively guaranteed at the time of the first contact with national authorities, migrants who would be entitled to be recognised as asylum seekers are, instead, considered to be 'irregular'. Here, a direct connection with the political intention to criminalise and deliberately muddle different legal regimes applicable to migrants is detectable: at rule-enforcing level, legal regimes whose boundaries are

[5] See *infra*. In contradiction with the populist will to reaffirm the centrality of the popular will betrayed by liberal and technocratic elites.

clearly drawn in legislation are likely to be confused due to the inadequacy of the guarantees effectively enforced (Cortese 2017); at political level, the misperception of different categories of migrants is deliberately ridden in order to convey the idea of an unlawful exploitation of the refugee status by migrants as a mass of individuals and to consider asylum not as a legal status with solid constitutional and European grounds, but, instead, as an *escamotage* employed by migrants to occupy the space belonging to citizens (Algostino 2018: 1175); at social level, this narrative contributes to strengthen the feeling of a 'siege' from outside to end which extraordinary measures must be passed to protect the safety and well-being of 'proper' citizens. The circle between social, political and legislative levels is ultimately closed.

The Italian Way to Migration: Was It 'True' Populism?

The Italian way to migration management is characterised by a recurrent use of key concepts—emergency crisis, national security and public order, fight against irregular migration—which are deliberately channelled by political narratives in a two-fold direction: downwards, the mantra of migration as national emergency contributes to artificially build a social environment, which is inclined to metabolise policies, which more or less explicitly contrast migration fluxes, when they are not explicitly against migrants; upwards, by basing legislative choices—largely ratified through exceptional legal sources (decree laws, emergency ordinances)—on the need to react against unexpected and extraordinary events in order to guarantee public order and national security. Thus, this narrative seems to be win-win: nonetheless, is this enough to consider this approach as populist? Are we experiencing a *structural* populism, capable of rewriting constitutional fundamentals of the form of state? Or rather, can it be qualified as *contingent* populism, which connotes migration policies merely in a sporadic and limited way, and which is, instead, the expression of a widespread approach of closure towards migrants within EU Member States?

In order to answer these questions, two issues will be tackled: the existence of a continuity between different governments; the reaction of counter-majoritarian bodies to hypothetical populist pushes, by analysing major trends detectable within the case-law of the Italian Constitutional Court.

During the above-mentioned two seasons of arrivals at the Italian borders, different coalitional governments in power made use of emergency measures in order to cope with mass migration. Both the '*larghe intese*' coalition government (we will focus on the Gentiloni government)—expression of the elite according to the populist rhetoric—and the 'yellow-green' one—where two different types of populism found representation (Newell 2018)—adopted decree-laws, respectively aimed at speeding up asylum procedures and fighting illegal immigration (Decree-Law no. 13/2017, converted into Law no. 46/2017, known as the 'Minniti-Orlando Decree'), on the one hand, and at introducing urgent measures on international protection and security on the other (Decree-Law no. 113/2018, converted into Law no. 132/2018, known as the 'Salvini decree') and on public order and security (Decree-Law no. 53/2019, converted into Law no. 77/2019, known as the 'Salvini bis').

Although the decree-laws mentioned above were an expression of different—even dichotomous—political backgrounds, they have been traced back, by Italian legal scholarship, to a common understanding of migration as an emergency event intrinsically linked to public security (Cavasino 2018: 14). Accordingly, the 'Salvini decree' was placed in a seamless common path with previous measures adopted in the past years, which would identify as their 'northern star' the combination between immigration and public security (Algostino 2018). So, how far does this political continuity go, when we consider that normative choices stem from different political cultures and refer to different 'peoples'?

The hypothesis is that a cultural discontinuity coexisted with a normative continuity (Cetin 2015); and that, with regard to the latter, a change in the cultural matrix of migration policies caused them to be reduced merely to public security issues. Thus, if a continuity is detectable, as emerges from the substance of the decree-laws mentioned, it was subject of an 'escalation', which took place while the 'yellow-green' coalition was in power (Cavasino 2018: 15–16). The paradigm shift was formally ratified by the coalition 'agreement' (*contratto*) between the two movements. The section dedicated to migratory policies was titled 'repatriations and stop business' and expressed main issues that would fill the government's agenda: further criminalisation of asylum seekers (to provide new crimes that, when committed by asylum seekers, cause their immediate removal); delocalisation of asylum procedures to countries of transit or origin; increase of the number of repatriation centres (CPR), the number of which had already been increased by the 'Minniti-Orlando Decree'; the transfer of financial resources from the reception of asylum seekers to the repatriation of irregular migrants. The ideological nature of this approach to migration management is self-evident, if one considers the intentional utilisation of slogans ('stop business') in official documents, the simplification of the factual and normative complexity produced by mass migration and the underestimation of the duties in terms of reception of asylum seekers and procedures deriving from European Union law (Bonetti 2018). Does this change in the cultural and political matrix find expression also in the substance of the acts adopted by the two (classes of) governments?

If we consider the political context from which firstly the 'Minniti-Orlando' and then the 'Salvini' decrees stem, it is possible to detect at least two areas of conjunct intervention, which are especially relevant, as they express the 'essentials' of Italy's way of dealing with migration: the systematic implementation of de facto administrative tools, which often lack legal grounds and are mainly based on un-formalised praxes, is proven by consolidation of the 'hotspot' approach; the implementation of the Memorandum of understanding signed by Italy with the government (or rather, one of the governments) of Libya, which is part of the process of externalisation of national borders and thus of migration management to foreign authorities. With regard to the hotspot approach and the Memorandum with Libya, a political continuity is clearly detectable. Both were activated during the '*larghe intese*' governments and went on to become some of the key tools for the tightening implemented by the 'yellow-green' coalition. The Memorandum with Libya has been particularly functional in reducing until almost complete exhaustion arrivals by sea, in the light of a political plan formally in line with European standards—as it was aimed at fighting trafficking and irregular migration—but which effectively had the indirect (probably not unwitting) effect of also stopping the fluxes of asylum seekers and thus of significantly curtailing the number of asylum requests.

Therefore, the cultural matrix shift produced found pre-existent legal grounds, which were then implemented in conformity with a rhetoric that can be qualified as populist. Particularly emblematic is the case of the closure of ports by the former Minister of the Interior, Salvini, who was formally able to exploit the conditions and implement the procedures set forth in the context of Themis, a Frontex Joint Maritime Operation (Carrera and Cortinovis 2019): the provision of the criterion of the closest port to the rescue zone for identification of the place, where migrants must be disembarked, a principle that is hardly compatible with the prohibition of refoulement and the criterion of 'safe harbour'; the reduction of the patrolling and intervention marine area. This implementation undeniably took place in line with a very different cultural and political mindset compared to that of previous governments (see the humanitarian nature of *Mare Nostrum* Operation).

A similar process is detectable also with regard to communication methods and policy implementation tools. The semantics of the political discourse related to migration completely changed during the time the 'yellow-green' government was in power; they undoubtedly contributed to the process of separation between concrete and perceived reality of the phenomenon that affected Italian society (see data above). The reiterated reprise of expressions (slogans?), such as 'sea-taxis', in reference to the NGO vessels operating in the Mediterranean with search and rescue functions; 'cruise', in reference to the routes followed by migrants, which not only statistics but also common sense should consider in their dramatic force and complexity; 'clandestine', used to indiscriminately label anyone who arrives on Italian coasts; 'holiday', to qualify the national reception system for those applying for international protection, identified as 'alleged refugees' on social media with the clear intention of suggesting a condition of illegality[6]; these are just some of the expressions that have been conveyed at political and institutional level in the public debate on migration (Dimitriadis 2019). They decisively contributed to the construction by the mass media of a perceived reality that does not correspond to the factual and legal situations, but that had the function of fostering social acceptability of highly restrictive policies, practices and regulations.

With regard to the methods of enactment of populist policies—and the cultural project of which they are expression—we experienced the exacerbation of a *modus operandi* typical of the Italian approach to migration management, which is directly connected to the binomial immigration-(in)security and to the emergency approach systematically adopted: the implementation of systemic reforms by means of administrative praxes, which are formalised at legislative level ex post facto. In order to highlight the chronological continuity of this approach, it is possible to refer once

[6] Il Post, Gli immigrati e gli alberghi, 17 June 2015 (https://www.ilpost.it/2015/06/17/immigrati-alberghi-di-lusso-salvini/).

again to the implementation of the hotspot method, which symbolically expresses a gradual 'administrativisation' of migratory policies and migrants' rights (Savino 2015). Also from this perspective, during the period in which the last Italian government was in power, there was an escalation, which is linked to populist dynamics and can be qualified as 'announcement effect' or, more generally, as mediatisation of migration policies. In this case, however, the social impact of political declarations ends up subrogating the lack of a formal legal act able to legitimate the effects thus generated.

A paradigmatic case, which undoubtedly constitutes a further element of discontinuity (Villa 2018),[7] can be found in the practice of ordering the closure of ports to prevent the disembarkation of migrants rescued at sea, in particular by NGOs (Cusumano and Gombeer 2018). This was also to avoid the duties of rescue, reception and protection imposed by national and European law; the 'announced' closure of ports, which had extraordinary media exposure (Sea Watch, Open Arms, Sea Eyes, Diciotti), was not preceded by the issue of formal acts by competent authorities (Carta 2018).[8]

In this case, the media power of the statements of the holders of top public functions ended up replacing the legal force of acts that should have formalised administrative measures concretely adopted. It is not arbitrary to identify in this strategy the expression of one of the characteristics of populist discourse, according to which populist leaders must do what the people want, even at the risk of setting aside 'The formal structures of liberal democracy (…) if they are preventing the populist leader to fulfil his role' (Bugaric 2019: 393). The legal manifestation of this political and cultural strategy took place only ex post facto: the 'Salvini bis' decree intervened to criminalise *de jure* those actions—connected with the search and rescue of migrants—previously stigmatised de facto, providing for a pecuniary sanction (with confiscation of the ship in case of reiteration) in case of non-compliance with limitations or bans on the subjects of order, public security and immigration (Article 2, Legislative Decree 53/2019, converted into Law no. 77/2019).

[7] According to Villa (2018): 'it is important to note that although the Gentiloni government had asked NGOs in the summer of 2017 to either sign a "code of conduct" or stop their SAR operations at sea, until May this year the Italian government had never openly and actively opposed search and rescue operations per se'.

[8] Legal Studies on Migration Association (ASGI), Accesso civico ai Ministeri dell'interno e dei Trasporti: nessun provvedimento formale di chiusura dei porti, 10 January 2019 (https://www.asgi.it/media/comunicati-stampa/chiusura-porti-accesso-civico/).

The semantic, ideological and methodological discontinuity becomes nuanced when interpreted on a strictly legal level, as it has been implemented through the 'populist' employment of existing rules and procedures. This 'heterogony of ends' has facilitated the jurisdictionalisation of populist policies, which have been legitimised and have undoubtedly been grafted onto a legal terrain which is fertile, or in any case not entirely refractory to accept their social and cultural sustainability. The concrete manifestations of this paradigm shift are manifold, and not limited to the decrees analysed. Limiting ourselves to two areas that symbolically express this trend, we shall focus on the abolition of the humanitarian protection status and the reform of the asylum seekers' reception system.

Decree no. 113/2018 (Section 1) repealed the status of humanitarian protection, replacing it with alternative forms of protection intended to cover fewer cases and to guarantee lower standards of protection. This change is symbolic from a two-fold perspective: it concretises the rhetoric of an instrumental and excessively 'bleeding-heart/liberal' determination of international protection, which is allegedly caused by an alliance between migrants/the 'Others' and judges/the 'elite', who support a broad implementation of the concept of 'humanitarian reasons' contrary to the letter of the law; and it demonstrates how legislative reforms based on populist rhetoric can produce a striking contraction of the scope of application of constitutional guarantees, as the possibility of granting a status for humanitarian reasons guarantees the full and complete enactment of the constitutional right to asylum (Article 10, third paragraph, of the Constitution; Benvenuti 2018).

Legislative enactment of populist rhetoric materialised also in the field of asylum seekers' reception. In this case, the symbolic role of the reform is even more patent: the exclusion of asylum seekers from the ordinary reception system, now reserved only for holders of international protection and for unaccompanied minors, has had the immediate effect of excluding them from involvement in reception projects aimed at their social integration; thus, the most vulnerable categories of migrants—asylum seekers—are actually deprived of a comprehensive linguistic, psychological and social support. In this way, reception is not formally denied to this category of people, but they are provided with a purely emergency-focused and reduced version: they will be allocated to extraordinary reception centres, where only primary and basic assistance is ensured (Article 10, Legislative Decree 142/2015). The result is likely to be paradoxical, since the inevitable outcome will be to further increase the percentage of people 'hosted' in extraordinary reception facilities, which are precisely those in which distortions and inefficiencies—or even actual illegalities—are more frequent. Additionally, the indirect result will be to reduce ordinary reception, founded on the principle of rebuilding individual autonomy and subsequently integrating the migrant through pre-authorised and assessed ad hoc projects implemented at the local level, to a merely symbolic function. In this case, the symbolic function of the law becomes particularly dominant, unless the real purpose was to hinder the stay and social inclusion of those who—as asylum seekers—have the right to stay and to enjoy adequate reception conditions (see European Court of Human Rights, Khlaifia and Others v. Italy, GC, 15 December 2016).

Migration Policies and Constitutional Pluralism: How Sustainable Are Populist Strategies?

Given the complexity that characterises the most recent seasons of migration policies in Italy, it is now necessary to return to the premises from which we started: Is it possible to trace populist policies back to a sustainable implementation of constitutional principles? In this light, it must be assumed that—avoiding any Manichaean setting (Martinico 2019: 73)—a populist interpretation can be also considered the expression of the pluralist nature of the constitution, within the limits of due respect for its essential core. In order to assess the concrete scope of this compatibility, the case-law of the Italian Constitutional Court has been chosen as benchmark: What is the reaction to laws which are 'carriers' of populist policies?

From this point of view, the Constitutional Court has not ruled on the merits of the aforementioned decrees. In broader terms, it is possible to identify two tendencies within constitutional case-law, which refer respectively to issues related to entry and stay and to the conditions for the enjoyment of social rights of foreigners.

With regard to the first issue (entry conditions, expulsion, status determination), the discretionary power of legislature reaches its highest density, as it is connected to the need to protect essential public interests such as border control, security and public order. With regard to legislative choices on entry and status determination of migrants, the Constitutional Court usually implements the paradigm of 'citizenship', according to which public interests prevail on the protection of individual freedoms; accordingly, the legislature enjoys a wide margin of appreciation in the selection of public interests which are likely to determine a limitation of non-citizens' freedoms (Savino 2017). Consequently, the Constitutional Court's scrutiny is weak: political choices will be illegitimate only when manifestly unreasonable or arbitrary. This approach leads the Court to frequently take refuge in procedural decisions, thus avoiding ruling on the merits of political choices by identifying grounds of inadmissibility due to a lack of legitimacy to sue (Salvini Decree, Judgment no. 194/2019; Libya Memorandum, Order no. 163/2108) or of relevance of the question referred (case related to the 'deferred refoulement', Judgment no. 275/2017). In some cases, when the Constitutional Court perceives that the democratic-representative circuit of sovereignty has produced a legislative framework that stretches excessively—even without breaching it—the balance between opposing constitutional interests, it may ask the legislature to intervene in order to trace the tension produced back to physiology.

An opposite paradigm—based on 'territoriality'—is adopted for foreigners' access to social rights. In this context, legislative choices limiting the enjoyment of these rights are assessed in the light of a plurality of parameters (residence in the territory, concrete needs, nature of the social provision), which considerably compress the political discretionary space (Savino 2017: 60). Therefore, the scrutiny will be strict and will usually quash laws that impose unreasonable conditions (such as an excessively extended number of years of residency in the territory) which directly or indirectly discriminate against foreign citizens.

In conclusion, the implementation of the 'citizenship' paradigm leads the Court to reiterate, more or less consciously, the traditional statist paradigm of tradition, through which a very broad margin of choice is granted to the majority of the citizens-insiders; regrettably, it occurs precisely when the risk of a limitation of migrants' rights becomes higher, that is, the determination of the conditions for the entry and stay of migrants (Savino 2017: 68). On the contrary, the adoption of the 'territoriality' paradigm allows the Constitutional Court to define in a clear-cut way the boundary that limits laws that express the implicit purpose of excluding foreigners—even those legitimately resident in the territory—from welfare benefits. Therefore, the Court identifies the limits between policies which are somehow linked to the pluralistic nature of constitutionalism, albeit with the indirect effect of excluding specific groups of people in need of assistance, on the one hand; and clearly defined populist strategies, which produce in 'flag laws', which are manifestly illegitimate from the very beginning but correspond to a logic of political rhetoric and propaganda, on the other hand (Corsi 2018: 1184). Thus, the attitude of the Constitutional Court seems to be dualistic: it applies a severe self-restraint when the need to protect public interests, such as public security and order or border control, is at stake; on the contrary, it becomes activist in those cases in which the need to protect such public interests is replaced by the need to effectively guarantee migrants' fundamental rights (right to health, right to education, right to social assistance, maternal rights).

All Populism, No Populism? Populism as a Constitutional Antigen

We started this analysis by supporting the idea that 'pure' populism is inherently incompatible with the essentials of constitutionalism. We referred to Berlin's distinction between 'true' and 'false' populism, where the latter is defined as 'simply the mobilization of certain popular sentiments – say hostility to capitalism or to foreigners or Jews, or hatred of economic organization or of the market society, or of anything you like – for undemocratic ends' (Berlin 1968: 12–13, quoted by Halmai 2019). Additionally, we highlighted the 'irresistible' attraction between some of the basics of populism (the insurmountable clash between 'Us' and the 'Others', an exclusive approach against the expressions of social pluralism) and those of current migratory policies (emergency and securitisation). We then detected three degrees of possible attraction between populism and migration. These were identified in cultural rhetoric, political narrative and legal action, intended as different contexts where the connection between populist strategies and migratory management can flourish. Coherently with a non-Manichaean attitude towards the populism-constitutionalism relationship, we suggested that laws and policies built on populist rhetoric could also be the expression of constitutional pluralism: in this way, we shifted the paradigm from an irreducible ideological incompatibility towards a possible constitutional sustainability of 'populist-based' laws.

In the second part of the paper, we applied this scheme to the Italian social, political and legal context. We identified two seasons both of migrants' arrivals and coalitional governments: on the one hand, we experienced normalisation and then reduction in flows, which however continue to be tackled essentially with emergency measures; on the other hand, the two types of coalition governments in power are the expression respectively of the idea of the 'people' ('yellow-green' coalition) and of the 'elite' (*grandi intese* coalition) channelled by populist semantics. We then tried to understand whether a line of continuity was detectable between the strategies adopted during the current season of migration management: on the one hand, we stressed a cultural and political discontinuity, due to an undisputable shift of ideological and rhetorical matrices; on the other hand, we observed a potential continuity when assessing those legislative measures concretely adopted. In the latter case, we identified an escalation in the implementation of a securitarian and exclusionist strategy which, linked to the paradigm shift that occurred at cultural and political levels, led to legislative and administrative measures barely compatible with the principle of legality (measures enacted in a lack of formal legal ground, as in the case of the closure of ports) and the rule of law (the limitation of the concrete scope of application of constitutional rights, such as in the case of the abrogation of protection for humanitarian reasons). In very synthetic terms, populist strategies have benefited from—or have exploited—the presence of a long-lasting normative approach to migration, essentially based on securitisation of policies and crimmigration of migrants. Therefore, in order to understand the concrete impact of populist strategies on the constitutional infrastructure, it is necessary to go beyond the surface of the populist rhetoric and assess whether—and to what extent—the latter can be traced back to the constitutional discourse.

Thus, if a populist shift occurred in Italy, it was *contingent* and not structural.

If we agree with this reconstruction, then the populist season experienced in Italy can be considered an *antigen*, rather than a parasite, within the constitutional system, able to activate antibodies which are traditionally linked to the core of constitutionalism: the central role of counter-majoritarian bodies; the separation of powers; the limitation of popular sovereignty, which must find implementation within the limits and through the forms set forth by the Constitution; a truly pluralistic social and cultural debate. Otherwise, it is destined to resurface, as a karstic phenomenon, especially if European democracies refuse to realise that the systematic adoption of policies which put excessive pressure on constitutional principles involved in the context of migration, may eventually lead to structural and not merely contingent populist drifts.

References

Algostino, A. (2018). Il decreto 'sicurezza e immigrazione' (decreto legge n. 113 del 2018): estinzione del diritto di asilo, repressione del dissenso e diseguaglianza. *Costituzionalismo.it, 16*(2), 167–199. Available at www.costituzionalismo.it

Alterio, A. M. (2019). Reactive vs Structural Approach: A Public Law Response to Populism. *Global Constitutionalism, 8*(2), 270–296.

Armillei, R. (2017). Boat Arrivals and the 'Threat' to Italian National Security: Between a 'Moral Panic' Approach and the EU's Failure to Create a Cohesive Asylum-Seeking Policy. *Journal of Applied Security Research, 12*(1), 141–159.

Baer, S. (2018). The Rule of – And Not by Any – Law. On Constitutionalism. *Current Legal Problems, 71*(1), 335–368.

Benvenuti, M. (2018). La forma dell'acqua. Il diritto di asilo costituzionale tra attuazione, applicazione e attualità. *Questione Giustizia, 2*, 14–27.

Berlin, I. (1968). To Define Populism. *The Isaiah Berlin Virtual Library*, (6). Available at http://berlin.wolf.ox.ac.uk/lists/bibliography/bib111bLSE.pdf

Bin, R. (2007). Che cos'è la Costituzione? *Quaderni costituzionali, 27*(1), 11–52.

Blokker, P. (2018). Populist Constitutionalism. In C. de la Torre (Ed.), *Routledge Handbook of Global Populism*. London: Routledge.

Blokker, P. (2019). Varieties of Populist Constitutionalism: The Transnational Dimension. *German Law Journal, 20*(3), 332–350.

Blokker, P., Bugaric, B., & Halmai, G. (2019). Introduction: Populist Constitutionalism: Varieties, Complexities, and Contradictions. *German Law Journal, 20*(3), 291–295.

Bonetti, P. (2018). Editoriale. *Diritto Immigrazione Cittadinanza, 20*(2), 2018.

Bugaric, B. (2019). The Two Faces of Populism: Between Authoritarian and Democratic Populism. *German Law Journal, 20*(3), 390–400.

Campesi, G. (2017). Chiedere asilo in tempo di crisi. Accoglienza, confinamento e detenzione ai margini d'Europa. In C. Marchetti & B. Pinelli (Eds.), *Confini d'Europa. Modelli a confronto e inclusioni informali*. Milano: Cortina.

Campesi, G. (2018). Seeking Asylum in Times of Crisis: Reception, Confinement, and Detention at Europe's Southern Border. *Refugee Survey Quarterly, 37*(1), 44–70.

Carrera, S., & Cortinovis, R. (2019). *Search and Rescue, Disembarkation and Relocation Arrangements in the Mediterranean Sailing Away from Responsibility?* CEPS, 10.

Carta, S. (2018). Beyond Closed Ports: The New Italian Decree-Law on Immigration and Security. *Immigration and Asylum Law and Policy*. Available at https://eumigrationlawblog.eu/beyond-closed-ports-the-new-italian-decree-law-on-immigration-and-security/

Casolari, F. (2016). The EU's Hotspot Approach to Managing the Migration Crisis: A Blindspot for International Responsibility? *Italian Yearbook of International Law, 25*(1), 109–134.

Castelli Gattinara, P. (2017). The 'Refugee Crisis' in Italy as a Crisis of Legitimacy. *Contemporary Italian Politics, 9*(3), 318–331.

Cavasino, E. (2018). Diritti, sicurezza, solidarietà e responsabilità nella protezione della persona migrante. *federalismi.it, Focus-Human Rights, 6*(3), 1–24. Available at www.federalismi.it

Cetin, E. (2015). The Italian Left and Italy's (Evolving) Foreign Policy of Immigration Controls. *Journal of Modern Italian Studies, 20*(3), 377–397.

Chetail, V. (2019). *International Migration Law*. Oxford: Oxford University Press.

Corsi, C. (2018). La trilogia della Corte costituzionale: ancora su requisiti di lungo-residenza per l'accesso alle prestazioni sociali. *Le Regioni, 46*(5–6), 1170–1187.

Cortese, F. (2017). La difficile "classificazione" dei migranti. In M. Savino (Ed.), *La crisi migratoria tra Italia e Unione europea: diagnosi e prospettiva* (pp. 141–172). Napoli: Editoriale Scientifica.

Cusumano, E., & Gombeer K. (2018). In Deep Waters: The Legal, Humanitarian and Political Implications of Closing Italian Ports to Migrant Rescuers, *Mediterranean Politics*. https://doi.org/10.1080/13629395.2018.1532145.

Dimitriadis, I. (2019). *Working Paper on the Construction of the Crisis-Invasion Discourse by Different Stakeholders in Italy*. Available at https://www.magyc.uliege.be/wp-content/uploads/2019/07/WP3-D.3.3-The-construction-of-the-crisis-invasion-discourse-Unimi.pdf

Doyle, O., Longo, E., & Pin, A. (2019). Populism: A Health Check for Constitutional Democracy? *German Law Journal, 20*(3), 401–407.

Fournier, T. (2018). From Rhetoric to Action – A Constitutional Analysis of Populism. *EUI Working Papers, 8*, 1–27.

Halmai, G. (2018). Is there Such Thing as 'Populist Constitutionalism'? The Case of Hungary. *Fudan Journal of the Humanities and Social Sciences, 11*(3), 323–339.

Kaidatzis, A. (2018). *Populist Constitutionalism as a Critique on Liberal (or Legal) Constitutionalism*. Oñati: International Institute for the Sociology of Law.

Martinico, G. (2019). Fra mimetismo e parassitismo. Brevi considerazioni a proposito del complesso rapporto fra populismo e costituzionalismo. *Questione Giustizia, 38*(1), 71–78.

Mény, Y., & Surel, Y. (2002). The Constitutive Ambiguity of Populism. In Y. Mény & Y. Surel (Eds.), *Democracies and the Populist Challenge*. London: Palgrave.

Moreno-Lax, V., & Lemberg-Pedersen, M. (2019). Border-Induced Displacement: The Ethical and Legal Implications of Distance-Creation Through Externalization. *Questions of International Law, Zoomorphology, 56*, 5–33.

Mudde, C. (2017). Populism: An Ideational Approach. In C. R. Kaltwasser, P. Taggart, P. O. Espejo, & P. Ostiguy (Eds.), *The Oxford Handbook of Populism* (pp. 27–47). Oxford: Oxford University Press.

Mueller, J.-W. (2017). Populism and Constitutionalism. In C. R. Kaltwasser, P. Taggart, P. O. Espejo, & P. Ostiguy (Eds.), *The Oxford Handbook of Populism* (pp. 590–607). Oxford: Oxford University Press.

Newell, J. L. (2018). Living in Interesting Times. *Contemporary Italian Politics, 10*(3), 215–217.

Penasa, S., & Pretto, C. (2016). The Italian Reception System. In P. Minderhoud & K. Zwaan (Eds.), *The Recast Reception Conditions Directive: Central Themes. Problem Issues, and Implementation in Selected Member States* (pp. 97–112). Nijmegen: Wolf Legal Publishers.

Savino, M. (2015). "L'amministrativizzazione" della libertà personale e del due process dei migranti. *Diritto Immigrazione Cittadinanza, 17*(3–4), 50–71.

Savino, M. (2016). The Refugee Crisis as a Challenge for Public Law: The Italian Case. *German Law Journal, 17*(6), 981–1004.

Savino, M. (2017). Lo straniero nella giurisprudenza costituzionale: tra cittadinanza e territorialità. *Quaderni costituzionali, 37*(1), 41–72.

Savino, M. (2019). Refashioning Resettlement: From Border Externalization to Legal Pathways for Asylum. In S. Carrera, A. P. L. den Hertog, M. Panizzon, & D. Kostakopoulou (Eds.), *EU External Migration Policies in an Era of Global Mobilities: Intersecting Policy Universes* (pp. 81–104). Leiden: Brill-Nijhoff.

Stoyanova, V. (2018). Populism, Exceptionality, and the Right to Family Life of Migrants Under the European Convention on Human Rights. *European Journal of Legal Studies, 10*(2), 83–124.

Stumpf, J. (2006). The Crimmigration Crisis: Immigrants, Crime and Sovereign Power. *American University Law Review, 56*(2), 368–419.

Taggart, P. (2017). Populism in Western Europe. In C. R. Kaltwasser, P. Taggart, P. O. Espejo, & P. Ostiguy (Eds.), *The Oxford Handbook of Populism* (pp. 342–362). Oxford: Oxford University Press.

Trimikliniotis, N. (2019). *Migration and the Refugee Dissensus in Europe: Borders, Security and Austerity.* London: Routledge.

Tushnet, M. (2019). Varieties of Populism. *German Law Journal, 20*(3), 382–389.

Villa, M. (2018). Sea Arrivals to Italy: The Cost of Deterrence Policies. *ISPI Commentary.* Available at www.ispionline.it

CHAPTER 14

Does a Sub-State Dimension of Populism Exist?

Alessandro Sterpa

Populism Contained in the Nation-State

The following considerations seek to analyse populism with reference to the institutional events that have occurred in some member countries of the European Union (EU), especially at the regional level, with a specific focus on the Italian situation.[1]

In recent years, a plethora of definitions of populism have emerged (see Allegri et al. 2019). The legal sciences have tentatively offered a description that meets the requirements of the law and have duly borrowed instruments from the social sciences (Incisa 2004). From a legal perspective, populism consists of the presumed superiority of the contingent will of the people (or better, part of the people), regardless of any legal

The text was translated from Italian into English by Sonia Maria Melchiorre, researcher at the University of Tuscia, unless otherwise noted.

[1] For the purpose of this chapter, we shall mainly focus on ordinary Regions.

A. Sterpa (✉)
Tuscia University, Viterbo, Italy
e-mail: sterpa@unitus.it

G. Delledonne et al. (eds.), *Italian Populism and Constitutional Law*, Challenges to Democracy in the 21st Century,
https://doi.org/10.1007/978-3-030-37401-3_14

restrictions imposed by the law on that will (Sterpa 2019b). In this sense, the analysis of populism is based on two legal concepts: the *people* as the constituent element of the state; and the *limits* of people's sovereignty. The very definition of people is one of the three elements (along with the territory and the internal and external sovereignty of a country) that traditionally constitute a contemporary nation-state. It is founded on the belief that a nation consists of a certain cultural consonance resulting from a common language, religion and history, shared by the resident individuals within a given territory. For these reasons, according to the approach presented in this contribution, populism must be studied by legal experts as part of the dynamics of the typical European state organization, internationally recognized as a model of the institutionalized power of the people. Some possible explanations are given below (and as a matter of fact, all three elements have been deeply affected by the profound social and political changes of the last few decades).

The concept of people can be ascribed to the notion of a stable community residing within the borders of a state and sharing a typical national cultural character. Presently, more than five million Italians are permanent residents of foreign countries and millions of foreigners permanently reside in Italy. The life of each individual is therefore increasingly detached from a specific territorial location, resulting in an unprecedentedly fragmented and disjointed situation.

The territory of a certain state is no more than a tool for the selection and protection of a specific community of individuals; first, because human mobility has reached an inconceivable level and second because functional geography has totally superseded physical geography. Such global mobility is now connecting parts of the territory of several different states in a finalistic way, thereby creating a "*new Hanseatic*" model where the state is only partially involved. Moreover, these portions of the territory are unevenly connected through time because the relationships between them are very dynamic.

The external sovereignty of the state is in turn mismanaged by the global connection via forms of "*local law*" or "*the law of privates*". In Europe, this process is exemplified by the increased competence of the EU, that is, a legal system that produces rules to impose on its member states. The supremacy of European law is formalized in the rigid constitutions of the member states (in Italy, it is specifically established by arts. 11 and 117, par. 1, of the Constitution) and affects more than ever the expression of popular sovereignty.

In fact, populism reconsiders the people, territory and sovereignty as key elements. Thus, as regards the internal state, within a specific territory, popular will, even if it is only the expression of part of the people, must prevail over any other will. Moreover, outside the state, it necessarily recovers the condition of the state's sovereignty within the international community, affirming the notion of a territorial "border" (souverainism).

Therefore, from the legal point of view, populism must be analysed in the light of the crisis of the three constituent elements of the European nation-state, that is, the people, territory and sovereignty.

Populism and the State Definition of People

Consequently, the people as the fulcrum of populist dynamics constitute a subject at state level. For the purposes of our study, it will be useful to consider the sub-state dimension of the term "people" and to ask whether the "fractions of people" belonging to autonomous territorial legal systems (the regions) can produce populist dynamics, as is the case with "people as a whole" at the state level.

Particularly interesting in this respect is the case law of the Italian Constitutional Court that, despite grappling with a transformation of the modalities of expression of popular sovereignty, has always denied the existence of the very concept of people outside the state dimension. When the Regions, called upon to adopt the new *Statuti* governing their organization following the Constitutional Reform of 1999, tried to define the Regional Council with the *nomen iuris "Parliament"* there was a reaction by Constitutional Court, clearly prohibiting the provision (judgment n. 106 of 2002). In fact, the Constitutional Court has made clear that "the relationship between the Parliament and popular sovereignty undeniably represents an element of democratic-representative principles, but does not describe the terms of an identity relationship. Consequently, the thesis according to which, as stated in our Constitution, popular sovereignty would essentially find expression in Parliament without territorial autonomy, helping to shaping its essence, cannot be shared in its absoluteness". Therefore, as acknowledged by the Court, "article 1 of the Constitution, in establishing, with a clear and definitive formulation, that sovereignty 'belongs' to the people, prevents us from believing that there are places or premises of the constitutional organization in which it can be fully established. The forms and ways in which the sovereignty of the people can take place, in fact, do not only find expression in the representation, but permeate the entire constitutional framework. They are refracted, as a matter of fact, in a multiplicity of situations and institutions, and take on such a wide configuration that they certainly include recognition and assurance of territorial autonomy". In any event, the judgment of the Constitutional Court has not prejudiced the concept of people, as the Court has specified that "the nomen Parliament has no purely lexical value, but it also has a qualifying value, connoting, with the entity, the exclusive position it occupies within the constitutional organization. Precisely this peculiar connotative strength of the word helps prevent any possible declination aimed to keep within restricted territorial circles the function of national representation that only the Parliament can represent and that is inevitably evoked by the use of its nomen".[2]

The Constitutional Court has confirmed the existing difference between the regional body and the Parliament regarding the condition of the representatives elected by the people in their respective political bodies that hold legislative power. As to the liability regime, the Constitutional Court has clarified that "the formal identity of the statements referred to in articles 68, first paragraph, and 122, fourth paragraph, Cost. does not refer to a full assimilation between the assembly of parliamentary members and regional councils. This Court has already established that, unlike the functions assigned to the chambers, 'the prerogatives of the regional councils are to be intended, instead, as the expression of autonomies guaranteed by the Constitution, and do not represent any possible national sovereignty *(judgment n. 306 of 2002; judgment n. 81 of 1975)*'" (judgment n. 301 of 2007).

These decisions, which refer to concepts of national representation, have therefore drastically limited the expansion of the political choices expressed by territorial fractions of people. We additionally find this form of disempowerment—in an indirect form—in the considerable constitutional jurisprudence that since 2003 has systematically reduced the autonomies of the constitutional provisions introduced between 1999 and 2001. Here, the provisions concerning the values, principles, rights and obligations contained in the Regional Statutes, "even when contained in a legal-act [source-act], cannot be recognised as having any legal effect, primarily expressing the several political convictions extant in the regional

[2] It is also interesting to stress the case of Sardinia, whose *Statuto* was prevented from using the word "*sovranità*" referring to the regional people by the Constitutional Court in judgment n. 365 of 2007.

community in the moment of the approval of the Statute" (judgment. n. 372, n. 378 and n. 379 of 2004) (Sterpa 2015). These changes have stimulated the Constitutional Court to establish that "regional people" do not exist (Morrone 2012). Indeed, in recent years, the region of Veneto has taken some very peculiar legal initiatives, including a regulation to hold a regional consultative referendum concerning a draft constitutional law proposed by the region itself to broaden the autonomy of Veneto. As a result, the Constitutional Court has clarified that "whereas the people under review may intervene as last instance and entirety [art. 138 Cost.]. This is evoked by the regional law in its partiality of autonomous fraction residing in a fraction of the national territory, as if in our Constitution [...] people, giving form to the political unit of the nation, did not exist and as if more people existed" (judgment n. 496 of 2000). In short, "pluralism and autonomy do not permit the regions to classify themselves as sovereign bodies and do not permit their governmental organs to be treated as equivalent to the representative bodies of a nation" (judgment. n. 118 of 2015).[3]

The first point considered in the present discussion therefore revolves around the concept of populism that presupposes that of people. From a legal perspective, it does not in fact exist at the regional level. This statement may provide support for the thesis that if people do not exist, populism cannot exist. Unfortunately, the question is not so simple. The "will" of what is defined as the "regional body of electors", rather than the "regional population", is nevertheless expressing a political stance that, as has been seen at the national level, tends to overcome the regulatory limitations typical of constitutional democracies.

In short, the behaviour of this "component of people" is subjugated, like the people itself, by a legal system of limitations akin to every power or fraction of power that constitutionalism attributes to institutional pluralism, as well as how "people as a whole" would surmount the system of limitations.

Populism and the Limitations of Popular Sovereignty

In fact, in the act of organizing contemporary institutions, constitutionalism has endorsed the principle of democracy intended—albeit very briefly—as the capacity of the recipient subjects of the forms of exercise of

[3] As translated on the website of the Court, www.cortecostituzionale.it

public authority (*in primis* the creation of legal rules) to legitimize and influence content. This is testimony to the system of limitations imposed by the Constitution on popular will (art. 1 Cost.) and by international and European regulations (arts. 2, 10, 11 and 117, Cost.), as it refers to both the forms of popular sovereignty and the content of the choices made (values, principles, organization of rules and procedures).

The system of formal and substantial limitations to the exercise of popular sovereignty, stated in the first article of the Italian Constitution, represents the bulwark to a self-destructive attitude of democracy. First, populism represents a risk for constitutional democratic systems regardless of the ideological relevance of its positions, as it originates in the negation of the principle of plurality, the initial connotation of constitutionalism that imposes limitations on people's power. Second, constitutionalism aims to fragment the three traditional powers of the state, thereby limiting each power within a "balanced" system.

If, on the one hand, populism (like any other ideology) insists on the affirmation of a historical truth, this irrefutable axiom is not only legally relevant *for the solution* occasionally proposed to a collective problem (true or alleged), but also *for the method*. Certainly, the main characteristic of populism is the assertion of a "truth" that is presented as popular will (whether it represents the majority or not) against "non-truths". The very essence of populism is the negation of pluralism, which conversely constitutes the foundation of democratic constitutionalism.

As already mentioned, it is not a coincidence that souverainism is no different from populism, as it represents its exteriorization. In fact, the assumed supremacy of a partial popular will within national borders necessarily leads to the affirmation of the supremacy of one people's will over others.

As a result, populist and souveranist policies result in a clash with those subjects that manage the forms and limitations of popular sovereignty. This is the case with the President of the Italian Republic, the Judiciary authority and the Constitutional Court. Given that the restrictions are produced at the international level, among those subjects that are attacked by populism and souverainism we also find EU bodies or supranational judges responsible for the safeguarding of international regulations and fundamental rights. As to the internal political bodies of the state, the regions may be forced by regional people to make decisions to formalize acts that generally exceed the legal limits imposed by the regulatory system on popular sovereignty.

Among the many expressions of this "regional populism", we find both regulatory acts that attempt to extend or recognize rights and obligations that are not included in the national legal framework and to expand concepts and bodies (i.e. "*common goods*"), as far as cases of legal measures (erroneously) are deemed capable of increasing (social and public) security levels. One example is provided by cases where the Regions have developed a fund to ensure free patronage to subjects tried for their excessive reaction to robberies in their own premises (Liguria and Veneto) (Sterpa 2019a). Indeed, "*protectionist choices*" have been formalized that exclusively favour residents (recently Friuli Venezia Giulia and Veneto, Const. Court, judgment n. 83 of 2018) or that attribute legal relevance to values, principle and regional identity issues (see the Statute of the Regions Veneto or Lazio). These choices cannot be qualified as more or less "populist" owing to their different repercussions on the whole legal framework and their association with conservative or progressive policies. They actually represent "expressions of territorial populism" only when the choices are proposed with a view to garnering electoral support, to the detriment of constitutional values.

The Italian Republic safeguards national axiological unity, in the first place monitoring the sources of the regional law that must conform to the Constitution, both for the limitations and the form. A regional law that clashes with the constitutional framework is declared unconstitutional by the Constitutional Court, compromising its impact, as its "subversive thrust" is rejected by the system.

It is hence understandable that in some situations, the ordinary mechanism may not be sufficient to tackle the problem. In such a case, the system might be based on constitutional predictions that envisage effective controls and sanctions of regions and local entities. For instance, art. 126 provides for the regions that "[t]he Regional Council may be dissolved and the President of the Executive may be removed with a reasoned decree of the President of the Republic in the case of acts in contrast with the Constitution or grave violations of the law. The dissolution or removal may also be decided for reasons of national security" (par. 1). In order to incur such a serious penalty, the region will not only violate the legal provisions in force, but also encourage wilful non-compliance with the governing rules. As has already been fully demonstrated in the jurisprudence of the Constitutional Court, constitutional limitations to the full exercise of popular sovereignty also apply to the regional electoral body. This happens not simply because the regional regulations must respect the

Constitution (and the international obligations and the EC's requirements), but also because "when intended in its broadest sense, autonomy cannot [...] be invoked to support and give legal form to referendum campaigns concerning fundamental choices of constitutional relevance" (judgment n. 496 of 2000). This approach has led the Court to clarify on several occasions that "regional referendums, including consultative referendums, cannot involve choices impinging upon constitutional law (judgment n. 365 of 2007, n. 496 of 2000 and n. 470 of 1992)" (judgment n. 118/2015).[4] One of these "choices of constitutional relevance" is the unitarian dimension of the state, which is the one symbolically regarded as a form of "regional populism".

The "Limit" of the Principle of Unity of the State

Through formal acts taken by institutional bodies, the popular will of a regional community can thus also formalize political choices, at odds with the Constitution. The question we ask is the following: is national unity a value and a constitutional obligation that qualifies a certain political choice that undermines it as populist? Or rather, is it something that is not a value to be considered like others, but that simply represents a mere material presupposition (as opposed to an axiological principle) of the national state?

In the words of the Constitutional Court, the unity of the Republic represents "one of those very essential elements of the Republican legal system excluded from any possible constitutional revision (judgment n. 1146 of 1988)"; "the republican order is also based on principles including social and institutional pluralism and territorial autonomy, in addition to an openness to supranational integration and international law; however, these principles must be developed within the framework of the Republic alone: 'The Republic, which is one and indivisible, shall recognise and promote local government' (Article 5 of the Constitution)" (judgment n. 118 of 2015)[5] (see Esposito 1954; Staiano 2017).

The positioning of national unity in the field of the "pre-constitutional" means that every attempt to modify it (that is, modify the territorial and national integrity of the Republic) involves an *extra ordinem* action (see Constitutional Court, judgment n. 118/15) (Martinico 2019). This leads to the following question: why is the modification of the integrity of a

[4] As translated on the website of the Court, www.cortecostituzionale.it

[5] As translated on the website of the Court, www.cortecostituzionale.it

political territory, governed by public authorities, defended by the Constitution?

The response has historical roots (Ferraiuolo 2016). It must be considered that territorial integrity has been called into question over the years without invoking the repression of an *extra ordinem* choice. One example is the expansion and reduction of certain national borders while the Constitution was in place, as seen in examples like the reunification of the territory of Trieste in 1954. Of course, the fact that Italy "rejects" war (art. 11) can imply that the immutability of the national territory is to be intended in both the expansionist and restrictive sense. However, according to our perspective, the core issue is altogether different.

The territory is intended in its entirety as a precondition of the Constitution to the extent that it qualifies and delineates the space of action and constitutional principles; that is, it creates the material conditions of the "agreement" of co-existence based on constitutional principles such as social and institutional pluralism, active personality and solidarity. The territory therefore identifies the community committed to achieving such a constitutional agreement of co-existence and economic development. It signifies no more than this, especially now that the notions of nation and identity are being substantially revised.

Considering the instruments used to achieve such a legal finalization of this "functional unit", we realize that they are often ascribable to both symbolic (such as the flag) and solidarity-based elements. It is hence necessary to consider this aspect further.

The flag of the Republic, as worded in art. 12 of the Italian Constitution (it is no coincidence that the *tricolore* is considered a "fundamental principle"), was included in the Constitution to specify, in terms of international relationships, "the banner of one's own nation" (Meuccio Ruini, in a speech to the Constituent Assembly), that is, "distinctive mark of the personality of the state on international level" (Const. Court, judgment n. 183 of 2018).

Further, the legal rigidity of the flag—as noticed by the Constitutional Court—aims to transform the "*tricolore*" into a symbol of national unity that cannot be modified by the political majority of the moment.

In judgment no. 189 of 1987, the Court had already noted that if in an authoritarian state the flag represents the symbol of "national sovereignty of a state that 'does not recognize' any values other than those that it embraces and implements", within a changed political climate flags "no longer represent the emblem or symbol of territorial sovereignty conceived of in the meaning mentioned above, but rather symbolically designate a certain country, the identity of a certain State" and "potentially the ideals that it promotes on international level" (Const. Court, judgment n. 183 of 2018).

No less important is the assumption of some scholars regarding the solidarity-based function of national unity, which would be rendered devoid of purpose in the case of secession (the so-called *patrimonial populism*). As already observed, the extent to which the state redistributes national wealth ensures rights and obligations on the entire territory of the country and provides the equalization of resources and opportunities Indeed, "[t]he idea of solidarity [...] is ingrained in the common elements of every legal system" (Nicotra 2019; Catelani 2018; Giuffrè 2002).

At this stage of the discussion, looking to the "territorial issue" in Europe (for instance, Catalunya or Scotland), the question is as follows: if it were possible to guarantee the respect of constitutional values and principles without retaining the territorial entirety of the national state, would we really be in the presence of an *extra ordinem* populist attempt? If, for instance, the fundamental principles of the Constitution of the state can be considered the same pursued by and legally protected in the Treaties of the EU, would it make sense to deem every secessionist will populist and thus disruptive of the constitutional order? Could a populistic choice be considered "secession by the state but not by the European Union"?

Populism, Self-Determination or Simple Re-organization of Public Authority?

At this point, the following question arises: when separating the idea of the people from that of the nation-state, in the context of an internal community of the state, where would the divide between populism and the right of self-determination stand? It is true that "[t]he democratic state cannot fear a confrontation with the ideals pursued by peoples of other states and different nations" (judgment n. 189 of 1987) and that a comprehensive body of literature and jurisprudence that deals with the idea of minority and self-determination exists, but it unfortunately does not help to solve the question.

It must be remembered that the Treaty on the European Union provides that "[t]he Union shall respect the equality of member states before the Treaties as well as their national identities, inherent in their fundamental structures, political and constitutional, inclusive of regional and local self-government. It shall respect their essential State functions, including ensuring the territorial integrity of the State, maintaining law and order and safeguarding national security. In particular, national security remains the sole responsibility of each member state" (art. 4, par. 2). Such a provision, agreed upon by the member states, can only be understood as a declaration of the absolute neutrality of the Union in relation to the national territorial dynamics of each country. Countries are thus left to manage the integrity of their own territories, with the Union having no jurisdiction on the subject matter. Notwithstanding this pro-state approach, such a prediction represents an attempt to define territorial integrity as functional fact, detached from the mere state organization when identified as one of its "essential functions".

What the EU obviously protects, together with an international law system and the Italian Constitution, are minorities' rights. It is no coincidence that the Veneto region has legally pursued the protection of minorities' rights to try to identify a "Venetian people" and has adopted rules with the aim of giving "effect" to the Framework Convention for the Protection of National Minorities, completed in Strasbourg on 1 February 1995 and ratified and executed in Italy with Law no. 302/1997. On that occasion, the Constitutional Court clarified that regional "law precepts" identifying "Venetian people" as a national minority are in conflict with "the task of determining the elements identifying a minority to be protected [which] must fall to the State legislator, because these must necessarily be uniform throughout the entire national territory" (judgment n. 81 of 2018).[6] On the other hand, "the state lawmaker is in the most favourable position to safeguard the differences because it is able to guarantee commonalities. It therefore represents the most appropriate body to make pluralism compatible with uniformity (judgment n. 170 of 2010) as well as the implementation of art. 5 Cost." (ibidem).

The reason preventing the sub-regional lawmaker from "identifying or representing their own community as a minority, 'being clear that, as a general rule, the local political and administrative body contained within a larger national territory and legal framework shall not automatically be regarded as corresponding – as is equally relevant – to part of the 'people', meaning a 'general' community, into unlikely fractions' (judgment n. 170 of 2010). Officially acknowledging that the regional lawmaker has such power implies introducing an element of fragmentation into the national community, in conflict with arts. 2, 3, 5 and 6 Cost" (judgment n. 81 of

[6] As translated on the website of the Court, www.cortecostituzionale.it

2018). The Italian Constitutional Court therefore clarifies that the Convention recognizes an individual right and "does not provide for [the] collective rights of minorities".

On the other hand, what kind of Constitution, based on the unity of a community being at least a factual tenet if not cultural (nation), would even consider a provision for self-dissolution? Moreover, the EU provides for the right of withdrawal (art. 50 TEU), presenting us with criticalities regarding its effective implementation (Savastano 2019). The Catalan case reminds us that the right to secession is not legitimate in the Constitution of a nation-state without undermining the historically allocated principle of unity. Nevertheless, it must be considered that not all legal orders of states are so rigid. The growing tendency, as several legal experts have observed, is to consider secession in a more dynamic way (Caravita 2009), that is, less as "the withdrawal of a group from a larger, pre-existing entity" (Attinà 2004) and increasingly as "the process through which a group aims to win the territorial withdrawal from a larger territorial entity, regardless of the achievement of their purpose" (Margiotta 2005).

The clearest example is Canada. The Supreme Court has described the secessionist intention of Quebec as "a right to negotiate the withdrawal" and has also indicated how in the case of Scotland (and in contrast to Catalunya) (Ferraiuolo 2016; Poggeschi 2018), a referendum was held for secession without causing a reaction on the part of the nation-state (Caravale 2014). The diverse approaches of national legal systems to the possible regulation (or management) of secessionist thrusts clearly demonstrates that "the question is not yet clearly defined". Moreover, regardless of the regulation applied by each legal system, not all secessions can be compared to a constitutional system.

When the secessionist impetus aims to create a new constitutional system that is consistent with the values of its predecessor or that is even willing to stay in the EU, can we really describe it as "populism", that is, as an attack on the legal limitations of power? Certainly, remaining as part of a new state in the Union is not a populist pretension of souverainism if it remains within the constitutional system of limitations of the public authority.

The reasoning behind this discussion is therefore simple: if, on the one hand, populism generally asserts the supremacy of popular will against imposed constitutional limits, on the other, it does not necessarily imply that the will to establish a new territorial legal subject, detached from the nation-state, can substantiate that limit and instead become a simple act of the re-organization of public authority in the framework of European federalism. Populist state experiences, in support of the dogma of "popular truth", deny pluralism and tend to develop political models that can be identified as authoritarian in their management of power (for example, Turkey, Hungary). This is an element that is not usually part of secessionist "pretences" in the states of the EU. On the other hand, many countries that are today part of the EU were formed by separating from other states (for example, Czech Republic, Slovakia, Slovenia, Croatia) or via the dissolution of supernational unions (Estonia, Latvia, Lithuania). The American federation also originated in an act of secession that broke the unity of the public authority (1776–1787).

What is the EU if not an attempt to create a federal state with a larger territory and the free movement of people, resources and regulations and where a "European people" legitimize the existence of a parliament and governmental bodies based on constitutional rules (treaties and conventions)? Is the bottom-up reorganization of people, territory and sovereignty not a form of populism? It would be regarded as such if it occurred within a nation-state.

On the other hand, if it is true that the three traditional elements of the Constitution of a state (i.e., people, territory and sovereignty) are being questioned, are we sure that the preservation of nation-states as conceived in the twentieth century would be able to support the development of constitutional democracy?

Beyond the nation-state, if popular will were included in the Constitution of a new constitutional order (a new state resulting from a separation, or a new state with origins in supranational integration) and complied with the values of the Constitution of the former state, could we establish with certainty that we are facing forms of populism, or rather, should we verify that we are witnessing the "re-organization" of public authority after the crisis of nation states' sovereignty?

Populism and souverainism are symptoms of the crisis of the nation-state to the extent that they would recover the previously existing conditions of the state. The response to the situation cannot be simplistic, that is, to re-establish national unity and to re-propose the traditional instruments previously used in the organization of public authority. The answer to the question must instead be to reconstruct constitutionalism, regardless of the state. The agony of the "immortal" state cannot end in the re-constitution of something that is anachronistically inadequate in managing public authority and that would prejudice constitutionalism and with it human freedom.

References

Allegri, G., Sterpa, A., & Viceconte, N. (Eds.). (2019). *Questioni costituzionali al tempo del populismo e del sovranismo*. Napoli: ES.

Attinà, F. (2004). Secessione. In N. Bobbio & N. Matteucci (Eds.), *Dizionario di politica* (pp. 867–868). Torino: Utet.

Caravale, G. (2014). Il referendum del 18 settembre 2014: *Scotland Chooses the Best of Both Worlds*. *federalismi.it*, *12*(18), 1–36. Available at www.federalismi.it

Caravita, B. (2009). *Lineamenti di diritto costituzionale regionale e federale*. Torino: Giappichelli.

Catelani, E. (2018). La tutela dei diritti sociali in Europa. I rischi della differenziazione. *federalismi.it*, *16*(5), 29–52. Available at www.federalismi.it

Esposito, C. (1954). Autonomie locali e decentramento amministrativo nell'art. 5 della Costituzione. In C. Esposito (Ed.), *La Costituzione italiana. Saggi*. Padova: Cedam.

Ferraiuolo, G. (2016). *Costituzione federalismo secessione*. Napoli: ES.

Giuffrè, F. (2002). *La solidarietà nell'ordinamento costituzionale*. Milano: Giuffrè.

Incisa, L. (2004). Populismo. In N. Bobbio & N. Matteucci (Eds.), *Dizionario di politica* (pp. 732–737). Torino: Utet.

Margiotta, C. (2005). *L'ultimo diritto. Profili storici e teorici della secessione*. Bologna: Il Mulino.

Martinico, G. (2019). Preserving Constitutional Democracy from Populism. The Case of Secession Referendums. *National Journal of Constitutional Law*, *39*(2), 139–157.

Morrone, A. (2012). Avanti popolo... regionale! *Quaderni costituzionali*, *31*(3), 615–618.

Nicotra, I. A. (2019). La 'sfida' secessionista e il valore "unificante" della solidarietà territoriale. L'ultima frontiera della protesta populista. *federalismi.it*, *17*(16), 1–20. Available at www.federalismi.it

Poggeschi, G. (2018). *La Catalogna. Dalla Nazione storica alla Repubblica immaginaria*. Napoli: ES.

Savastano, F. (2019). *Uscire dall'Unione europea. Brexit e il diritto di recedere dai Trattati*. Torino: Giappichelli.

Staiano, S. (2017). *Art. 5*. Roma: Carocci.

Sterpa, A. (2015). *Il pendolo e la livella. Il "federalismo all'italiana e le riforme"*. Torino: Giappichelli.

Sterpa, A. (2019a). *La libertà dalla paura. Una lettura costituzionale della sicurezza*. Napoli: ES.

Sterpa, A. (2019b). Il teorema di Pitagora: come si rapportano Costituzione, populismo e sovranismo? In G. Allegri, A. Sterpa, & N. Viceconte (Eds.), *Questioni costituzionali al tempo del populismo e del sovranismo* (pp. 11–49). Napoli: ES.

CHAPTER 15

Populism and Criminal Justice in Italy

Nicola Selvaggi

The Defining Problem

Any reflection on the phenomenon of "crime-related populism" cannot fail to acknowledge its complexity and its multiple effects on society, legislative policy, the administration of the criminal justice system and the media.

In order to avoid inappropriate generalisations, initially, a distinction should be drawn between types of populism that are, strictly speaking, "political" and those that are more specific to the criminal domain, even if there is a natural link between the two.

The label "political populism" often refers, including as it is portrayed in the media, to a wide variety of movements and parties, which are not infrequently in the grip of charismatic leaders and around which certain values—either real or imagined—relating to identity revolve; whereby these movements and parties also tend to ascribe crucial significance to a "rhetoric" of the people, of which they are apparently both the guarantors and the interpreters (see Costa 2019; Diamanti and Lazar 2018; Müller 2017; Mastropaolo 2010).

N. Selvaggi (✉)
Department of Law and Economics, Mediterranea University of Reggio Calabria, Reggio Calabria, Italy
e-mail: nicola.selvaggi@unirc.com

G. Delledonne et al. (eds.), *Italian Populism and Constitutional Law*, Challenges to Democracy in the 21st Century,
https://doi.org/10.1007/978-3-030-37401-3_15

A rhetoric that drains the meaning out of collective belonging built around great ideals (Catholic, communist, democratic, liberal, etc.) ultimately deprives politics of its essential role as an instrument for mediating social conflicts; and does so under a banner signifying a vast dumbing-down (Violante 2014).

Hence, we see confirmed the notion that the task of politics is not to govern society, but rather to pander to it.

Here, critical thinking is replaced by suggested messaging, which, the more banal and easily understood it is, the more effective it becomes.

Certain themes—the "self-made-man", the "healthy virtues" of the middle class—offered as alternatives to the vices and privileges of the elites, the counter-formalist criticism of the excessive complexity of institutions, come together in a confused composite that appeals directly to the people and serves as a way of destabilizing the establishment and attacking the "powers that be".

A political programme is replaced by a set of slogans, while the success of politicians is not measured by the social utility of their initiatives, but by the number of their TV appearances.

What matters is not finding the solution to a problem; it is enough to just point the finger at whoever is allegedly responsible for it.

"Penal Populism"

In the political sphere, the populist wave tends to marginalize rational arguments and to emphasize more "emotional" ones; and, in the process, they give the illusion that the relevant situation has now been taken under control.

In the criminal sphere, these pathologies cause additional problems.

In the case of Italy in particular, some phenomena also to be found, not least, in a number of other European countries, are associated with specific factors that have been well established for over thirty years.

To be sure, any discourse on criminal justice populism has to take into account the fact that one of the most significant institutional transformations occurring in Italy, which brought about the end of traditional parties, also saw a decisive role played by the criminal justice system. Insofar as this transformation has become, more or less explicitly, one of the main expressions of anti-system sentiment, this has occurred even though criminal prosecutions have actually been directed, as one might expect, against very serious, widespread criminal manifestations, starting with corruption.

It should not be forgotten in this context that, based on the reconstructions of one of the protagonists of the time, popular support for the various investigations announced under the newspaper headline "Clean Hands" ("Mani Pulite") began to decline significantly once the investigations started to consider corruption mechanisms that did not necessarily affect the political or economic system; instead, they focused, for example, on possible conspiracies between individuals responsible for identifying tax offences involving small businesses or corrupt practices aimed at ensuring the cancellation of major fines for road traffic offences. This meant that, with regards to the public opinion prevailing at the time, the prosecutors and the courts enjoyed widespread support until their efforts gave voice to the anti-system feelings that were already very widespread; whereas, in contrast, an objective sense of legality was not in evidence, or at least, was not widespread.

Despite its contradictory aspects, the transmission to the criminal justice system of a series of mass (popular) expectations represents an extremely significant aspect of the Italian experience and is fundamental to any understanding of it.

Another aspect that should not be overlooked is the relationship between the increasing resort to the criminal justice system and the difficult macro-economic situation.

Our intention here is not just to highlight how economic and social hardship are capable of being translated into calls for criminal justice, with the latter evidently propelled strongly by a widespread malaise among the public (Gallo 2018).

What interests us here is to demonstrate how, because of—inter alia—the high level of public debt that afflicts Italy, the political echelon is more prone to implementing a facile "programme of promises". Interestingly, it does so by enacting criminal law reforms that have no need of specific financial coverage.

Put differently, it may be simpler (and more electorally convenient) to reassure citizens by introducing new immigration offences, or by increasing the penalties for medical malpractice, than by devising measures that require a prior warning that the resulting costs will need to be covered by State finances.

Of course, none of this means that criminal legislation does not entail real costs; quite the opposite, in fact.

Consider, for example, what it might mean to expand the number of offences for which particular methods of obtaining evidence may be available (e.g. wiretapping or bugging) or else the cost that the introduction of alternatives to detention or other measures needed to counteract recidivism might involve; or, again, the introduction of new offences that could result in a significant extra workload for the courts—given that, in Italian law, the principle of mandatory prosecution applies.

Despite these considerations, it is the case that laws that provide for the introduction of offences or amendments to rules governing criminal proceedings do not need to contain any specific reference to further financial costs to bear.

It is also because of these factors that the criminal justice system is becoming a method of obtaining and manipulating popular consent.

The experience of recent years shows that, in parliamentary practice, the criminal justice system has often been reduced to a mere technique for accommodating demands for punishment originating from society and the mass media (Violante 2014).

The criminal code no longer seems to be a type of Magna Carta governing the treatment of offenders but has now replaced the constitutional Magna Carta in the political arena (Violante 2014).

In relation to social problems of varying degrees of gravity, criminal prosecutions are constantly being called for in order to deal, in the most politically advantageous way, with the problems posed by security and the need for collective reassurance. And while this "primacy" of the criminal justice system unleashes a dangerous chase after ever harsher punishments and ever stricter treatment of offenders, the associated penal legislation tends to be formulated in an increasingly vague way, so as to widen its potential applicability.

In turn, the average citizen thinks "the more criminal prosecutions the better" may be the way forward and tends to evaluate the behaviour of politicians on the basis of their tendency to invoke the need for criminal punishments.

In this way, the criminal justice system becomes easy territory in which to battle and achieve consensus. It is used widely as an instrument for turning crime and punishment not just into "social sedatives" designed to appease more or less well-founded collective anxieties and insecurities but also to excite the most irrational feelings of "revenge"; this, in turn, may trigger reactions not always consistent with the principles of strict necessity and proportionality that ought to accompany the wielding of criminal sanctions.

It is emblematic, in this regard, that there is currently a tendency to redefine a not inconsiderable proportion of public policies in terms of criminal policy, with all that this entails, including over-criminalization and the associated deviation from the principle of criminal law as a last resort (*extrema ratio*).

The selection of criminally relevant facts is thus carried out in accordance with the moods of public opinion, to which the task of modelling new types of perpetrators is delegated, accompanied by different punitive statutes: the unlawful foreigner, the corrupt and/or corrupting politician, the reckless driver, the fraudulently negligent employer, to name but a few.

Imposing "law and order" and "doing justice" are the political imperatives of entities charged with providing security. As such, the latter aim at satisfying the need for societal reassurance and relevant media pressures; if need be, by calling for zero tolerance towards the "enemy" (Lacey 2019).

Hence, the legislator pursues the growing demand for punishment by betting on the potential of the criminal justice system as an effective—and electorally successful—instrument for sophisticated defence of the community. Irrational impulses aim to confront the emergencies of the day, without actually being able to solve them: the reality of the statistics, however, especially when they refer to the categories of criminality characterized by hardly any figures in the black, points to an almost total systematic failure, as evidenced by facts, of the "law and order" policies involving mere deterrence as their endpoint.

Criminal law scholars, for their part, after devoting themselves to the problem of populism with both breadth and depth of thought, are now struggling to come up with a rationale that would involve a reversal of these trends, especially in terms of possible options for legislative policy (Risicato 2019; Tripodi 2019; Scoditti 2018; Various Authors 2016; Violante 2014; Pulitanò 2013; Fiandaca 2013).

This is because the demagogic use of crime and punishment is met with growing support, in a context in which society, the media and political power are clamouring for the legislator and judges to combat the type of perpetrators that populism likes to conjure into life from time to time.

You may even wonder whether the criminal justice system itself is *inherently* populist (Fiandaca 2013).

This is a provocative question to a certain extent, since criminal justice intrinsically has an extremely close relationship with the self-perceived identity of a particular community.

Behind these reflections is Jellinek's famous theory that the criminal justice system reflects the "ethical minimum" of a people in a given historical context (Fiandaca 2013). In this regard, it is clear that this ethical minimum refers to the cultural identity of a people, as it results from the prevailing values that characterize it. From this point of view, the criminal justice system would constitute, even before being an instrument of protection, a symbolic marker of values, the observance of which defines the perimeter of an identity and any associated group membership.

A Loss of Humanity?

It is generally felt that the major cost of the trend described above is paid in terms of the ineffectiveness of criminal justice itself.

In fact, one of the characteristics of the legislation of recent years is represented by the recurrent presence of excessive sanctions, "manifesto standards" and "exemplary" prosecution models, which are signs of a system often denounced as merely symbolic, in which an excessive number of punitive offerings provide no guarantee of any genuine reduction in levels of crime (Paliero 2011; Forti 2000).

In other words, whether the intention is to neutralize die-hard or aspiring terrorists, pursue a "zero tolerance" policy against undocumented migrants, combat administrative or road traffic offences, the impression given is that of a model that has basically failed: profoundly "inequitable", but nonetheless capable of creating "redundancy", whereby the more it is acknowledged to be ineffectual, the more it continues to be used more or less ritualistically.

Ultimately, therefore, we end up with a "multi-speed" system, as expensive as it is inefficient, consisting of a labyrinth of subsystems whose stated infidelity to the "grammar of the criminal law" (Fletcher 2007) seems to buttress a "spendthrift mentality" shared with a general approach in this area that promises much more than it actually delivers.

These observations, which should certainly be welcomed, nevertheless need further clarification.

It is correct to speak of ineffectiveness when referring to the inadequacy of an instrument intended to achieve the objective of preventing serious crime.

On the other hand, resorting to criminal law with this level of frequency and, in particular, the tendency to introduce new offences and to increase the level of penalties already legislated for, clearly does not come at zero cost. The result is a dehumanisation of the criminal justice system. And this direct shift from ineffectual shouting to use of the law itself, without any knowledge or reason being involved, risks being a really retrograde step in criminal justice.

A few years ago Mario Sbriccoli wrote that the history of criminal justice system is one of a long and arduous process of liberation from the idea of mere revenge and, therefore, also from the dead weight of prevarication (and violence) that have always been liable to accompany revenge (Sbriccoli 2009).

Of course, this assertion hit the mark and still hits the mark today, because the very legitimacy of criminal law, as a discrete legal discipline, should always be linked to the need to establish a set of principles and techniques designed to ensure that the punishment—a profound and perhaps inevitable type of human intervention—is carried out under the sheltering arms of reason and humanity (Paliero 2012).

It is precisely here, as we all know, that the need to take away from the victim all punitive power, strictly understood, in order to entrust instead to the public authorities, begins; and here too originates the need, consecrated by the Enlightenment and by the work of Cesare Beccaria in particular, to advance criminal science as a predictor of the limits properly attributable to the *ius puniendi*; and in such a way as to favour, together with the promise of finally abandoning the infliction of "sublime torment" (Foucault 1993), the notion of punishment as an act of last resort—which must only be administered within the limits of the strictly necessary—and in favour of the criminal justice (also) as a kind of "Magna Carta for offenders".

To sum up, the most significant perspective is that which aims to fully implement the principle of humane punishment, when seen not only as the inspirational rationale for a vision of the consequences that characterize criminal justice but also when seen as including the more immediate effects of this principle throughout the system of criminal liability.

Today, we are witnessing the real risk of a turnaround, however.

We are witnessing the emergence of a "passion for punishment" in the form of a resurgence of ancient, irrational instincts of revenge; a simplification of criminal justice to the detriment of its most important enlightenment and liberal sources (Donini 2019).

Anti-Elite Criticism and the Criminal Justice System

Moreover, since the history of criminal justice consists of all kinds of court proceedings, neither "passion for punishment" nor "symbolic" recourse to the criminal law are considered to be, in themselves, phenomena peculiar to "penal populism".

Instead, they have acquired a meaning that relates specifically to the phenomenon under examination here, whenever they are considered to be an expression of a feeling of criticism or "repulsion" towards the elites.

In an extremely wide variety of sectors (although with particular emphasis on a number of fields, such as economic and entrepreneurial activities), in practice, criminal statutes tailored to certain subjective figures (e.g. the "employer" or "corporate manager") are starting to be created.

The number of "enemies" to be fought using the criminal justice system is multiplying, well beyond the categories devised by theorists of the relationship between power and the criminal law.

Thus, the emergence of functional dangerousness associated with the structure of a criminal justice system that reflects the needs of the hegemonic classes (i.e. the bourgeois society), as based on Michel Foucault's reinterpretation, is compounded in the current situation by the tendency to "criminalize" people who perform productive, economic and professional work; these people once occupied a "privileged" status in the system, but today, at least in some respects, they have been more or less relegated to a kind of continuum of "abnormality" (Sgubbi 1990).

As is well known, while portraying the ways in which criminal justice systems change, Foucault also points to the alteration of a "strictly legal structure"; whereby to this should be added, together with a number of other factors, the development of legal systems themselves in a way that focuses on the offender (to an extent now regarded as increasingly the norm), which therefore, also necessitates the design and implementation of measures and, in general, regulatory instruments (also) suited to this approach (Foucault 2013).

The view of this writer is that schemes of strict liability, which were developed in the context of civil law to meet the requirements generated by economic processes and the corresponding technological innovations, have now become, in a certain sense and to a limited degree, a model for the criminal justice system.

In particular, the concept of risk initially "impoverishes" the case facts underlying civil liability, simultaneously removes any profile of personal guilt, and then, almost "virally", travels in the direction of criminal law, where it re-emerges to address the "offender" or even just in the territory of the "excluded" or the "marginalized"; and in so doing, it directs the justice system to emphasize the nature of the individual, as opposed to relying on an interpretation of the case facts.

Accordingly, the punishment is not understood to be imposed for a criminal act; it rather focuses on the subjective disposition or attitude of the offender (Fletcher 2007).

In the author's own words: "In a very general way, I would say that we need to emphasize the importance that accidents came to have, especially in the later years of the nineteenth century, and not just for the law, but also for the economy; as well as the likelihood of their occurrence and whatever can be done to compensate for their effects, etc.; and finally, the significance of their impact on the economy. (…). Now all of this has meant that the concept of civil liability has had to be reworked. (…) Civil liability has had to be broken up, separated from any reference to subjective fault and relieved of the requirement to prove the existence of personal fault"; hence the hypothesis that "in a rather strange way, it was the break-up of civil liability that constituted a model for the criminal law (…). After all, who is a born criminal, who is a degenerate, who has a criminal personality, if not someone who, based on a chain of causation difficult to reconstruct, achieves a particularly high score on the index of likely criminal behaviour? Someone who is, basically, a walking crime risk?" Finally, the conclusion reached by the reasoning here is as follows: just as civil liability can be established without "guilt", but in view of the risk created against which it is necessary to have some protection, in the same way, it is possible to "(…) render an individual criminally liable without having to determine if they were a free agent, and therefore if there was any guilt on their part; whereby the act committed is linked to the risk of criminality constituted by his/her specific personality". As a consequence, the same sanction will no longer be set aside for punishment, since "instead, it will have the task of reducing, as much as possible, either by elimination or by exclusion or by means of restrictions of various types, or even using treatment options, the risk of criminality posed by the individual concerned" (Foucault 2013).

As already mentioned, the interesting aspect of the current populist reversal of the spirit of the legislation in this area is the fact that the State's "punitive power" is directed not only at the "marginalised" and the "excluded" but also at the so-called "elites".

In the case of Italy, the coexistence, under the same roof, of "securitarism" and draconian legislation targeting economic and administrative crime is a clear confirmation of our assertions in this regard.

Legislative Populism: How Criminal Law, as We Know It, (Can) Die

These considerations can be more accurately understood by making a distinction between "legislative" populism and "judicial" populism.

As regards the former, the populist use of criminal legislation may consist in showing severity that could be pursued effectively or else is merely symbolic; it may perhaps be an expression of good intentions in terms of protection of public goods, but at the same time, it may also cause discrepancies that would scarcely be compatible or even completely incompatible, to say the least, with the principle of equitable treatment/reasonableness.

This trend generally manifests itself in a series of recurring scenarios.

As already stated, an offence is devised with a type of person in mind rather than a type of fact; the relevant provisions are generally of a casuistic nature and may contain general closure clauses; the legislative technique is generally of poor quality, while the rules introduced are almost foreign bodies insofar as they do not take into account the drafting style and the logic that in principle characterize the criminal code.

It is often the case that genuine, specialised criminal statutes are created, which refer to particular categories of persons: thus, criminality increasingly becomes a "social risk", in which—as it has been noted previously—the "who" prevails over the "what" (Sgubbi 1990).

The tendency to resort more and more frequently to criminal law also translates into a criminalization of social phenomena that would otherwise require different treatment by the legislator: in these cases, the criminalization option risks being reduced to a mere *marketing operation* (Manes 2019a; Nobis 2018; Pratt and Miao 2017; Pratt 2007; Salas 2005).

The other fundamental trend is, as we have stated, the obsession with punishment itself; thus, the severity of penalties constantly increases and more comprehensive reforms are enacted with the aim of ensuring the effectiveness of punishment.

In this way, either the severity of punishment is increased or else the legislation governing the circumstances of offences is applied in such a way as to prevent the mitigating effect of general legal standards. Action is also taken on the rules governing the limitation period of offences as well as on the code of criminal procedure itself, which makes it increasingly difficult to access special proceedings and diversion mechanisms. Finally, reforms of the penitentiary law are intended to restrict prisoners' opportunities to avail of alternative benefits and measures other than detention.

That there has been a "regression" of the legislation is quite clear, because after decades spent studying how to move the prison sentence from centre-stage, prison is now back with full attention as the heart and soul of the penal system.

Immigration and Criminal Law

It is sufficient to consider the recent regulatory solutions offered in the field of immigration.

In the face of the growing social alarm induced by the chaotic management of migration flows, the legislator has responded by focusing almost exclusively on the criminal justice system; it has done this, however, without conducting any proper assessment of the options available for instituting essential non-criminal measures to control and prevent unlawful immigration.

Moreover, the way this has been done has a particular leitmotiv, according to which, the most effective response to the "problem of immigration" always consists exclusively of adopting public order measures based on progressively more severe punishments (Caputo 2012; Sicurella 2012).

Symbolic in this regard is the offence of unlawful entry into, and unlawful residence in, the territory of the State (Art. 10-bis of Legislative Decree No. 286/1998, as introduced by Art. 1, par. 16, Legislative Decree No. 94/2009), which punishes foreigners who enter or remain in Italy in breach of the administrative provisions aimed at regulating, respectively, the general conditions of entry and residence in the territory of the State (Legislative Decree No. 286/1998) and short stays for visits, business, tourism and study (Legislative Decree No. 68/2007).[1] This is conduct

[1] Thus, the perpetrators of the offence concerned are not only, as in the original bill, the real illegal immigrants, that is, foreigners who have illegally entered Italian territory, using stealth to cross our borders by land or by sea, but so too are the so-called "overstayers", that is, persons who, even though they may have entered our country based on a legitimate entitlement (for example, a residence permit or a tourist visa), have nevertheless remained here illegally after that entitlement has ceased to apply (for example, after the expiry of a residence permit or tourist visa).

punishable by a fine only, which, exceptionally, cannot be turned into a cash settlement.

Here we will not dwell on the many concerns raised by the law in terms of compliance with the constitutional principles of equality, the harm principle and the principle of culpability.[2]

We note only that Art. 10-bis seems to refer to a presumption of dangerousness on the part of a clandestine immigrant; and therefore, it shows itself to be a provision with a major propaganda element, lacking any real capacity for prevention; something which is also due, not least, to the nature of the unlawful act as a mere misdemeanour, rather than an act that was initially intended to be classified as a crime (Manna 2011).[3]

For our purposes, it is important primarily to note that the rule appears to be merely symbolic in terms of its effectiveness, for the obvious reason that the fine provided for is likely to remain unenforceable in most cases; this being due to the insolvency of the convicted person, who is usually without any source of income and is also frequently untraceable.

This is quite apart from the obvious redundancy of this same set of factual elements, owing to its almost complete overlap in terms of applicability with the set of factual elements underlying administrative expulsion, as pertaining to the rules governing lack of impediment (Art. 10-*bis*, par. 4) and the dismissal of proceedings (Article 10-*bis*, co. 5), and also expulsion, which is meant to operate as a sanction that substitutes for the fine imposed for the offence. All of this is without taking into account the further delicate problems surrounding the actual enforcement of an expulsion order, problems that the complex provisions of Legislative Decree No 94/2009 do not give any plausible guarantee of being able to address or resolve effectively.

On the other hand, there is no question that the real punishment here consists of the expulsion of the foreigner, which must be carried out administratively or a substitute for a fine.

Basically, we are dealing with a type of offence intended to function as an *instrument of expulsion*, within a regulatory framework that aims to *exclude* the illegal immigrant and certainly not to *re-educate or re-socialise* him or her, as the Constitution would require.

[2] Some of these issues have been deemed groundless by the Italian Constitutional Court: see Corte Cost., sent. no. 250/2010, in *Dir. pen. proc.*, 2010, 1187 ff.

[3] The original formulation of the case elements referred to in art. 10-bis (deriving from art. 9 of draft law AS No. 773) constituted the offence of illegal entry and residence in the territory of the State, not as an infringement, but as a crime, punishable by imprisonment of from six months to four years.

Opting for a criminal sanction, therefore, seems to be justified only by virtue of the greater symbolic charge that distinguishes it from its administrative counterpart and in order to give an idea of the special punitive attention given by the legislator to the problem of unlawful immigration.

In the context of the security legislation on the subject of immigration, the aggravating circumstance of the "clandestinity" provided for by Article 61, No. 11-bis, of the Italian Criminal Code, which was introduced by the "security package" of 2008 and declared unlawful by the well-known constitutional judgement No. 249/2010, is also highlighted (Pulitanò 2013).

Without dwelling on the reasons for the unconstitutionality of this law, we confine ourselves here to pointing out that the judgment just cited recognized the contrast between this aggravating circumstance and Art. 25, par. 2, Const., which places an "act" as the basis of criminal liability and thus requires that a person is punished for their conduct and not for their personal attributes. According to this provision, which was declared unconstitutional, the status of "unlawful" immigrant—which is acquired at the time of illegal entry into Italian territory or else at the time of detention after expiry of a visa permitting a stay in the country, including owing to the culpable failure to renew it within the deadlines set—was considered a kind of "stigma"; and it was intended to serve as the foundation for more severe criminal treatment, following the logic of a "perpetrator-based" view of criminal law (Bartoli 2011; Donini 2009). This logic, in turn, is based on the mere *suspicion* that an illegal immigrant, as such, could behave dangerously (Pelissero 2007; Caputo 2012).

The gravity of this scenario, on the other hand, is now on the increase, as a result of the most recent measures taken and, in particular, the "Security bis" decree, which was enacted into law in July of this year.

The "Spazza Corrotti" Law

A further example of *legislative populism* can also be found, in our opinion, in a recent law, namely Legislative Decree No. 3/2019 ("*Misure per il contrasto dei reati contro la pubblica amministrazione, nonché in materia di prescrizione del reato e in materia di trasparenza dei partiti e movimenti politici*"), better known as "Spazzacorrotti".

This law has had an impact on the area of criminal law affecting public authorities—which has always been politically very "sensitive" anyway. In this context, it has focused mainly on a conspicuous tightening of the system of sanctions, through solutions that in some cases are not subject to any criteria of reasonableness or proportion at all, but are also in breach of the constitutional principle of the rehabilitative aim of punishment (Gambardella 2019; Manes 2019a, b; Manna 2018; Camon 2018; Pisani 2018).

In this vein, we point to, among other things, the inclusion of several offences against public administration within Article 4-bis of Legislative Decree No. 354/1975, which mentions a series of offences, the sentence for which precludes access to the benefits provided for by the penitentiary law.

Here it should be noted that, historically, this provision was created in order to combat mafia-type organised crime, in the belief that a custodial sentence was a mandatory option in all such cases. This was also done in order to break the link between an individual mafia member and the family (and locality) to which they belonged.

The inclusion in Art. 4-bis of a number of serious offences against public administration has brought about an "irrational" normative alignment of political-economic crime (of the "white collar" variety) with organised crime of the mafia variety, but leaves out of account the profound differences that still divide them (Pulitanò 2019; Manes 2019a, b).

And this has taken place in an area in which new legislation, despite its unfavourable consequences, is capable of being applied retrospectively, owing to the absence of a transitional rule requiring it to be applied in the future (*pro futuro*) only; whereby, in fact, case law is geared towards applying the principle *tempus regit actum* with reference to enforcement provisions in the criminal sector.

By amending Article 317-bis of the Criminal Code, the legislator extended the list of offences leading to the application of (perpetual/temporary) disqualification from public office, as well as to the "unprecedented" punishment of prohibition from contracting with any governmental entity.

The previous provision, following the amendment made by Legislative Decree No. 190 of 2012, referred only to peculation (Article 314 of the Criminal Code), extortion (Article 317 of the Criminal Code), direct bribery (Article 319 of the Criminal Code) and corruption in judicial acts (Article 319-ter of the Criminal Code). The following have now been added to the list: bribery for the performance of a duty (Article 318 of the Criminal Code), undue influence (Article 319-quater of the Criminal Code), bribery of persons in charge of a public service (Article 320 of the Criminal Code), incitement to corruption (Article 322 of the Criminal

Code), international corruption (Article 322-bis of the Criminal Code) and trafficking in unlawful influences (Article 346-bis of the Criminal Code).

There has been talk in the *media* of a life ban for corrupt and corrupting individuals, as if to convey the idea that the response by the criminal justice system to this issue is infallible and its consequences potentially permanent and unalterable. It is hard to argue with the fact that *slogans*, however legally incorrect, are very effective when it comes to the media.

This recent reform has also altered the rules governing rehabilitation to some extent. As has been observed, the general rule contained in Article 178 of the Criminal Code states that rehabilitation extinguishes collateral penalties, unless the law provides otherwise. As an exception to this rule, Decree No. 3/2019 added a last paragraph to Article 179 of the Italian Criminal Code, to the effect that rehabilitation granted pursuant to the provisions of Article 179 of the Italian Criminal Code has no effect on perpetual accessory penalties.[4]

Finally, the additional action taken with regard to the rules governing limitation periods, an area in which the previous government had already intervened (see the so-called Orlando reform), is illustrative of the trends discussed in general terms in the previous paragraphs.

In this case, the decision was made to provide for a suspension of the limitation period following conviction at first instance. The intention here was to support the demand for justice. However, it is clear that this cure risks being worse than the disease: a mechanism like this may, in fact, cause trials to last longer, at least after a conviction at first instance, which would undoubtedly have a detrimental effect on the accused, who is always waiting for a rapid outcome. In this regard, the arrangement may have a critical effect on both the presumption of innocence and the principle of reasonable duration of trials.

Judicial Populism?

As regards the different kinds of "judicial populism", it is worth noting, first of all, that nowadays the criminal justice system is crushed by the prevalence of criminal procedure that transforms trials into methods of social control rather than places where liability for criminally relevant acts is ascertained.

[4] However, after a period of not less than seven years from rehabilitation, perpetual accessory punishment must be declared extinguished, provided the convicted person has provided genuine, consistent evidence of good conduct.

The Code of Criminal Procedure of 1988 had identified criminal trials as the place where evidence is gathered (Luparia 2017; Gialuz 2017). In order to confirm this choice, the Code had—among other things—prohibited the dissemination of prosecution documentation, by means of rules on secrecy, on the prohibition of publication of documents or images and on the creation of court records.

Over time, the centre of gravity has inexorably returned to the investigative phase.

This has been brought about by many factors: it is enough to think of the press conferences set up with great clamour by the Public Prosecutor's Office, of the prominence of certain investigators, of the "personalization" of the struggle against certain forms of alarming criminality, as well as the transfer into the public arena of "irrefutable" accusatory documents, which often devote ample space to the entire transcript of recordings, which are irrelevant in themselves for the purposes of the investigation, but which are apt to provide evidence of the "immorality" of the actors concerned.

All of this has provided the basis for the unilateral formation of a reality independent of legal proceedings, which, among other things, demands "journalistic" haste and shows intolerance of the long time it takes for courts to determine responsibility (Violante 2014).

The problem is due, not least, to the fact that interest in punishment is increasingly focused on talk shows, opinion polls and TV debates that now dictate the agenda of criminal policy.

This is also due to the fact that the mediatisation of justice caused by the impact of mass media, the uncertainty of interpretation brought about by ambiguous legislation that has been deliberately devised to offer the interpreter vast swathes of unsupervised discretion and the fragmentation of what were originally uniform categories—all these have transformed the process into a theatre, where the confrontation between the prosecution and the defence has become just a game of cunning involving procedural *gimmicks* and has ceased to constitute any real measuring of criminal liability.

Increasingly, the dialectic of court proceedings no longer involves any evaluation of the evidence, but rather, its legitimacy.

Substantive criminal law remains confined to the periphery of the system, while the real punishment risks becoming the criminal proceeding itself.

On the other side, the figure of the combined "judge/tribune" has sometimes emerged, who now and then purports to assume the role of the authentic representative of the "peoples'" expectations of justice, styling him or herself as a substitute for the court, even in open conflict with the official political establishment. Thus, in the end, the main source of legitimacy of one's own actions comes to be derived from popular consent, rather than from an exclusive bond with the law (Fiandaca 2013).

Concluding Remarks

Faced with this scenario, it is not surprising that crime, trials and punishment all tend to take on new (or perhaps old) vindictive demands, replete with certain moralizing and quasi-healing functions, since removal from the public system of those who are allegedly guilty is viewed as having the salutary effect of eliminating areas of dysfunction and fighting crime. If problems persist, it is said, it is not a sign that the remedy was wrong, but that the punishment was not severe enough; and so, it is necessary to make the punishments harsher, the checks more penetrating and the police investigations more extensive (Violante 2014). Intransigent moralizing and a lack of liberal culture fuel a kind of "penal extremism".

The repressive trends of the seventies and eighties of the last century, when the political classes responded to new criminal phenomena or to a resurgence of the traditional ones with procedural constraints, restrictions on personal freedom and increased penalties, while nevertheless keeping intact the traditional categories of criminal offences, and in any case not departing from their managerial role in this area, have thus now been replaced by the "populist illusion", whereby the latter is completely at variance with the categories of offences mentioned (Violante 2014).

The experiences of recent years should have taught us that a strong antidote to populism is the ability of politics to renew itself profoundly, so as to regain credibility and a real capacity for providing guidance to the public (Fiandaca 2013). At the same time, the principle of the division of powers should be kept firmly in place, so as to avoid undue encroachment between the different spheres of public activity; and also to raise consciousness generally that the criminal justice system must be "taken seriously" and must not be allowed to become a mere mechanism for seeking popular consent.

References

Bartoli, R. (2011). Il diritto penale dell'immigrazione: strumento di tutela dei flussi immigratori o mezzo di esclusione e indebolimento dello straniero? *Questione Giustizia, 2*, 17–32.

Camon, A. (2018). Disegno di legge spazzacorrotti e processo penale. Osservazioni a prima lettura. *Archivio Penale, LXX*(3), 799–813.

Caputo, A. (2012). I reati in materia di immigrazione. In F. Palazzo & C. Paliero (Eds.), *Trattato teorico-pratico di diritto penale* (Vol. IX, pp. 223–235). Torino: Giappichelli.

Costa, V. (2019). *Élite e populismo. La democrazia nel mondo della vita*. Catanzaro: Rubbettino.

Diamanti, I., & Lazar, M. (2018). *Popolocrazia. La metamorfosi delle nostre democrazie*. Bari: Laterza.

Donini, M. (2009). Il cittadino extracomunitario da oggetto *materiale* a tipo d'autore nel controllo penale dell'immigrazione. *Questione Giustizia, 1*, 101–133.

Donini, M. (2019). *Populismo e ragione pubblica*. Modena: Mucchi Editore.

Fiandaca, G. (2013). Populismo politico e populismo giudiziario. *Criminalia, 8*, 95–123.

Fletcher, G. (2007). *The Grammar of Criminal Law. American, Comparative and International. Volume One: Foundations*. Oxford: Oxford University Press.

Forti, G. (2000). *L'immane concretezza. Metamorfosi del crimine e controllo penale*. Milano: Raffaello Cortina Editore.

Foucault, M. (1993). *Sorvegliare e punire*. Torino: Einaudi Editore.

Foucault, M. (2013). *Mal fare, dir vero. Funzione della confessione nella giustizia*. Torino: Einaudi Editore.

Gallo, Z. (2018). The Penal Implication of Austerity: Italian Punishment in the Wake of the Eurozone Crisis. *European Journal of Criminology, 16*(2), 147–169.

Gambardella, M. (2019). Il grande assente nella nuova "legge spazzacorrotti": il microsistema delle fattispecie di corruzione. *Cassazione penale, LIX*(1), 44–73.

Gialuz, M. (2017). The Italian Code of Criminal Procedure: A Reading Guide. In M. Gialuz, L. Luparia, & F. Scarpa (Eds.), *The Italian Code of Criminal Procedure. Critical Essays and English Translation* (pp. 17–53). Padova: Cedam.

Lacey, N. (2019). Populism and the Rule of Law. *London School of Economics*, Working Paper, 28, 3–27. Available at http://www.lse.ac.uk/International-Inequalities/Assets/Documents/Working-Papers/III-Working-Paper-28-Lacey-Populism-and-the-Rule-of-Law.pdf

Luparia, L. (2017). Model Code of Broken Dreams? The Italian Criminal Procedure in a Comparative Perspective. In M. Gialuz, L. Luparia, & F. Scarpa (Eds.), *The Italian Code of Criminal Procedure. Critical Essays and English Translation* (pp. 1–17). Padova: Cedam.

Manes, V. (2019a). Diritto penale no-limits. Garanzie e diritti fondamentali come presidio per la giurisdizione. *questionegiustizia,it*. Available at www.questionegiustizia.it

Manes, V. (2019b). L'estensione dell'art. 4-bis ord. pen. ai delitti contro la p.a.: profili di illegittimità costituzionale. *Diritto penale contemporaneo, 2*, 105–122.

Manna, A. (2011). Il diritto penale dell'immigrazione clandestina, tra simbolismo penale e colpa d'autore. *Cassazione penale, 2*, 446–457.

Manna, A. (2018). Il fumo della pipa (il cd. populismo politico e la reazione dell'Accademia e dell'Avvocatura). *Archivio penale, 3*, 1–12. Available at www.archiviopenale.it

Mastropaolo, A. (2010). Democrazia e populismo. In M. Bovero & V. Panzè (Eds.), *La democrazia in nove lezioni* (pp. 64–84). Roma/Bari: Laterza.

Müller, J.-W. (2017). *What Is Populism ?* Philadelphia: University of Pennsylvania Press.

Nobis, F. (2018). Strafrecht in Zeiten des Populismus. *Strafverteidiger, 38*(7), 63–74.

Paliero, C. (2011). *Il principio di effettività nel diritto penale*. Napoli: ES.

Paliero, C. (2012). L'agorà e il palazzo. Quale legittimazione per il diritto penale? *Criminalia, 7*, 95–117.

Pelissero, M. (2007), Logiche di esclusione e di inclusione nella politica criminale sulla immigrazione. *Questione Giustizia, 4*, 684–705.

Pisani, N. (2018). Il disegno di legge "spazzacorrotti": solo ombre. *Cassazione penale, LVIII*(11), 3589–3592.

Pratt, J. (2007). *Penal Populism*. London/New York: Routledge.

Pratt, J., & Miao, M. (2017). *Penal Populism: The End of Reason*. The Chinese University of Hong Kong Faculty of Law, Research Paper No. 2017-02.

Pulitanò, D. (2013). Populismi e penale. Sulla attuale situazione spirituale della giustizia penale. *Criminalia*, 123–149.

Pulitanò, D. (2019). Tempeste sul penale. Spazzacorrotti e altro. *Diritto Penale Contemporaneo, 3*, 235–250.

Risicato, L. (2019). *Diritto alla sicurezza e sicurezza dei diritto: un ossimoro invincibile?* Torino: Giappichelli.

Salas, D. (2005). *La volonté de punir. Essai sur le populisme pénal*. Paris: Fayard.

Sbriccoli, M. (2009). *Storia del diritto penale. Scritti editi e inediti*. Milano: Giuffrè.

Scoditti, E. (2018). Populismo e diritto. Un'introduzione. *Questione Giustizia*. Available at www.questionegiustizia.it

Sgubbi, F. (1990). *Il reato come rischio sociale. Ricerche sulle scelte di allocazione dell'illegalità penale*. Bologna: Il Mulino.

Sicurella, R. (2012). Il controllo penale dell'immigrazione irregolare: esigenze di tutela, tentazioni simboliche, imperativi garantistici, percorsi di riflessione critica. *Rivista italiana di diritto e procedura penale, LV*(4), 1425–1477.

Tripodi, A. (2019). Dal diritto penale della paura alla paura del diritto penale. Spunti per una riflessione. *Quaderno di storia del diritto penale, 1*, 263–273.

Various Authors. (2016). La società punitiva. Populismo, diritto penale simbolico e ruolo del penalista. *Diritto penale contemporaneo*, 1–44. Available at www.penalecontemporaneo.it

Violante, L. (2014). Populismo e plebeismo nelle politiche criminali. *Criminalia*, 197–211.

Index[1]

A

Accountability, 46, 52, 53, 64, 70, 129, 131, 177, 192, 207, 211n20, 215n28, 216, 217

Amendment, 4, 15n2, 23, 24, 77, 92, 102, 103, 103n4, 105, 107–109, 108n8, 129, 130, 157, 160, 162, 170, 202n3, 213n24, 227, 294, 304

Anti-elitist ideologies, 6, 235

B

Berlusconi, Silvio, 3, 18, 21–25, 24n6, 27, 28, 31–33, 43, 43n3, 65n51, 112, 113, 123, 125, 130, 140, 160, 205

Border defence, 7, 255

Budget, 5, 88, 128, 129, 143, 147, 153–159, 158n2, 160n3, 161–171, 168n10

Budgetary populism, 153–171

Budget rules, 157, 158, 158n2, 160

C

Casaleggio, Davide, 75, 75n3

Casaleggio, Gianroberto, 245

Constitutional amendment, 4, 15n2, 16, 27n11, 48–50, 76n9, 87, 88, 108–114, 159–161, 166, 167, 185

Constitutional change, 4, 86, 104–108, 113, 136

Constitutional Court (Corte Costituzionale), 2, 4, 5, 7, 25n8, 26n9, 43, 43n4, 50, 56, 76, 78, 86, 89–91, 105, 107, 111, 129, 147, 156, 158, 159, 167, 168n10, 169, 170, 180, 180n7, 180n8, 180n9, 181, 187, 188, 191n26, 201–203, 214, 226, 232, 234, 235, 243, 244,

[1] Note: Page numbers followed by 'n' refer to notes.

G. Delledonne et al. (eds.), *Italian Populism and Constitutional Law*, Challenges to Democracy in the 21st Century,
https://doi.org/10.1007/978-3-030-37401-3

Constitutional Court (*cont.*) 247n14, 251, 264, 270–272, 279–285, 280n2, 287, 288
Constitutionalism, 1–3, 6, 7, 11–17, 20, 21, 31, 33, 97–102, 101n2, 104–106, 108, 114, 124, 156, 166, 171, 177, 192, 199, 199n1, 200, 247, 255–258, 272, 273, 281, 282, 289
Constitutional politics, 3, 12, 15, 28, 34, 101, 106, 112
Constitutional reform, 3, 4, 11–35, 43, 76, 76n6, 79, 88, 98, 99, 108–114, 130, 138, 160, 215n26
Constitutional replacement, 4, 102, 104–106, 108–114
Conte government, first, 2, 4, 5, 7, 120, 125–130, 143–147
Conte government, second, 129, 131, 139n4
Contract for Government, 139–143, 143n8, 147, 148
Corruption, 22, 42, 46n11, 292, 293, 304, 305
Criminal justice, 8, 291–307
Criminal law, 179, 191, 258, 293, 295–303, 306
Crucifix, 249, 249n20, 250n21

D
Democracy, 2, 3, 8, 11–14, 17, 20, 24, 29, 30, 32–35, 41, 75–78, 78n12, 80, 82–86, 90, 101, 101n2, 106, 107, 121n3, 122, 124, 131, 137–140, 137n2, 154–156, 166, 177, 180, 187, 208, 209, 211, 212, 214–217, 215n29, 223–238, 241, 242, 245, 251, 252, 256, 268, 273, 281, 282, 289
Di Maio, Luigi, 66, 67, 127, 140–142, 146, 148, 169n11, 206
Direct democracy, 4, 6, 35n14, 75, 76, 83, 84, 200, 204, 208, 209, 211n22, 245, 252n27

E
European Union (EU), 2, 5, 62, 79, 79n13, 80, 82, 85, 87n25, 103, 112n11, 129, 129n12, 143, 154, 156, 159–166, 165n8, 178n1, 182n13, 190, 261, 264, 266, 277, 278, 282, 286–289
Executive power, 26

F
Fake news, 6, 177–192, 206
Five Stars Movement, 125, 127, 241, 242, 244, 244n11, 245, 247–249, 250n24, 251, 252, 252n27, 262

G
Golden rule, 164, 165n8
Government, 2, 15, 42, 76, 102, 120, 135–148, 157, 177, 201, 228, 241, 260, 284, 305
Grillo, Beppe, 185, 185n19, 186, 205–207, 212, 213, 213n24, 227, 228, 245

I
Identity, 7, 78n12, 104, 104n5, 105, 165, 167, 247, 255, 279, 280, 283, 285, 286, 291, 295, 296
Identity politics, 7, 248

Immigration, 68, 248, 249, 252, 258, 258n1, 265, 268, 293, 301–303
Internet, 6, 44, 52–54, 66, 70, 177–192, 200, 201, 204–208, 214, 217, 245
Italian parliament, 26n10, 30, 41–70, 89n27, 90, 169, 185, 191n24, 215, 227

L
Law-making process, 4, 119–131, 146, 167
League (Lega; Lega Nord), 161
Legislative procedure, 52, 119–124, 120n2, 130
Legitimation, 31, 32, 107, 108, 236
Letta, Enrico, 45n10, 65n52, 112, 112n11, 113, 113n12, 144, 160, 206, 262
Limitations of popular sovereignty, 281–284

M
Majoritarianism, 3, 13, 14, 21–27, 34, 120
Majority, 2, 5, 15, 15n2, 17, 20–26, 23n5, 25n8, 26n9, 27–28n11, 28n13, 32, 33, 42, 43, 49, 56–60, 63, 67, 70, 76n6, 77, 81, 81n16, 86–88, 98, 100–106, 109–111, 119, 120, 122–126, 130, 131, 140, 142, 143n8, 145, 146, 148, 154–156, 158, 163–165, 170, 171, 200n2, 205, 209n15, 225, 231, 234n29, 243, 247, 256, 271, 282, 285
Mattarella, Sergio, 62, 144, 144n9, 164, 165n7, 200n2
Migration, 7, 43n3, 141, 146, 179, 255–273, 301
Ministers, 23–25, 28, 29, 45n10, 64, 66–68, 113, 141, 143–147, 145n10, 165n8

N
National security, 7, 255, 257, 260, 264, 283, 287
National state, 8, 284, 286
Non-legislative procedures, 41–70
Non-validated therapies, 230, 235, 236

P
Parliaments, 3, 17, 41, 76, 109, 120, 157, 191, 202, 224, 244, 262, 279
Partitocrazia, 1, 19, 20, 138
Political parties, 1, 6, 19, 42, 46–48, 49n20, 53, 81, 122, 138–141, 144, 148, 164, 199–203, 202n3, 202n4, 205–209, 211, 213–217, 242, 245, 246
Politics of immediacy, 78
Populism, 1–8, 11–35, 43, 44n7, 50n22, 75–92, 97–114, 119–131, 135–148, 153–171, 177–192, 199–217, 223–238, 241, 244–250, 252, 255–273, 277–289, 291–307
Prime Minister, 5, 21, 24, 27, 30, 32, 124, 136, 138, 139, 139n4, 141–146, 143n8, 145n10, 148, 148n15, 160, 162, 206, 244, 246, 250, 252
Public discourse, 43, 177–192

Q
Qualunquismo, 120

R

Referendum, 4, 21, 43, 75–92, 103, 130, 185, 215, 245, 281
Religion, 7, 241–252, 278
Renzi, Matteo, 3, 18, 21, 22, 24–27, 29, 30, 33, 43, 45n10, 76, 88, 112, 112n11, 113, 161, 262
Representative democracy, 4, 6, 75–78, 101, 141, 155, 199, 200, 203, 211, 211n22, 214, 215, 217
Resentment, 33, 34, 155

S

Salvini, Matteo, 66, 68n63, 88, 139n4, 140–142, 146, 148, 161, 205, 206, 245, 250, 250n21, 262
Savona, Paolo, 144
Science and democracy, 179, 235–238

T

Transparency, 4, 44, 52–55, 68, 70, 120, 131, 207, 212, 215, 215n28, 216, 230, 249

U

Unconstitutional constitutional amendments, 98, 107

V

Vaccines, 225–230, 235, 236

The manufacturer's authorised representative in the EU is Springer Nature Customer Service Centre GmbH, Europaplatz 3, 69115 Heidelberg, Germany. If you have any concerns regarding our products, please contact ProductSafety@springernature.com

Printed and bound by CPI Group (UK) Ltd, Croydon, CR0 4YY
30/09/2026
02225459-0013